THE DRAMA OF SOUTH AFRICA

This is the first comprehensive account of drama and performance in twentieth-century South Africa. It discusses both well-known figures such as Athol Fugard and the many lesser-known actors, directors and impresarios who have given the theatre of South Africa its uniquely syncretic character.

This original and outstanding book challenges the familiar binary oppositions that have conventionally defined the field: black/white, imported/indigenous, purist/hybrid, and text/performance. It also shows that the simple opposition between European and African has been complicated by the contribution of American and African-American influences, such as musicals, the Beats and Black Power.

As well as discussing conventional dramatic texts, the book investigates the impact of sketches, scripts and manifestoes. It also examines the oral preservation of scripts that were banned or forgotten. Kruger highlights the contribution of women and minorities such as South Africans of Indian descent, as well as the work of dissident Afrikaners, and concludes with a discussion of post-apartheid performance since 1994.

Loren Kruger is Associate Professor of English, Comparative Literature, and African and African-American Studies at the University of Chicago. She is the author of *The National Stage* and currently editor of *Theatre Journal*.

THE DRAMA
OF SOUTH AFRICA

Plays, pageants and
publics since 1910

Loren Kruger

London and New York

First published 1999
by Routledge
11 New Fetter Lane, London EC4P 4EE

Simultaneously published in the USA and Canada
by Routledge
29 West 35th Street, New York, NY 10001

© 1999 Loren Kruger

Typeset in Baskerville by
J&L Composition Ltd, Filey, North Yorkshire
Printed and bound in Great Britain by
TJ International Ltd, Padstow, Cornwall

British Library Cataloguing in Publication Data
A catalogue record for this book is available from the British Library

Library of Congress Cataloging in Publication Data
Kruger, Loren.
The drama of South Africa/Loren Kruger.
p.   cm.
Includes bibliographical references and index.
1. South African drama (English) – History and criticism.
2. Theater – South Africa – History – 20th century.   3. South African
drama – History and criticism.   I. Title.
PR9361.2.K78   1999   98–54712
822–dc21   CIP

ISBN 0–415–17982–3 (hbk)
ISBN 0–415–17983–1 (pbk)

CONTENTS

FIGURES

ABBREVIATIONS

AAC	All-African Convention
AAM	Anti-Apartheid Movement
AJP	African Jazz Pioneers
ANC	African National Congress
ANT	African National Theatre
AREPP	African Research and Educational Puppetry Program
ARM	African Resistance Movement
ATKV	Afrikaner Taal- en Kultuurvereeniging (Afrikaans Language and Cultural Union)
AZAPO	Azanian People's Organization
BCM	Black Consciousness Movement
BDS	Bantu Drama Society
BMSC	Bantu Men's Social Centre
BPC	Black People's Convention
BPT	Bantu People's Theatre
BW	*Bantu World*
CAPAB	Cape Performing Arts Board
CAW	Creative Arts Workshop
CPSA	Communist Party of South Africa (1919–50)
DOCC	Donaldson Orlando Cultural Club
FAK	Federasie vir Afrikaner Kultuur
FUBA	Federated Union of Black Artists
JATC	Junction Avenue Theatre Company
JPL	Johannesburg Public Library
KCAL	Killie Campbell African Library (University of Natal, Durban)
LAMDA	London Academy of Music and Dramatic Art
LANGTAG	Language Task Action Group
MDALI	Music, Drama and Literature Institute
NAC	National Arts Coalition
NAPAC	Natal Performing Arts Council
NELM	National English Literary Museum, Grahamstown
NEUM	Non-European Unity Movement

NGO	Non-Governmental Organization
NP	National Party
NTO	National Theatre Organization
NUM	National Union of Mineworkers
NUSAS	National Union of South African Students
PAC	Pan-African Congress
PACOFS	Performing Arts Council of the Orange Free State
PACs	Performing Arts Councils
PACT	Performing Arts Council of the Transvaal
PET	People's Educational Theatre
SA	States Archives (Pretoria)
SABC	South African Broadcasting Corporation
SABTU	South African Black Theatre Union
SACHED	South African Council on Higher Education
SACP	South African Communist Party (underground, 1950–90)
SADF	South African Defense Force
SAIRR	South African Institute for Race Relations
SAR	South African Republic, former Boer republic (1838–1902)
SASO	South African Students Association
STC	Strange Theatre Collection (JPL)
TECON	Theatre Council of Natal
UDF	United Democratic Front
UDW	University of Durban–Westville
UNICUS	University of Natal – Black Section Theatre Co.
UwB	*Umteleli wa Bantu*
UWC	University of the Western Cape
WAVE	Women against Violence and Exploitation
WRF	Wits Rural Facility

Note: isiNguni orthography currently calls for a lower-case class prefix (e.g. kwa) and capitalizing the proper name that follows (e.g. Zulu). I have followed this usage except where published sources indicate otherwise.

ACKNOWLEDGMENTS

This book has taken ten years to write and more than another ten to incubate, since I began to observe theatre in South Africa in the early 1970s. In that time, I have garnered many debts, from the teachers who took high school girls to plays probably not intended for their eyes and ears, to the theatre practitioners who have enlightened and entertained me over the years. I would like to begin by acknowledging the South African theatre practitioners and scholars who took the time to answer my questions and query my answers: Tim Couzens, Bhekizizwe Peterson, Jae Maingard, and Patricia Watson at the University of the Witwatersrand (Wits), as well as Maishe Maponya and Carole Steinberg, who have moved from Wits to government arts administration; Carolyn Hamilton, Reyda Becker, and Elizabeth Dell of the Museums Forum at the same institution; Barney Simon, late of the Market Theatre; Vanessa Cooke, Mncedi Dayi, and Phumudzo Nephawe of the Market Laboratory; Ismael Mahomed, Irene Menell, Gcina Mhlophe, Peter Ngwenya, and Malcolm and Colin Purkey, past and present theatre practitioners in Johannesburg; Kriben Pillay and Suria Govender in Durban; Muthal Naidoo in Giyani; Mike van Graan in Cape Town; Temple Hauptfleisch in Stellenbosch, and Clive Evian, Judith McKenzie, Shirley Ngwenya, Helene Schneider, Shereen Usdin, and Mhlalabesi Vundla, variously involved in theatre and health education. I am especially grateful to Ian Steadman, whose example and advice have been unsurpassed.

Several archives provided me with print and visual material. Thanks are due to the South African Library (Cape Town); Cory Library, Rhodes University; the Western Cape and KwaZulu/Natal archives; the Johannesburg Public Library; the Market Theatre Publicity Office; Nasionale Pers; the Argus Group; Bailey's African History Archive, and Northwestern University's Africana Library. Michele Pickover at Cullen Library, Wits, and her colleague, Ann Stuart, at the Performing Arts Library; Ann Torlesse at the National English Literary Museum (Grahamstown); Kathy Brookes at Museum Afrika (Johannesburg); Louana Brewis at the State Archive (Pretoria); Rita Ehlers at the Performing Arts Council of the Transvaal (Pretoria), and Joan Simpson at the Killie Campbell Africana Library (Durban) have been particularly helpful, as has Ruphin Coudyzer, whose beautiful images have greatly enhanced this book. Visits to archives, theatres, and other venues in South Africa, as well as the reproduction of images, have been made possible by funds from the National Endowment for the Humanities, the Fulbright Foundation, the University of the Witwatersrand travel fund, the Chicago Humanities Institute, and the Visitors' Committee at the University of Chicago.

Many colleagues and friends at Chicago and elsewhere have offered valuable criticism and encouragement: at the University of Chicago: Jean and John Comaroff, Ralph Austen, and other members of the African Studies Workshop; Tamara Trojanowska, Larry Norman, Sabine Haenni, Arno Bosse, and other members of the Theatre Studies Workshop, also Ken Warren, in English, and African and African-American Studies; at Northwestern University: Tracy Davis, Sandra Richards, and Tony Eprile; at Northwestern's Institute for the African Humanities: director Jane Guyer, and guests Kofi Anyidoho and Jabulani Mkhize; at the University of Minnesota: Tamara Underiner, Megan Lewis, and other members of the postcolonial theatre seminar. I would also like to thank Ann Wilson (Guelph), Albert Wertheim (Bloomington), Dennis Walder (London), Erika Munk (New York), Neil Lazarus (Providence), Liz Gunner (London, now Pietermaritzburg), Helen Gilbert (Brisbane), Joachim Fiebach (Berlin), Chris Balme (Mainz), and David Graver (Chicago), whose contribution to our jointly written article jump-started this book, and whose support of this project is otherwise incalculable.

Portions of this research in various forms have appeared in the following journals: *New Theatre Quarterly* 19 (1989) (with David Graver); *Diaspora* 1, 3 (1991); *Transition* 59 (1993); *Modernism/Modernity* 1, 3 (1994); *Modern Drama*, 38 (1995); *The South African Theatre Journal* 9, 1 (1995), *Theater* 25, 3 (1996); *Theatre Research International* 21, 2 (1996); *Journal of Southern African Studies* 23, 4 (1997), and the following anthologies: *Imperialism and Theatre*, J. Ellen Gainor, ed. (London: Routledge, 1995) and *Crucibles of Crisis: Performance and Social Change,* Janelle Reinelt, ed. (Ann Arbor: University of Michigan Press, 1996).

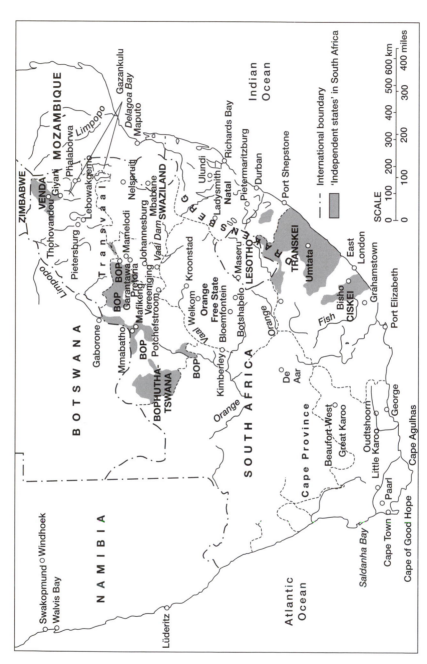

1   South Africa immediately prior to 1994, showing the apartheid "homelands".

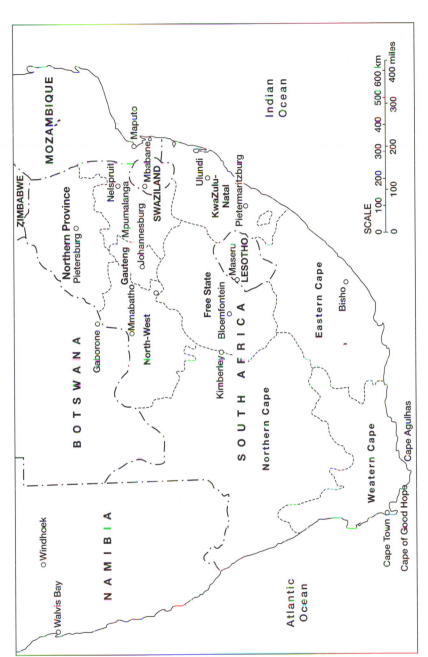

2 South Africa in 1999, showing new provinces and provincial capitals.

1

INTRODUCTION
The drama of South Africa

On 10 May 1994, South Africa's first democratically elected government staged the inauguration of Nelson Mandela as the first president of a new South Africa. Taking place on a hill in Pretoria, erstwhile bastion of Afrikanerdom, in the amphitheatre-courtyard of the Union Buildings, Sir Herbert Baker's monument to British Empire and white supremacy and still the seat of executive government, witnessed on television by millions worldwide, and in person by 150,000 people on the lawn below the buildings, this event was understood by participants and observers alike to inaugurate not only the new president but also the new nation.[1] At the center of the proceedings was the swearing in of the president who took the oath of office "in the presence of all those assembled here" while standing in a small pavilion, open to the VIPs in the amphitheatre but sealed with plexiglass at the rear end facing the crowd below. The official enactment of the new state and its representative actors in this privileged space was, however, framed by performances outside, which preceded, succeeded, and accompanied the act of inauguration itself.

The other performances may have lacked the indicative force of law of the act of inauguration but carried nonetheless the subjunctive power of prayer, prophecy, play, or occasionally doubt about the resolution of conflict in this drama of South Africa.[2] An hour or more before Mandela and his entourage entered the site, the arrival of national and international delegates was accompanied by choirs, some black, some white, some more or less integrated, whose informality contrasted with the formal mien of the delegates ushered in by (mostly white) members of the South African Defence Force (SADF) or (mostly black) *UmKhonto we Sizwe* [isiNguni: Spear of the Nation; MK], the former ANC guerrilla army.[3] The act of inauguration was immediately preceded by South Africa's competing anthems of modern nationhood, "Die Stem van Suid-Afrika" [The Voice of South Africa – the Afrikaner national anthem] and "Nkosi sikelel' iAfrika" [God Bless Africa – the anthem of the African National Congress (ANC)], and by the *izibongo* [praises] of *izimbongi* [praise poets] vying with one another to hail the arrival of the new nation and its leaders in a manner that recalled without quite restoring the role of the court *imbongi*. It was succeeded by prayers from representatives of South Africa's international religions: Hinduism, Judaism, Islam, and Christianity.

1

"Traditional" and "modern" elements in this celebration of invention were perforce mediated by the apparatus of electronic broadcasting and the local and global marketing of the recorded event and associated memorabilia as commodities.[4]

The events in the amphitheatre were followed by a series of entertainments on a stage in front of the crowd on the lawn, featuring performances that mixed people and materials from different ethnic groups under the rubric, "many cultures, one nation." The opening act, the African Jazz Pioneers, recalled in personnel (black and white) and in repertoire (jazz laced with *kwela* and swing) the integrationist politics and syncretic aesthetics of the 1950s, which were being celebrated at the same time but in *Sophiatown*, the play (first performed 1985; published JATC 1994), revived at the Market Theatre in Johannesburg especially for the election. AJP's performance, like the production of *Sophiatown*, underscored the link – at once nostalgic and hopeful – with the urbane modernity exemplified by its name-sake, the most famous intercultural "bohemian" neighborhood to be destroyed by apartheid. Others included Ladysmith Black Mambazo's deftly urbane reformulation of the *isicathamiya* [walking like a cat] dance developed by Zulu migrant workers, and a collaboration between Savuka, whose lead singer, "white Zulu" Johnny Clegg, sang of Mandela's former imprisonment in "Asimbonanga Mandela" [We do not see him, Mandela] in a combination of rock and *maskanda* (itself a fusion of Zulu migrant song and a European instrument: the electric guitar), and the Surialanga Dance Company, who interpreted the song by way of *Bharata Natyam*. The range of languages, from Afrikaans via English to Zulu, and music, from the *boeremusiek* of Nico Carstens to the *isicathamiya* of Ladysmith Black Mambazo, was matched by visual diversity, in dance, from *Bharata Natyam* to *tiekiedraai*, and in formal and informal costume from one *imbongi*'s *imvunulo* (Zulu festive attire, including skins) to another's designer shirt, or from the diplomatic blue "Western" suit – competing with the daishiki or the *boubou* (in homage to West Africa) – in the amphitheatre above to the T-shirt emblazoned with "Nkosi sikelel' iAfrika" or with Mandela's face or clan-name (Madiba) on the lawn below.

This amalgam of visual and aural diversity as well as the active responsiveness of participants, whether members of parliament or citizens on the lawn, to the words, images, and music mediated by screen and microphone, dramatized the act of union proffered by the official slogan, "many cultures, one nation." While some responses were predictable enough, such as black and white ANC MPs swaying enthusiastically to Soweto choirs in the amphitheatre, others offered more idiosyncratic but no less striking performances of reconciliation on the lawn: a black woman danced a *tiekiedraai* [Afrikaans: turning on a threepenny piece] which she claimed to have learnt "in [her] *boerestaat*" (separatist Afrikaner state), playfully defusing the explosive idea of white secession (which had been behind the bombs that had threatened the election); an Afrikaner woman selling (and wearing) "Madibamobilia" despite her "usual" National Party (NP) affiliation answered the question "Are you ANC?" with "Today, what else can I be?" (Gevisser 1994a: 9). Despite the security barriers separating the presidential party

2

and the crowd below and the fence between entertainers and audience on the lawn, the audience danced, sang, and waved flags in response to the ceremonies in the amphitheatre, even cheering on the former apartheid airforce because it was now "saluting our freedom" (Gevisser 1994a: 9).

This public response anticipated and answered – in the most immediate ways – the opening words of Mandela's thoroughly mediated (scripted) inauguration address: "Today, all of us, by our presence here, and by our celebrations in other parts of the country and the world, do confer glory and hope on new-found liberty" (Mandela 1994: 4).[5] As the addressee of the speech and implied subject of the sentence, "we the people of South Africa . . . tak[ing] possession" of a "new nation" and a "common victory" for "justice, for peace, and for human dignity," those present assumed the role of national audience and national protagonist. In embracing in this single "we" those whose crimes subjected "our country" to the "human disaster" of "racial oppression," and those "heroes and heroines who sacrificed their lives so that we could be free," (p. 5) Mandela's inaugural speech did not obliterate the past and present of "poverty, deprivation, suffering and gender and other discrimination" but, for its willing participants, it performed, if only momentarily, the "miracle" of national unity (p. 5). In the eyes, ears, bodies, hearts, and minds of those present, and in reports across all but the most extremely separatist terrain agreed, this was no mere "imagined community" – as Benedict Anderson categorizes the notion of nation in the "mind of each citizen" all of whom cannot be literally present to each other (Anderson 1983: 15) – but an experience of simultaneous presence *as* national belonging.

While television and press reports highlighted consent rather than dissent, they obliquely acknowledged the persistence of discord and dramatic conflict in the national celebration. Most visible in the ex-ministers of the "old" South Africa who appeared unable or unwilling to sing "Nkosi sikelel' iAfrika" or the anti-apartheid activists turned MPs chortling ironically as they sang "Die Stem," dissent was occasionally more explicit. Newly inaugurated *imbongi yeSizwe* [people's poet], Zolani Mkhiva, dressed to signify the new South Africa in a loose white garment, topped with a skin hat festooned with new South African flags, staged this dissent in "A luta continua," his *izibongo* to ANC leaders including not only Mandela but also Jay Naidoo, formerly trade union leader and now Minister of Telecommunications, alluding to the class struggle many in the ANC elite would rather put behind them. While his later *izibongo* on the podium, "Halala Mandela," saluted Mandela unconditionally, "A luta continua" was delivered in the style of the mass movement rally, dramatizing the difference between the militant language, emphatic tone, and bold gestures of the struggle, and Mandela's subdued mien as he turned to face the assembly through the plexiglass to call (in Afrikaans, the language associated with apartheid), for the overcoming of the past – "Laat ons die verlede vergeet. Wat verby is, is verby" [Let us forget the past. Bygones *are* bygones] (emphasis added).

Mandela's call to reconciliation and the audience's performances in direct or indirect response prompted at least one reporter – observing from the lawn rather

3

than, as the SABC crews were, from the amphitheatre – to call this "political theatre," which "blurred the distinction between audience and players to such an extent that . . . the . . . event became a living enactment of this country's possibilities" (Gevisser 1994a: 9). This attribution of theatricality to the event is paradoxical because it appears to celebrate the transcendence rather than the restoration of theatrical form. While it did not enact a dramatic fiction in the conventional sense, the inauguration was theatrical in its formal staging and script, and in its distinction from ordinary speech and behavior. Gevisser's celebration of a blurring of the boundaries between actors and audience, conventionally associated with (Western, modern, bourgeois) theatre and manifest here in the security barriers separating the presidential party and the crowd below, may seem *antitheatrical* to the extent that it posits an authentic experience of collective belonging that belies the formal orchestration of the official enactment. But the moniker "political theatre" also alludes to the anti-apartheid drama which, although performed on stages for audiences, has been largely understood to have provided the place and occasion for representing an alternative nation, one that achieved full legitimacy with the inauguration of 1994. The analogy between theatre and inauguration is a casual one, but it is precisely this casualness that draws attention both to the pervasive authority of theatre in South Africa and to the difficulty of defining "theatre" and "South Africa" and thus provides this introduction with its point of departure.

The brief account of the inauguration and its surrounding celebrations that I have outlined here does not exhaust the semiotic and ideological complexity of the event nor does it pretend to plumb the depths of the not quite compatible passions it conjured up in participants and observers. What it does provide is a series of intersecting scenes, whose consonant and dissonant performances outline the parameters for the drama of South Africa. This outline allows me to begin to trace the ties and the ruptures among plays, pageants, and their publics, and the social, political, and historical conditions that these performances have inhabited and animated; to sketch the links and boundaries among the terms that frame this study; and to argue both for the distinctiveness of these South African formations throughout the twentieth century and the heterogeneity of cultural practice in this place and time. Rather than attempting at the outset to define terms – such as performance, theatre, and drama, or modern, civilized, and postcolonial – I shall use the points at which they coincide or conflict with each other as points of departure for plotting this drama of South Africa.

Performance and theatrical nationhood

As the print and televisual record of the inauguration suggests (and the memories of many confirm), the impromptu as well as the official enactments appear to carry the force of performance in its most emphatic sense. In inaugurating the new nation, these performances were seen to "actualize" a "potential" action (Bauman 1989: 3, 262–63), completing that action in the world as well as on stage

(Turner 1982: 13), and thus constituting an efficacious enactment of social transformation rather than just an entertaining representation of fictional action
(Schechner 1988: 120–24). In other words, these enactments were felt to have
the power of rites of passage or *liminal* performances (Turner 1982: 54), in that
they marked a fundamental and collectively acknowledged breach in the life of a
community, as well as the resolution of that breach in the reassembly of the nation.
At the same time, the combination of the formal ritual of national installation and
unification and the aleatory acts of individual participation, such as the black
woman dancing the *tiekiedraai* or the NP member selling (and wearing) "Madibamobilia," suggests performances of a *liminoid* character, not only because the latter
were idiosyncratic and playful (Turner 1982: 54), but also because they introduced
a self-reflexive, ostentatious, *theatrical* pause into the visual and narrative representation of collectivity, as well as a reminder of the ways in which this immediate
experience is mediated by local and global commodity circulation.[6]

While this enactment of the nation is performative in both strict and playful
senses, it is also more specifically theatrical. As an instance of *theatrical nationhood* it
signifies "nationhood" because it purports to summon the nation, its unofficial as
well as official representatives, to ratify the event (Kruger 1992: 3). It does so
"theatrically" because it is a performance by actors for an audience at a designated site, and because this performance follows scripts that call on the actors to
take on roles not quite their own, from Mandela speaking in Afrikaans to the
dancing black woman who declared "I am black. I am white. I am coloured. I am
Indian" (Gevisser 1994a: 9). These scripts are only partly verbal – culled from the
discourses of modern statehood and armed struggle, liberal democracy and ethnic
affiliation. Their force arises out of their embodiment in what Richard Schechner
has called "twice-behaved behavior": the "symbolic" and "reflexive" (and in that
sense, "theatrical") representation of once-behaved behavior in a new context
(Schechner 1985: 36–37). As Schechner notes, this restoration may have an
ambiguous, if contradictory relationship to its source; or, as Raymond Williams
might sharpen the contrast, it may restore residual practices understood as
tradition or offer a subjunctive sketch of an emergent, contestatory practice
(Williams 1977: 121–28). What is at stake in these performances is not merely
the restoration or even the revision of the past, but the transformation of received
material in the inauguration of a new model that might provide the basis for
future restoration.

The intersection of residual and emergent scripts was manifested not only in the
SABC camera's attention to ways in which the formal attire and movement of the
nation's official representatives, their retinue, and guests, reclaimed the rituals of
modern statehood, but also the ways in which these rituals are "subject to
revision" (Schechner 1985: 37), when newly legitimate actors, such as newly
inaugurated people's poet Mkhiva and his better-known colleague, Mzwakhe
Mbuli (in designer tie-dyed silk shirt), contested in dress and comportment as
well as in speech the normalization of the South African state. By praising the
militancy of the anti-apartheid organization rather than any single leader and by

calling for ongoing struggle, Mkhiva used the performance and political repertoire of the struggle to challenge the decorous behavior and the formal gravity of Mandela's appeal to reconciliation. On the other hand, he also challenged assumptions about the traditional role of the *imbongi* praising the court by invoking a militant form of political *izibongo* that had already revised the deferential behaviors attributed to (but not always assumed by) precolonial *izimbongi* and by highlighting instead the affinity of his performance repertoire with the script of modern revolution and international class struggle as well as with local practice that has historically "mixed veneration and criticism" in so-called "praises" (Vail and White 1991: 43).[7] The dramatic conflict in the revision and restoration of performance repertoires could also be more subtle, especially when subordinated to the representation of cultural unity. The fusion of Indian dance, Zulu lyrics, and syncretic musical form in "Asimbonanga," for instance, submerged but did not quite erase the history of Indian/Zulu tension in its performance of intercultural collaboration.[8]

Placing the occasion

As designated site for this national drama, the Union Buildings functioned as both proscenium and threshold. As proscenium, they directed the audience's attention to the physical and historical definition and boundedness of the official stage and the relatively unmarked entertainment stage below, shadowed but not surrounded by the erstwhile colonial structure. As threshold, the structure called attention to not one but several passages into a world deemed by participants to be modern and civilized. Built as a monument to the partially postcolonial moment of Union, when, in 1910, Boer leaders (but not all their followers) quashed the anti-British antagonism still simmering after the Anglo-Boer War to join English South Africans under the shield of Britannia and "the civilised nations of the world" (as the Historical Pageant in Cape Town represented the moment) in the creation of a sovereign but segregated state (*Historical Pageant* 1910: 8) (Figure 1.1), the Union Buildings had also provided a literal and figural vantage point from which to view the culmination of another, quite different pageant: the conclusion of the Voortrekker Centenary celebrations with the laying of the foundation of the Voortrekker Monument on the facing hill in 1938 (Figure 1.2). In both instances, women appeared as silent emblems of the nation rather than as national protagonists. But the Union Buildings were also the endpoint of demonstrations against the minority white government, such as the Women's March of 9 August 1956 (now Women's Day), before it became the place and occasion for "South Africa's transition to democracy" (Mandela 1994: 4) and its international recognition as an enlightened modern society, characterized by "peace, prosperity, non-sexism, non-racialism and democracy" (p. 4). While in this case, women protesters carried and expressed national agency, they did so as auxiliaries rather than principles in a national struggle still implicitly gendered male (see chapters 2, 5, and 7).

Figure 1.1 "The partially postcolonial moment": Boer and Briton before Britannia in *The Pageant of Union*, Cape Town, May 1910. *Source*: South African Library

Claimed by succeeding occasions and players, this place cannot be seen only through the eyes of its most recent actors. Rather, as a site on which national prestige – the legitimacy and renown of the nation in the eyes of its citizens and its rivals – is staged, acknowledged, and contested, this place and others like it are overdetermined by the imprint of successive and competing occasions. Traces and echoes of earlier occasions are apparent not only in the monumental structure, but also in the script and staging of this event as the definitive marker of South African maturity and modernity. Despite the inauguration oath, whose injunction to "honor all people in the republic" carries the force of law, and despite the overarching appeal to the reconciliation of former antagonists, the event fused (and sometimes confused) different discourses and behaviors of a still not quite postcolonial South Africa.

The persistence of residual scripts in this place and occasion of the new nation complicates any clear-cut delineation of a postcolonial threshold. In Mandela's speech, as in the dances, the *izibongo*, or the informal comments from the crowd, the discourses of modern statehood, of the liberation struggle, and, in vestigial form, of precolonial, colonial, and neocolonial pasts fuse and fissure.[9] By using the language of universal enlightenment and its barbaric other – the "human disaster" of apartheid (Mandela 1994: 4) – to describe South Africa's return to

Figure 1.2 Women as silent emblems of the Afrikaner *volk* at the Voortrekker Centenary, 16 December 1938. *Source and permission*: Nationale Pers

the civilized world, Mandela highlights his country's claims to exemplary status in that world, as a model of reconciliation that others should follow. This model brings together an enlightenment conception of reconciliation by reason rather than by war, with what Archbishop Desmond Tutu (whose Christian prayer closed the formal inauguration ceremony) has since called the "restorative dimension of African jurisprudence" (Maja-Pearce 1996: 53), but Mandela's final endorsement of that achievement sounds an unexpected note: "The sun shall never set on so glorious a human achievement" (Mandela 1994: 5). This allusion to the boast of the (British) Empire on which the sun was supposed never to set is doubtless ironic, but the irony draws attention not only to the shadow cast by the building in front of the speaker's pavilion but also to clouds on the horizon (in the form of ongoing civil strife) not quite dispelled by this invocation, which seems thus more contemplative than triumphant.

When was postcolonial?

As a liminal event commemorating the act of national renewal after the "country [tore] itself apart in a terrible conflict" (Mandela 1994: 4), the inauguration lays claim both to uniqueness, in that it marks the singular threshold of South Africa's unrepeatable passage into the postcolonial era, and to exemplarity, in that it purports to be the definitive moment in a *series* of liminal events, which it claims to surpass and thus to end. Balanced paradoxically between the unique and the iterative, this postcolonial moment has both modernizing and archaizing aspects. Notwithstanding the power of this rite of passage to transform the site of the Union Buildings into the moment of the "non-racist, non-sexist, democratic South Africa," the combination of colonial place and postcolonial time confounds those who might wish to give this rite of passage a single meaning. Multiple claims – the culmination of armed struggle and the obliteration of the old regime; or the recapitulation and incremental modification of earlier occasions on the same spot, or the inauguration of a coming restoration of an essential African identity obscured by the legacy of colonialism – are all present here, but none triumphs. What emerges from this event and other instances of South African theatrical nationhood is not an authoritative *teleology* of performance that might lead to a single national identity, but rather multiple *genealogies* of performance, the analysis of which might clarify the place of the past in the present (Roach 1996: 25), or the different Nows (and Thens) enacted and embodied by the actors (cf. Bloch 1977: 22).

The combination of modernizing and archaizing impulses in the inauguration and, I would argue, in South African theatrical nationhood generally, resists attempts to assimilate the drama of South Africa to the influential formulation of postcolonial culture as "all the culture affected by colonization from imperialism to the present day" (Ashcroft *et al.* 1989: 2). The virtue of this formulation is that it highlights not only the irrevocable impact of colonization but also the significance of earlier as well as later resistance, whether as anticolonial agitation and rebellion or as negotiation with colonial power and neocolonial hegemony, cultural as well as political, whose syncretic and strategic appropriations of imported practices and institutions can be called postcolonial in orientation if not yet in actual fact.[10] The problem with this generalized idea of the postcolonial condition and its corollary, the notion that postcolonialism is "not a temporal concept" but rather a "mode of reading" and of "textual/cultural resistance" (Gilbert and Tompkins 1996: 2), is that it "suspends" history, including the history of cultural imperialism and the past and present of uneven development, in the name of a generalized "resistance" (McClintock 1992: 88). The attribution of anticolonial force to textual complexity under the aegis of a postcolonial "resistance" also attempts to validate as "postcolonial" those formal techniques that have more to do with metropolitan modernism and postmodernism, thus potentially reinforcing rather than deconstructing the hegemony of metropolitan cultural and critical norms, while neglecting other forms, from "tribal sketches" to "historical pageants," which, despite association with colonial and neocolonial institutions, such as mission schools, have been used by Africans to assert their own modernity and sovereignty.

Although the inauguration of Nelson Mandela and a democratic government represents a distinct *political* break from the ideas and practice of white supremacy, the difference between this event and earlier instances of South African theatrical nationhood marks and masks a *formal* connection to an as yet barely investigated genealogy of national enactments.[11] This history juxtaposes the national pageants of white supremacy, such as the pro-British Pageants of Union (1910) and of South Africa (1936) or their Afrikaner Nationalist rivals, the Voortrekker Centenary (1938) and the Tricentenary of Jan van Riebeeck's arrival at the Cape (1952), with the majority-rule inauguration of 1994 and its most recent successor, the opening and closing ceremonies celebrating South Africa as "rainbow nation" on the occasion of the Rugby World Cup (1995).[12] It ought also to include perfor- mances of unrealized emancipation, such as the Emancipation Centenary Celebration (1934) or the protests of the ANC's Defiance Campaign, launched on the same day as the Van Riebeeck Tricentenary (6 April 1952). As chapters 2 and 4 will show, these enactments of quite different South Africas had in common the attempt to re-present and re-member the past in the present, and so to offer a subjunctive enactment of a desirable future, not merely through declarations and documents but above all through the embodiment of ideas and ideologies in the performance of citizen-subjects. Staging or mise-en-scène, as Jean-François Lyotard argues, "inscribes" a message "on human bodies . . . transmitted by these to other bodies" (Lyotard 1977: 88) and so highlights mise-en-scène as a site of conflict over legitimate script and representation.

This process of imposing, transforming, reclaiming the scripts and behaviors of the past in the present in the enactment of the nation deploys what Joseph Roach has called *surrogation*. The "imaginative" action of collective memory, enacted in pageants, plays, historical sketches, or contemporary celebrations responds to "perceived vacancies in the network of social relations" (Roach 1996: 2), attempt- ing to fill these gaps, inconsistencies, or outright contradictions in the record or its recollection. As Roach suggests, surrogation may sometimes succeed in acting as (second) nature, but more often it succeeds only partially, leaving a deficit, or excessively, creating an unmanageable surplus, the production of which may disrupt the legitimation of a particular national enactment.

Interpreting the difference between deficit and surplus or between the recup- erative and provocative moments of surrogation requires us to raise the questions of agency, intent, and control. At its most controlled, surrogation may proceed quite literally by means of the authorized impersonation of a historical figure. In the 1910 Pageant of Union, for instance, Sokobe, son of the legendary Sotho king, Moshoeshoe, played his own father in the last episode in which the latter made a pact with the president of the Orange Free State and so lent the authority of his person to the legitimation of the white Union government. This surrogation can sustain the Union's cherished "historical fiction" of benevolent despotism because the pageant ends in 1854, occluding the sub- sequent history of British, Boer, and Basotho conflict (Merrington 1997: 13); the annexation of Lesotho and that part of the Free State on which diamonds had been discovered by the British in 1867; and the massive transformation of the region by the discovery of diamonds in 1867 (see Thompson 1990: 107–10). By contrast, black impresario Griffiths Motsieloa's recitation of the Gettysburg Address at the Emancipation Centenary Celebration in 1934, while it did not quite entail an impersonation of Abraham Lincoln, still less of Frederick Douglass, represented an attempt to use surrogation as critical rewriting of the script handed to them, and succeeded in appropriating the textual and corporeal scripts of the African-American Emancipation for the South African stage. At the 1994 inauguration, Mandela's Afrikaans epilogue to his English speech enacted reconciliation through impersonating the former Afrikaner antagonist, an act of surrogation that may have reassured his Afrikaner predecessor, F. W. de Klerk, but that doubtless disturbed many of his ANC supporters. Johnny Clegg's performance status as a "white Zulu" has been generally received as a benign homage to the culture of South Africa's largest ethnic group and thus enhanced the legitimacy of "Asimbonanga," but it does not erase the less than benign historical figure of the "white Zulu" exemplified by nineteenth-century colonial landowner and political intriguer, John Dunn, whose act of "going native" did not prevent his betrayal of the Zulu king to the British (see chapter 3). Each of these performances marks the breach, but also the link, between bondage and freedom, tradition and modernity, subordination and sovereignty, revising the scripts of previous rites of passage, and thus reconstructing new genealogies of performance. Even at the moment that appears to us now as the most dramatic rupture of 1994, this process retraces but never quite clears the slate.

If the term "postcolonial" is to help us in plotting the drama of South Africa, it has to illuminate these asymmetrical and asynchronic enactments of South African modernity and maturity and the multiple appropriations of the actors, whose surrogations draw on the scripts, behaviors, and sites of apparently incompatibly South African occasions, and thus to acknowledge, as Homi Bhabha has it, the "disjunctive" character of the "enunciative present of modernity" (Bhabha 1991: 195). The ambiguous temporality of the impersonations and enunciations at play here does not therefore mean that we should abandon the term "postcolonial," but rather that we should pay due attention to each of the stages on which they might appear.

Theatre and the public sphere

Calling the inauguration and its surrounding performances "theatre" highlights simultaneously the effective enactment of the nation *and* the subjunctive, perhaps fictive, even illusory dimension of theatrical nationhood. It stresses not only the multiple modes of performances, whether identified as theatre or not, which have competed for authority on the South African stage since its first – partial – enactment as a nation in 1910, but also the contribution to national representation of theatre in the narrower sense – the staging of dramatic fictions by actors more or less trained to embody characters and the institutions – social, economic, and political, as well as cultural, supporting (or constraining) this activity and its audiences. Moreover, it draws attention to the limits in the South African context of definitions of theatre that rely on the generic specificity of aesthetic forms. Theatrical forms, I would argue, can be properly evaluated or even seen as theatrical only through the investigation of the ownership, contestation, and appropriation of institutions, understood as organizations located in social and economic structures (and sometimes in actual buildings) and as the prevailing conventions that determine the identification and legitimation of certain practices as "theatre," certain people as audiences, and certain combinations as "national." Legitimate definitions of theatre – not only in South Africa, but also throughout the modern world – do not rest on invariable formal features or aesthetic value but rather, as Pierre Bourdieu notes, take their shape as capital in response to the pressure of legitimation and contestation in the social and economic as well as the cultural field (Bourdieu 1993).

The limits of an aesthetic definition of theatre can be seen not merely in the overtly political performances in South Africa but even in the metropolitan institutionalization of Shakespeare, whose aesthetic value is often taken for granted. The canonization of the Shakespearean text (and its subsequent dissemination as the exemplar of English culture throughout the Empire) bears witness to the entwinement of the discourse of universal aesthetic value with that of social discipline and exclusion. The attempts of cultural conservatives, such as Samuel Coleridge, to preserve the poet Shakespeare from the ravages of the stage in the early nineteenth century, a period of rapid industrialization, urbanization, and national redefinition in the context of empire, was not an overdue recognition of Shakespeare's literary genius but a historically specific response by the "cultivated classes" to what they saw as the vulgarity of the stage – the textual bowdlerization of producers and the habits of performance (virtuoso gesture and ad-lib declamation) that encourage and reflect the noisy participation of the "unlettered audience."[13] The defense of the autonomy of Shakespearean poetry is thus predicated on assumptions about the proper occasion and place for appreciating Shakespeare. The appeal for the decorous contemplation of dramatic poetry as autonomous art is, in the historical context of anti-Jacobin England, linked to the *heteronomous* demand for maintaining rank in a patrician social order. While the notion of autonomous aesthetic value does not owe its authority directly to these social relations, the institution of that authority makes sense only in terms of the relationships legitimately established between aesthetic authority and social and political hegemony and the ways in which both are sedimented in the apparatus and in the form and function of the texts performed there. Conversely, the capacity of theatre to resist political power emerges from its liminal character: its condition as both autonomous (an aesthetic practice at one remove from daily life) and heteronomous (a practice engaged with political, economic, and social pressures, even as it resists them).

The analogy between national enactment and theatre in the broad sense in South Africa, with which I began, draws its power from the historical part played by theatre in the narrower sense in contesting official definitions of the South African nation and in constituting an assembly that could be considered, against the manifest illegitimacy of the apartheid state, a nation in the making. This is the theatre conventionally associated with the anti-apartheid movement, the theatre of *testimony* variously identified with "protest" and "resistance," and with the names of Athol Fugard, John Kani, or Barney Simon (see chapters 5 and 7) or, less frequently, with the theatrical activities of political groups such as the Communist Party in the 1930s and 1940s (see chapters 3 and 4), the Black Consciousness Movement in the 1960s and 1970s (see chapter 6), or the United Democratic Front in the 1980s (see chapter 7). While these men and their theatre in no way exhaust the field, their impact is exemplary as well as influential; for this reason, they serve as key points of reference in this introduction. This testimonial theatre can be said to constitute a *virtual public sphere*, a site and a mode of counter-publicity where South Africa could be depicted as it could have been and might yet be, as well as where actual conditions might be critically represented in the guise of dramatic fictions, at times when direct action was dangerous or impossible.[14] In its juxtaposition of apparently alien languages and conventions culled from European, American, and African practices, this theatre has performed the syncretizing character of South African culture, even at historical moments when the ruling class and race insisted on racial purity and cultural separation.

The virtual publicity of anti-apartheid theatre took concrete shape in real time and space in the performance and reception of such plays as Fugard, Kani, and Ntshona's *Sizwe Banzi Is Dead* (first performed 1972; published by Fugard, Kani, and Ntshona 1986). This play moved its initial, predominantly white audience at the independent Space Theatre in Cape Town to laughter and tears, but provoked the black audience in the players' home township, New Brighton, to enact questions of immediate social urgency, such as their enforced subjection to the passbook and the arbitrary tyranny of white bosses, so that the event retained its subjunctive character within the relatively safe bounds of an entertainment space in an otherwise politically risky environment (see chapter 7). This virtual publicity was also manifest at events where the connection with contemporary politics was more oblique – such as the coincidence of *Moshoeshoe* (first performed 1938; published Dhlomo 1985), by the prolific but at the time largely unpublished Herbert Dhlomo (now canonized as the "pioneer of modern black drama" [Visser and Couzens 1985: xv]), with unofficial but nationwide commemorations of Moshoeshoe Day, in honor of the Sotho king's magnanimous treatment of his enemies, black and white; or the performance at the Emancipation Centenary (1934) of scenes from slave life reminiscent of *Uncle Tom's Cabin*. Despite their marginal visibility outside the small circle of educated Africans and liberal white patrons, these performances nonetheless retained their subjunctive force (in the representation of an unacknowledged African history and possible African future) for a target audience that ideally included less than elite Africans as well (see chapter 3).

"'Theatre' is not part of our [African] vocabulary"

If drama in South Africa from Dhlomo to Fugard and beyond, performed under the aegis of urban institutions from the Bantu Men's Social Centre (1920s–1950s; sustained by white philanthropists and black professionals and teachers) to the Market Theatre (1976–; sponsored by foundation grants and donations from South Africa's liberal capitalists), is generally acknowledged as a key player in the creation of counter-publicity and, eventually, of nationally legitimate publicity in South Africa, then how do we make sense of the charge, made by Sipho Sepamla (writer and editor of the influential black theatre magazine, *S'ketsh*) that "'theatre' is not part of our [African] vocabulary"? It is significant that this charge was made at a moment of intensive anti-apartheid theatre activity: 1981 saw the premiere of *Woza Albert!* (Mtwa, Ngema, and Simon 1983), one of the best-known examples of syncretic South African theatre form. The answer lies in part in the institutional as well as formal differences between the variety entertainments that have dominated urban black leisure since the 1920s and the imitation of European, especially English drama, by educated Africans, especially the generation schooled in the Anglophile mission institutions up to 1960. As Sepamla notes, urban and urbanizing Africans in this century have performed and observed a range of forms from "sketches" to "concerts" to "plays." If popular producers and audiences have not made "theatre" part of an African vocabulary, or have done so inconsistently, it is in large part because these entertainments and their impresarios have had little access (economic, legal, cultural) to the prestige of theatre and theatres, even if their shows may have included the performance of dramatic texts.

This institutional determination of "African theatre" does not render the question of forms irrelevant, however. What it does is remind us that drama at venues like the Bantu Men's Social Centre in downtown Johannesburg and later in halls in Soweto had to find a place alongside the "concerts" and "sketches" that had developed in the encounters between the commercial entertainments of European (and also American and African-American) capitalist culture and the *ingoma* [the general isiZulu term for music or performance] (Erlmann 1991) associated with ritual or other celebrations of the rural amaZulu, becoming, in the process of negotiating with segregation (and later, apartheid) capitalism, *ingoma ebusuku* [night music, or entertainment performed after work in enclosed spaces for money] (Ballantine 1993) and, in time, African variety.[15] For its audiences and practitioners, African variety was the purview of impresarios like Motsieloa, who drew on a range of models from the imperial Eisteddfodau and the missionary church choir to rural modes of storytelling – *izinganekwane* (isiZulu) or *ntsomi* (isiXhosa) – and praises – *izibongo* (isiZulu) *lithoko* (Sesotho), African-American jubilee, as well as the ambiguous representation of race in minstrelsy, "tribal sketches," and other vaudeville gags.[16] They appealed to black audiences from urban English-speaking elites to urbanizing *abaphakathi* [the people in between tradition and modernity] and attempted, with limited success, to match aspirations to cultural modernity with the accumulation of capital (see chapter 2). Among Motsieloa's successors, we can count Todd Matshikiza (composer of the Sophiatown "jazz opera" *King Kong* in 1959; see chapter 4), Gibson Kente (premier writer and producer of township musicals from 1960s to 1980s, see chapter 6), Mbongeni Ngema (best known for *Sarafina*, 1986; published Ngema 1995), and Walter Chakela, director of *Bloke* (adapted in 1994 from the 1962 autobiography of Sophiatown writer, Bloke Modisane), who have made this the most durable form of black entertainment in South Africa (see chapter 7).

Against the success of this syncretic music-theatre, the appeal of "theatre" associated with the British colonial curriculum and its African counterpart in the elite mission schools may seem slight, even if it was embraced by elite Africans keen to appropriate "European civilization" from those some called "white savages" (Kabane 1936: 187). This curriculum included Shakespeare and Shaw, but made more use of the drawing-room comedy of Sheridan and Wilde, as well as the "social drama" of John Drinkwater and John Galsworthy. This is the drama that shaped the secondary and tertiary education of white and black elites, including men like Dhlomo and Mandela as well as Sepamla, during the relatively Anglophile period (1910–50) of Union in the British Commonwealth.[17] While an English literary education and a theatrical repertoire of West End tours offered Anglophone whites membership in an ersatz or substitute public sphere that indulged their desire for the metropolitan glamour of the London stage and the legitimation of the neocolonial Union as a modern, "European" society, mission school education appeared – to its ultimately disillusioned graduates as well as to outside commentators – to grant its African participants an elusive if not illusory association with an English civilization remote from the reality of segregation (see chapter 3).

While the ersatz publicity of Anglophone settler culture in South Africa resembled formations elsewhere in the Commonwealth, the Afrikaner Nationalist state's appropriation of theatre and other practices of national enactment represented a more direct instrumentalization of culture in the service of politics. Afrikaans literary theatre, especially in the amateur heyday (1920s–1940s), shared with its Anglophone counterparts a desire for affiliation to Europe reflected in its practitioners' interest in translating the drama of Shakespeare, Lessing, or Ibsen. But this cosmopolitan moment was superseded by a nationalist commitment to the Afrikaans language and (white) identity. From the anti-British drama of the 1920s to the populist reenactments of Afrikaner suffering and triumph in national pageants (commemorating the Voortrekker Centenary in 1938 and the Van Riebeeck Tricentenary in 1952) to the more literary allegories of *Die Dieper Reg* [The Deeper Right, written by N. P. van Wyk Louw, a major Afrikaner poet, on commission for the Centenary] and *Die Jaar van die Vuuros* [The Year of the Fire-ox, prize-winner for the 1952 festival, written by W. A. de Klerk, later author of *The Puritans of Africa*], Afrikaans theatre endorsed, with minor reservations, the ideology of Afrikaner primacy in Africa (see chapters 3 and 4). Those authors who expressed mild dissent from apartheid policy (such as de Klerk) or criticism of

15

Afrikaner racism and hypocrisy – such as Bartho Smit who had one play, *Die Verminktes* [The Maimed, 1962], denied production, and another, *Putsonderwater* [Well without Water, 1965] marginalized by an unpublicized short run – still enjoyed support (as employees of state-run agencies such as the Performing Arts Councils [PACs] or quasi-state entities such as the Afrikaans presses) in the name of *volkseie* [ethnic identity] and *volkskapitalisme* [ethnically exclusive state subsidy], a privilege denied English-speaking dissenters, white or black (see chapter 5).[18] Only those blacks who submitted to the apartheid conception and organization of tribal identity (such as announcers and translators for Radio Bantu or authors of vernacular-language textbooks) received government subsidy – ironically, for the translations of European classics or for plays in the European manner extolling "traditional" rural Africa (see chapter 4).

It is the historical association of European dramatic forms with neocolonial – whether more apparently liberal Anglophone or more emphatically segregationist Afrikaner – institutions that has led critics at home, such as Mafika Gwala, Sepamla's younger contemporary, to dismiss this inheritance as irredeemably colonial and therefore unsuitable for a properly African National Theatre (Gwala 1973: 131). It has also led some abroad to argue that pioneering African writers, including the now much-feted Dhlomo, were producing merely mission literature (Gérard 1971: 236) or "sterile unimaginative plays bearing little relation to African theatrical expression" (Coplan 1985: 125). Such condemnations of the neocolonial legacy in South African writing correspond in part to debates else-where in Africa, articulated most notably by Frantz Fanon and Ngũgĩ wa Thiong'o, who argue that only cultural practices that harness indigenous forms to the representation of current popular concerns can fully represent postcolonial society (Fanon 1968: 220–27; Ngũgĩ 1986: 4–33).

This rejection of literary drama is in large part a reaction to the a priori definition of drama propagated not only by the mission schools but also by respected ethnographers of "oral literature in Africa," such as Ruth Finnegan, who argued that, "while dramatic elements [such as impersonation, props, costume, and the representation of interaction among characters] enter into several different categories of artistic activity in Africa . . . there are few or no forms which include all these elements" (Finnegan 1970: 501). As Nigerian-born critic Biodun Jeyifo has noted, even pioneering work like Finnegan's *Oral Literature in Africa* or Graham-White's *Drama of Black Africa* (1974) is problematic to the extent that it brings to African practices an a priori idea of what drama should be without fully acknowledging the derivation of this idea from canonized European practices; thus it cannot explain its failure to find this idea fully realized in Africa (Jeyifo 1996: 153–56). As Jeyifo's discussion suggests, these scholarly accounts seem, despite their pioneering surveys of the field, still touched by the vestiges of a (neo)colonial essentialism that possessed white educators of black performers of an earlier era. This essentialism or nominalist attachment to an essential idea of "theatre" is what allowed avowedly missionary organizations like the British Drama League to applaud the spontaneity of African performers while regretting

their apparent lack of dramatic knowledge, and apparently friendly white collaborators, such as Harry Bloom (amateur librettist for the hit *King Kong*) to think of
his colleague, the more experienced professional Matshikiza, as a "part-time
musician," unskilled in "proper theatre" (Bloom *et al.* 1961: 15).

The "tenacious logocentrism" (Jeyifo 1996: 155) of neocolonial essentialism,
which diminishes African theatrical practices by finding them incompatible with
European ideas of *the* theatre, has provoked in some Africanist circles an equally
tenacious "ontologization" of an essential Africanness (Jeyifo 1990: 37) which
reverses but does not radically challenge neocolonial essentialism. Africans in this
tradition have generally proceeded either by dismissing "theatre" as a colonial
import or, more often, by arguing the reverse: that "theatre" ought to apply not to
colonial dramatic literature but to precolonial oral performance practice. The first
line of argument underlies Sepamla's assertion at the outset of this section; the
second finds its South African spokesman in self-described "witchdoctor" Credo
Mutwa, who has argued that theatre has its African origin in *umlinganiso* [imita-
tion]. Sepamla's line of argument is more useful here because it draws attention to
the production and reception and the place and occasion of performance *practices*
rather than, despite his polemical statement, getting caught up with definitions,
and thus to the processes that Jeyifo calls, revising Hobsbawm and Ranger's classic
formulation, the "*re*invention of tradition" or the "reappropriation" of a "suitable
past" as tradition (Jeyifo 1996: 157). As the examples mentioned here suggest,
theatre in South Africa is not *essentially* European or African; rather it *takes place*
between and within practices, forms, and institutions variously and contentiously
associated with Europe, Africa, America, and – to complicate the standard
oppositions – African America.

Subjunctive enactment

The institutional determination of aesthetic value or, more precisely, of what may,
in a given place and occasion, be identified as theatre art, suggests that, while it
may be historically necessary or currently pragmatic to distinguish theatre,
syncretic or otherwise, from other forms of performance (Balme 1995: 10–11),
and even political or what I've called *testimonial* theatre from related practices such
as *izibongo* at political funerals, choral singing at union rallies, and the like, it is not
clear that aesthetics is the most appropriate criterion. To insist on aesthetics –
form, fictionality, autonomy – as the distinguishing term of theatre, in this
context, threatens to reintroduce surreptitiously the nominalist attachment to
an a priori idea of "theatre" against which actual practices are measured and,
by implication, found wanting. This nominalism would not necessarily entail a
return to narrowly Eurocentric tastes in the name of artistic value, but it would
obscure the irreducibly *impure autonomy* of theatre, in South Africa, or indeed,
elsewhere, as a cultural practice that combines in unstable but productive ways
aesthetics and politics, autonomy and heteronomy (whether in the form of
confirmation of or resistance to prevailing social relations), fictional plots and

factual representations. The impure autonomy of theatre means that it can only approximate the status of an artistic work but also that its incomplete approximation is its distinguishing feature. In this peculiar way both more and less than art, theatre straddles the border country between the aesthetic state and the political, and provides the stage on which the contradictions between them can be enacted.

What is at issue in the differences between theatre and related practices is not aesthetics but rather the historical and current determination of the *friction* as well as the functional association of differently restored behaviors, conventions, or scripts, on the occasions of their performance and reception as "theatre," as cultural practice judged to have aesthetic and social legitimacy. Particular forms (for instance, dialogue, consistent impersonation of character or portrayal of plot) are less determinative than theatre's capacity for subjunctive enactment. Where performances like the act of inauguration and the speeches and songs at rallies (or, for that matter, the re-creation of the Voortrekker migration) have a subjunctive component, their power depends on their convincing representation of an unmediated, authentic, *indicative* link between performers and the roles they enact. In contrast, in its various institutional manifestations from the performance by professional actors with no intrinsic connection to the dramatic text mounted on a stage in a specially designed building for a paying audience to variety sketches displaying and undoing racial stereotypes to simulations of worker/boss conflicts to even the black women doing the *tiekiedraai* at the inauguration, theatre's action is subjunctive. In other words, it maintains a relatively fictional, autonomous, and, in this sense, aesthetic distance from indicative action, however political its explicit aims. Although most obviously applied to the utopian dimension of anti-apartheid theatre's evocation (in performing defiantly under duress rather than by depicting future conditions) of post-apartheid South Africa, subjunctive action can also apply to what some might call the "bad fictionality" of enactments of and in the ersatz public sphere of settler culture or the segregated public sphere of *volkseie* [ethnic identity]. Despite their very different meanings, these enactments have in common the representation of fictions that attempt, in the restoration – or contestation – of scripts, conventions, and behaviors in dramatic conflict, to realize a new South Africa on stage.

The languages of South African theatre

Language is a key site and medium for this contestation. Where debates on indigenous authenticity elsewhere in Africa have focused on language as well as performance forms, black South African theatre practitioners have tended to treat the questions of indigenous language and indigenous form pragmatically. With the exception of theatre by and for Afrikaans-speaking coloureds, black urban theatre has usually consisted of English dialogue, with jokes and songs in a range of vernaculars, performed for bilingual or multilingual audiences. The argument for indigenous authenticity or, in Ngũgĩ's more dynamic formulation, radical decolonization, certainly has the virtue of highlighting the eclipse of indigenous languages by the global reach of capitalist social relations and international languages and thus the marginalization of those who speak only local languages or who prefer to perform in the home languages of their target audiences. It does not take full account, however, of the range of local transformations undergone by the English language and dramatic conventions in South Africa, to say nothing of the history of Afrikaans, whose development as a creolized descendant of Cape Dutch influenced to a greater or lesser degree by the creoles spoken by (Asian) slaves and indigenous Khoisan was for a long time distorted by Afrikaner Nationalist claims for the "European" character of *suiwer* [pure] Afrikaans.[19]

Moreover, insisting on authenticity or an absolute difference between European and African, imported and indigenous, literary and oral, threatens to repeat the neocolonial essentialism that it purports to critique. Because the discourse of ethnic essentialism has historically been associated with segregation, even Africanist advocates for authentic or, more precisely, *autochthonous* language or modes of performance have found only a limited, usually ethnically exclusive following. The promotion of indigenous language education has, until recently, been linked with the apartheid policy of divide and rule by way of (re)tribalization and the attempt to deny Africans full access to English. It has also been associated with ambiguous figures, such as Mutwa, whose appeals to precolonial authenticity were undermined by connections to apartheid structures.[20] On the other hand, the historical association of English with the power of the British Empire and the hegemony of colonial culture has not prevented its past and present function in South Africa as a sign, if not a direct means, of emancipation (Hartshorne 1992: 186–217) and continues to function as a key aspiration of black parents and students (Heugh 1995), in addition to its role as a primary (but not exclusive) medium for theatre.[21]

While endoglossic (indigenous) language theatre has become slightly more visible on subsidized stages since 1994, most performers rely on English (supplemented by the most widely spoken vernaculars, especially in the isiNguni group), to reach multilingual audiences, engaged in the local appropriation of a range of englishes. Acknowledging the ongoing pervasiveness of English in South Africa, we should nonetheless be cautious about celebrations of postcolonial englishes as unequivocal signs of resistance to imperial legacies (Ashcroft *et al.* 1989: 41–44), since such celebrations dwell on and in ex-settler colonies where English has either obliterated indigenous languages or accorded them minority status. Commentators on South African englishes cannot lose sight of the paradox that, while only about 10 per cent of the population speaks English as mother tongue, ever more theatre is produced in englishes by those who have acquired the language through formal or informal education (see articles by Buthelezi, Mesthrie, and Branford and Claughton, in Mesthrie 1995a). The transformations of the linguistic and dramatic conventions of English in South Africa should include not only those of anti-apartheid testimony in drama or the public poetry of political funerals, but also the incomplete but arresting combination of the literary history play, *izibongo*, and African Nationalist hymns in plays like Dhlomo's *Moshoeshoe* (see chapter 3) and Ronnie Govender's "Indian" English in such plays as *The Lahnee's Pleasure* (1972) (see chapter 6), as well as the better-known plays of Fugard. Fugard's contribution is noteworthy not just because he has been the most widely published and produced playwright from South Africa but rather because he was the first to create on stage a fully colloquial South African English, as opposed to the self-conscious literariness that affects writers as different as Dhlomo and the established white poet and professor, Guy Butler. Shaped by the Afrikaans that many of his characters would plausibly speak more readily than English, especially in *The Blood Knot* (1961), *Hello and Goodbye* (1966), and *Boesman and Lena* (1972), Fugard's mature plays created a South African idiom that could be national, local, and intimate all at once. Refusing initially to work with the state-subsidized (and therefore segregated) PACs, Fugard nonetheless enjoyed access, as a white English-speaking man (with an unfinished BA), to the resources of liberal universities or informal theatre groups to produce these plays about the constrained lives of black, brown, and poor white. By contrast, Adam Small, a "brown/black Afrikaner" (with an advanced degree) who wrote plays on similar topics in *Kaaps*, perhaps the original Afrikaans dialect, saw his 1965 play, *Kanna, Hy Kô Hystoe* [Kanna's Coming Home], produced by a coloured student group only in 1972, and appropriated by the all-white Performing Arts Council of the Transvaal (PACT) in 1974, whose production he could attend only by special permit (see chapter 5).

The dramatic and theatrical idiom of Fugard's solo literary work can be described as a *synthesis* of the scripts of domestic drama, existentialism, and anti-apartheid testimony. However literary they might be, Fugard's plays from *No-Good Friday* (1958) on are locally grounded in a way that marks a crucial departure from the provincial self-consciousness of plays like Lewis Sowden's *The Kimberley Train*, written in the same year. Fugard did not, as has been claimed, inaugurate either a dramatic tradition of writing on South African themes or "political theatre in the Western mode" (Mda 1995: 39). The first honor should go to writer and actor-manager, Stephen Black, whose farces and melodramas were popular in the early twentieth century; the second to groups like the Bantu People's Theatre (1930s and 1940s), and their European socialist collaborators. What Fugard did was to make "political theatre in the Western mode" visible, available, and ultimately legitimate to a degree impossible for the small, beleaguered interracial groups associated with liberals or communists in the 1930s and 1940s.

Fugard's theatrical collaborations, with the African Theatre Workshop in the 1950s, the Serpent Players in the 1960s, and, most famously, the team of Kani and Ntshona in the 1970s, were also not the first of their kind, but their national and international success prepared the ground for the growth of the *syncretic* or, more precisely, *syncretizing* practices now generally associated with South African theatre. The syncretism of *Sizwe Banzi Is Dead* (first performed 1972), their signature

20

collaboration, consists not only of its formal combination of anti-apartheid testimony, naturalistic dialogue, and African variety gags (especially in Kani's impersonation of characters ranging from his white boss to township cockroaches) or its concatenation of the occasions of theatre and political debate, but also of a more subtle engagement with a largely unwritten history of photographic as well as dramatic depictions of African aspirations thwarted by racism (see chapter 7). This theatre of testimony, from *Sizwe Banzi Is Dead* (1972) to *Woza Albert!* (first performed 1981; published Mtwa *et al.* 1983) to *Born in the RSA* (first performed 1985; published B. Simon *et al.* 1986, 1994), produced by institutions like the Market Theatre and their associates and competitors, can be called *syncretizing*, because it marks an ongoing negotiation with forms and practices, variously and not always consistently identified as modern or traditional, imported or indigenous, European or African.

With the transformations – and disappointments – of the 1990s, the moral conviction that sustained several generations of theatre activists and cultural workers since the 1930s and that culminated in such memorable political theatre events as the performance of *Sizwe Banzi* (1972), *Woza Albert!* (1981), and *Born in the RSA* (1985) has given way to a variety of not-quite-compatible political persuasions and cultural practices. Theatre in South Africa is now more diverse but also more conflicted. The performance of satirist Pieter-Dirk Uys, for instance, at his recent show, *Truth Omissions* (1996) (Figure 1.3), as Winnie Madikizela Mandela draped in a Nelson Mandela T-shirt gives us not only the spectacle of an "Afrikaner-Jewish drag queen" impersonating the woman still known as "mother of the nation" (despite her own appearance as the accused in the hearings of the Truth Commission), in the manner in which he has previously posed as Evita Bezuidenhout, wife of a fictitious Afrikaner ambassador to a non-existent bantustan. Uys's stature is such that he has entertained and teased new South African politicians (including Mandela) in Evita drag on the steps of the Union Buildings in full view of the national TV audience (Uys 1995). In these encounters, but even more pointedly in this impersonation of the "mother of the nation," Uys challenges South Africans to think sceptically about national icons and founding fictions when competing appeals for national, regional, and ethnic affiliation continue to echo across the country. More modestly, perhaps, post-apartheid theatre, by and for local communities, has attempted to combine theatrical performance and religious expression to grapple with the conflicts arising with the falling-away of anti-apartheid certainties in the absence of radical social transformation, as in *Zombie*, which uses the resources of practicing diviners, church elders and their choir, and talented worker-actors, to dramatize the struggle of the Kokstad/Bhongweni community (in the underdeveloped Eastern Cape province) to cope with the accidental (but actual) death of twelve schoolboys and the seemingly fated conflict between young comrades who blame old women as witches for stealing the souls of the dead and the church elders who attempt to break the witchhunt and bury the dead – or undead (see cover of present volume). Where the idea and practice of dramatic synthesis may imply the achievement of

Figure 1.3 An Afrikaner-Jewish drag queen plays mother of the nation: Pieter-Dirk Uys as Winnie Madikizela Mandela, Standard Bank National Arts Festival, 1996. *Source and permission*: Grahamstown Foundation

an organic or at least a literary whole (legitimated, in Fugard's case, by international publication and canonization), that of syncretizing theatre foregrounds the ongoing and unfinished work of appropriation (in the double sense of seizure and making one's own) as well as the historical and contemporary constraints on that work. The history and legacy of that work is the drama of South Africa and the subject of this book.

THE PROGRESS OF THE
NATIONAL PAGEANT

On Sunday, 3 June 1934, African artists and intellectuals, American Board Missionaries, liberal whites associated with the Joint European/African Council movement and a "New African" (educated and, to a degree Europeanized) audience gathered at the Bantu Men's Social Centre (BMSC) in central Johannesburg for a National Thanksgiving or Emancipation Centenary Celebration, commemorating the abolition of slavery in the British Empire in 1834. The Celebration was framed by speeches by American missionaries and leading Africans, such as R. V. Selope Thema (editor of *Bantu World*) and Dr. A. B. Xuma (later president of the ANC) and incorporated chamber music by Mendelssohn and Schubert, extracts from Handel's *Messiah*, Elgar's "Land of Hope and Glory," hymns composed by Europeans, Africans, and Americans, including "Negro spirituals," and the Gettysburg Address, delivered by African variety impresario and Trinity College (London) graduate, Griffiths Motsieloa. It culminated in a "dramatic display," the subject of which was not, as might have been expected, the emancipation of slaves in Africa or the Caribbean, but the lives of slaves in the United States.[1]

While its primary occasion was the commemoration of emancipation, this National Thanksgiving was also in part a reproach to the South African government for its increasingly aggressive disenfranchisement of Africans. As a reproach, this event responded not only to present discrimination but also to the racialist ideology and practice of the state established by the opening of the first South African parliament and its commemorative performance, the South African Pageant of Union. This pageant, which premiered in Table Bay two days before the opening of parliament on 31 May 1910, displayed before the mayor and city council of Cape Town, members of parliament, and the Duke of Connaught, a pageant of South African history involving over five thousand performers and the services of the new South African Navy. The pageant presented historical sketches from the European (Portuguese, Dutch, and British) "discovery" of the native inhabitants to the appropriation of their lands by treaty or conquest, epitomized, in the last episode, by the meeting between Moshoeshoe and President Hoffmann of the Orange Free State in 1854. By ignoring the subsequent impact of the British annexation of Lesotho and that part of the Free State where diamonds were discovered in 1867, industrialization, and the forced proletarianization of

African peasants to work in the mines, the pageant represented the act of Union as a coming together of Boer and Briton and thus reenacted the familiar teleology of the "Progress of Prosperity" over "hordes of ignorance, cruelty, savagery, unbelief, war, pestilence, famine and their ilk" (*Historical Sketch* 1910: 93), whereby Europe brought "civilization" to what Hegel notoriously called the "unhistorical, undeveloped Spirit of Africa" (Hegel 1956: 99). The pageant acknowledged the historical role of some blacks – such as Moshoeshoe, or Sheik Yusuf, a Muslim cleric now credited with bringing Islam to the Cape while exiled there by the Dutch colonists – whose resistance to the Europeans was represented as benign acquiescence: Yusuf is identified merely as "a Javanese teacher" (*Historical Sketch* 1910: 78), although he was both slave-owner and anticolonial rebel. But Africans were largely relegated to the category of Hegel's "unhistorical" while Europeans and their surrogates in the new parliament were "historical heroes" (*Historical Sketch* 1910: 95) flanked by "maidens in white" (p. 94).

The differences between these two events are noteworthy, but so are their points of contact. The Pageant of Union differed from the Emancipation Celebration not merely in content – in the depiction of white conquest as opposed to black endurance – but also in form and scale of performance. The earlier event displayed the full force of state power, alongside the conspicuous consumption of colonial culture, especially in apparently minor episodes, such as the scene depicting the ball arranged by Lady Anne Barnard, wife of the secretary of the first British colony at the Cape (1795–1803). The later event exposed the relative poverty and powerlessness of even elite Africans, who were dependent on the neocolonial state as well as liberal white patrons. At the same time, however, the participants in the Emancipation Celebration shared with those in the Union Pageant a belief in the universal value of European civilization, represented here by the music of Handel and the Gettysburg Address as well as by the promise of enfranchisement and other liberal freedoms. Even those Africans who criticized the actual "savagery" of whites in Africa and who sought therefore to a degree to "provincialize Europe" by relativizing its claim to the universal (Chakrabarty 1992: 20), used the language of the European Enlightenment to defend the idea and practice of universal rights.

The scripts of the later event explicitly cast the African participants as New Africans, as opposed to the "tribal" Africans featured in the Union Pageant and the "Savage South Africa" show in London (1899–1900) and other colonial expositions (Dell 1993). By including Lincoln's 1863 text and African Nationalist songs composed since the founding of the ANC (1912), the program pointed beyond the nostalgic iconography of the Union Pageant toward an as yet utopian democratic future in South Africa. More concretely, the institutional as well as formal representations of New Africans in this event would be repeated in the context of official events in Johannesburg, South Africa's most modern city, such as the Empire Exhibition (1936), as well as non-official and perforce less visible events, such as "Africa – a revel pageant" (1940), "depicting the march of progress of the Bantu."

24

The syncretism of these events and their forms provided New Africans with occasions in which they could represent themselves as modern agents, even in the performance of "tribal sketches," and thus contest the state's exclusive claims to modernity. While New Africans could not contest the state on the scale of the Union Pageant or the Empire Exhibition, they could attempt to appropriate and refunction the forms of these enactments. Taking into account the precarious nature of New African aspirations and the contradictions between the invention of "authentic" tradition and the reality of a "shattered rural order" (Erlmann 1991: 150), or between the prospect of emancipation held out by "European civiliza-tion" in the abstract and the actual constraints on African freedoms in the Union of South Africa, this chapter investigates the ways in which performance, especially the flexible format of variety and the pageant, created a space for the representation and negotiation of these contradictions unavailable in the legit-imate public sphere of neocolonial institutions and practices.

New Africans, New Negroes and the paradoxes of neocolonial modernity

Although the Emancipation Centenary Celebrations focused on a representation of African modernity, their use of the pathos of slave life in the manner of *Uncle Tom's Cabin* in the "dramatic display" complicates the heroic portrayal of black struggle offered by the ANC repertoire. Written by noted Zulu writer Rolfes Dhlomo and directed by his brother Herbert (journalist, dramatist and musician), the "dramatic display" borrowed freely from Harriet Beecher Stowe's portrayal of "life of the lowly." As reports in *Bantu World* and *Umteteli wa Bantu* (major African papers in Johannesburg) suggest,[2] the portrayal of "the suffering of the American Negroes on the slave market, in the cotton fields and at home, until the joyful news of the liberation" and the "feelings of joy and relief, which the right ending of the struggle for freedom had brought" highlighted the pathos of the slaves' misery and their relief and gratitude for the act of emancipation.[3] This pathos was modified, however, by the inclusion of such songs as "Sixoshiwe [emsebenzini]" ["We are being expelled (from work)"] by Reuben Caluza, composer and collector of Zulu folksongs, and visiting fellow at Columbia University. While the full import of these songs might have been lost on the whites in the audience, it is likely that the Africans would have been familiar with these and other nationalist songs such as "Silusapo or iLand Act" (the first ANC anthem, also by Caluza) (Erlmann 1991: 119–47). Likewise, speeches such as the Gettysburg Address in the mouth of master elocutionist Motsieloa resonated differently from the praise heaped on British "emancipators" such as David Livingstone.

Politically charged as this event certainly was, it thus had no single political meaning. Tolerated by the neocolonial state and applauded by white liberals, it was well received not only by the members of the BMSC but by a more diverse audience in Eastern Native Township the following week. The performance eludes the dichotomy between white colonial hegemony and the oppressed black masses (or between high English culture and working-class practices), a dichotomy that has pervaded South African criticism and underlies key formulations of postcolonial theory elsewhere.[4] In this schema, members of the New African elite, the small intermediary class of clergymen, teachers, and other professionals, who organized events such as the Emancipation Celebration, are distinguished by their attachment to European civilization and thus by their alienation from the masses of black people, whether this alienation is read as the irredeemable result of their colonial assimilation and distance from popular African cultural expression (Gérard 1971; Coplan 1985) or as a measure of the odds against their attempts to represent African masses (Orkin 1991: 45–51; Steadman 1990: 212–16). This retrospective judgment still haunts current debates but it does not fully acknowledge the fluidity of these class and ethnic affiliations or the volatility of African identification with "European civilization" in the 1930s.

The uncertainties of New African life can be summed up by the "ambiguities of dependence," felt especially in the tension between the "mid-Victorian idea of progress" on the one hand and the "fact of subordination" on the other (Marks 1986: 54). However much betrayed in neocolonial practice, the liberal ideals of the Enlightenment, the concept of individual autonomy in the political and economic spheres, offered a compelling if utopian image, and a weapon not only against segregationists but also against communism, which was feared by African conservatives as well as most Europeans. Selope Thema joined the American Board Mission in cautioning his readers against the unchristian tactics of the Bolsheviks and to "honor the great emancipators" such as Livingstone or Lincoln whose example shows the way to "rescue [the world] from the thraldom of nationalist and racial passions."[5] Even Africans who expressed skepticism about European intentions to honor the promise of universal rights implied by the centenary nonetheless used the language of the European Enlightenment to make their case. As the editor of *Umteteli wa Bantu* wrote:

> it is true that Natives can no longer be bought and sold . . . but they are still in bondage as a people and there is a determined stand by Europeans against the grant to them [sic] of that full liberty to which all men are entitled. . . . Natives are not slaves, but they are not freemen.[6]

In pointing to the entrenchment of racial discrimination despite formal freedoms, this editorial drew explicitly on the insights of W. E. B. du Bois, whose landmark work, *Souls of Black Folk* (1903), vividly described the oppression of African-Americans after emancipation (Du Bois 1989: 28–29). In doing so, it not only challenged the authority of white segregationists but also criticized those Africans who, for various and not always consistent reasons, supported some version of separate development as a form of African autonomy. The Emancipation Centenary Celebration was thus both more and less than a commemoration. It reminded its audience, white philanthropists as well as New Africans, of the lacunae in the narrative of liberation, while also speaking against attempts, on the part of some African leaders as well as the Union government, to restrict emancipation in the name of African autonomy.

The New African position in the 1930s was made even more precarious by African as well as white threats. The conservative ascendancy in the ANC, led by Pixley ka Seme and John Dube (president of the Zulu-dominated Natal branch), tended to see in the state's program of "separate development" an opportunity for what might be called *retraditionalization*.[7] Just as tradition has less to do with the "persistence of old forms, but more to do with the ways in which form and value are linked together" (Erlmann 1991: 10), retraditionalization implies not so much a return to premodern rural life as a reappropriation of the memory of clan custom as the means to a tangible if limited autonomy in the present, consolidating the power of the chiefs eroded by the emergence of the New Africans on the one hand, and the mass migration of landless peasants to the cities on the other.[8] Conservative chiefs welcomed new parliamentary bills – the Native Representatives Act, which would remove the last Africans from the Common Roll in favor of an advisory Native Representative Council, and the amendment of the Land Act that provided for a fraction more land in the reserves supervised by the chiefs. The Christianized intellectuals who founded the Zulu Cultural Society in 1937 mobilized a form of Zuluness that responded to European notions of national identity forged by linguistic affinity and a diffuse sense of contiguity rather than to the complex and personalized interrelation of vassal and patron that had maintained the authority of the precolonial Zulu clan (Harries 1993: 110).

Retraditionalization is thus not so much a rejection of modernization as an attempt to appropriate certain aspects of modernity, especially vernacular literacy, the mastery of new technologies, and the refashioning of remnants of the precolonial record into a unifying national heritage, so as to reinvent the habitual acknowledgment of clan affiliation as the obligatory but natural respect for traditional authority. Retraditional*ization* is a more appropriate term than the usual "neotraditionalism," which more adequately describes an ahistorical, or dehistoricized, view of tradition as intact, timeless, and immune to present politics. What is at stake here are rather the *processes* of negotiating the relationships between tradition and modernity and the agency of that negotiation.

This retraditionalist tendency collided with the convictions of New Africans, who held by and large to the belief that the benefits of modernity would ultimately outweigh the disruption of communal life and clan loyalties caused by colonization. Selope Thema, for instance, defended African appropriation of the benefits of European civilization, such as literacy and individual rights, and, while acknowledging the value of precolonial communal organization, severely criticized tribal custom, especially ancestor worship, as the weight of the "dead . . . on the living."[9] Profoundly suspicious of European definitions of the authentically African promulgated by apologists for development along the "Native's own lines," New Africans such as Thema and the Dhlomo brothers did not, however, abandon traditions they saw as African. Rather, by participating in networks established by graduates of mission schools such as Lovedale (founded 1832), Adams (1855), and Marianhill (1884), as well as cultural institutions such as the Gamma Sigma debating societies (1918), the BMSC (1924) or the Eisteddfodau (1931), festivals of choral singing and dramatic monologues loosely based on Welsh or rather British imperial models, they hoped to enrich, elevate, and legitimate the African inheritance as well. As the program for the Emancipation Celebration indicates, however, the African traditions in view here were those reinvented by a precariously placed elite, rather than any intact precolonial legacy or the leisure practices of an urbanizing, not yet quite proletarian working class.

The mission school syllabus, which supplemented the canon of Shakespeare, the post-Romantic poets, and the musical repertoire of the European courts with the imperialist fiction of Rudyard Kipling and John Buchan, provided only one model for the cultural refashioning of the New Africans. They drew also on a variety of American and African-American practices whose status as high culture was not secured by the imperial decorum of the great tradition. The abolitionist melodrama and "Negro spirituals" in the Emancipation Centenary program complemented and competed with a range of vaudeville, ragtime, jazz, and minstrel turns, which reached a wider African audience in the dance halls and often makeshift musical venues frequented by growing numbers of *abaphakathi* [the people in between – neither fully assimilated to "European" modernity nor any longer at home with indigenous custom].[10] New Africans saw in the metropolitan, modernizing impulse of the New Negro an alternative to neocolonial retribaliza-tion or the mission schools but they also hoped to combat the allegedly degraded forms of urban culture, especially jazz and *marabi*, which they saw as corrupting the *abaphakathi*.[11]

New Africans found in the distance traveled by African-Americans from slavery to visible (if uneven) participation in American life – as well as the distance still untraveled – a crucial point of reference for criticizing the curtailment of civil rights for black South Africans. Like the New Negro, who challenged white society's "sentimental interest" in black traditions and the "double standard" of the "philanthropic attitude" among white American liberals (Locke 1992: 8–10), the New African was suspicious of those who expressed concern for "Native" traditions while remaining either indifferent or hostile to black aspirations to transform society as a whole. As a mission school-teacher wrote:

> the Negroes on the other side of the Atlantic have made "gigantic progress"; all the same we are making a steady advance to the same goal. . . . They have shown . . . that this much debated "arrested development" is practically unknown among the Negroes.
>
> (Mdhluli 1933: 48–49)

The figure of Du Bois, cosmopolitan yet tireless in his defense of the disenfran-chised, offered an alternative to the retraditionalist views of Seme, Dube, and others who tended to support the deferential model of development put forward by Du Bois's most famous rival, Booker T. Washington.[12]

Despite their identification with the African-American elite, in Du Bois' phrase, the "talented tenth," New Africans acknowledged that the appeal of African-American popular culture, including jazz, flowed in part from African-American assertions of pan-African affiliation.[13] In the 1920s, the indirect influence of African-American culture on Africans in South African cities could be traced in jubilee hymns as well as minstrel groups such as the African Darkies and the Midnight Follies offering coon songs and skits borrowed from recordings and sheet music from Britain and the United States (Coplan 1985: 124).[14] By the 1930s, these had grown into polished variety troupes such as the African Own Entertainers and the Darktown Strutters, whose repertoires mixed jazz, ragtime, and comic sketches with the jubilee and church [amakwaya] music favored by the black elite (Ballantine 1993). Women's groups, though less common, were also popular and, as names such as Dangerous Blues and the Merry Makers imply, did not confine their repertoire to "respectable" music.

New African negotiation of these African-American currents thus blurs any simple divide between British imperialism and African resistance, between imported art and indigenous practice or, indeed, between modernity and its apparently premodern, "savage" other. Far from being merely a prelude to the much-celebrated "Sophiatown era" of the 1950s (Kavanagh 1985; Nixon 1994), the engagement between New Africa and African-America that took place in a number of venues in 1930s Johannesburg was if anything more complex, more diverse, and more autonomous than the cultural activity that, in the later period, was confined to, as well as defined by, Sophiatown, as the last integrated city neighborhood. While the urban entertainments of 1950s Sophiatown may have imitated more aggressively the popular idiom of American mass culture, their practitioners were losing ground to European interlopers and apartheid law. The cultural producers of the 1930s still had a margin of control over the means of their production – measured by access to papers edited by Africans and to groups run by African impresarios, such as Motsieloa, and by exemptions to the pass laws for educated Africans – which allowed for a relative autonomy and diversity of performance and reception that would be impossible in the strained circumstances of Sophiatown's final years. If the emergence of an urban African modernity in South Africa is to be compared to the Harlem Renaissance (Nixon 1994: 13–31), it is the New African dawn, however darkened by neocolonial clouds, rather than the twilight of Sophiatown, that should be the point of reference.

Performance culture as virtual public sphere

New African exploration of the routes crossed by African, American, and European culture was both contradictory and productive. It involved often passionately inconsistent appropriations of English cultural artifacts, American

29

popular entertainments, and indigenous traditions, in which the transformation (but not the destruction) of "Africanness" through colonization formed the basis for a thoroughly modern syncretism. While New African aspirations to legitimate South African citizenship were certainly constrained by mission schooling, the political and economic pressures on African newspapers, and by white philanthropist manipulation of organizations such as the BMSC, as well as by the government's more overt racial discrimination, they were not completely controlled by it. At a moment when political rights for even elite Africans were curtailed, culture, whether seen as arts or entertainment, became a crucial site for the contestation of the legitimacy of African participation in a South African public sphere.

At its most instrumental, culture operated as social control. Mining executives argued that monitoring their employees after hours was a "good business investment" (Koch 1983: 167), and missionaries like Ray Phillips, author of the assimilationist *The Bantu Are Coming*, organized Chaplin evenings for mineworkers. Like his fellow missionaries, he hoped to curb social and economic unrest and the "swaggering, sweeping claims of Communism" by "moralizing the leisure time of the natives" (Phillips 1930: 51, 58). R. W. H. Shepherd, director of the Lovedale Press, the single most influential publishing venue available to Africans, argued that literature should not only "equip the Bantu for the demands of the new day" but also offer a "substitute of a satisfying kind to take the place of so much that has passed from them" (Shepherd 1935: 76). More subtle, perhaps, were the aspirations of African retraditionalists such as Dube and Caluza, who saw in the state's interest in preserving "Native ways" an occasion for reestablishing rural practices fractured by colonization.

In the space between the instrumentalization of culture in the production of modernized subjects and the evocation of culture as a retraditionalized refuge from the ravages of modernization, the ambiguous notion of the disinterestedness of culture offered an escape, at once compelling and imaginary, from daily humiliations. This relative autonomy could and did give New African performance culture an affirmative cast, in Marcuse's sense, by providing an imaginary refuge from it (Marcuse 1968: 116), but it also offered at least the framework for the subjunctive enactment of a free African agency. As the Emancipation Celebration suggests, "dramatic displays" and other public performances commemorating events in the New African calendar offered a key site on which the legitimate public representation could be contested. Marginalized in a general South African public sphere defined in racially exclusive terms, and largely ignored by the white organizers of the official "South African Pageants," New African theatre articulated what I have called a virtual public sphere. At stake in the subjunctive enactments of this New African publicity is the attempt to seize the idea of modernity – citizenship, emancipation, individual and collective agency – from its prevailing colonial representation: the attempt, in other words, to "deploy, deform, and defuse" neocolonial institutions and formations so as to make "many modernities" out of colonial modernization (Comaroff and Comaroff 1993: xi, xii).

The modernity of the tribal sketch

The retraditionalist road to African self-representation was, of necessity, paved with stones of colonial manufacture. Nowhere was the ambiguity of this self-representation more vividly portrayed than in the "tribal sketch." Understood by New Africans and missionary educators alike as "reconstruction of native custom in dramatic form" (Peterson 1990: 229–31), these short representations of customary rituals bore an unmistakable resemblance in form and content to the scenes that formed a central part of commercial and ethnographic displays of Africans in metropolitan shows from the Exhibition of Zulu Kafirs (1853) to the Savage South Africa Show, initially part of the Greater Britain Exhibition of 1899 (Dell 1993: 151–90).

The central site for this retraditionalization was paradoxically also the crucible for elite modernization: the mission schools, such as Lovedale, Marianhill, Amanzimtoti – later Adams – College, or the Ohlange Institute, John Dube's counterpart to the Tuskegee Institute in Alabama. One of the first such performances in what might be called "redefined Zulu folk idiom" took place not in South Africa but at the Hampton Institute in Virginia, where Madikane Cele, a graduate of Ohlange and nephew of its founder, John Dube (Curtis 1920: 58), "acquainted his black American students with Zulu folklore and music" culminating in 1913 in "the presentation of 'For Unkulunkulu's Sake'" (Erlmann 1991: 72). Madikane Cele was named for the founder of the Cele clan, which was among those stigmatized by the Zulu hierarchy as *amaLala* [slow-witted] and, for this reason perhaps, among the first to adopt Christianity (Hamilton 1985: 478–84). As a Christian, Cele would have encountered the story in its missionized form which rendered *Unkulunkulu* as God the Creator, but he may also have been aware of the argument that the oral tradition lent a historical rather than theological cast to this "originator" (Callaway 1870: 124), whose character depended on the historical moment of reappropriation (Hamilton 1985: 74–84). The representation of Zulu tradition by this bicultural New African thus rewrites successive conflicts as a common myth of origin, whose recovery is made possible ironically by the European disruption of Zulu hegemony.

This ambiguous but powerful association of "salvaging" a precolonial tradition with the modernizing mission of Hampton and its South African counterparts was to define later African pageants. This does not mean that New African interest in "tribal" sketches could be explained away as mission dressage, however. The shows of one particularly influential group, the Lucky Stars (1929–37), confirm the appeal of retraditionalist images but they also illuminate the modernity of this retraditionalizing gesture. Founded in 1929 by Esau and Isaac Mthethwa of Amanzimtoti College, the Lucky Stars performed dances and sketches in reconstructed Zulu costume and in isiZulu.[15] The titles of such sketches as *Ukuqomisa* [courting] and especially *Umthakathi* [diviner, sorcerer, trickster] allude to the ambiguous legacy of the tribal sketch, which includes the "smelling out" of the diviner as an outright imposter impeding the civilizing mission (Caldecott 1853:

26), an interpretation that recurs in the Centenary Celebration of the American Board Mission in 1935.[16] However, the several parts of this show – sketches, dancing, and choral singing of Zulu "folk" songs of the national kind, as well as quite varied places of performance – suggest a more complex mesh of occasion and meaning than either a reconstruction of precolonial practices or a replication of colonial prejudices. An account by a white observer is illuminating:

> This new departure among the black races is valuable in presenting to the public scenes of native domestic life with a realism which would be otherwise unobtainable. Such education of the white man is a necessary preliminary to his understanding of Bantu problems. . . .
>
> . . . these plays are presented with a naivete which would be impossible for the white man to imitate. The style of acting is much more free than we have been accustomed to see on the more civilized stage. The producer is an educated Zulu [Isaac Mthethwa] but the players have only a rudimentary knowledge of reading and writing. Consequently, the parts are learned by word of mouth and no strict adherence to the original wording is insisted on. . . . This induces a freshness and vigor of presentation which is a welcome relief from the too conscious presentation of our own stage.
>
> (Lloyd 1935: 3)

This account rehearses the familiar colonial opposition between jaded metropolitan culture (whether the "public" clamoring for performances "at the hotels and socials in Durban" or the "too conscious" artifice of the "civilized" actor) and the fresh naïveté of the "black races." At the same time, it concedes the artifice of this native naïveté , in the shape of Mthethwa's guiding hand, in the fact that the lines were learnt, and in the possibility that the "education of the white man" might be the object and not merely the incidental result of this performance. Even the natural setting, "the lush sub-tropical bush of the Natal coast," is framed by the thoroughly modern contrivance of the illusionist set: "The scene was set by . . . a canvas sheet with a painting of a Zulu hut." If the content of the sketch harks back to "scenes of native domestic life," this canvas backdrop points to the power of naturalist illusion for mission-educated Africans. The modern character of the show as a whole, over and above the content of the sketches, is confirmed by the "historical songs" that concluded the performance. Lloyd's description of the songs – "they traced the record of the Zulu nation through their kings. They sang of those who had wielded supreme power, whether good or bad" (Lloyd 1935: 3) – suggests the historical consciousness of "Elamakosi" [Of the Kings], Caluza's song popular with Zulu audiences in the 1930s.

Although shaped in large part by elite places and occasions, the sketches of the Lucky Stars were enthusiastically received by black workers and those on the fringes of the formal economy, especially in less industrialized Natal, where audiences found these "idealized images of a rural past" a welcome escape from their alienation from "civilization" (Coplan 1985: 127). Nevertheless, claims that the Lucky Stars produced a variant of black political theatre (Gérard 1971: 197) preparing the way for the anti-apartheid theatre of the 1970s (Kavanagh 1985: 45), ought to be treated with caution. The origins of the sketches in the mission school did not prevent them from being appropriated by a diverse popular audience, but the ethnic emphasis of the sketches reflected the Zulu pride of the performers, most of whom came from the Zulu-identified Amanzimtoti College, more than a desire to challenge the social and economic discrimination against all Africans. Performed in isiZulu and in historically reconstructed Zulu costume (rather than the mixed attire worn in rural Zululand at the time), the critical edge in the sketches would have been only partially accessible to speakers of other Bantu languages who saw the shows, whose response may have been affected as much by the music and the tangible presence of African actors, as by the authentic details of their attire or speech.

While groups such as the African Own Entertainers (founded, like the Lucky Stars, in 1929) and the Darktown Strutters (active by 1931) were taking their variety shows of music, comedy, and sketches on the road in the Union and beyond, the Lucky Stars were based mostly in Natal. "Discovered" by Bertha Slosberg, Jewish South African impresario and later talent scout for Zulu actors for the film *King Solomon's Mines*, starring Paul Robeson as an African prince, at the Bantu Sports Club in February 1936 (Slosberg 1939: 194), they performed under her auspices at the Durban City Hall in March, the BMSC in Johannesburg in May, together with the Darktown Strutters in "An African Entertainment," and at the Empire Exhibition in October.[17] Slosberg's claim to have discovered both these groups testifies not only to the arrogance of the white impresario but also to an ambiguous desire to give Africans their due. Slosberg insisted that she paid the performers well and that she associated with them despite scandalized response from members of the white press (Slosberg 1939: 210–13), but her aspirations to honorary Zuluness have to be matched against the material advantages conferred by her membership in white South African society (Figure 2.1). Isaac Mthethwa's acquiescence in this arrangement reflects above all the obstacles faced by African performers attempting to make a living as artists. Although producers such as Mthethwa and Motsieloa had functioned as professionals for more than half a decade, in the sense that they and their audiences took their performances seriously, they could not afford to abandon waged labor and were unable to maintain control over their own work. Racist custom as well as segregation law made hiring a hall difficult, the pass laws curtailed evening rehearsals, and lack of capital made African producers dependent on white benefactors.

The social and economic dependence of Africans reinforced the appeal of a primitivist nostalgia on the part of whites in the metropolis as well as in the Commonwealth, and encouraged impresarios like Slosberg to claim ownership of these shows even while emphasizing their exotic otherness. In this context, the spectacular fuses with the folkloric dimension and the thrilling dancing becomes the reason "to salvage from European influence, the remaining power, the native

Figure 2.1 The Mthethwa Lucky Stars and the Honorary Zulu (Bertha Slosberg). *Source*: Bertha Slosberg, *Pagan Tapestry*, London: Rich and Cowan, 1939

simplicity, the splendid savage grandeur of a dying pagan land" (Slosberg 1939: 192). The authenticity of the spectacle depends on its visible difference from the self-proclaimed modernity of the white spectators. From their perspective, a clear distinction between "native simplicity" and the "progress of the Union" is the *sine qua non* that confirms their affinity with Europe and thus with modernity. Only when the "splendid savage grandeur" is perceived to be "dying" can the modernity of the colony (or neocolonial Union) be assured, yet that "grandeur" continues to compel attention. Designed to vindicate and reinforce the legitimacy of modernity outside the metropolis, the Empire Exhibition, which incorporated performances of African entertainers as well as an Anglo-Afrikaans pageant, displayed the contradictions in that modernity.

Empire and its discontents: pageantry, archaism and modernity

Where New Africans faced with the dubious benefits of "civilization" sought an alternative route to modernity that led often through retraditionalization, the beneficiaries of colonial civilization, especially those who identified themselves as British subjects, were keen to translate their peripheral status into progress toward the center. The organizers of the Johannesburg Golden Jubilee (1886–1936) and the Empire Exhibition (the first held outside the British Isles) in 1936 saw themselves as participants in a celebration of the Union and of Johannesburg, Africa's most modern city, to be sharply distinguished from "Savage South Africa." This modernity was represented not only by a new version of the South African Pageant but also, in the model of the Great Exhibition of 1851, by the display of "Manufacture, Machinery, Raw Materials and Fine Art" (Dell 1993: 101), and, as indicated in the Exhibition's official poster (Figure 2.2), the new skyscrapers literally springing up by the dozen (Chipkin 1993: 94–95), all as signs of progress. Where South African pavilions at earlier exhibitions, such as the Colonial and Indian Exhibition (1886) and the Greater Britain Exhibition (1899), had represented South Africa as a source of raw materials and exotic "natives," those at the Empire Exhibition were to emphasize the host country's emergence into the company of civilized nations.[18] By displaying its "resources and potentialities," the government hoped to encourage trade and industrial development as well as to "gain worldwide publicity for the Union."[19] The primary purpose of the Exhibition, according to the *South African Mining and Engineering Journal*, was "to present a striking picture of the history, development and progress of the Union."

Though not in the British imperial lineage, the Chicago Columbian Exposition of 1893 also exerted an influence. Apart from some obvious connections – the description of the Exhibition site as a "white city,"[20] the memorialization of the era of imperial exploration in full-scale models of Van Riebeeck's ships (by analogy with those of Columbus), and the imitation of innovations such as a Women's Pavilion – the two exhibitions had in common an uneasy relationship between the products of progress and development displayed in the pavilions and the spectacle of indigenous people housed in poorly constructed and insanitary "native villages." Just as the Chicago city fathers were reluctant to admit black visitors on the same terms as whites, let alone allow the exhibition of modern African-American achievements, the organizers of the Johannesburg Jubilee offered only limited access to Africans, providing them with limited accommodation and, initially, demanding the same entrance fee as for whites.[21] In the South African case, the cracks in the national consensus were deepened by the prominent display of a model of the Voortrekker Monument that was to be erected outside Pretoria in time for the Centenary of the Great Trek of 1838.[22] The tensions between Boer and Briton, country and city, agriculture and manufacture, whose union was invoked by the official publicity poster of the Exhibition (Figure 2.2) as it had been by the celebrations of 1910, but, as the image suggests despite itself, South Africa's two "white races" remained apart; the Voortrekker confronts the City of Gold.

The Pageant of Southern Africa was intended to address the differences between Anglo and Afrikaner interpretations of history as well as to reinforce their commonalities. The pageant was performed only four times near the end of the Exhibition in December 1936, but its rehearsal nonetheless commanded attention for over a year, from the initial plans in mid-1935 for an amphitheatre

Figure 2.2 The Voortrekker confronts the City of Gold; Ernest Ullman's prize-winning poster for the Empire Exhibition, Johannesburg, June 1936. *Source*: The Argus Group; *permission*: J. P. Ullman

in the Milner Park grounds that would seat 12,000 people,[23] through the selection of the Belgian-born André van Gyseghem as a suitably bilingual pageant master in February 1936, to the recruitment and training of the provincial pageant leaders in the winter of that year and the performance several months later. Indeed, the prestige associated with the event is as palpable in the numerous photographs and profiles of the many young white women applying for these positions as in the commentary on the pageant itself. The protest in *Outspan*, the magazine organizing the selection, that "the Pageant is not merely a beauty competition" was belied by the portraits of would-be debutantes and the concession that "good looks" would play a role alongside "*some* elocutionary ability" (emphasis added).[24] The pageant master was in turn fêted more as a metropolitan messenger bearing the latest theatrical fashions from Europe than as an international director whose theatrical style had more in common with the European and American avant-garde than with the drawing-room comedy that dominated the stage in London or, indeed, in Johannesburg,[25] and who was also to become involved with African theatre groups such as the Bantu People's Theatre.

Like the 1910 pageant, the 1936 event comprised a series of scenes from South African colonial history culminating in the moment of Union. But, where the commemoration in 1910 relied on the representation of conquest and the opening of parliament to depict South Africa's maturity, the 1936 pageant attempted to combine the triumphal dramaturgy of theatrical nationhood with the representation of the industrialization and modernization which had transformed South Africa since the Union. The latter aspiration was, however, soon at odds with the attempt to respect British and especially Boer myths of origin. To write the text, he engaged the populist Afrikaans chronicler Gustav Preller, whose vivid accounts of the Voortrekkers in print and in film – *De Voortrekkers* (1916) was the first feature film in Dutch-Afrikaans – played a central role in the development of an Afrikaner Nationalist mythology.[26] The initial plan listed the episodes as follows:[27]

1   Zimbabwe the Magnificent
2   The Bushmen, at one time sole owners of the Continent
3   The Hottentots
4   The Beginning of History
5   The Landing of Van Riebeeck [1652]
6   Simon van der Stel welcomes the Huguenots [1690]
7   The British occupy the Cape [1806]
8   The arrival of the British settlers in 1820
9   Chaka, King of the Zulus, presents the Charter of Natal to Lt. Farewell [1824]
10 Piet Uys and his trek party are presented with a bible by the citizens of Grahamstown [1836]
11 Nagmaal [communion] after the Battle of Vegkop
12 Arrival of Louis Trichardt's trek party in Lourenço Marques
13 The vow taken to build a church should the Boers be victorious over Dingaan [16 December 1838]
14 Dingaan's Day: [Andries] Pretorius and Mpande [Dingaan's successor] on the Rock
15 Smith's Soldiers and the Lady Kenneway Girls [1840s]
16 Discovery of Diamonds [1867]
17 The Discovery of Gold on the Rand [1886]
18 Rhodes's *indaba* [conference] with Lobengula [king of the Matabele] [1889]
19 The arrival of the first train in Bulawayo
20 Election of Paul Kruger [to a third term] as president [of the South African Republic] in 1898
21 Final Tableau – Union – The National Convention Assembly in Cape Town

As might be expected, these episodes reproduced a neocolonial view of South Africa, whose history seems to begin only with the arrival of Europeans at the Cape (Figure 2.3). The original inhabitants appear either in prehistoric preludes or in capitulation to the imperial plan, as in Shaka's alleged signing-over of Natal

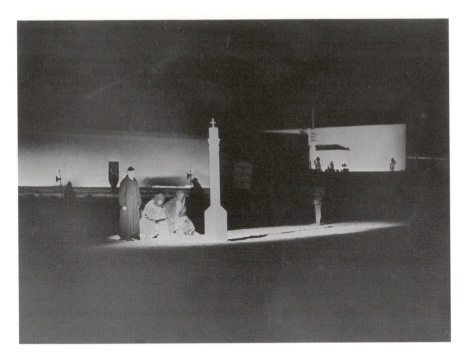

Figure 2.3 The Arrival of (European) History in *The Pageant of South Africa*, sc.1. Directed by André van Guyseghem for the Empire Exhibition. *Source and permission*: Museum Afrika, Johannesburg

to Lt. Farewell,[28] Rhodes's *indaba* with Lobengula, or the scenes leading up to the defeat of the Zulus at the Ncome [Blood] River. To emphasize the importance of this last episode, the pageant opened on 16 December (commemorated in the Afrikaner calendar as the Day of the Vow; now Day of Reconciliation).

This scene formed the core of a later pageant which took place on a scale that surpassed that of the Empire Exhibition or the Pageant of Union: the reenactment of the Great Trek in 1938 to commemorate the centenary of the vow taken by the *trekboers* at the Battle of Blood River in 1838 and a century of Boer resistance to the British. The Afrikaner Taal- en Kultuurvereeniging (ATKV; Afrikaans Language and Cultural Union) began by organizing a trek of two wagons from Cape Town but gained enough contributions from the members of its parent union, the South African Railways and Harbours, mostly recently urbanized and disaffected "poor whites," as well as from nationalist intellectuals, clerks, and teachers in the predominantly Nationalist Transvaal and Free State, to support the trek of nine ox-wagons from various points to retrace the *trekkers'* journey along what the official *Gedenkboek van die Voortrekker-Eeufees* [Commemoration Book of the Voortrekker Centenary Celebration] called the "path of South Africa" (*Gedenkboek* 1938: 57), the route from Cape Town to the old eastern frontier and northward to

38

Pretoria. Men in *boerekommandos* and women in *kappiekommandos* gathered in their thousands at points along the route and especially at the two culminating festivals – at the site of Blood River and in Pretoria. In Pretoria in mid-December, 200,000 people assembled to welcome the wagons, and, on 16 December, amassed on the hill outside the city, opposite the "British" Union Buildings, to witness the laying of the cornerstone of the Voortrekker monument, the "altar of Afrikanerdom" (*Gedenkboek* 1940: 815).

The days leading up to this moment featured speeches by ATKV and National Party leaders, *boeresport*, folk singing and dancing, and prayer, while the nights included spectacles such as the film, *Die Bou van 'n Nasie* (script: Preller, dir: Joseph Albrecht) (13 December), and the allegorical drama of national loss and recovery, *Die Dieper Reg*, written by the more highbrow poet, N. P. van Wyk Louw (15 December), directed by Anna Neethling-Pohl, noted theatre director and Afrikaner Nationalist.[29] *Die Bou van 'n Nasie* [marketed in English as *They Built a Nation*] and *Die Dieper Reg* [The Deeper Right] shared an explicit dedication to the priority of Afrikaner claims to represent South Africa; Louw's play may have been allegorical, but its central suffering protagonists were Voortrekkers in appropriate costume (Louw 1938: 7). The difference between the populist racism of Preller, whose script, like that for *De Voortrekkers* (1916), was inspired by D. W. Griffiths's notorious celebration of white supremacy in *Birth of a Nation* (1915), and the aestheticism of *Die Dieper Reg*, whose author later argued that "absolute beauty" rather than "fiery rhetoric" was the best way to support the "struggle of the volk" (Louw 1959: 29), nonetheless suggested that the festivities had not quite done away with class tensions among the Afrikaners. Despite considerable cross-class appeal and "middle-class support" (Grundlingh and Sapire 1989: 20, 24), the celebration of *volkseenheit* [unity of the people, or perhaps only of the tribe] was not without contestation, from above and below. On the one hand, the patrician elite of gentleman farmers, especially South African Party supporters in the Cape or internationalists such as Jan Smuts, disdained this spectacular display as a consolation for displaced and disaffected "poor whites," the constituents of the "purified" National Party, and even accused the ATKV leadership of promoting Nazism (Moodie 1975: 175). On the other hand, Afrikaners who identified with an international class struggle over *volkseie* [ethnic identity], such as the *kappiekommando* of unionized garment workers who wished to attend the centenary celebrations as socialists, were rejected as communist dupes.[30]

Despite these tensions, the Second Great Trek secured the national legitimation of the "sacred history" of Afrikaner suffering and humiliation at the hands of the British imperialists and their regeneration as God's chosen people (Moodie 1975: 180) because it was able forcefully to link the memory of suffering of the past, especially during the Anglo-Boer War, which Afrikaners across classes acknowledged, with the humiliations of the present, suffered predominantly by displaced Afrikaners in the "English" city. As the *Gedenkboek* put it, in the nationalist pathos dear to Preller, "the covenant was sealed at Blood River. . . . The continued existence of our People [*Volk*] is a miracle. . . . Our People were frequently in deep grief and divided, but always become united again" (*Gedenkboek* 1938: 55). This reenacted "*Voor*trek" [progress], toward a *volkstaat* and the promise of greater material prosperity associated with it, offered many Afrikaners, especially those ill-adjusted to industrial capitalism, a compelling alternative to the benign despotism of the British Empire. Their party, the purified National Party, was to emerge out of this reenactment to win the election (1948) and, eventually, to sever ties with the Empire (1961).

This shadow on the "white city" and the sun of Empire made itself felt already in disputes around certain scenes in the South African Pageant of 1936. Partly as a result of political pressure and partly as a result of logistical difficulties, the opening performance of this "magnificent historical spectacle" (as advertised by the organizers) offered only twelve episodes, ostensibly because the show was too long. The episodes that fell away could be described as too touchy politically (such as the Anglo-Zulu War of 1879 or the Day of the Vow) or too complex for visual representation (such as the exploitation of the gold and diamond fields and the miners who worked them). However, these omissions also reflected a departure from the modern(ist) proclamations of the Johannesburg Jubilee and a return to the colonialist nostalgia of 1910. As in 1910, this nostalgia was figured in the bodies of women. The substituted scene, which did not appear on the initial list but drew more acclaim than any other, revived the episode of Lady Anne Barnard's Ball at Cape Town Castle that had appealed to 1910 audiences. The episode had less to do with historical reconstruction than with the present-day pleasures of nostalgia and neocolonial prestige, reflected in the liveried footmen and the spectacle of debutantes in period dress (Figure 2.4).[31] Staging the past as a beauty pageant, this spectacle stole the show from history, as it were, but also reminds present-day readers of what Roach calls the "surplus of surrogation" (Roach 1996: 2). In this case, the invisible expropriation of African land wealth and productive labor is dis-placed and re-presented in the vivid display of the unproductive leisure of white women. This neocolonial representation of civilization as the leisure of "English ladies" contrasts significantly with the female performers of the Second Great Trek, whose refusal of ornament reflected not only Calvinist custom, but the historical role attributed to Voortrekker women as auxiliaries in the battle for *volkseie*. Their *kappies* are a sign of *volkseenheit* [ethnic unity] but also the index of dispute, since the headdress could cover a "communist" garment worker or a black servant as well as a *volksmoeder* [mother of the *volk*] (see Figure 2.5, p. 42).

The neocolonial glamour reflected in the portrayal of Lady Anne Barnard and the "striking picture of the history, development and progress of the Union" that impressed Anglophone critics, who favored "a pictorial representation of a period in history with a minimum of verbal comment" (Linscott 1937b: 16),[32] was as invisible to the black inhabitants of Johannesburg as they were in these episodes, since they were not allowed to attend "evening entertainments." Indeed, accounts of the Empire Exhibition in African papers were few in a period when African

Figure 2.4 The Past as Beauty Pageant at Lady Anne's Ball; *The Pageant of South Africa*.
Source and permission: Museum Afrika, Johannesburg

attention was focused on their imminent disenfranchisement at home and the
Italian invasion of Ethiopia abroad. Amid occasional articles noting that only
about 500 Africans attended daily as opposed to tens of thousands of whites, one
reporter recorded, perhaps ironically, that "The City Thanks Africans" for their
contribution to the growth and prosperity of Johannesburg, while concluding
that Africans "look forward to the day they will be granted the freedom of the
city."[33] Another reminded readers that, while the pavilions were educational and
celebrated the "pulsing life of modern commerce" rather than "the mysteries of
the past" in Africa, Africans with permission to visit in the evening would have
no entertainment except the amusement park.[34] While no African critic matched
the indignation of Frederick Douglass, who had condemned the Columbian
Exposition as a "white sepulchre" (Greenhalgh 1988: 99), all regretted the
Empire Exhibition's neglect of interested African visitors. Although it displayed
precolonial Africans (or their impersonators), the Exhibition excluded the urban
African spectator who might disturb the ethnographic pleasure of white
audiences.

The evening entertainments from which Africans were barred included ball-
room dancing, a series of one-act plays performed by members of the Associated
Repertories of South Africa, and ballet led by "Nedeja, a Russian who was in

Figure 2.5 Volksmoeders and servants and in the *kappiekommando* Voortrekker Centenary, December 1938. *Source and permission*: Nasionale Pers

Pavlova's Corps de Ballet."[35] Most popular, however, were the African entertainments, which ranged from the urban sophistication of the Darktown Strutters and their usual accompanying swing band, the Merry Blackbirds, through the Lucky Stars, to displays of Zulu dancing orchestrated by the pageant master himself. This last show, *Amangabeze* [exhortations – oddly glossed as "the dancing place"], was billed as "the Real Africa at last" and performed at least a dozen times (more often than the pageant). Van Gyseghem took pains to preserve what he understood to be the authenticity of the dances, often against the wishes of the performers themselves. As the British Drama League representative noted:

> He toured native territories, but the original ritual dances, untouched by European influence, could not be witnessed by Europeans and those dances that he did see definitely bore traces of White contact. The original costumes had been added to by brilliantly coloured cheap silks and other trimmings easily available at village and city stores.
>
> Eventually a troupe . . . was gathered together and before they appeared in the arena, a man, employed for the purpose, removed the superfluous apparel.
>
> (Kelly 1938: 2)

A reporter from the *Sunday Express* even attributed the authentic details of the show to the Native Affairs Department, which had been "most helpful in collecting and rehearsing dances and in giving advice about the authenticity of the costumes."[36]

This battle for the authenticity of the dance, waged against the preferences of the dancers, reveals the inextricable yet unmentionable association of modernity, capitalism, and neocolonial anxiety about both. The African dancers appear to be willing to see themselves as consumers as well as performers, if not producers, of a living syncretic culture; their promoters, on the other hand, seem consumed by the encroachments of modernity on "native territory." The involvement of the Native Affairs Department as expert advisor on maintaining traditional custom should remind us not only of the ideological character of "separate development" but also of the suspicion on the part of New Africans about Native Affairs enthusiasm for African traditions. As one African commentator wrote, "There is no objection to war dances provided they are staged by the enlightened Bantu. When they are staged by the uncivilized Native, it is a sign of retrogression" (*BW,* 16 April 1932, p. 8) and, as another reiterated more than a decade and a half later, "The proper people and place for *modernising* this primitive art are the Zulu Cultural Society" (emphasis added).[37]

The stake here is not the authenticity of the African object, but rather the legitimacy of African agency in determining the character and function of tradition. New Africans were particularly concerned that the revival of traditional custom should not cast them in a primitive light: "The joy that a civilised man gets when watching Zulus dance is the same kind of joy that he gets when looking at monkeys."[38] If the attachment of sympathetic liberals such as Lloyd or Slosberg to the authenticity of the spectacles cannot be described in quite the same way as the man viewing Africans as monkeys, it can nonetheless be understood as the anxious insistence on European authority by neocolonial subjects of the Empire. Native authenticity in this context is a relational rather than absolute term, whose meaning depends on the use to which it is put. The case of Bertha Slosberg is once again illuminating. Slosberg insisted repeatedly on preserving the specifically Zulu character of the Lucky Stars' performance and on her desire to represent this authentically to white audiences in London as well as Johannesburg. Yet, when this plan was thwarted by the South African government's refusal to grant passports to the group, she was ready to devote the same enthusiasm to a curtain-raiser for a play at the Drury Lane Theatre, *The Sun Never Sets [on the Empire?],* performed mostly by Nigerians and British blacks trained by herself (Slosberg 1939: 312–20). Like Slosberg, Van Gyseghem was unable to recognize the modernity not only of this reproduction of tradition but also of the agency of the performers. He and his fellow impresarios attempted to erase evidence of modernity in the spectacle, even as their own activity as producers and the Exhibition itself could not but highlight that modernity.

"Unity in Bantudom": the African
revue as national pageant

The African entertainments at the Empire Exhibition may have been closed to African spectators, but this did not prevent the event as well as the shows themselves from "influenc[ing] Johannesburg location performances" (Vilakazi 1942: 273). This influence was enhanced not only by performances in township halls and social clubs across the country, but also by the prestige garnered from appearances at the Empire Exhibition. Even though they did not get the publicity reserved for *Amangabeze*, the Lucky Stars and the Darktown Strutters portrayed an actual Africa more complex than the "real Africa" of the spectacle. The retraditionalist mode of the Lucky Stars was complicated by their incorporation of nationalist songs, while the Strutters' modernizing appropriation of American music and drama was in turn modified by the inclusion of sketches on precolonial African themes.

The Darktown Strutters and their successors, the Pitch Black Follies, were one of the longest-lived variety groups. Their longevity was due in large part to the management of their leader, Griffiths Motsieloa, but also to the patronage of Gallophone Records, who employed Motsieloa as a talent scout from the mid-1930s on and thus gave the group a rare measure of economic independence. Born in Basutoland (now Lesotho), Motsieloa was a childhood friend of Peter Rezant, later leader of the Merry Blackbirds, which often played together with Motsieloa's variety groups, and the husband of Emily (née Makanana), a pianist of renown who had led the all-women Dangerous Blues and continued to perform with the Strutters (Matshikiza 1956). He qualified as a teacher at Lovedale College and went on to study elocution at Trinity College of Music in London, where he earned the reputation of "London's Favourite Bantu Actor" (Skota 1931: 215). From the mid-1920s, he ran a series of variety groups, from the African Darkies in the 1920s to the Darktown Strutters in the 1930s and the Pitch Black Follies in the 1940s. These groups, like their accompanying band, the Merry Blackbirds, can certainly be characterized as "elite entertainment" (Coplan 1985: 131) for educated Africans and their white patrons of the kind that took part in the Emancipation Celebration, insofar as they looked askance at the *marabi* culture of the *abaphakathi*, while drawing liberally from the repertoire of the Eisteddfodau and the European bourgeoisie. Nonetheless, the fact that their repertoires tended to combine *amakwaya* with *marabi* music – as Motsieloa's music on the cassette accompanying Ballantine (1993) makes clear – and minstrel gags with more sustained dramatic representation of the modern African (and African-American) condition, using Sesotho and isiZulu as well as English, and that they regularly performed at venues other than the respectable BMSC, suggests that their audiences were more diverse that the "elite" label allows. Performing in places as far away from their Johannesburg base as Queenstown in the Eastern Cape, Serowe in Bechuanaland (Botswana) and Lourenço Marques (now Maputo) in the Portuguese colony of Mozambique,[39] they also had to offer a broadly appealing program that crossed class lines and the ethnic boundaries maintained, for instance, by the Lucky Stars' concentration on their Zulu heritage.

Reviews of the Darktown Strutters in the African press suggest a willingness on the part of performers and audience alike to celebrate the African, European, and African-American aspects of the show without regarding them as separate elements. Thus a reviewer of the Strutters/Blackbirds show in Queenstown praises Petrus Qwabe, the group's leading comic mime, as the "Zulu king of laughter and mirth" and his partner, the tap-dancer and choreographer, Johannes Masoleng (like Motsieloa, of Sotho origin), as "South Africa's Stephen [*sic*] Fetchit."[40] While the allusion to Stephin Fetchit might alarm present-day readers, its appearance in this review is likely to be entirely complimentary. In so far as Stephin Fetchit, like other "coon" stereotypes, was the image of a "successful and self-conscious urban black," he represented a positive role model (Erlmann 1991: 63). At the very least, the virtuoso *impersonation* was worthy of emulation.

Renamed the Pitch Black Follies in 1938, the group became more ambitious and shows included dramatic performances more complex than the routine comic sketch. An evening at the BMSC in February 1938 included the following plays:

1   The Xhosa prophet Ntshikana: Ntshikana's vision, tribal dance, Ntshikana the prophet sees the coming of the white man (led by Victor Mkhiza)
2   Jim Utakata Kanje [Jim the Trickster] (Petrus Qwabe)
3   Die Oorlams Mense [the streetwise people] van Vrededorp
4   "The Recruiter," a two-act play by J. Mathews [*sic*], "written by a Negro during the early days of the USA's entry into the Great War."

This was complemented by an "imitation of a bell" calling to prayer by Motsieloa and the "singing of the First Native hymns" by John Knox Bokwe and Tiyo Soga.[41] "The Recruiter," or "Cruter" (Matheus 1975) by the African-American folklorist, John Matheus (1887–1983), is particularly interesting for two reasons. The first was its topical subject: the recruiting of rural blacks for the factories of the Northern cities, the Great Migration, and the mass urbanization of African-Americans:

> At that time the negroes on the plantations were bound on contract to the cotton plantation owners, and the recruitment of labour for the factories was in consequence illegal. Led by promises of emancipation and riches, scores of negro youth left their homes where their forebears lived as "Squatters" for many generations.
> This play serves to illustrate the antagonisms of the negro youth to the superstitions and willing subjection of their parents.
>
> (SAIRR, AD843/Kb28.2.2)

45

The references to squatters is an oblique but telling reference to the consequences of the Land Act in South Africa, while the final sentence of the outline equates the urbanization of the youth with their emancipation from superstition. These were clearly issues of great interest to New Africans at a time when the Union government was placing ever greater constraints on African mobility and employment in the cities. Equally important, however, was the institutional status of this text. Written by an African-American intellectual and published in *Opportunity*, the organ of the National Urban League (USA), the play not only addressed the pressing questions of modernity, urban life, and economic self-sufficiency for Africans, but also demonstrated that this modern theme could be legitimately addressed in folk idiom.[42]

This negotiation of the border country between the modern and the folk in the quest for emancipation was a keynote of the Pitch Black Follies' shows. A description of "Africa – a revel pageant" in 1940 recalls a performance "depicting the march of progress among the Bantu, from the primitive stage right up to that of the 'Upper Tenth,' the academic class, with a didactic climax – the necessity of 'Unity in Diversity' in Bantudom."[43] This suggests an emphasis on evolutionary modernization rather than on notions of authenticity. Calling the show a "pageant" and a "masque," the reviewer emphasizes its affinity with European forms, while noting the show's comparison of Africans with African-Americans. At the same time, he notes the inclusion in the program of comic sketches and standard minstrel numbers like "Lost in the Shuffle." This particular performance took place in the state-administered "community hall" in Western Native Township and its audience would have included industrial and service workers as well as intellectuals. As the program implies, the group was attempting to entertain as well as enlighten a diverse audience. This description of "Africa" echoes the aspirations of the Emancipation Centenary rather than the primitivist nostalgia of Slosberg's "dying pagan land," insofar as it reiterates the evolutionist views permeating the earlier event, but it also draws on the retraditionalized sketches developed by the Lucky Stars.

This combination of uplift and self-mocking exaggeration relied for critical as well as entertaining effect on a knowledgeable (urban, African, and relatively educated) audience that could interpret this syncretic show as a pageant of a nation in the making. Over the next decade, however, the intimate relationship between groups like the Pitch Black Follies and their audience was subject to some strain. On the one hand, the phenomenal growth of urban industry due to World War II brought a new generation of Africans to the cities who did not share the cosmopolitan tastes of the New Africans. On the other, service with the troops brought the Pitch Black Follies and other variety groups in closer contact with more whites who saw themselves as entrepreneurs "discovering" the "real Africa." Thus, while the Liberty Cavalcade for American soldiers in Cape Town in 1944 gave the Pitch Black Follies and the Merry Blackbirds the opportunity to perform for people that band-leader Peter Rezant admired as representatives of "Harlem and Chicago," it also gave one Lt. Ike Brookes the chance to put together a "large variety company from the South African Native Military Corps" (Coplan 1985: 150). Brookes went on to produce the variety show *Zonk* in 1946, which absorbed members of several groups such as the United Bantu Artists and Jabulani Concert Party, as well as the Pitch Black Follies, and to claim that he had trained the ensemble "from scratch," despite ample evidence of their long-standing experience as performers (Coplan 1985: 151). Herbert Dhlomo commented on this appropriation of African talent:

> After seeing the Nu-Zonk revue many Europeans were amazed at so much African talent. . . . On the African side, there have been some heart-searchings. Why do we neglect our talent? . . . Why cannot we organize and efficiently manage ourselves? Why must there always be a European behind us?[44]

The answer to these questions lies in large part in the state's restrictions on African entrepreneurs in the cities, which were to become a stranglehold after the Afrikaner Nationalist victory in 1948. Also significant was white audiences' preference for "tribal sketches" to the "march of progress of the Bantu."[45]

In the context of the commercial and ideological pressure brought to bear on African performers by "the public," the legitimate and therefore unmarked (but usually white) arbiters of taste, New African criticism of jazz and vaudeville looks more complicated than mere elitist disdain. On the same page as the favorable review of "Africa – a revel pageant," *Bantu World*'s "Critic at Large" challenged the popularity of jazz and vaudeville, which, he argued, "deafen our appreciation for art" including the "greater beauty and entertainment" of drama.[46] Herbert Dhlomo, regarded by himself and other New Africans as a "capable interpreter of the desires and ambitions of his people" (Skota 1931: 143) and a spokesman for an "African tradition grafted onto the European," was critical not only of the commodification of African tradition as "exotic crudities"[47] but also of its embalming as "static museum-like plays" (Dhlomo 1977e: 39). As an alternative, Dhlomo proposed an African National Theatre that would harness the best of European and African forms to the representation of the historical and present condition of Africans. That proposal, its achievement and its contradictions, is the subject of the next chapter.

3

NEW AFRICANS, NEOCOLONIAL THEATRE, AND "AN AFRICAN NATIONAL DRAMATIC MOVEMENT"

Modern drama is not a mere emotional entertainment. It is a source of ideas, a cultural and educational factor, an agency for propaganda and, above all, it is literature. What part will the new African play in modern drama? On its physical side, he can contribute strong, fast rhythm, speedy action, expressive vigorous gesture and movement, powerful dramatic speech – no small contribution when modern plays drag so tediously. . . . We want African playwrights who will dramatize . . . African History. We want dramatic representations of African Serfdom, Oppression, Exploitation, and Metamorphosis. . . . The African dramatist . . . can expose evil and corruption and not suffer libel as newspapermen do; he can guide and preach to his people as preachers cannot do. To do this he must be an artist before a propagandist; a philosopher before a reformer, a psychologist before a patriot; be true to his African 'self' and not be prey to exotic crudities.[1]

This passage from Herbert Dhlomo's essay "The Importance of African Drama" (1933) marks a crucial moment in the history of South African drama not only because it argues for plays that speak of and to the suffering and aspirations of Africans, but also because it suggests the complex history of cultural developments now classified as "modern black drama in South Africa," the pitfalls as well as potential of these developments for articulating an emergent national identity.

As a playwright, poet, and critic as well as impresario for the Emancipation Centenary Celebration in 1934, Herbert Dhlomo grappled in an exemplary way with the oppositions between elite and popular, imported and indigenous, literate and oral practices that traversed the terrain mapped out by New Africans. Although now canonized as the pioneer of modern black drama in South Africa, he was until recently dismissed by some present-day critics in search of authentic and univocal South African cultural expression, whether defined in terms of ethnic authenticity or in terms of a unified urban working class, as a writer of "sub-Wordsworthian" mission literature (Gérard 1971: 236) or "sterile unimaginative plays bearing little relation to African theatrical expression" (Coplan 1985: 125). Only in the last decade or so has he been revived in South Africa as "the pioneer of modern black drama" (Visser and Couzens 1985: xv; Peterson 1990: 229–45; Steadman 1990: 208–28). His status as a source for a buried intercultural lineage that might have been more forceful now "had it been easier for him to publish or produce his work" (Orkin 1991: 49) is not unproblematic, but it does bear witness to his participation in the formation of a tradition that could be simultaneously African and modern.

The career of Herbert Dhlomo (1903–56), graduate of Amanzimtoti College, vice president of the Bantu Dramatic Society, journalist on *Bantu World* and *Ilanga lase Natal*, and, in his later years, an African Nationalist struggling against the hostility or indifference of his erstwhile white sponsors, articulates the contradictions of this formation. His dramatic work includes African themes that run the gamut from an evangelical treatment of the Xhosa prophetess Nongqause in *The Girl Who Killed to Save* (1936; his only published play) to the portrayal of historical African leaders such as *Moshoeshoe, Cetshwayo*, or *Dingane* (1936–38), and the representation of the travails of urban blacks, from the miscegenation melodrama, *Ruby and Frank* (1939), to the indictments of contemporary race and class oppression in *The Workers* and *The Pass* (1941–43). In addition to this literary production, his activities as actor, director, and animator for a variety of different organizations make him a crucial point of reference for an investigation not only of the history of an "African National Theatre" but of the troubled relationship between theatre and social change in South Africa in general.

As "detribalised, 'progressive,' adapted adaptor of the modern South Africa" (Couzens 1985: 110) in the 1930s and 1940s, Dhlomo and his colleagues attempted to negotiate the interface between the imported and the local, European and African, urban and rural performance practices. This attempt not only articulated New African aspirations but also offered a significant, if largely unacknowledged, challenge to the neocolonial character of the theatre institution in South Africa. At this time, commercial managements like African Consolidated Theatres (run by the Schlesinger family, who also controlled African Consolidated Mines) were primarily interested in sponsoring touring companies from London. Local amateurs like the Johannesburg Repertory and the Little Theatre in Cape Town followed a slightly more adventurous program, performing modern plays which had enjoyed successful runs in London or New York, as well as English classics from Shakespeare and Sheridan to Wilde. Members of the Bantu Dramatic Society and the Bantu People's Theatre, working irregularly with considerably less financial and cultural capital at their disposal, attempted on the other hand to include in their repertoire plays by black and white South Africans. While hampered by fragmentary education and limited access to local and touring performances in the white theatres, these groups were no more amateur than their white counterparts. In their desire to draw on traditions as different as African seasonal celebrations and workers agitprop, the European avant-garde and the English drawing-room comedy, moreover, they were often more daring than white amateurs or than white academic "experts" on African affairs allowed.

In the absence of a comprehensive history, accounts of South African theatre have tended to be insider chronicles of particular groups (e.g. Hoffman 1980) or, more recently, revisionist reconstructions of an adversarial, mostly black, theatre (Kavanagh 1985; Orkin 1991), played out against a blurry backdrop of the so-called legitimate stage in South Africa. Neither group has explored in any detail the contradictory character of this legitimacy, which is marked not only by its neocolonial character but also by the relative freedom granted "non-professional" enterprises away from the glare of metropolitan publicity. Before we can begin to examine New African negotiation of and resistance to the "legitimate" South African theatre, we ought at least to delineate the features of this institution.

Stages of legitimacy: neocolonial theatre, ca. 1930

In the introduction to his account of "South African drama and discursive struggle" (Orkin 1991: 15), Martin Orkin writes off theatre in early twentieth-century South Africa as follows:

> In the early decades of the twentieth century, Stephen Black . . . dramatised and satirised Cape social behavior and referred to social and political issues in a series of plays which were very popular. None of these plays was published at the time of performance. . . . Potentially important early attempts at the displacement of the colonial centre, they had little or no practical influence beyond perhaps encouraging those who had participated in productions to continue with work in theatre.
>
> (Orkin 1991: 6–7)

This write-off is problematic for several reasons. Perhaps the most obvious is the insistence on the absolute legitimacy of print, despite the fact that the playwright in question was, like his counterparts in London and New York, more interested in box-office receipts than in publication that might have reduced his earnings by making the play available to competing managements (Gray 1984: 21). Second, the meaning of "practical influence" is left ambiguous. The bulk of the repertoire in this period did not, to be sure, undertake to "displace the colonial centre." Over and above dramatic texts, however, the institution of theatre and theatre-going, with its characteristic vacillation between imitating metropolitan trends and sporadic attempts to buck those trends, offers a more likely scenario for articulating the contradictions of neocolonial culture and the attempts to get beyond it than the rehearsal of militant dissent that Orkin demands. Finally, it is not clear that encouraging participants to continue "to work with theatre" constitutes a failure of influence or an abdication of social action.

Rather than attempt to redeem theatrical activity of this period as nascent protest theatre (an attempt that does justice to neither protest theatre nor 1930s theatre), we ought to look beyond the content of the drama, published or not, to the workings of the institution of theatre, the place and occasion of its performance, the tastes of its target audience and, equally important, the uses to which those outside this circle put this theatre. Theatre in Johannesburg and Cape Town in the decades after Union was neocolonial to the extent that the season was driven by touring groups from metropolitan centers, especially London and, to a lesser extent, New York, or by local productions of plays that had already been tested in the metropoles. However, the notion of "metropolitan drama" does not take into account the diversity of, say, the Johannesburg season of 1911, which included *The Girl Who Lost Her Character, Richard III, The Pageant of Great Women* (Cicely Hamilton's homage to women's struggle for freedom and equality, originally staged in London by Edy Craig, Ellen Terry's daughter), and *Love and the Hyphen* (Stephen Black's aforementioned satire on social and racial mores in Cape Town, including the neocolonial foibles of its self-described aristocracy).[2] Though both were metropolitan in origin and theme, the formulaic "woman with a past" plot of *The Girl Who Lost Her Character* had little in common with the suffragist *Pageant. Love and the Hyphen* (first performed 1902; published Black 1984), on the other hand, may have departed from metropolitan norms in incorporating local topics and dialect, but its generic mix of drawing-room comedy, social satire, and broad farce was exactly the combination that was popular in metropolitan and provincial theatres in Britain and North America at the time.

Furthermore, plays did not have to be locally written to have topical local relevance; Stephen Black's production in 1917 of *Damaged Goods*, Eugène Brieux's drama about the social consequences of syphilis, provided a public forum for this question which had been taboo in South Africa; the Johannesburg Rep's performance of *The Red Robe* by the same author in 1930 drew the remark from Black that "smug lawyers will no doubt reassure themselves (and their clients) by saying 'well, of course, it isn't like that *here* . . .' But my own experience has been rather that French law is more . . . *merciful* than English or Roman Dutch law."[3] The members of the Bantu People's Theatre production of Eugene O'Neill's *The Hairy Ape* in 1936 drew on their knowledge of the day-to-day oppression of Africans as well as expressionist stage techniques for its portrayal of the alienation of workers in capitalist modernity. Distinctions between the center and the periphery, between imported and indigenous production, between affirmative and critical culture, are thus not as straightforward as some commentators may wish to claim. Any argument for the overall neocolonial character of theatre in Johannesburg in the early twentieth century needs to take into account not only the nationality or ethnicity of the playwright but also the workings of the institution of theatre.

The first three decades of the twentieth century saw a few local producers, such as Black and Leonard Rayne, penetrate a field dominated by management sponsoring tours from London (such as the Schlesinger group's African Consolidated Theatres). By the 1930s, the scarcity of local capital, the growing competition of the cinema, and perhaps also greater class differentiation among the white population, left the commercial field practically monopolized by African Consolidated's tours, while opening up a space for repertory companies run by leisured, relatively well-educated amateurs in regional centers from Pretoria to Cape Town. The Afrikaans repertories at the time included drama on nationalist themes (such as J. F. W. Grosskopf's plays about Paul Kruger and the economic plight of contemporary Afrikaners) (Kannemeyer 1988: 90–91), patriotic tear-jerkers, like *Sarie Marais*, alongside translations of English, German, and Scandinavian drama. However, the English language groups (in particular, the Johannesburg Repertory Society [1928–78; the longest running group] and the Jewish Guild (also in Johannesburg) or the Little Theatre in Cape Town), showed relatively little interest in local playwrighting, preferring instead to balance the drawing-room comedies of Wilde, Coward, and others, with Shakespeare and Shaw and, somewhat more adventurously, modern European and American playwrights including Nicholai Evreinov and Karel Čapek along with the more familiar Chekhov, Pirandello, Giraudoux, and O'Neill.

This attachment to drama sanctioned by the metropolis did not mean that local drama was entirely absent, however. In 1937 the Repertory Reading Group performed *Red Rand*, a play about the white miners' strike of 1922, by Lewis Sowden, critic for the *Rand Daily Mail*.[4] Measured against the only other South African play of note on the subject of the goldfields, Stephen Black's *Helena's Hope Ltd.* (first performed 1910; published Black 1984), which satirizes individual capitalists and rapacious land-sharks but follows the classic melodramatic plot in which the dispossessed yet genteel Helena eventually outwits the villainous land-grabbers to reclaim her inheritance, *Red Rand* is remarkable for its serious engagement with the social consequences of mining capitalism. Yet its treatment of militant workers, their families, and their antagonists, while critical, remains within the bounds of "social concern" (the Edwardian phrase) rather than revolution. Like John Galsworthy's *Strife* (1910), which was hailed as a play of national importance at its London premiere (Kruger 1992: 101–24), *Red Rand* portrays the militants as heroic but misguided manual laborers, whose grievances against Capital, in this case, the Chamber of Mines, are justified but whose armed resistance is shown to be the last resort of desperate men. *Red Rand* also shares with *Strife* the predominantly domestic setting for the public drama that occurs largely off-stage. The conventions of action in this space threaten to domesticate the struggle; in both plays, the single public scene – a workers' meeting – smells of barely suppressed violence. As one of the instigators, marked in the stage directions as a fanatic, remarks: "I've got no time for moderate men. . . . Those who know history know that it is only by force that great reforms are effected" (Sowden 1937: I, 70). The violence of the Chamber of Mines and the military, on the other hand, remain off-stage, as a shadowy but powerful force whose machinations are impenetrable. This has the partial effect of generating sympathy for the underdog miners but it also evades direct attribution of responsibility to the state or the Chamber for the miners' suffering.

Despite the ostensible focus on the labor struggle, the actual center of the play is not the labor leader, Will Mullins, but his educated brother, John, who has the last word:

> That's the trouble with you strikers. You go about shouting and waving the Red Flag but you don't know the first thing about the force you set in motion. . . . You've got to know as much as the other side know before you can beat them. . . . And they've learnt a good deal from books. . . . Without geometry, you couldn't sink a shaft, without knowledge of history, you wouldn't know how to govern. You've got to learn and learn before you can have power.
>
> (Sowden 1937: II, 48)

The ending – John is shot by the mining police while trying to retrieve his books, while Will reiterates his brother's plea for education rather than direct action – endorses an alliance between intellectual and manual labor, while saying little about the ongoing violence of the South African state and next to nothing about the fate of black workers caught between white state and white labor. The racist aspect of the strike, especially the miners' defense of the Colour Bar, is glossed over, as is the occasional reference to the deaths of black miners. The only black in the play, the Mullins's servant, Samuel, is portrayed as loyal but naïve. He is willing to work for no pay (an ironic reflection of the miners' refusal to consider higher wages for their black co-workers) and is killed, not in heroic action but by a stray bomb while watching the planes from the roof. Likewise, isiZulu features only as a minor part of the domestic scene, rather than as one of the languages of the mines. Thus, while this play pays ample attention to conflicts among the workers and gives a relatively sympathetic portrayal of their grievances, racism remains its structuring absence. Africans were also excluded from the theatre event, since they were not admitted to the Library Theatre without special permit.

This dramatic silence on the racist heart of South Africa received a curious but telling endorsement in a contemporary article defending South African dramatists against criticism from abroad, in the person of the "Distinguished Visitor" looking for drama about the "particular problems of this country . . . between Boer and Briton, and between Black and White" (Celli 1937: 13). The author relies on the pragmatic but false claim that "the reason our dramatists cannot write plays about either problem is the simple fact that . . . these plays would not be allowed to see the inside of a theatre" (in fact, plays, especially in Afrikaans, about the tensions between Boer and Briton were certainly produced, though usually not by commercial managements). More telling, however, is her insistence that "the great South African play will need to deal with some aspect of the fundamental human being" rather than "national peculiarities." The appeal to the authority of universal art functions here, as Marcuse has argued, as a refuge from an unpalatable reality (Marcuse 1968: 118) as well as neocolonial resistance to the perceived inclination of "distinguished visitors" to reduce white South Africans along with blacks to raw material for the portrayal of "particular problems."

In South Africa, as in the other Commonwealth dominions, such as Canada and Australia, in this period, the idea of theatre art was fueled by the metropolitan aspirations of a neocolonial leisured class of tastemakers.[5] To assimilate this class completely to a "ruling class" is misleading, however, since such a move ignores the gap between those with cultural rather than financial capital and the state as such, the distance between metropolitan tastemakers and their followers in the periphery, as well as the ambiguous character of their interrelation.[6] Further, the habitual emphasis on the *scale* of racial discrimination in South Africa may lead one to overlook the structural similarities among the dominions as well as the generalizable aspects of neocolonial culture and its leisured amateur practitioners. "Amateur" should be understood in the full range of its meanings, as the activities of those who love theatre rather than those who sell it, the informal association of leisured patrons rather than the regulated production of workers in a culture industry. The *idea* of amateur theatre in the metropolis provided a case against competing arguments for a theatre accessible to a popular audience. As Harley Granville-Barker, chief sponsor of an English National Theatre, wrote:

> Leisure is not so much an opportunity as a . . . quality of mind. . . . But the mass of the world's work . . . is too highly specialized to call for . . . well-balanced faculties. So much the worse for . . . workers. That . . . is the retort. Although articulated in terms of a commitment to art as such, the theatrical activity of these leisured classes, is that which art, with its sole concern for man's complete humanity, must make.
>
> (Granville-Barker 1922: 286–87)

The case for art's "complete humanity" thus rests on its a priori exclusion of the working majority.

Expressed in terms of a commitment to art, the theatrical activity of leisured amateurs drew its strength from the desire for metropolitan prestige rather than from a commitment to radical experiment. Even productions of modern plays apparently remote from the drawing-room conventionally associated with amateur theatre, were redolent of the mustiness of that well-upholstered interior. The Johannesburg Rep's revival of *R.U.R* ("Rossum's Universal Robots"), Karel Čapek's apocalyptic vision of a robot revolution and the nightmare of technology, in 1936, the same year in which the Empire Exhibition celebrated the power of technology, was apparently so "insipid" and "uninspired," played "for all the world like men's football on a Sunday afternoon" (Linscott 1936: 15), that the critic felt moved to (mis)quote Roy Campbell's indictment of neocolonial gentility:

> We note the great restraint with which you write
> We're with you there, of course.
> You use the snaffle and the curb all right
> But where's the b——y horse?[7]

The misquotation is significant not only because it deflects Campbell's attack on genteel critics as well as their targets but also because it authorizes neocolonial conventions of gentility even as it upbraids them.

The Bantu Dramatic Society and the teleology of modernity

Although certainly generated by a neocolonial elite, the desire for metropolitan cultural capital was not confined to this class but also affected the activities of New African groups. Even before making informal contact with the white repertories, New Africans were, as we have seen, exposed to drama as an integral part of their mission school education. The first production of the Bantu Dramatic Society (BDS) was Oliver Goldsmith's *She Stoops to Conquer*. The most plausible basis for this choice was not, as has been claimed (Hoernlé 1934: 224) and repeated (Orkin 1991: 25), "a visiting English company at His Majesty's Theatre in Johannesburg" (there was none), but the experience of members, such as Dan Twala, who had performed the play at Lovedale College (Couzens 1985: 51) and went on to become secretary of the BDS on the one hand, and the example of the Johannesburg Rep's production at His Majesty's in 1932, on the other.[8] Subsequent productions, such as *The Cheerful Knave* (1934) and *Lady Windermere's Fan* (1935), remained firmly within the framework of a genteel conception of European modernity (Figure 3.1). On the other hand, a production of John Drinkwater's *Abraham Lincoln*, proposed for 1935 and supported by materials and advice from the British Drama League (Kelly 1934: 3), did not go forward. Furthermore, André van Gyseghem's suggestions of American socially critical drama such as *The Hairy Ape* and *The Emperor Jones* by Eugene O'Neill and *Stevedore* by Paul Peters and George Sklar, were not taken up, apparently because they were "not sufficiently genteel" (Kelly 1938: 3).

She Stoops to Conquer opened on 28 April 1933 for two weekends only at the BMSC and was followed, in each case, by a dance with music provided by the Merry Blackbirds. African critics thought the event worthy of front-page news, in part because the performance demonstrated African assimilation of European culture but chiefly because of BDS's inaugural aim to "perform European drama [only] from time to time [and] to encourage Bantu playwrights and to develop African dramatic and operatic art" (Kelly 1934: 2).[9] White commentators treated the activities of the BDS with varying degrees of patronizing concern. Hoernlé commended the players for "the way in which they surmounted every conceivable handicap" (Hoernlé 1934: 224) but praised mostly for an allegedly "natural aptitude for acting" (p. 225). J. D. Rheinhallt Jones, director of the Institute for Race Relations and honorary patron of the BDS, opined that "the group would benefit from guidance from an experienced European."[10] Sybil Thorndike, liberal veteran of the Old Vic, forerunner of the English National Theatre, was more generous: "In holding the black man back, we are holding back the best in ourselves. . . . We are not so clever that we cannot learn from him."[11] All had in common the familiar emphasis on Africans' apparently "natural aptitude for acting," rather than on African agency in the choice of genres and conventions of

Figure 3.1 African theatre and European gentility in *Lady Windermere's Fan*; Bantu Dramatic Society, 1932. *Source: Bantu World*

performance. They were, however, willing to criticize clumsy propaganda such as *uNongqause* by the missionary Mary Waters, the second BDS production, which dealt with the starvation of the amaXhosa as a result of the cattle-killing prescribed by the prophetess of the title and their redemption by missionaries, who dominate the play despite the title. Far from approving of the play's "proselytizing" (Orkin 1991: 31), Hoernlé dismissed the play as a "harangue" by a "Bible-reading missionary" (Hoernlé 1934: 226), while the British Drama League report criticized a "lack of dramatic knowledge on the part of the dramatist" and noted African audiences' indifference (Kelly 1934: 2).

The performance of *uNongqause*, coupled with his New African suspicion of missionary drama artificially constructed in "Native idiom,"[12] encouraged Herbert Dhlomo, BDS member and commentator on African drama, to write his own play on the subject, *The Girl Who Killed to Save* (first published in 1936 but written in 1934 or 1935; Dhlomo 1985), as well as a series of articles on the nature and function of African drama. Where Waters' *uNongqause* portrayed Xhosa custom as merely primitive and therefore doomed, Dhlomo's play treats the cattle-killing "as a tragically mistaken tactic rather than as immature futility" (Orkin 1991: 35). *The Girl Who Killed to Save* begins by juxtaposing Nongqause's doubts about her visions with her fervent desire to help her people repel the invaders and ends with the vision of a dying convert, Daba, who translates Nongqause's divination into the premonition of Christianization. Yet, although the end of the play casts Nongqause in the role of "Liberator from Superstition and the rule of Ignorance" (Dhlomo 1985: 29) and thus unwitting contribution to

56

her people's Christianization, these words were first heard in the mouth of a zealous European, Hugh, endorsing the most radical kind of social engineering (p. 18):

> Nongqause may accomplish in a short time . . . what in the ordinary course of events would have taken generations of Christianity and education . . . to do. The only thing to ask is whether or not the price she has asked the people to pay is not too costly. . . . If we believe in the doctrine of the survival of the fittest then we may excuse her by saying that those who survive her purging and liberating test will be individuals physically and intellectually superior to the others.

The edge of cruelty in the speech cuts against the liberating claims of the speaker and reminds us of the brutality of colonization. At the same time, Hugh's reference to those people who "have already shown their intellectual independence by being sceptical and refusing to kill their cattle" does allow space for those amaXhosa whose independence of mind shows the way forward to a critical appropriation of the tools of modernity – skepticism, rational thought, improvisation – which may be used against the teleology of neocolonial modernity that treats Europe as the alpha and omega of progress. To borrow the terms of Stephen Greenblatt's discussion of European possession of the New World, the ability to improvise and a capacity of "appropriative mimesis" enabled the colonizers to undermine the structured but inflexible order of the amaXhosa; these attributes were, however, subject to a counter-appropriation against the colonizers (Greenblatt 1991: 4, 99).

The teleology of modernity may drive the plot of *The Girl Who Killed to Save* but it does not entirely determine its form. To be sure, the key moments of crisis in the play – the private confrontation between Nongqause and her sceptical suitor, Mazwi; the showdown between paramount chief Kreli and doubters among his subjects; the debate between intervention and inaction among the Europeans; as well as the conflicting dialogue between white settlers and the indigenous population on the colonial frontier – are rendered in a language that recalls the heightened prose naturalism of contemporary English writers such as Drinkwater and Shaw and, for one reviewer of the published text, even the expressionist intensity of Ernst Toller's portrayal of collective anguish and individual alienation in *Masses and Man* (1921).[13] Yet dialogue between autonomous subjects, which have come to be associated with modernity (Williams 1995), is not the only dramatic device operating here. The original manuscript was accompanied by five songs, written by Dhlomo.[14] The last song, a hymn that begins "Nkosi kawu sikelele" [God bless you], is in the tradition of *amakwaya*, Xhosa hymns, and church music, and, inserted in the final scene as the converts gather at Daba's deathbed, reinforces the power of Christianization. At the same time, however, its first line recalls "Nkosi sikelel' iAfrika," the familiar ANC anthem, with its associations of national longing if not nationalist struggle. The other four songs, which are interspersed in the first two scenes, which introduce the life and customs of the tribe, are more in line with the folk music disseminated by Dhlomo's cousin, Reuben Caluza. Like Caluza's songs, these bear witness not only to the invention of a tradition, but to the desire to draw from an African/European syncresis the means to fashion an African present and future.[15]

Despite the authority of Anglophilic gentility over the BDS, their project encouraged members to push further the limits of neocolonial modernity through the use of syncretic aesthetics and politics, in plays such as *The Hairy Ape*, which combined a metropolitan pedigree with more substantial social themes than the drawing-room comedy. Although English "experts" had previously dismissed the play, a new group called the Bantu People's Theatre (led by Dan Twala, secretary of the BDS) approached Van Gyseghem about *The Hairy Ape* in 1936. The play was performed under Van Gyseghem's direction, with Twala in the leading role of Yank at the BMSC in December and revived at the Witwatersrand University Great Hall in June 1937.[16] Although set ostensibly in America, the play's dramatization of an absolute gulf between rich and poor, parasites and workers, clearly resonated in the context of racial and economic conditions in Johannesburg and was praised for its "stark, symbolic treatment of the action" (Linscott 1937a: 15). This production signaled a departure from the practice of the BDS at several points: its subject was the exploitation of urban workers, rather than the lives of precolonial tribes or English gentry; it used language more appropriate to this milieu – the "American slang was translated into the Bantu idiom of English" (Kelly 1938: 3), which may have been Fanagalo, the pidgin spoken on the mines (Kavanagh 1985: 46) – and it called for a performance style marked by staccato delivery and expressionist gesture quite different from the decorum of drawing-room comedy.

This direction was certainly noteworthy, but it did not automatically put the Bantu People's Theatre in the vanguard of a new political movement. In 1936 at least, its members were careful to reassure prospective patrons such as Rheinhallt Jones that they were "entirely dissociated from political movements and parties"[17] and the company's draft constitution states its goal as the cultivation of art rather than politics:

(a) The Bantu People's Theatre stands for the cultivation of Bantu Art and Drama
(b) It aims at improving the undiscovered talents of Bantu Art in Drama
(c) to be non-political.[18]

This statement was probably designed to deflect queries from prospective patrons as to the political complexion of plays like *The Hairy Ape*. The very terseness of the final clause suggests an afterthought and a certain dissonance between the nationalist potential of the first two clauses and the disavowal at the end.

In the political context of the mid-1930s, the draft constitution of the Bantu People's Theatre is likely to have been a defensive maneuver. The Hertzog Acts of

1936, the impotence of the All-African Convention (AAC) called at intervals since December 1935 in a vain attempt to halt this legislation, the lukewarm response of even liberal whites to the anger of educated Africans, and the spectacle of European barbarity in Spain and Ethiopia all combined to undermine the authority of "European civilization." As D. D. T. Jabavu, convenor of the AAC, had it:

> All Africans as well as other non-White races of the world have been staggered by the cynical rape of Italy of the last independent State belonging to indigenous Africans. After hearing a great deal for twenty years about the rights of small nations, self-determination, Christian ideals, the inviolability of treaties . . . the glory of European civilization, and so forth, the brief history of the last eight months [since the summoning of the Convention in December 1935] has scratched this European veneer and revealed the white savage hidden beneath.
>
> (Kabane 1936: 187)

What is striking about this speech is that, for all the fury of the attack on white savagery, the author sustains a certain faith in an ideal of civilization, which has been betrayed by particular Europeans rather than by Europe as such. By stripping the "European veneer" from the faces of "white savages," he can criticize the actual brutality of colonization while appropriating the values of modernity. The more conservative Selope Thema makes a related, though less corrosive, point when he writes that:

> tribal life is not a peculiarity of the African race; it is a stage through which all the great nations of today have passed . . . we have a right to decide our own destiny and to make our distinctive contribution to the world's civilizations.[19]

While these statements do not resolve the contradictory impulses of colonial modernization, they do attempt to hold in view the idea of modernity as progress and enlightenment, even if the European realization falls far short of the ideal.

"History . . . and metamorphosis": Dhlomo's Africa

Dhlomo's work after 1935 was influenced by this increasing skepticism about "European civilization": but also by an ongoing desire to "graft African tradition onto the European" (1977a: 7). In a series of essays written between the inauguration of the Bantu Dramatic Society in 1932 and the first (recorded) performance of one of his plays, *Moshoeshoe,* in 1939, Dhlomo moved closer to an affirmation of "native drama" than he had been when he criticized the revival of Shaka as a "new kind of tribalism . . . [that] encourages non-progressive institutions among the people."[20] At the same time, however, he remained vigilant against the

59

commodification of African practices in the "African Entertainments" for predominantly white audiences, dismissing them as "exotic crudities" (Dhlomo 1977a: 7) or "static museum-like plays" (Dhlomo 1977e: 39). These essays chart Dhlomo's navigation of the fault-lines between, but also within, African and European cultural practices, a process that reveals the syncretic and contradictory character of supposedly monolithic traditions, while his plays of this period, grouped together in a potential collection that he called "This is Africa," plot a way forward through building on these traditions.

Even the early essay cited at the beginning of this chapter offers a trenchant critique of simple oppositions, while examining the prospects and pitfalls of an African National Theatre. In this essay, Dhlomo defends the value of literary drama, yet he insists that the strong performative dimension of African oral traditions should inform any African National Theatre. He calls for the dramatic representation of social injustice – "African Serfdom, Oppression, Exploitation, and Metamorphosis" – but also argues that the modern African dramatist should be artist before propagandist. This inconsistency certainly expresses the tension between the precepts of Dhlomo's missionary education (which affirmed the timelessness of art against the contingencies of politics) and the pressures of the historical moment that pushed him and his peers toward commitment, but it also speaks for the concept of art, in this case theatre, as a form of negative critique of the status quo.

The appeal to art before propaganda should not therefore be read as a capitulation to imposed norms of gentility. Rather, it attempts to use the notion of artistic autonomy to negotiate cultural space for the contestation of oppression in an environment in which more direct action (from political mobilization to adversarial journalism) was increasingly curtailed. Framing the revitalization of tradition in the generalizing terms of African nationalism, Dhlomo challenges both white and black separatists when he argues, in an essay entitled "Why Study Tribal Dramatic Forms?" (1939), that this revitalization should transform not only African forms but also modern drama as a whole by "infus[ing] new blood into the weary limbs of the older dramatic forms of Europe" (Dhlomo 1977e: 35). The hint of deference is more than offset by the critical reference to the "weary limbs . . . of Europe" or, in the earlier essay, to the "tedium" of modern (by implication, genteel English) plays. This disdain for the "acting plays" of the professional theatre in favor of "literary drama" (Dhlomo 1977e: 39) that might also propagandize for social change echoes the aspirations of the advocates of the "new social drama" in Britain, who criticized the frivolity of the musical comedy and drawing-room drama that dominated the commercial stage. Like this "drama of social concern," however, it stops short of a radical abolition of naturalist aesthetics and domestic interiority, in the manner of Brecht's *Lehrstücke* or the proletarian agitprop in the United States as well as Britain in this period (Kruger 1992: 101–107; 145–51).

The example of metropolitan social drama, its attempt to be both literary and engaged, independent of the pressure to make a profit, yet able to draw an audience, exercises a significant but not overwhelming influence on Dhlomo's reflections on drama and the African. Whereas his suggested themes – exposing corruption and representing metamorphosis as well as oppression – may confirm the influence of Shaw or Galsworthy, his ideal institution of theatre differs from that of the "new drama" in England, whose producers, such as Granville-Barker, operated within a modified version of the commercial theatre institution. Against this commodification of drama, Dhlomo highlights, in "The Nature and Variety of Tribal Drama" (1939) the close relationship between the occasion of performance and the commemoration of rites of passage, seasonal festivals, and the like (Dhlomo 1977d: 28–35) and argues that traditional African drama shares with the classical Greek its integration into the social fabric (Dhlomo 1977d: 30). This evocation of a theatre of ritual power does not entail a nostalgic revival of tribal community, but rather the reverse: "The African artist cannot delve into the Past unless he has first grasped the Present. African art can grow and thrive not only by . . . excavating archaical art forms, but by grappling with present-day realities" (Dhlomo 1977e: 40). Instead of "static museum-like drama based on primitive tradition and culture" (Dhlomo 1977e: 39), Dhlomo envisaged an African National Theatre that might appropriate those African performance forms that lent themselves to a critical engagement between past and present.

While highlighting the public character of these forms, however, he insists that they be evaluated as "ends in themselves," in aesthetic as well as functional terms (Dhlomo 1977d: 27). He appropriates the courtly tradition of *izibongo*, rather than the more demotic convention of *izinganekwane* [folktales], which suggests a desire to legitimate a tradition of high culture as universal as Greek tragedy in the European pantheon. However, his appeal to tradition rests on a distinctly modern invention of a term, *izibongelo*, to bolster his claim that the panegyric form contains within it the traces of dramatic structure and that its function, like that of drama, is to "tell the story of the nation" (Dhlomo 1977d: 24,35).[21]

These essays thus record the impact of retraditionalist rhetoric but do not submit to it. They appeal to a "sacred inheritance" (Dhlomo 1977e: 37) as the "ground on which a great original African drama can be built" (Dhlomo 1977d: 35), even as they speak to New African skepticism of the "museum-like" construction of ethnicity. They also register the strain in New African faith in modernization through Europeanization at a time when white suspicions of African resistance to "Serfdom, Oppression, and Exploitation" were fueling the drive toward more explicit segregationist legislation. The appeal of segregationist policy and its ideological justification as development "along the Native's own lines" was a response to the perceived threat of mass action on the part of a growing African working class. As politician, novelist, and arch-racialist George Heaton Nicholls argued, this policy defended the "maintenance of chiefdoms" as a bulwark against an emerging "native proletariat" (quoted by Dubow 1987: 86). New Africans responded to this trend by insisting on their rights to full citizenship. As ANC leader, D. D. T. Jabavu wrote in response to the Herzog bills restricting African franchise:

There are Black men today fully capable of sitting and representing their people in the House of Assembly. . . . These bills were framed on the assumed basis that the Black race is a race of children who will continue to be children for all time.

(Jabavu 1935: 25–26)

Both apologists for and opponents of the segregation laws emphasized the continuity between the program of Herzog and Nicholls in the 1930s and the policy, implemented by Theophilus Shepstone, secretary for Native Affairs from the 1840s to the 1880s, of maintaining tribal custom under the ultimate authority of the colonial administration (Couzens 1985: 134–36). Admirers, such as the writer Sarah Gertrude Millin, called Shepstone, "the greatest native administrator South Africa has ever had" (Millin 1925: 47). Critics such as Jabavu and Dhlomo argued Shepstone's policy of separate development was the cornerstone of contemporary segregation (Couzens 1985: 138). Both sides of the debate, however, acknowledged the persistent influence of Shepstone's ambiguous but forceful synthesis in his dealings with African and especially Zulu leaders, of the assertion of imperial supremacy, and the insistence on the integrity of indigenous institutions, even when, in the 1930s, those institutions were thoroughly integrated into the segregationist state.

Dhlomo's most developed history play, *Cetshwayo* (written 1936–37; first published Dhlomo 1985), speaks both to the historical conflict and the contemporary debate. Depicting the betrayal of Cetshwayo, the last autonomous Zulu king by Shepstone – whose participation in key events such as the coronation of Cetshwayo (1873) had earned him the honorific Somtsewu – and his allies after the Anglo/Zulu war in 1879, the play is also Dhlomo's most explicit dramatic indictment of segregation and disenfranchisement conducted in the name of civilization and Empire. The representatives of the British imperial order, Governor Lord Chelmsford, as well as the ambiguous figure of John Dunn, English adventurer and "white Zulu," speak of imperial power as the irresistible force not merely of conquest but also of modernization, while Cetshwayo and his followers evoke the utopian image of "Africa for the Africans." Shepstone's presence, as a character and a subtext, is more complex than a mere agent of imperialism. On the one hand, Dhlomo incorporates Shepstone's role as kingmaker from the tradition cultivated not only by Shepstone and his friend, the imperial novelist Rider Haggard, in his purportedly historical account *Cetywayo and His White Neighbours* (1882) but by Mpande, who gave him a Zulu name, Somtsewu, and the paternal authority of Shaka at the investiture of Cetshwayo as official heir in 1861 (Hamilton 1998: 75). On the other hand, he modifies the record of Zulu endorsement to highlight Shepstone's cunning manipulation of Zulu ceremony and thus heighten the conflict between Cetshwayo and Shepstone.

Dhlomo readily exploits the theatrical potential of Shepstone's king-making as well as the portrayal of history as the struggle of great men, drawn from Shepstone's mentor, Thomas Carlyle, as well as Carlyle's student, Drinkwater.

However, he also modifies the historical record by collapsing two events: the nomination of 1861, at which Shepstone arrived to a tense reception which he turned to his advantage, and the coronation, to which Cetshwayo invited him, only to conduct a secret ceremony ahead of time and to keep Shepstone waiting for his role in the event (Hamilton 1998: 80–85). The investiture scene in the play incorporates the tension of the nomination scene. It begins with the rivalry between the declining King Mpande and his combative heir, Cetshwayo, which is in turn amplified by the contest between Mpande's chief advisor, who stresses the authority of the past, and the unnamed bard who praises Cetshwayo as the "New Light from the East" (Dhlomo 1985: 121) and who will later compose *izibongo* [praises] for the historic (if short-lived) Zulu victory at Isandhlwana (pp. 159–60) and introduces Shepstone, capable of flattering the Zulu army with praises of Zulu might. Whereas Shepstone's praise of the king and proclamation of himself as the king's servant (pp. 123–25) recapitulates the traditional role of king-maker, Cetshwayo's anger at his presumption marks Dhlomo's resistance of this tradition. At the same time, using Rider Haggard's admiring account to critical effect, he makes his Shepstone more of an overt imperialist by having him insist not only on the power of the British army: "Like waves, the men roar and charge, . . . never die, can never be exterminated" (p. 125; cf. Haggard 1882: 7–8) but also on the supremacy of the Empire: "I have come to perform a sacred Duty. Why do you refuse to obey the sacred Voice?" (p. 125).[22]

In the final silent action of the scene, in which Mpande covers Cetshwayo with the royal robe while Shepstone crowns him with a headdress of "brass and leather" (pp. 125–26), Dhlomo vividly depicts Shepstone's power within as well as his potential disruption of Zulu power, but also attempts to redeem Cetshwayo's royal authority from conflicting accounts that threaten to denigrate it. Dhlomo's "brass and leather" headdress appears to correspond to the curious hybrid of Zulu, British, and Roman Imperial form fashioned by the tailor of the British regiment at Shepstone's request. However, his image of the royal robe departs sharply from the small cloak worn by Cetshwayo in a photograph of the proceedings (Hamilton 1988: 129) (see Figure 3.2), which Shepstone apparently borrowed from "the Natal Society's amateur dramatic group" (Dominy 1991: 73). The emphatic transformation of this diminutive object into a "a huge tiger skin" and the transfer of the act of draping it from Shepstone to Mpande (Dhlomo 1985: 125) suggests that Dhlomo is reacting to *The History of the Zulu War* by Frances Colenso, daughter of Bishop Colenso, Shepstone's most ardent antagonist. Colenso has Shepstone envelop the king in a "little scarlet mantle – formerly a lady's opera cloak" and crown him with a "pasteboard, cloth and tinsel crown" and Cetshwayo react with dual awareness of the indignity of the ceremony and the necessity of the event for his alliance with the British (Colenso and Durnford 1881: 11): Shepstone is thus cast in the villainous light Dhlomo was likely to approve.[23]

This scene, like the play as a whole, enacts not merely the plot of imperial conquest but rather the complexities of colonial legitimation. The debate between

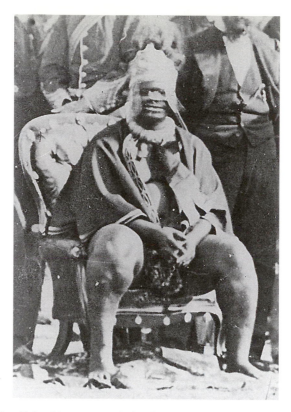

Figure 3.2a The Zulu king wrapped in English amateur dramatic costume; King
Cetshwayo at his coronation in 1873, wearing an opera cape borrowed
from the Pietermaritzburg Drama Society and a crown designed by the British
colonial army. *Source and permission*: The Killie Campbell Africana Library,
University of Natal, Durban

Shepstone and his clerk Park at the center of the play takes up this question of
legitimacy. When Shepstone claims that he wants "the Native to develop along his
own lines" (p. 143), Park exposes the constitutive contradiction in Shepstone's
policy:

> You want Natives to develop on their own lines. Yet, even now, you are
> compelled to dictate those lines. For the truth is that they are develop-
> ing along their own lines at present. But you are against it. . . . You
> intend creating many petty Chiefs, who will have no real power. . . .
> [they] will be your police and puppets under a Native Affairs Dept. that
> will see that they never get absolute liberty or full rights or enter the
> centre of the maelstrom of progress.
>
> (p. 144)

Figure 3.2b Crown worn by the Zulu king at his coronation in 1873. *Source and permission:* The Killie Campbell Africana Library, University of Natal, Durban

Civilization, like liberty and progress, is, in Park's view, absolute. Yet, despite this defense of universal rights, Park concedes that Shepstone's policy is a "most ingenious and effective instrument for maintaining white supremacy" because it will "advance European interests . . . under the guise of . . . benevolent guidance of the Native" while appearing to "give them recognition and [to] preserve their racial integrity" (p. 145). In other words, it provides the ideological underpinnings for hegemony, for *consent* to domination (Williams 1977: 110).

The conclusion of the play exposes this mask of benevolence as "protection that is destruction" (p. 149). The "sunset of Zulu power" that Chelmsford celebrates as Ulundi burns (p. 165) is reflected in the deterioration of cultivated land that had been well tended and in the squabbles between Cetshwayo's would-be successors, exploited by adventurers like John Dunn. Where Shepstone covers the fist of domination with the glove of diplomacy, Dunn speaks plainly but, like the Vice in a morality play, only to the audience:

> What conflicting forces! Shepstone and the Government, Mpande and the old tribal order, Cetshwayo a new revolutionary force. . . . Great God, there must be an explosion soon . . . and it must blow up poor Dunn to some mighty position.
>
> (p. 122)

As a settler who had adopted Zulu mores and married Zulu wives, all the while retaining white privilege, Dunn does not merely straddle two worlds as an individual; his character functions as a device highlighting the ambiguity of colonial relations and to implicate Shepstone in those relations.[24] Where the historical Cetshwayo lived to plead his case for Zulu autonomy to Queen Victoria in 1882 and to be reinstated – again by Shepstone, but under firm British control – in 1883, Dhlomo attempts to redeem his protagonist from this capitulation by giving him a dignified death and by suggesting the ongoing struggle for freedom. He does not resolve the discrepancy between Cetshwayo's admission of failure – "When I was nothing, I thought I was something. Now that I am lost, I know that . . . [n]o man can live for others before . . . living in himself" (p. 175) – and the promise of a future when "Black kings shall watch over vast dominions" (p. 176) but ends the play nonetheless with the prophecy of a destined emancipation: "What was will be/We shall be free" (p. 176).

History, agency, and the aporia of colonial modernity

Like *The Girl Who Killed to Save*, the drama of *Cetshwayo* unfolds mainly through dialogue; the songs and praises comment on the action but do not deflect the forward drive of the plot. For all Dhlomo's argument for African forms and conventions, the dramaturgy of *Cetshwayo* is mostly Aristotelian or, more precisely, Hegelian and Schillerian, in that it focuses on a national hero, whose unwillingness to act decisively against the machinations of his enemies brings about his tragic defeat. Although there is no conclusive evidence that Dhlomo read any plays by Friedrich Schiller (1759–1805), he was certainly familiar with Drinkwater's history plays and with Drinkwater's mentor (and Hegel reader), Thomas Carlyle and his *On Heroes, Hero-Worship and the Heroic in History* (1841), which were available at the Carnegie Non-European Library. Drinkwater's *Mary Stuart* (Drinkwater 1925), in particular, follows Schiller's play of the same name (first produced in 1800) quite closely, emphasizing the inner conflict of both Mary and Elizabeth and including the famous, but fictitious, confrontation between the rival queens (Drinkwater 1925), but all the plays share with Schiller's historical dramas – such as *Don Carlos* (1787), *Die Jungfrau von Orleans* [*The Maid of Orleans*, 1801], and

Wilhelm Tell (1804) – the primary focus on a self-reflective protagonist, whose heroism often emerges in the resistance to, as much as in the engagement with, conclusive action. Cetshwayo's final reflection on the discrepancy between leadership and personhood owes a debt to this tradition.

This focus on reflexive subjectivity, sometimes in conflict with decisive agency, is for Schiller's contemporary, the philosopher G. W. F. Hegel, the hallmark of modern drama (1974: 1173, 1224–25). Hegel's theory of drama as the "product of a . . . developed national life" (1974: 1159) resonates in Schiller's plays, as in Dhlomo's, in which the struggle for national identity at a time when the nation in question is not yet firmly established is embodied in the person of the protagonist (1974: 1224). The historical conflicts with which Schiller and Hegel were concerned, the French Revolution and its impact on German nationalist agitation, were, to be sure, different from the situation in which New Africans found themselves. Nevertheless, the tension between the promise of emancipation and national self-determination embodied by the French Revolution and its legacy, and the actual conditions of subjection by a paternalist state, are structurally similar. Dhlomo's critical writing, especially the essay on "African Drama and Research," reflects an interest in a theory of history which suggests at least the imprint of Hegelian philosophy:

> Our ideas of Past, Present and Future do not rest on an unchangeable rock of finality, but on the plastic wax of time, conditions, progress. . . . Man's life is an unfolding, a revealing of new colours and designs . . . It is this process of birth and revelation that writers should record.
>
> (Dhlomo 1977c: 19–20)

He also shares the conviction that these ideas are formed in and embodied by individuals, through their desires and actions in human society, so the passionate confrontations between individuals become the principal site of historical change (Hegel 1956: 23; Dhlomo 1977c: 20).

Materialist critics of Hegel (and Schiller), in particular, Bertolt Brecht and Augusto Boal, have objected to this emphasis on individual agency and subjectivity as a form of bourgeois individualism that overemphasizes the protagonist's interiority as the driving force of the action (Boal 1979: 87) or the priority of the subject's idealism over the realistic portrayal of the social conditions that belie that idealism (Brecht 1967, vol. 16: 747). Dhlomo's portrayal of Cetshwayo certainly makes full use of the conventions of bourgeois drama to encourage empathy with the protagonist, while highlighting his exemplary character as a "great African genius" (Dhlomo 1977c: 19). At the same time, he modulates this variation on "great man history" by stressing the necessity of "historical and anthropological research" into the life of "the masses" (p. 21) who appear not only in the rousing warriors' choruses that punctuate the action but also in the scenes devoted to everyday life and its disruption by civil strife.

This emphasis on collective agency in the drama of history does not, however, make Dhlomo's dramaturgy "Brechtian" (Orkin 1991: 42). The moments when his characters (especially John Dunn, the villain of the piece) comment on the repercussions of their actions, owe more to the Vice in the medieval morality play, or perhaps to the villain in Victorian melodrama, than to the techniques – distantiation, acting in the third person, critical demonstration rather than the embodiment of character – of *Verfremdung* ["distantiation," mistranslated as "alienation"]. Brecht developed the concepts of *Verfremdung* and historicization in opposition to heroic representation of character at a time when "great man" history was used to glorify those in power; his deconstruction of the demonization of Hitler in *The Resistible Rise of Arturo Ui* (1934) is a good example. Dunn's malevolent manipulation of Cetshwayo, on the other hand, serves as a foil to highlight the king's heroism and to encourage, rather than to diminish, audience identification with the hero's goals of national emancipation. We can, however, only speculate on the effect of this play on Dhlomo's contemporaries, since it was neither published nor publicly performed.[25]

Moshoeshoe was rather less adversarial than *Cetshwayo*; the play portrayed the wisdom of the legendary Sotho statesman, revered not only for his ability to resolve conflicts between his subjects and refugees from the Mfecane (isiZulu)/ Lifecane (Sesotho) – the mass migration caused, in part, by Zulu expansionism in the 1820s – but also as a model African leader whose perspicacity was sadly missed a century later. The play's emphasis on Moshoeshoe's statesmanship highlighted the success of the Basutoland Protectorate's resistance of attempts at incorporation by the South African government. By placing at the center of his play a *pitso*, [people's assembly], Dhlomo also called to mind the disputes of the ANC and AAC at that time and thus implied that the wise counsel of the great leader and his council of elders could not alone heal African disunity.[26] As the performance of the play by the Bantu Dramatic and Operatic Society at the BMSC in May 1939 was in honor of Moshoeshoe Day, these connections to contemporary politics would have been explicit.[27]

The significance of *Moshoeshoe* does not lie solely in an analogical representation of a modern African state in embryo. Equally important is the play's attempt to negotiate a new association of form, content, and occasion of performance. Although *Moshoeshoe* was written (but not published) text marked by the conventions of European drama and the pressures of neocolonial publishing, it drew also on the recurring motifs of African oral traditions: narratives that recount, recall, and re-present the origin and progress of the clan (Miller 1980: 2) or *auriture*, the performance of narrative or drama fully realized only in the ears of the participants (Coplan 1993: 81), however mediated by European commentary (e.g. Lagden 1909). Chief among these motifs would have been the opposition between Shaka, represented in Sesotho narratives as a "Lord of Chaos who both devoured the people of the region and set them to devour each other" (Coplan 1993: 87), and Moshoeshoe I, who not only maintained peace amongst Basotho but also gave refuge to destitute people displaced by the Lifecane. Dhlomo also included in his play the figure of Mohlomi, a diviner of the Bakoena (a Basotho) clan who is said to have advised Moshoeshoe to make peace even with the "devouring" travelers, by attending to the cause rather than the symptom of social disorder and to have prophesied the Lifecane, though he did not live to see it (Coplan 1993: 87–88). By including in a play set in this momentous time a character whom the historical record marks as already dead, Dhlomo follows a procedure that can be compared to auriture as well as to Shakespeare. He telescopes the events in the record to intensify the power of the play as subjunctive enactment of "African history. . . and metamorphosis" and so to amplify the historical resonances of the present occasion.

Contemporary reviews duly noted these resonances but also exhibited the influence of modern notions of antiquarian authenticity. R. W. H. Shepherd, director of the Lovedale Press, had the previous year judged the text of *Moshoeshoe* "artificial"[28] and, although the performance was praised in the African press for portraying an exemplary African leader, and for its evocation of Sotho custom, "legend and reality, action and philosophy,"[29] the attempt to render Sesotho in English received a mixed response. Whereas the *Bantu World* reviewer praised the play as the first indigenous drama combining the efforts of Zulu (Dhlomo and the composer Caluza) and Sotho (the choreographer, A. P. Khutlang, and songwriter, Salome Masoleng) and justified the flowery verse and choppy syntax by claiming that the play's "chief charm lies in the dialogue which is a literal translation from the language in which it was originally written,"[30] his *Umteteli* counterpart maintained that "there was too much of the refined" in the dialogue and accused the actors of not being "typically Masotho." Songs in Sesotho rather than English, he argues, "would have contributed much to making the play a strong living drama of a significant episode in our national life."[31] This dispute reflects the pressure on New Africans from white "experts" and African retraditionalists to write literature in the African vernaculars rather than English.[32] It suggests the strain in the language of the play between a desire for idiomatic authenticity and an aspiration to poetic language that might transcend local specificity, "find the changeless in the changing, the fundamental in the ephemeral" (Dhlomo 1977c: 20). It also confirms that the question of authenticity could not be resolved in terms of form or stable literary value but rather in terms of the significance of the occasion of performance.

The occasion of the performance was likewise subject to strain. Although the play was performed at the BMSC and not, for instance, at the mountain setting of Thaba Bosiu where Moshoeshoe held his *pitso*, or its namesake in Pimville, near Johannesburg, where political meetings were held,[33] its loosely linked scenes – the *pitso* at the center, framed by suitors' quarrels and encounters between the Basotho and refugees from the Lifecane, mediated by Mohlomi, the wandering bard, and ending with a harvest festival (Dhlomo 1985: 229–66) – suggest a commemoration rather than a singular story, which would incorporate varied accounts of past events of ongoing significance. The music for the performance, like that for the Emancipation Centenary, would have at least alluded to melodies already familiar from Caluza's songs of national sorrow such as "iLand Act" and "Elamakosi."

Dhlomo would have liked to legitimate his play in the eyes of an African public by drawing on the immediate authority of the Convention as well as numerous Moshoeshoe Day rallies but this legitimation was far from secure. The social authority of the story of Moshoeshoe, as a drama of national pride, might be considerable, but its political effectiveness was hampered by the neocolonial South African state and British imperial interests.

While reviewers and audience alike would have made the connection between the *pitso* and the rallies, the harvest festival that concludes the play does not quite bring in the yield. The festival envelops but cannot incorporate the missionaries who praise Moshoeshoe's genius only to cast doubt on the enactment of his legacy: "Moshoeshoe . . . a man consumed by the smouldering and devastating fire of . . . great expectations unfulfilled, of plans and ambitions whose very attainment would give birth to plans and ambitions never to be attained" (pp. 260–61). This ambiguous praise strikes a cautionary note against the soaring *izibongo* at the end. The allusion to the citadel of Thaba Bosiu and to "Moshoeshoe the man-mountain, the mountain-mind" (p. 265) has the status of tradition but not the force of historical inevitability.

In this pregnant juxtaposition of a nourishing if fragile inheritance and a still-born emancipation, *Moshoeshoe* struggles to express New African conviction in "African Evolution and Emancipation" (Dhlomo 1977e: 40), while enacting the historical constraints on that conviction. Even as it raises the thoroughly modern standard of "Emancipation from the tyranny of custom and taboo," the play appeals to a precolonial "sacred inheritance," which, as Dhlomo argues in "Why Study Tribal Dramatic Forms?" (1939), should provide "contact with the culture, the life, the heart of forefathers" (Dhlomo 1977e: 37). Responding to this question, the performance attempted to treat this contact as the simultaneous presence of ancient custom and modern evolution:

> The *izibongelo* . . . are, as it were, an extensive, dense forest, where we may go to gather sticks to fight our literary and cultural battles, timber to build our dramatic genres, wood to light our poetic fires, leaves to decorate our achievements. . . . They are the essence of our being, the meaning of our name.[34]

By summoning the "sacred inheritance" as a precious resource *essentially* present to the nation, Dhlomo implies that the spirit of precolonial ceremonies of harvest gathering and community assembly ideally infuse the celebrations of Moshoeshoe Day, a modern invocation of a past and future national unity in the face of its present absence.

This invocation of the present and the future as the embodiment rather than the developmental result of the past does not in any simple way turn *Moshoeshoe* into a ritual act to conjure up the nation through "sympathetic magic" (Dhlomo 1977d: 35), nor does it revive the ancestor worship condemned by Dhlomo's elder contemporary, Selope Thema, as the "iron hand" of the dead. It does nevertheless speak to faith in the simultaneous presence of current experience and ancestral memory and in the embodiment of that memory in surviving, if fragmented, forms and institutions that do not fully submit to modern distinctions between secular history and religious divination. As two recent researchers on South African *izibongo* put it, this kind of drama is "history with the metaphysics included" (Vail and White 1991: 73). It wields metaphysics with a sceptical edge, however. Offering contemporary audiences the simultaneous depiction of Moshoeshoe's autonomy, imperial encroachment, and the image of this contra-dictory legacy in the Moshoeshoe Day celebrations, *Moshoeshoe* is critique as well as celebration. The performance of this play gives voice and body to the inheritance of Moshoeshoe, while staging the gap between that inheritance and the limits of contemporary agency.

In dramatizing the discrepancy between the celebration of the African exemplar and the implied deflection of his legacy without providing a resolution, *Moshoeshoe* represents the historical impasse faced by the New Africans. In 1934, the Emancipation Centenary Celebration was still able to sustain the legitimacy of liberal paternalism, bolstered by the conviction of the promoters, participants, and many in the audience in the necessary conjunction of emancipation, modernity, and European civilization. In 1939, however, this New African conviction was evaporating in the white heat of European savagery. In the decades to follow, a revitalized African nationalism was to break the impasse and galvanize resistance to the segregationist state. *Moshoeshoe*, with its juxtaposition of incompatible elements, its lack of resolution, in short, its *in*authenticity, does not offer a model for the literature of protest and resistance, which would characterize much black South African writing from the 1950s to the present. Nonetheless, the flaws and fissures in the text of the play and the occasion of its performance speak more truly than any tragic catharsis or resounding fictional triumph to the pressures of the historical moment, the aspirations of New Africans, and the fundamental incoherence of colonial modernity.

4

COUNTRY COUNTER CITY:

Urbanization, tribalization, and performance under apartheid

"Country," as Raymond Williams notes in *The Country and the City*, comes from *contra*, meaning "against" or "opposite." "City," on the other hand, comes from *civitas*, meaning "community" or, more broadly cast, "citizenship" (Williams 1973: 307). This etymology complicates the familiar contrasts between the city as "achieved centre" and a place of light and the country as a "place of backwardness" or, conversely, between the country as the site of a "natural way of life" and the city as a place of "worldliness, ambition" and, one might add, corruption and decadence (Williams 1973: 1). As metonyms for collective identity, "city" and "country" are not simply opposites but both mutually reinforcing and mutually repellent. In the South African context, in a period of rapid urbanization during World War II, the meanings of "country" and "city" emerge not only out of the contest between competing ideas and practices of citizenship, progress, and tradition, but also out of the peculiarity of the neocolonial environment in which both country and city are, as it were, "in the country," the "hinterland of the metropolitan centre" (Skurski and Coronil 1993: 232).

This peculiarity can be located in the aporia at the heart of colonial modernity, in the incommensurability between the promise of emancipation in the city and the practice of retribalization and poverty in the country. Increased industrialization, spurred by wartime isolation, severe droughts, and a temporary relaxation of influx control, led to the expansion of the urban African population (Thompson 1990: 178)[1] and, in time, to organized resistance in the form of effective bus-boycotts and a spectacular, if ineffective, strike by migrant miners, as well as to a newly militant ANC spurred on by the Youth League (led by Anton Lembede, Nelson Mandela, and Walter Sisulu) in 1944 (Thompson 1990: 179–84; Lodge 1985: 18–20).[2] When the Afrikaner National Party came to power in 1948, however, it attempted to reverse African urbanization, assimilation, and politicization. Responding to Afrikaner ideologues' calls for complete separation of the races, the state tightened restrictions on African labor, social and residential mixing, and non-racial political opposition, while it consolidated existing segregation, forcing Africans onto the reserves that would eventually become bantustans. Drawing its support primarily from farmers or displaced "poor whites," the National Party spoke an anti-urban, even anti-modern language, arguing for an innate tribal connection to the soil for the Afrikaner and, in debased form, for Africans as well. In practice, however, apartheid legislation aided the expansion of Afrikaner capital and an Afrikaans labor aristocracy, which depended on a labor reserve of unskilled Africans, even as it made permanent African residence in the cities increasingly difficult.

Whatever their differences, Afrikaners and English-speaking whites in 1950s South Africa shared an attachment to the country rather than the city as the source of cultural value. While English-speaking whites may not have embraced the Afrikaner mythologization of *land* and *volk*, they inherited a distaste for the city and an attachment to a mystified gentlemanly pastoral which shaped English and Commonwealth views well into the twentieth century (Williams 1973: 31–32). As an ever larger majority of whites from both groups moved to urban areas, this attachment had less to do with country life than the idea of the country as counter-city. In an ironic reversal of the classic modern paradigm where, even in the periphery, the city represents progress against what Marx famously called the "idiocy of rural life," the postcolonial city – especially Johannesburg – came to signify the threat of barbarism. This threat was conventionally represented by the urbanizing black masses flocking to the cities but it also took the form of a more ambiguous figure: the English-speaking, intellectual "native." Against this alleged monstrosity born of urban hybridization, the Afrikaner Nationalists (and their English fellow-travelers) proposed a perverse modernity defined not by urban civility, but by isolation on the land.

From their ideological vantage point on the land, Afrikaner ideologues led by Hendrik Verwoerd, then minister of Bantu Affairs and later prime minister, saw the greatest threat to Western civilization in Africa in integrated urban enclaves such as Sophiatown. Settled by blacks since the turn of the century, Sophiatown was the last remaining Johannesburg suburb in which Africans held freehold title.[3] Although increasingly overcrowded as blacks were pushed in from other city areas designated "white," and although troubled by the symptoms of enforced poverty from unsanitary conditions to gangsterism, Sophiatown boasted a vibrant cultural life. Its rebellious urbanity defied apartheid norms of racial purity and the ideology of rural belonging. The syncretic performance practices that had characterized urban African culture in Johannesburg, Durban, and smaller centers like Bloemfontein and Port Elizabeth in the 1930s were in the 1950s concentrated in Sophiatown. This concentration, as well as the imminent threat of removal, enabled the late flowering of an intercultural urban milieu, which has become the subject of much nostalgic rediscovery in the last ten years. The tone of many Sophiatown intellectuals, from Bloke Modisane to Lewis Nkosi, was ironic, even cynical, rather than politically committed (Chapman 1989: 186; Gready 1990: 152–53), but their adherence to this wilfully urban, partially integrated enclave nonetheless challenged the prevailing reverence for land and race.

In this milieu, the city "native" appears more urbane, more metropolitan, more international than the "countrified" representatives of European civilization. Indeed, the confluence of practices that has come to be dubbed "Sophiatown" synthesized influences from Europe, America, and what might be called African-America, as well as South Africa, into a culture that was as cosmopolitan, urbane, and postcolonial as the apartheid system would allow. Especially in its performance practices, from music to drama and points in between, Sophiatown demonstrated the strength of the hybrid plant in difficult terrain. In contrast, Afrikaners, the self-described guardians of Western civilization in Africa, favored a culture of nostalgia that was at once postcolonial, in its anti-British moment, and premodern, in its controlling fiction of autochthony and rural belonging in defiance of the facts of conquest and displacement. Here too, performance, in the shape of national pageants as well as literary drama, provided an exemplary place, occasion, and form for the articulation and management of the contradictions contained in the multiple connotations of the word "country."

African National Theatre and international modernity

Among the metropolitan natives most disliked by Afrikaner Nationalists were those Africans who turned from the contradictions of colonial modernity toward the discourse of international socialism. Where African theatre production had in the 1930s been only fitfully engaged in the representation of urban life and steered well clear of class conflict, the members of the revived Bantu People's Theatre in 1940 described their program in explicitly socialist terms:

> Here [in South Africa] the economic disintegration, the breakdown of tribal economy, and the impoverishment of Europeans, with the massing of classes in their trade unions and employer organizations, is enriched by the emotional complications of race and color.[4]

This program for the BPT Drama Festival at the BMSC explicitly yoked anti-colonial and class struggle: "our situation is symptomatic of the world-wide travail of all repressed communities and dominated classes" (Kabane 1936: 188). At the same time, the plays clearly address an African audience. Alongside *The Dreamy Kid*, a one-act play by Eugene O'Neill set "in the Negro quarter of New York," the festival included two plays by the communist trade unionist and amateur theatre veteran, Guy Routh, who was later to leave the country under pressure from the Suppression of Communism Act (1950).[5] *The Word and the Act* exposed the hypocrisy of the Hertzog Bills, while *Patriot's Pie* addressed the contradictions in Union policy on African enlistment. Setting both plays in the home of Sonke ("all of us") in one of the townships, Routh emphasized the urban African environment, while using a domestic frame to bring the action closer to home.

The following year, their performance in the Gandhi Hall in Fordsburg under the title of "African National Theatre" (ANT), was greeted by *Inkululeko* [Freedom], a Communist Party organ, as the advent of a theatre with national aspirations.[6] The program included the group's first play by an African, *The Rude Criminal*, by Gaur Radebe, later leader of the Alexandra bus boycotts, which dealt with the pass laws.[7] *The Rude Criminal* opened with a "policeman" striding into the hall, demanding passes from members of the audience. Africans were so alarmed, according to Routh's account (1950b: 23), they left abruptly. This strategy antici-pated by more than twenty years the direct assault on audiences that was to become a familiar device in protest plays like Workshop '71's *Survival* (1976). The review in *Inkululeko* focused above all on *Tau*, by I. Pinchuk, also a trade unionist, which dealt with the expropriation of African land in the reserves and the "cruel way in which Africans are treated on the farms," while also suggesting that, "when a tribe is united, it can fight for its rights and win."[8] The play was written primarily in Sesotho and featuring Dan Twala, by now a well-known radio personality and secretary of the Bantu Sports Club, as well as Yank in O'Neill's *The Hairy Ape*. It was probably the first play written in the vernacular to tackle contemporary politics, certainly the first vernacular production from an explicitly socialist perspective. By tackling the plight of African farmers, the ANT demon-strated an astute political grasp of the links between country and city, rural expropriation and urban poverty, which South African theatre was not to achieve again until the work of Zakes Mda in the 1970s.

The organizers of the ANT saw no contradiction between African nationalism and international socialism. Stressing, in the 1940 program, that the BPT con-stitution was modeled on that of the Unity Theatres in Britain they linked their endeavor with similar projects abroad. Like Unity Theatres in industrial Manchester, Liverpool, Glasgow, as well as London, and the Theatre Union in New York (which had staged *Stevedore*, one of the plays suggested to the BDS by André van Gyseghem), the ANT targeted urbanized and urbanizing workers and intellectuals. But, where their counterparts in Europe and the United States could expect subsidy from well-established unions, the South African theatre could not. While state harassment and lack of funds were probably the primary cause of the group's demise, in addition to the "pressures of war" (Routh 1950b: 23), the lack of a literate membership (and universal primary education), able to contribute written plays and criticism for wider circulation, is also significant. This was especially the case since the BPT organizers' conception of drama largely relied, like that of the Unity Theatre movement, on plays with a domestic setting rather than the short agitprop sketches of the Workers' Theatre Movement (Britain) and the League of Workers' Theatres (USA), whose mass choreography did not depend as much on naturalist acting techniques or on players learning written lines (Samuel *et al.* 1985). Yet, brief as the South African experiment was, its national aspirations, its intercultural membership, and the topical themes of its plays are remarkable as was its case for a people's theatre grounded on class as well as racial affiliation.

The influence of the ANT, now hardly remembered, can be seen in the work of Herbert Dhlomo, whose unperformed plays, *The Workers* (1941) and *The Pass* (first written 1943; see Dhlomo 1985), suggest a closer, if uneven engagement with contemporary urban life under pressure from apartheid capitalism than his better-known plays about African historical leaders. Rather than an agitprop version of drama as strike tool, *The Workers'* portrayal of the reification of factory workers more closely resembles the abstract, telegraphic style and dark, often elegiac treatment of the menace of a mechanized society and the alienation of labor that were the stock in trade of drama in the expressionist tradition, such as Georg Kaiser's *Gas* trilogy. The play "portrays working-class conditions" after a fashion, but this abstract, often fragmented text does not really respond to the "need to develop proper unions as well as tactics for strike action" (Orkin 1991: 48). The trade unionist, a chauffeur for the "Nigger-Exploitation Slave Crookpany," calls for union organization, but the impact of the massed workers is described in almost mystical terms: "Don't speak of the close of day. It is here and now!" (Dhlomo 1985: 213). The manager's defense of machines over men recalls the technological juggernaut of Karel Čapek's *R.U.R.* (revived by the Johannesburg Rep. in 1936), rather than the pro-union agitprop of the Workers' Theatre Movements in 1930s Britain and America or, indeed, its equivalents in 1980s South Africa.

> The machines must not stop . . . even if men die like flies. . . . Machines are rare and costly, men are cheap and common. . . . We no longer believe in the myth of the soul and the dignity of Man but we know that machines have a soul . . .
>
> (Dhlomo 1985: 216)

Even though the manager's position is undermined by stage directions that describe him as "almost hysterical" (p. 216) or "childish" (p. 226), the final scene in which the workers physically overwhelm management and police only to die in large numbers in the final explosion (p. 227) suggests an expressionist apocalypse rather than disciplined revolutionary action.

The Pass offers more plausible evidence of "a writer in touch with urban realities . . . rooted in a more clearly defined political vision" (Steadman 1990: 216). Compressed into less than twenty-four hours, the action of the play tracks the impact of the pass laws and arbitrary police power on a group of Africans arrested in a random sweep one night in Durban. The strength of the play lies not merely in its graphic portrayal of police brutality or in its exposure of their venality, but in the concrete representation of different cases, including, among others, an elderly woman shamed by the arrest, a burglar whose scorn for the police earns him a certain respect from other men in the jail, and Edward Sithole, an educated professional who is nonetheless not immune to arrest. Although Sithole is ultimately acquitted, thanks to a legal loophole that exempted educated Africans from the obligation to carry passes, the play makes clear that the pass laws will radicalize an otherwise quiescent population: "The pain and hate in our hearts will mould and be suckled by our children of the next generation. When these children grow up, the white man will regret [it]" (Dhlomo 1985: 200).

Tribal cultures, white supremacy and a "new South Africa"

In its foreshadowing of the anger as well as the suffering of blacks in South Africa, *The Pass* looks forward to the Defiance Campaigns of the 1950s and beyond to the defiance that has characterized much South African drama since the 1970s. The emergence of a theatre of defiance in this period was curtailed, however, by Afrikaner suppression of political mobilization and cultural assimilation of the African majority in the name of a chimeric tribal identity. After their electoral victory, the National Party organized cultural activity along tribal lines. State-subsidized and urban-based institutions, such as the South African Broadcasting Corporation (SABC) – which included Zulu slots from 1941 and organized programing in seven African languages under Radio Bantu from 1962 – and the exclusively white National Theatre Organization (NTO, 1947–62), were harnessed to the production of ethnicity, rural identification, and white supremacy. Radio drama, such as *Chief Above and Chief Below* by Zulu newsreader and Shakespeare translator, King Edward Masinga (1944), was broadcast in 1941, accompanied by music composed by Masinga and edited for "authenticity" by white ethnographer, Hugh Tracey. Set in a rural community, the play emphasized the authority of precolonial custom and the hereditary chiefs. *Izinkwa* [Bread] by Dan Twala was broadcast in 1948 (Steadman 1985a: 82). Unlike Masinga's play, *Izinkwa* dealt with economic hardship in the cities but its concluding emphasis on resignation marked the gulf separating the urban and progressive ANT and the narrow confines of the Bantu Education Act of 1953. The ideological project driving Bantu Education could be described as *neotraditionalism*: the attempt to discredit urban cultural assimilation in favor of rural tribal identity for Africans, while nonetheless exploiting their labor in the cities.

The passage of the Bantu Education Act in 1953 closed the mission schools whose liberal instruction was considered unsuitable for those whom Bantu Affairs Minister Verwoerd thought "had no place in the European community above certain forms of labor" (Omond 1985: 80). While Bantu Education met with significant if ultimately unsuccessful resistance in the Cape and Transvaal, the situation in Natal was complicated by the history of negotiation between Native Affairs and local retraditionalists such as the Zulu Society. The ambiguity of this revival is especially striking in the revisionist treatments of Shaka, the Zulu king. As Hamilton (1998) demonstrates, the legacy and the legend of Shaka and a Shakan model of integral Zulu culture provided the focus for long-standing debates about distinctive African culture and African self-government. Although well aware of the apartheid state's manipulation of these ideas in the interest of white supremacy and black subordination, Dhlomo and his contemporaries, such as the poet B. W. Vilakazi, took part in the revision of Shaka as a prophetic leader, "nation-builder" and "patron of the arts," rather than the bloodthirsty tyrant of European – and New African – legend (Couzens 1985: 321–23). Revaluating the authority of the chiefs, and in particular the legendary power of Shaka over a now scattered Zulu nation, Herbert Dhlomo, the director of the Emancipation

Celebration, argued that those invoking Shaka defended the glories of the past rather than civil rights in the present and were advocating a "new kind of tribalism . . . [that] encourages non-progressive institutions among the people and made the government the supreme chief and dictator."[9]

The performance of Herbert Dhlomo's play about *Dingane*, Shaka's assassin and successor, illustrates the complexity of this revisionism. Directed by (white) instructors, William Branford and Walter Pople, with "African music" by Charles Marivate, the play was first performed by students at the University of Natal Medical School ("Non-European" section) in May 1954, almost twenty years after its composition, and revived at the Durban City Hall in August as a "milestone in the indigenous theatre of this century."[10] Dhlomo's stage version was based on the manuscript, written in 1937, but departed from it at several points.[11] The most obvious addition is a narrator, who introduces the action:

> My work tonight is to tell you what cannot be shown. It is a story of the kings of long ago . . . written in books . . . but that is not the real story. The real story is in darkness . . . there is no-one left to show us the truth. But some of the old men tell the story like this, and we must not contradict them.
>
> (Dhlomo 1954: 1)

This prologue, performed by Branford, is part homage to oral tradition and part condescending explication. The most striking alteration was in the treatment of the confrontation between Boers and amaZulu. The 1937 version provides an elabo-rate prelude to the Boers' arrival – a discussion among the *indunas* [advisors to the king], in which they impersonate Boer behavior and comment on the latter's disrespect for royalty (Dhlomo 1985: 85) – followed by Piet Retief's audience with Dingane in which they perform military drills and answer (or evade) questions about cattle theft and demands for land (pp. 88–89). Only after Dingane hears that the Boers have broken Zulu taboo by talking to girls in the king's *isigodlo* [harem], does he authorize punishment. Although the killing is not staged, the text describes a dance designed to dazzle the Boers, their confused response, and Dingane's signal (raising the shield) that interrupts the dance and closes the scene (pp. 97), in a precisely orchestrated dramatic climax. The stage version both concentrates and dilutes this dramaturgy. It concentrates the action by cutting the first audience and by having the news of the violation of taboo follow immediately after the *indunas'* discussion and lead directly to the ambush, while diluting the effect of this climax by moving it off-stage and by having the narrator remind the audience, with the security of full house-lights, of the historical consequences:

> Dingane did not get rid of all the white men by killing a few of them . . . The gun and horse of the white men were too much for Zulus armed only with assegais and shields, and thousands of warriors were sent to battle, never to return.
>
> (Dhlomo 1954: 21)

This speech acknowledges the impact of the Ncome [Blood] River battle without naming it, but spells out the white victory only hinted at in the original text by Shaka's ghost prophesying ruin like Caesar's ghost in Shakespeare's play. The final comment – "There is nothing left but to mourn for the wreck of Zululand, and there are not words for that" (p. 36) – speaks to the current as well as the historical moment but, in light of the place and occasion of performance, does so equivo-cally. The broad sweep of the drama certainly evokes the "mighty epic" that Dhlomo had in view for all his plays on the Zulu kings, but the narrator's cautious interpretation of the action, as well as the stage presence of the white teacher in this role, brings the play back to the constrained circumstances of the 1950s. This play on a "traditional" Zulu subject does, however, acknowledge the neotradi-tional pressures of the moment, using subaltern ethnic histories to explore the limits of tribal culture.

If the term "tribal culture" has hitherto implied the neotraditional events sanctioned by Bantu Education, it can also apply to the *volkseenheit* that gave a chauvinist cast to Afrikaner postcolonialism. The drift of bankrupt Afrikaans *bywoners* [tenant farmers] to the cities (by 1948, more than half the Afrikaner population lived in urban areas) fanned anti-English and anti-capitalist sentiment as well as the invention of a divine pact between Afrikaners and the land. This pact cast Afrikaners as the *natural*, if not original inhabitants, premodern post-colonials dispossessed by English capital, erasing the history of Dutch and later Afrikaner expropriation of African farmers on the one hand, and more recent Afrikaner urbanization on the other. In the colonial agon between civilization and barbarism, Empire and Africa, modernity and backwardness, Afrikaners appeared to take up both positions. They claimed as the descendants of white settlers to represent the vanguard of European manifest destiny, while at the same time cast themselves in the role of autochthonous, indeed *African*, victims of British imperialism.[12]

This potent ideological mix expressed itself not only in the reenactment of the Great Trek in 1938, but also in Afrikaans drama in the 1920s and 1930s, whether in a sentimental vein – as in André Huguenet's adaptation of Jochen van Bruggen's *Ampie* (1930) – or melodramatic, as in J. W. Grosskopf's *As die Tuig Skawe* [When the Harness Chafes] (performed 1926; published Grosskopf 1940), which blamed the destitution of Afrikaans farmers largely on Jewish moneylenders, a character-istic gesture of this period (Coetzee 1988: 79), as well as the drama of historical martyrdom.[13] The legitimation of this tradition as a national theatre that began with the Voortrekker Centenary reached its apogee only after the Nationalists' political victory. In the Tricentenary of Jan van Riebeeck's landing at the Cape on 6 April 1652, the Afrikaner Nationalist government found the appropriate occa-sion for the performance of the triumphant volk. The festivities, which were conducted mostly in Afrikaans, included a mass pageant on the model of the Voortrekker Centenary of 1936, and more conventional dramatic representations produced by the National Theatre Organization (founded in 1946). The organizers of the pageant, led by the Federasie vir Afrikaner Kultuur (FAK), recast Van Riebeeck – a representative of the imperial Dutch East India Company, who set up a refreshment station for his company's ships in 1652 – in the role of founding father of an *anti*-imperialist Afrikanerdom.

In this national drama, Van Riebeeck was "a symbol of white rule as a whole" but not in *opposition* to Afrikaner priority (Rassool and Witz 1993: 449). Rather, the Nationalist sympathies of the FAK, the public relations officer, W. A. De Klerk, pageant mistress Anna Neethling Pohl, author Gerhard Beukes, and the precedent of the Voortrekker Centenary of 1938, led to an event that endorsed the priority of Afrikaner Nationalist claims to represent European civilization in Africa. While the 1952 pageant included popular motifs from the South African Pageants of 1910 and 1936, such as the replicas of Van Riebeeck's ships in Table Bay and the glamorous display of Lady Anne's Ball, and cast the bilingual André Huguenet in the role of Van Riebeeck, the overall teleological thrust was the legitimation, not of Union, but of Afrikaner independence. The pageant began with the conquest of the dark, masked figure of Africa over "Skoonheit, Geregtigkeit, Oorvloed, en Geloof" [Beauty, Righteousness, Prosperity and Faith], reducing all to "geestlike duisternis" [spiritual darkness] (*Official Festival Program* 1952: 100). Only the arrival of the Voortrekkers and the orderly occupation of the land by the Boers could reverse this condition of barbarism.[14] The second part focused on the Great Trek as the path of nation-building. It treated the Peace of Vereeniging that ended the Anglo-Boer War in 1902 as a defeat in which "the *volk* was defeated, confused and hopeless") (p. 39) and portrayed the recognition of Afrikaans as the second official language in 1925 as a moment of triumph rather than reconciliation, in which "the Boer was once again at home [*tuis*] in his own land") (p. 45).[15]

This event drew on the popularizing example of the Voortrekker Centenary, the reputation of Beukes who appealed to rural and small-town Afrikaners (Naudé 1950), and above all on the example of and the work of Gustav Preller. Like the Voortrekker Centenary, it represented Afrikanerdom as a nation born of a struggle on two fronts, against "British imperialism" and "Native barbarism." Unlike the earlier event, which was staged by a subaltern group vying for hegemony, the Van Riebeeck Tricentenary was produced by an Afrikaner state bent on the Afrikanerization of all "Europeans" through "Christian National Education."[16] The English South African elite, represented by Anglo-American Corporation and the Chamber of Mines, who had provided key support for the 1936 Empire Exhibition, responded to this Afrikaans bias by attacking the pageant as a "second Voortrekker monument" (Rassool and Witz 1993: 436). Anti-apartheid opposition from the Non-European Unity Movement (NEUM) and the ANC, who launched the Defiance Campaign on the very day – 6 April 1952 – of the tricentenary, indicted "white domination" as a whole, but targeted especially the Afrikaner variant of white supremacist ideology associated with the *Herrenvolk* ideology of National Socialism (p. 461).

While apartheid culture was certainly not *purely* Afrikaans, its primary impetus was. While the FAK appealed to the most chauvinist elements of the Afrikaner petite bourgeoisie, the National Theatre Organization (NTO) attempted to link South African drama to a metropolitan tradition and urban tastes. Its organizers, from educator P. B. B. Breytenbach to bilingual actor and director André Huguenet and international director Leontine Sagan, saw the NTO as a combination of the literary aspirations of the amateur repertories and state subsidy on the European (as distinct from the British) model and drew from both a repertoire of metropolitan classical and modern drama, while making a place for local talent, especially in Afrikaans (Huguenet 1950: 200; Stead 1984: 65).[17] Although the organizers insisted that they had a "permanent and firmly established people's theatre . . . within reach of the poorest," they acknowledged tensions between the metropolitan desires of a relatively well-off urban audience and the tastes of rural Afrikaners (Stead 1984: 66). They did not acknowledge the claims or experience of black theatre practitioners in the cities nor the vast majority of the population silently excluded from this "people's theatre."[18] As the repertoire of the opening seasons confirms, the horizons of the NTO were bounded on the one hand by metropolitan English drama and on the other by Afrikaans drama, including Afrikaans translations of European classics; the English company opened in 1948 with *Dear Brutus* by J. M. Barrie and continued with J. B. Priestley's *An Inspector Calls*, while the Afrikaans company opened with *Altyd, my Liefste*, an Afrikaans translation of G. E. Lessing's eighteenth-century comedy, *Minna von Barnhelm* and continued with *Nag het die Wind gebring* [Night Brought the Wind] (De Klerk 1947), which portrayed the conflicting loyalties of an Afrikaner family in the British Cape Colony during the Anglo-Boer War, rehearsing tensions between honest pioneers and subtle English interlopers similar to those in early American plays such as Royall Tyler's *The Contrast* (1783).

The NTO's participation in the Van Riebeeck Tricentenary confirms the hegemony, in Gramsci's sense of consent to power (Gramsci 1971: 12), of Afrikaner nationalism. The Afrikaans and English plays, which were performed for the Tricentenary celebrations, *Die Jaar van die Vuuros* [The Year of the Fire-ox], by W. A. De Klerk, and *The Dam*, by poet and advocate of South African English literature, Guy Butler, both explore the historic tensions between Boer and Briton and suggest their resolution in the marriage plot and both take for granted the primacy of Afrikaner claims to Africa. Written the year the state abolished the Native Representatives Council and the year after the enactment of the Group Areas Act, which accelerated the mass displacement of blacks from areas coveted by whites, *Die Jaar van die Vuuros* rewrites this legislation as the government's allocation of *white* land, here the Van Niekerk farm in South West Africa for African settlement. The state, in the person of Kemp, an idealistic member of parliament, appears to speak for African rather than Afrikaner interests but the claims of Ngondera, son of a family retainer Kasupi, now dead, remain on the margins, variously interpreted by Kemp and the male members of the Van Niekerk family and settled rather ambiguously at the end; after Pieter, the eldest Van Niekerk son has killed Ngondera, his brother Martin, the citified *verlore seun* [prodigal son] returned from medical service among displaced persons in post-war

Germany, promises "reg te maak wat verkeerd is" [to rectify what is wrong] (De Klerk 1952: 91).

The family in this tribal drama functions not only as a synecdoche for the nation but as its structuring principle. As J. M. Coetzee has written in a trenchant critique of "white writing," the fiction of the farm as a "kingdom ruled over by a benign patriarch, with, beneath him, a pyramid of contented children . . . and serfs" (Coetzee 1988: 6–7), depicts the nation as a collection of family farms and the citizenry as an assembly of patriarchs speaking on behalf of dependants who cannot – or should not – speak for themselves. Located on the imaginary frontier, even if in fact in the midst of settlement, the family farm marks the place and the moment of colonial penetration of the hinterland and dispossession of the Africans, even as it claims to represent the natural rights of the Afrikaner. As Orkin argues, following Bakhtin, in the chronotope of the frontier "[t]ime . . . thickens, takes on flesh, . . . likewise, space becomes charged and responsive to the movements of time, plot, and history" (Bakhtin 1987: 84–85); the tangible presence of the family homestead naturalizes colonial possession as natural right (Orkin 1991: 59–60). Furthermore, the juxtaposition of this wilderness and the confines of the homestead intensifies the sense of the latter as an environment in which space and time are contained by the bonds and bounds of kinship and which the modern individual – free, self-conscious and capable of onward movement – is reined in by the timeless claims of the tribe.

Vuuros takes the primacy of Afrikaner patriarchy as its point of departure, but it is not just a family drama. The tensions among family members in *Vuuros* are closely connected to the land dispute and to the constitutive contradiction of the premodern postcolonial: simultaneously native to Africa and avatar of European civilization. Although the old patriarch and Anglo-Boer war veteran appears in some ways out of touch with modern times, his dramatic authority is secured at the outset by his "Chair, which dominates the stage" (De Klerk 1952: 1),[19] by stage directions that insist that, despite his age, "his sun still shines high in the sky," and by a key assertion of land rights:

> You know how the first Van Niekerks came here to cleanse the world [die wereld hier kom skoonmaak het] . . . and, at greatest duress, paid for it with their lifeblood . . . Can you *now* imagine that Okonjenje belongs to anyone other than our posterity, especially since the disturbing things that happen these days on the reservation?
>
> (p. 27)

Spoken in rebuttal to Kemp's appeal to "human rights" (p. 25), this claim of ownership through blood is grounded in tribal sacrifice but also uses the language of realpolitik in the opposition between Afrikaner order and the "disturbances" on the reserves. This claim to the land rests on the myth of Afrikaner identity forged through transformation of the land, in which "the family fathers pay for the farm in blood, sweat and tears, not in money; they hack it out of primeval bush, they defend it against barbarism; they leave their bones behind in its soil" (Coetzee 1988: 85), but also draws on metropolitan models of political authority and even, in the claim to "cleanse the world," to set a global example of civilization.[20]

In this scenario, Afrikaners are both aggrieved victims and natural owners, hostile to metropolitan modernity and the most legitimate bearers of civilization. Pieter, the most stubbornly tribal of the general's three sons, may fit Kemp's scathing description (in English) of "those desperate Dixiecrats under Capricorn" (p. 27), treating Africans as "halfmense" [half-people] (p. 71) and English South Africans as imperialists, but he nonetheless boasts of his scientific agriculture (p. 27). The youngest son, Alexis, vows to abandon what he sees as small-minded nepotism but his point of reference remains that of the "great renewal" of the nation (p. 45). Martin, the protagonist of this drama, may sympathize with his younger brother's frustration, yet he defends the idea of white hegemony in South Africa by asserting the Afrikaner's unique claim to represent Europe in Africa:

> I got to know Europe, yes, but also my own country, precisely because over *there* I perceived for the first time what was after all unique in our national life . . . that we are a nation with a *history*, perhaps alone in our hemisphere.
>
> (p. 50)

This association of the rational authority of (written) history with the romantic appeal to "land *itself* and its story" borrows from European narratives of national origin. Like those narratives, this myth of origin is both modern and primitive, grounded in the enlightenment of the written record and steeped in primal blood-ties. This mix of race and reason is not unique to the Afrikaner.[21] What is peculiar is the insistence on singular legitimacy from the South, the claim to be both European and, in a distinct, limited, but enduring sense, African as well.

In this national drama, women are mothers and wives, not protagonists. Emma, Pieter's long-suffering helpmate, makes coffee, tends to the children, and cautions her husband, in vain, against precipitous action that might threaten family stability. Gillian, the widow of Desmond Hammond, brother to the Van Niekerk's jingoistic neighbor, is in part the lure that secures Martin's return to the land and in part the device which will ensure the unity of Boer and Briton and the future of white South Africa. Where white women have a partial voice in this drama, blacks are heard only as an untranslated but unsettling song in the background. The Africans, the loyal but dead Kasupi and his rather more militant son Ngondera, remain at an unconquerable distance. But, more than inchoate threats of black violence, it is the casual assumption of black labor and black dependence that is characteristic of this play. Emma's apologies for slow service due to absent maids and Martin's assurances to his father that he will do what is right for "their" people share an unspoken assumption that the patriarchal household is the natural basis for social order. It is on this basis, vividly if sentimentally painted by the final tableau – Martin and Gillian on the *stoep* [front porch] facing the rising sun (p. 92) – that De Klerk's "new South Africa" is ostensibly to be built.[22] The settlement of national conflict is thus contained in the resolution of domestic strife, foreclosing any working-out of the crisis that might go beyond the family circle.

The Dam, directed by Marda Vanne for the NTO in 1952, also draws analogies between marriage and national plot. Its protagonist, Douglas Long, English South African farmer, shares with Martin van Niekerk the sense of "shaping the land as he himself has been shaped by it" (Orkin 1991: 60), as well as the desire to harness this pre-rational intimation to modernity. By damming the river, Long aims to compel the "too hard sun" and "intruding stone" (Butler 1953: 8) of the Karoo to contribute to progress and development. His daughter Susan, like Gillian Hammond, feels that, despite her English heritage, she too belongs to "this land" (p. 69). But, while the union between Boer and Briton in *Vuuros* had securely attached this sense of belonging to the conviction of ownership and authority, *The Dam* is less certain. Long's desire to master the land by building the dam is beset by doubts about the legitimacy of his presence and objections of others, such as his old-time Afrikaner neighbor, Jan de Bruyn, to his disruption of the natural order; Susan is unable finally to yield to the proposal of Sybrand, Long's lieutenant and De Bruyn's son. The deferral of this resolution stems from Susan's preoccupation with the black slums where she does charity work, but it also registers a pervasive uneasiness about the impact of modernization.

This uneasiness permeates Long's most heroic vision. While the Christian motifs of the play and especially Long's struggle with his conscience may indeed suggest the themes of self-doubt and redemption of T. S. Eliot (Orkin 1991: 60), Long's consuming, if irresolute, desire to risk all in one bold action – "All men must choose – to risk themselves or not" (Butler 1953: 19) – calls to mind Goethe's Faust, that quintessentially modern protagonist, whose desire for mastery is matched only by his fear of his own weakness, personified in *Faust*, by Mephistopheles, and, in *The Dam*, by masked choral figures (Figure 4.1). Long's dam project recalls Faust's desire to harness "the purposeless power [*zwecklose Kraft*] of the unfettered elements" (Goethe 1981, vol. 3: 309).[23] Faust's quest takes the form of a pursuit of technological mastery of the natural environment and its premodern inhabitants; he attempts to reclaim land from the sea for the more efficient organization of production and the benefit of humankind. At its most seductive, Faust's vision transforms the sand dunes on the coast to a "green and fertile meadow" (p. 348; l.11565), cultivated by a "free people [*volk*] on free ground" (l.11580). This vision of arid ground made fertile by the power of the imagination (aided by silent but productive labor) recurs in Long's celebration of the finished dam:

What I . . .
Find so very precious is the sense
Of a larger, freer world.
          (Butler 1953: 63)

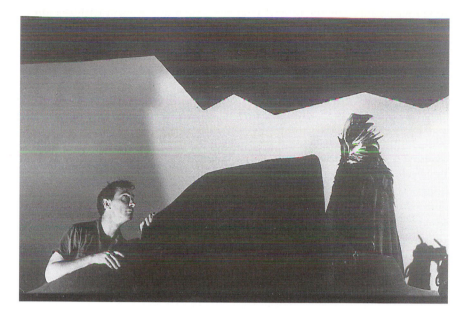

Figure 4.1 The Dam-builder meets his nemesis: Rolf Lefevre (L) as Douglas Long and Gerrit Wessels as the chorus in *The Dam* by Guy Butler, National Theatre Organization, 1952. *Source and permission*: State Archive, Pretoria

Freedom, in both cases, appears to emanate from the creative combination of mind and hands.

In each case, however, the mind of one controls the hands of many. As Marshall Berman notes (1988: 64), "Faust the developer" speaks eloquently of the liberation of human energy from the bondage of the "unfettered elements" even as he reduces his workforce to tools shaped by his mind – "One mind is enough for a thousand hands" (Goethe 1981, vol. 3: 346; l.11510), and treats resistance as an obstacle to development. At first glance, Long appears to possess the compassion that Faust lacks, as he appeals to God to "touch these semi-savage things that sweat for me" (Butler 1953: 62), but this paternalist concern grants the laborers no voice other than, as in *Vuuros*, incomprehensible song, "[w]ide and moaning at the indifferent stars" (p. 67). Faust's instrumentalization of his workforce, on the other hand, calls forth eloquent dissent from one of his victims who protests against the sacrifice deemed necessary for efficient production:

> Human sacrifices had to bleed
> Tortured screams would pierce the night
> Where from the sea blazes spread
> A canal would greet the light
> (Goethe 1981, vol. 3: 335, ll.11127–30)

Faust confronts directly the brutality of exploitation in this nightmarish vision of industrial production as well as in Mephisto's blunt exposure of Faust's vision of rational development and efficient labor as "colonization" (vol. 3: 339; l.11273). *The Dam*, on the other hand, camouflages, if rather thinly, the realities of colonization with appeals to God's grace and, as a bathetic aside to the celebration of a "freer world," a rather disingenuous worry about who "the next employer" of these casual workers may be (Butler 1953: 62).

The Dam is too burdened by liberal doubts to match the clash of forces in *Faust* or, on the other hand, the faith in the peculiar hybrid of paternalist modernization that grants *Vuuros* a certain authority – at least in the eyes of its target audience. But where *Vuuros* allows for no South African scene other than the farm, *The Dam* acknowledges the urban dimension of South African reality, especially the conditions of the most rapidly urbanizing section of the population, Africans in search of work:

> It can't be told, it must be met with all
> Five senses; the violence, and smells,
> Degradation, the lurid colours, the dark
> Of a primitive human storm – How sweet
> The air is here, how spacious, how secure . . .
> Into space one tenth the size of this farm;
> A horde of hovels, hedged between a white
> And well-lit suburb . . .
> And mine dumps, depots . . . on the other.
> (Butler 1953: 65)

Despite the urge to compassion that Susan expresses here, the evocation of a "primitive human storm" suggests not only the "paternalist aspects of assimilationist discourse" (Orkin 1991: 60) but also the alacrity with which benign paternalism shifts under pressure to fear of the "hordes" supposedly about to overstep the "secure" bounds of the homestead. While individual blacks may be objects of pity, collectively they appear either as a threatening mass or as helpless migrants "[p]laying a blind man's buff between the Mine Dump/And the mud hut, the war chant and the blues" (Butler 1953: 35). African laborers, like Faust's "hands," may be the means of modernization but, despite historical counter-examples such as the 1946 strike of 70,000 miners, are not to be represented as modern agents on the way to becoming city-dwellers.

The Sophiatown set: scenographies
of defiance and nostalgia

The "horde of hovels" between the white suburb and the mine dump in *The Dam* presents an overwrought view of Sophiatown. Butler's personification of Sophiatown's overcrowded but hitherto stable mixture of brick houses and backyard shacks as a predatory "horde" follows the *swart gevaar* [black peril] rhetoric of Hendrik Verwoerd. It reverses the actual movements of blacks, forced *out* into Orlando, Meadowlands, and other tracts of veld that would make up Soweto, and of whites, moving into central, mixed neighborhoods: Fordsburg, Mayfair, Vrededorp and eventually Sophiatown (renamed Triomf after it was declared "white"). Moreover, it renders invisible Sophiatown's urbanized African population, which included professionals, such as Dr. Xuma, political activists, such as the communist, J. B. Marks, writers, such as William "Bloke" Modisane, entrepreneurs of many sorts, whether legitimate, such as the bus company run by the Italian grandfather of the gangster (later writer) Don Mattera, or the stores owned by Indian or white immigrant South Africans, or "shady," like the shebeens [speakeasies], as well as city workers, and a floating population of outlaws, from rural migrants, whose search for work was made illegal by the pass laws to gangs of *tsotsis*, who defied the law.[24] It also denies the fascination of the place not only for white intellectuals, activists, and tourists, but also for blacks from all over the country.[25]

It is this image of Sophiatown, an embattled but vibrant urban settlement, a somewhat integrated but hardly harmonious community, a mode of living on the edge, which persists today. Part ghetto, part cultural bazaar, a meeting place of black radicals, bohemians of all colors, and organized and disorganized criminals, Sophiatown was an actual but thoroughly *imagined* place that came, despite the violence perpetuated by police as well as *tsotsis*, to symbolize a utopia of racial tolerance and cultural diversity, crushed by the apartheid juggernaut. This place was, in the words of Sophiatown writer and later exile, Lewis Nkosi, "on the verge of . . . a new and exciting cultural Bohemia" (Nkosi 1965: 24), not only for the "Sophiatown set" (Gready 1990: 140), writers who habituated the place, even if they did not inhabit it, but also for recent commentators looking for hybrid roots, or at least for evidence of an intercultural legacy that might nourish urban culture in South Africa today (e.g. Stein and Jacobson 1986; Schadeberg 1987; Nixon 1994). Sophiatown in this scenario risks becoming merely a set, a backdrop to enhance the enactment of current dramas, rather than the place and occasion of deeply felt historical experience.[26]

The Kofifi '50s, to give this place and occasion its local name, were in many ways the end rather than the beginning of an era. Sophiatown had been under threat since 1934, when the Urban Areas Act was extended to Johannesburg. The laws passed in the 1950s were undermining the already precarious pleasures of New Africans by eroding the exemption from the pass laws that had allowed them to enjoy cultural activity – such as theatre at the BMSC or His Majesty's – in the city center.[27] In Sophiatown, as well as Orlando, gang activity made entertainment a dangerous business. To a degree, *tsotsis* embodied a sort of outlaw glamour, displayed in their expensive American clothes and cars and in the perversion of official Afrikaans in an inventive *tsotsitaal* [tsotsi-lingo].[28] Their brazen defiance of white authority earned them admiration as well as fear from urban Africans (much as African-Americans in the Chicago ghetto treated the "shadies" amongst them), but they also preyed on ordinary people and extorted protection money from entertainers, kidnapped their favorite stars – such as Miriam Makeba – to bolster their prestige, and even killed those, such as Solomon "Zuluboy" Cele of the Jazz Maniacs, for allegedly playing for a rival gang (Matshikiza 1953). Established African impresarios – Motsieloa, Peter Rezant, Wilfred Sentso (leader of the Synco Fans and writer and director of township musicals) – were reluctant to play in townships while aspiring producers could not match the capital and mobility of whites such as Ike Brookes, producer of *Zonk*, and Alfred Herbert, who organized *African Jazz* and *Variety* (Coplan 1985: 163–64; 170–71) and who participated in 1952 in the founding of the Union of South African Artists, which was to help African performers secure royalties and rehearsal pay.[29]

The pressure of the "white hand," in the words of Job Radebe, boxing promoter, BMSC secretary, and one of the "African Advisors" for *Drum* magazine (Sampson 1983: 21), was a combination of handshake and manipulation, well-meaning liberalism and the search for profit. Like *Drum*, Union Artists attempted to fuse "African native talent and European discipline and technique" (Nkosi 1965: 19) at a moment when participants of both groups by and large acquiesced in this division of labor.[30] White associates, such as chairman Ian Bernhardt, producer Alfred Herbert, and part-time novelist and theatre novice Harry Bloom (writer for *King Kong*) claimed that they had "discovered" African talent; like Bertha Slosberg's before them, these claims were based more on assumptions about African "spontaneity" than on knowledge of African cultural practices. But they were also able to marshal the capital and legal skills to secure royalties and to organize benefits for the families of deceased members, such as Pitch Black Follies comedian Victor Mkhize, or non-members, such as *Drum* journalist Henry Nxumalo, killed by *tsotsis* in 1956. Initially less interested in drama than in music, Union Artists nonetheless lent rehearsal space to the African Theatre Workshop and Athol Fugard's *No-Good Friday* (1958), and later sponsored the "jazz opera," *King Kong* (1959), based on the life of the "Non-European" boxing champion, Ezekiel Dhlamini.

No-Good Friday was not the first play on urban African life nor the first collaboration between black and white but, unlike the work of the Bantu Dramatic Society and the Bantu People's Theatre in the 1930s and 1940s, it received mainstream critical attention and thus a certain legitimacy denied those earlier experiments. It has been praised for "verisimilitude" and "rootedness" in the township (Vandenbroucke 1986: 29) and lambasted for dwelling on alienation from rather than struggle against apartheid (Kavanagh 1985: 59–83). Fugard's reaction to the extreme conditions of Johannesburg was immediate if naive; he speaks of the "horror" of his job as clerk in the Native Commissioner's Court, dealing with thousands of Africans accused of "pass offenses" (Benson 1977: 78). Nkosi, who collaborated on the script, argued that "Fugard gave no sign of being directly interested in politics . . . [he] was interested in learning about how we lived and in practising his art. The politics of the South African situation touched him on these two levels" (Nkosi 1983: 139). He went on to fault the play for its sensationalist treatment of township violence (p. 140), but he shared Fugard's "concern with the trapped individual," especially the alienated intellectual, dubbed a "situation" by township toughs mocking the aspirations of educated Africans seeking white-collar "situations vacant," and the development of an urban intercultural bohemia. The workshop included Bloke Modisane, later author of *Blame Me on History* (1963), Nat Nakasa who, like Nkosi, had come to *Drum* via Adams College and John Dube's newspaper, *Ilanga Lase Natal*, and actors, men such as Zakes Mokae, Dan Poho, Stephen Moloi, Ken Gampu, Cornelius Mabaso and two women, Gladys Sibisa and Sheila Fugard.

While certainly acknowledging the hardship of Africans in the townships and their daily humiliations at the hands of white employers or the police, *No-Good Friday* shies away from direct representation of these conflicts. It dwells instead on the fatalism of the residents of a Sophiatown slumyard, including a waiter and an aspiring musician, as well as an ANC activist, Watson, and Willie Seopelo, correspondence B.A. student and "situation," a part initially written for Nkosi but performed by Moloi (Vandenbroucke 1986: 33). The action focuses on confrontations between these people and a gang of *tsotsis* who collect "protection money" every "no-good" Friday. While the *tsotsis* are portrayed as gratuitously violent rather than glamorous, they appear to be evils in themselves rather than products of the systematic deprivation of Africans. Resistance to the tyranny of the *tsotsis* appears to be futile; the ANC activist is portrayed as an opportunist, while those who offer individual resistance end up dead. Tobias, a rural migrant, is killed for refusing to pay up, and Willie, the *raisonneur* of the drama, who comes to see his indifference as a moral outrage and so tells the police, waits at the end for the *tsotsis* to come for him too.

Although set in Sophiatown at the moment of its historic destruction, the dramaturgy of *No-Good Friday* places a greater weight on individual integrity in the face of defeat than on political action against its causes. When Willie attacks his neighbors' fatalism – "You think we're just poor, suffering, come-to-Jesus-at-the-end-of-it black men and that the world's all wrong and against us" (Fugard 1993: 50) – and argues instead that "my world is as big as I am. Just big enough for me to do something about it" (p. 51), all he can propose is a private reckoning with his conscience in the face of probable death. Despite his dismissal of Christian suffering and his disdain, typical of the "situation," for the "simple man" from the reserves, Willie's final reaction reinforces the legitimacy of faith in Christian redemption and the unspoiled dignity of the tribe, which apparently enabled Tobias to defend his manhood against the decadent city that has made life "cheap." But Tobias's dignity is not an innate aspect of his "simple nature" as the Sophiatown pastor, Father Higgins (modeled on Trevor Huddleston and played by Fugard himself) argues, but rather an idealistic view of the dignity of rural labor relations.

This idealization of rural paternalism is striking not merely because it writes a paternalist English gentleman farmer into the space occupied by Afrikaans over-seers of near slavery conditions on the farms,[31] but because it follows a literary example closer to *The Dam* than the streets of Sophiatown. That example is Alan Paton's novel *Cry the Beloved Country* (1948). What is famously explicit in the story of the pious Zulu pastor, Stephen Kumalo – his odyssey from rural Natal to Johannesburg in search of his son and sister, who have fallen into evil ways, and his return to rebuild the church, with the help of the local English farmer-patriarch, as a bulwark against urban immorality – is whispering in the wings of *No-Good Friday*. Although this play is set in the city, its moral center lies in a lost rural idyll: where most urban Africans, except the *tsotsis*, are shown to lack agency, it is the reticent Tobias and his self-appointed spokesman, Father Higgins, rather than the activist or the intellectual, who point the way beyond the "B-type Gangster film" milieu of the *tsotsis* (Nkosi 1983: 141). Sophiatown becomes a backdrop for a morality play rather than a plausible urban environment, and its characters players in either the "B-movie" or the parable of fall and redemption. Like Alan Paton's characters, these are projections of white desires for "simple Africans" rather than representations of actual city-dwellers (Nkosi 1965: 5–7).

The performance of *No-Good Friday* only reinforced this equivocation. Staged initially at the BMSC on 30 August 1958, it garnered enough attention to secure four nights at the Brian Brooke Theatre. Since Brooke did not allow an integrated cast to perform for an all-white audience, Nkosi played Fugard's part, Father Higgins, which, in Nkosi's (later) view, exposed the implausible character of his moral exhortations (Nkosi 1983: 141). It also suggests the participants' ambivalence about European culture. Noting his improbable appearance "a thin hungry black cat in a white priest's robes exhorting the 'natives' to stand up to the criminal elements" – Nkosi also acknowledges his "surprised nostalgia" about this moment (1983: 141). Bloke Modisane, who played the *tsotsi* leader, Shark, claims that the group acquiesced to please Fugard (Modisane 1986: 291) yet laments his exclusion from "white society": "I want to listen to Rachmaninoff [*sic*], Beethoven, Bartok, and Stravinsky . . . I am the eternal alien between two worlds" (Modisane 1986: 218). These outbursts are not merely expressions of alienation in the "bohemian no-man's land between the black masses and the white world" (Kavanagh 1985: 62). Rather, they articulate the "fantastic ambiguity, the deliberate self-deception" of the African's enactment of figments of a white imagination (Nkosi 1963: 7) that Du Bois dubbed "double consciousness" (Du Bois 1989: 3) and that postcolonial writers Albert Memmi and Ashis Nandy call the colonized's internalization of the mythical portrait imagined by the colonizer (Memmi 1965: 87; Nandy 1983: 109). They *perform* the volatile ambivalence of the "situation" in the situation, of the urban African intellectual faced, in the demolition of Sophiatown, with the destruction not simply of his environment, but of the in-betweenness that constituted his identity.[32]

King Kong, the (relatively) big-budget musical designed to showcase African singers and musicians as well as the predominantly white production team, reflected the showbiz ambitions of Union Artists more than the literary interests, collaborative method of the amateur and relatively democratic African Theatre Workshop. Indeed, an influential critic has argued that the spectacle of multiracial harmony under white direction reflected the interests of the show's most powerful sponsor, the Anglo-American Corporation, whose director, Harry Oppenheimer, had argued that the "disintegration of traditional African society" was a necessary step in the development of a "modern state and society built on European foundations" (Kavanagh 1985: 89). It is certainly true that the Anglo-American Corporation sponsored African entertainment but not the African franchise, provided scholarships for individual students but no political pressure for universal education, supported African stars in white-run shows but not African impresarios competing with white unions. But it is also true that the white – predominantly Jewish – intellectuals, philanthropists, and amateur and professional artists who collaborated on *King Kong* constituted a dissident class faction at one remove from the Anglo-Saxon economic elite and several from the overtly anti-semitic Afrikaner political class.[33] This dissidence sometimes meant open revolt, as in the case of communists Joe Slovo and Ruth First. More often, as with *King Kong* producer Leon Gluckman, musical director Stanley Glasser, writer Harold Bloom, and facilitators, Clive and Irene Menell, it meant commitment to the "tenuous liberalism and humane values" that "tempered the harsh social order of apartheid" (Nkosi 1965: 19). While we cannot deny the differences in wealth and privilege that separated liberal Jewish patrons and practitioners of the arts from Africans such as Nkosi, nor ignore the charge that, in "tempering" apartheid, liberalism encouraged adjustment to it, we ought to note that this alliance stemmed from a shared affinity for the cosmopolitan, syncretic potential that made "Johannesburg alive and absorbent in a way no other city in the Republic was" (p. 19) and a shared aversion to the myths of rural belonging that had captured the Anglo-Saxon as well as Afrikaner imagination.

If Jewish South Africans were the catalyst that brought about "the fusion of Africa and Europe" (p. 19), America was the base. On the one hand, the Manhattan Brothers followed groups like the Pitch Black Follies in borrowing from African-American bands like the Inkspots. On the other, the producers of *King Kong* drew on the American musical; mid-50s Broadway hits, *West Side Story* (music by Leonard Bernstein; book by Stephen Sondheim, 1957) and *The Threepenny Opera* (music by Kurt Weill; adaptation of Brecht's text by Mark Blitzstein, 1956), featured in discussion as well as in the musical and lyrical idiom of *King Kong*.[34] The most telling exemplar was *Porgy and Bess* (1935). Although written by a composer of Jewish descent, George Gershwin, and based on the play by white Southerners, Dorothy and Du Bose Heyward, this "jazz opera" appeared in *Drum* – at the time of its world tour (1950–53) – as "the Negro show sweep[ing] the world."[35] *Porgy and Bess*'s influence can be seen not only in the subtitle, but in the division of labor between black talent and white organization and can be heard in the overall orchestration of *King Kong* as well as the echoes of "Summertime" in the overture. *King Kong* was not a simple imitation, however. Its musical numbers – and the Nguni lyrics – were written by Todd Matshikiza, composer, journalist and musician familiar with African-American and European music as well as African styles from the genteel *amakwaya* to *marabi* and *kwela* street music;

the English lyrics (by journalist Pat Williams) and the book (by Harry Bloom, based on a synopsis by Williams, Clive and Irene Menell, with input from Matshikiza) drew on the *tsotsitaal*-inflected English favored by African writers on *Drum*.[36]

In a context where Africans were barred from professional associations and specialized training, the issue of expertise was thoroughly overdetermined. At its crassest, the disparaging comments of Bloom, himself a rank amateur (Bloom *et al.* 1961: 9), on actors such as Moloi, Poho, and Gampu, whose performances in *No-Good Friday* and in films like *The Magic Garden* (1951), had given them experience to match most white amateurs, reflect the limitations of the writer rather than the performers. The characterization, by Bloom and Mona Glasser, *King Kong* "chronicler," of Matshikiza as an "unknown musician" and razor-blade salesman, reveals more than ignorance, however. Matshikiza was not only an accomplished pianist who worked with several bands from the Harlem Swingsters to the Jazz Dazzlers (led by saxophonist, Mackay Davashe, who led the *King Kong* band), but was also *Drum*'s music editor, writing jazz reviews, social commentary, "How Musicians Die" (1953), and an informal history of African jazz, "Jazz Comes to Jo'burg" (1957). Unlike *Drum* writers such as Nkosi or Can Themba, who professed indifference to African custom in their pursuit of modernity, Matshikiza combined "Music for Moderns" (the title of his *Drum* column) with Xhosa themes, as in his musical praise poem, "Makhalipile" ["The Undaunted One," 1953], in honor of Trevor Huddleston, and "Uxolo" [Peace], a cantata for 200 voices and a 70-piece orchestra, commissioned for the seventieth anniversary of Johannesburg in 1956 (Schadeberg 1987: 52). The misrecognition of Matshikiza's contribution to South African culture is not a matter of individual oversight but a symptom of the tension between African aspirations to modern agency and white tendency to *naturalize* Africans.

This tension structures the plot of the opera and the relationship between text and performance. Nat Nakasa's account in *Drum* follows the trajectory of Dhlamini's life from mission school and petty crime to his triumph as a champion but undisciplined boxer, and on to his murder conviction and subsequent suicide by drowning; it also includes his secret humiliation by the white champion and the violence of the police, so as to highlight the contradictions in his social situation as well as his character (Nakasa 1959: 27). Although he suggests that Dhlamini was a "symbol of the wasted powers of the African people" (Bloom *et al.* 1961: 17) and has *King Kong*'s manager, Jack, comment bitterly on the discrimination against African "champions" (p. 77), Bloom's script focused on the decline of a glamorous but brittle legend, from "the winner" (p. 31) to "a man [with] writing on him – bad, rubbish, gangster" (p. 78) (Figure 4.2). The performance of Nathan Mdledle, lead singer for the Manhattan Brothers, complicates this melodramatic image of a muscle-man gone bad, however. A "tall rangy man with expressive hands" (Glasser 1960: 21), Mdledle's deft movement and supple baritone granted the character more subtlety than his "Marvellous Muscles" lyrics implied. Played by Moloi, the character of Jack acquired a reflective quality at odds with the swagger

Figure 4.2 "A man [with] writing on him – bad, rubbish, gangster": Nathan Mdlele as the eponymous hero of *King Kong* by Harry Bloom *et al.*; directed by Leon Gluckman, 1959. *Photograph*: Ian Berry; *source*: National English Literary Museum, Grahamstown; *permission*: Magnum Photo

of the stereotypical boxing manager and at a certain remove from the other singing parts, particularly the outlaw glamour of the gangster Lucky (Manhattan Brother, Joseph Mogotsi) and his (briefly, King Kong's) shebeen queen Joyce (Miriam Makeba), backed by their signature tune, "Back of the Moon" (named after an actual Sophiatown shebeen).

Although written into the published script, these modifications respond to the actors' interpretation of their roles rather than to the writer's preconceptions (Glasser 1960: 33–34) and suggest an understanding of the social context and the resources of dramatic and musical representation beyond the bounds of the dialogue and the initial conception of a musical bathed in the outlaw glamour of the shebeen. Most overt in Jack's bitter comment and in the intermittent chorus of washerwomen, whose remarks point to the discrepancy between King Kong's legend and the shabby reality of township life, social criticism also surfaces in the ironic use of musical themes and stage vignettes; thus, during King Kong's prison term, Joyce throws a party to a flashier version of "Back of the Moon," while Jack trains a substitute for King Kong to a "ragged version" of "Marvellous Muscles" (Bloom *et al.* 1961: 56–58). While this critical comment through comic gesture and musical phrasing apparently responded to the difficulty some actors had with English (Glasser 1960: 17), it also resembled the vignettes of the Pitch Black

Follies, with which the Manhattan Brothers and other older members of the cast would have been familiar. The allusion to variety format, rather than the "continuous dramatic line" (Glasser 1960: 13) of "straight" drama does not mean an assent to assumptions about African ignorance of "proper theatre" (Bloom *et al.* 1961: 15). It suggests that the stylistic and thematic references – from the American musical and European drama to African variety (itself a syncretic product of African-American vintage) – available to cast and production team may have been heterogeneous but were nonetheless too intertwined to be reduced to simple oppositions.

If the performance of *King Kong*, rather than its musical and verbal notation, keeps the conventions of the American musical in contact with African variety, it also reveals the syncretic character of the African forms that the text marks as "traditional." The two songs with isiNguni (isiXhosa/isiZulu) lyrics, written by Matshikiza, are important not simply because the text uses the "authentic" languages of Sophiatown and so speaks to the African audience largely indifferent to or puzzled by "talky" theatre (Kavanagh 1985: 109), but because the music and lyrics in combination evoke a multi-layered tradition of *Africanizing* performance that has historically absorbed outside conventions without being overwhelmed by them. The overture, for instance, is identified in the program by the English title "Sad Times, Bad Times" but consists of a Xhosa saying in proverbial form, sung to a jubilee choir melody underlaid with the swing beat, as the gangsters cross the stage and disrupt the early morning routine:

Ityala lalamadoda	Men learn the hard way to sleep [or keep quiet]
nguAndazi noAsindim'. .	It's "I don't know" and "it's not me" . . . .
Alaziwa-mntu	Nobody knows

(Bloom *et al.* 1961: 27)[37]

While the lyrics allude to township passivity in the face of gangsterism in the present, the music resembles less the *kwela*-inflected jazz of King Kong's signature than the national laments written a generation earlier by composers like Caluza to music that combines *amakwaya* with ragtime. The Zulu song, "Hambani madoda," which registers the gloomy mood after Joyce's dismissal of King as "rubbish" but speaks also to the trials of urban Africans plagued by *tsotsis* and impossible work conditions, likewise echoes these earlier songs:

Hambani madoda	Keep moving, men
Siy' emsebenzini	We are going to work
Sizani bafazi	Stand with us, women
Siyahlupheka	We are suffering
Amakhaza nemvula	Cold and rain
Ibhas' igcwele	The bus is packed

Sihlutshwa ngotsotsi	We are preyed on by *tsotsis*
Basikhuthuza	They rob us of what we have
Siyaphela yindhlala	We are half-dead with hunger
Nemali ayikho	There is no money
Hambani madoda	Keep moving, men
Isikhathi asikho	Time is short
Hambani madoda	Keep moving, men
Isikhathi asikho	Time is short

(Bloom *et al.* 1961: 82–83; Kavanagh 1985: 111; trans. modified)

Although it opens with the staccato rhythms and masculine bass of the migrant work song, this is not the choir of "a thousand [male] voices" that Kavanagh associates with mass struggle. Sung as a restrained lament, this has more in common with the *isicathamiya* of Solomon Linda's Evening Birds (and, more recently, Ladysmith Black Mambazo) than the mass rallies of the Defiance Campaign. Combined with the women sopranos in the ensemble, an addition unthinkable in *isicathamiya*, the song acquires an intimate quality reminiscent of Caluza's Double Quartet. Even though the song itself is not repeated and the finale leads to a conventional reprise of King Kong's signature, the note struck by this restrained lament returns in the reaction to his death in an image that sings of both mourning and celebration (Figure 4.3).

Figure 4.3 Mourning and celebration at the end of *King Kong*. *Photograph*: Ian Berry; *source*: National English Literary Museum, Grahamstown; *permission*: Magnum Photo

95

Matshikiza's appropriation of the choir music of the New African elite does not mean that these songs have nothing to do with protest; on the contrary, they mine a long tradition of singing protest against the grain of the apparently genteel choir melody, but they suggest tenacious survival rather than heroic defiance. It is also significant that the locus for this survival is not, in the first instance, the modern political organization of the ANC nor the culture of the city, but the music and the subdued subversion associated – especially by Matshikiza's more aggressively modern contemporaries – with migrants, the rural missions, or, to a certain degree, with women. By including these songs in a musical environment that is otherwise thoroughly modern, Matshikiza is not retreating into a neotraditional refuge of the kind promoted by Bantu Education but rather extending the boundaries of the modern and, albeit implicitly, challenging the masculinist cast of Sophiatown culture.

"Music for moderns": the legacy of Sophiatown

The significance of Sophiatown as the crucible of modern South Africa was legitimated only in the 1980s but the place lived on after its demolition in the nostalgic musical theatre of its erstwhile denizens. Before he left South Africa for good, Matshikiza composed *Mkhumbane*, a cantata for 200 voices, with text by Paton. It dealt with life in Cato Manor, a soon-to-be-demolished township outside Durban, in an idiom close to Matshikiza's Nguni songs in *King Kong*.[38] As cultural contacts with whites declined under pressure from Group Areas segregation and police harassment, especially after the Sharpeville massacre (1960), shows by African impresarios dominated the townships. Produced by musicians, these shows has lively numbers loosely wrapped around a plot. *Washerwoman* (1959) and *Frustrated Black Boy* (1961) by Wilfred Sentso, performed at the Johannesburg City Hall but were most successful in Soweto. *Back in Your Own Backyard* (1962), by Ben "Satch" Masinga (who had played Jack's flashy side-kick, Popcorn, in the London production of *King Kong*), was performed in Soweto with Union Artists' support, as a vehicle for Masinga and singers such as Letta Mbuli and Tandi Klaasen.[39] This combination of star turns and a melodramatic plot of love thwarted – often by female infidelity – held together by the dominant personality of the actor-manager-composer, was to become the successful formula of popular theatre in the townships, developed above all, by Gibson Kente, but its treatment of Sophiatown was mostly nostalgic.

The 1980s revival of Sophiatown, which culminated in the play *Sophiatown* written and produced by the Junction Avenue Theatre Company (JATC) in 1986, had its nostalgic elements too. Nonetheless the play drew not only on the memories and memoirs of writers like Modisane and Mattera but also on more than a decade of radical historiography (associated with the South African History Workshop from 1977, modeled on the University of London original where many of its members trained) that had reconstructed the social life and cultural aspirations of urban blacks and demonstrated the resilience of this culture despite suppression by

96

apartheid (Bozzoli and Delius 1990). From its inception in 1976, JATC participated in this effort to unearth competing South African pasts so as to better understand its conflicting presents. *Randlords and Rotgut* (JATC 1995), JATC's second play but the first with an integrated cast, opened the second History Workshop in February 1978.[40] Like the scholarly paper (by Charles van Onselen) whose title it borrowed, *Randlords and Rotgut* exposed the hypocrisy of mining capitalists who denounced drunkenness while profiting from the sale of liquor on their property, and showed how such moralizing served to rationalize the interests of capital in a workforce that would be sober often enough to be efficient but drunk often enough to be dependent on their wages rather than any income from the land.

Randlords and Rotgut animated this materialist analysis of race and capital in South African history with techniques drawn from music hall as well as Brecht. The "dastardly" capitalists, Sammy Marks, owner of the Hatherley Distillery, and Sir Lionel Philips, chairman of the Chamber of Mines, recalled – in dress, gesture, and singing delivery – the politicians and arms merchants of Theatre Workshop's *Oh, What a Lovely War!* (London 1963), as well as the stockbrockers in Brecht's *St. Joan of the Stockyards* (1938).[41] Following Brecht, JATC attempted to demonstrate the legacy of the past in the present and thus also to remind its (predominantly white dissident) audience that they inherited the evils as well as benefits of mining capitalism in South Africa. If JATC's representation of capital was satirical, their portrayal of workers owed more to contemporary anti-apartheid resistance, whether in the Soweto street marches or on the stage in plays like *Survival* by Workshop '71, some of whose members joined JATC. These influences combined to produce a theatre that focused on public rather than private action, social rather than personal relations, and men rather than women (the only woman in the play is a foreign white prostitute).[42]

Whereas *Randlords and Rotgut* was caustically satirical in the Brechtian manner, *Sophiatown*'s treatment of its subject was more redemptive. The performance of the play, along with the publication of interviews collected by the company (Stein and Jacobson 1986), and the re-publication of banned texts like *Blame Me on History*, encouraged the rediscovery of a historical model, however flawed, of an integrated urban South Africa. The play was based on a serious prank: Nakasa and Nkosi advertised in *Drum* for a Jewish girl to come and stay with them and apparently they found one (Purkey 1993: xii). Out of the interaction between the visitor, Ruth, and the members of a Sophiatown household – from the matriarchal owner, Mamariti (Gladys Mothlale), and her daughter, Lulu (Doreen Mazibuko), to the gangster, Mingus (Arthur Molepo), and the "situation," Jakes (Patrick Shai) – JATC recreated a microcosm of the Sophiatown milieu, while also probing the connections and disconnections between the "bohemia" of the "fabulous fifties" and the tentative integration of the 1980s. The situation of the "situation," Jakes, and perhaps also Ruth (Megan Kriskal), articulated the mixture of alienation and celebration in urban life (Figure 4.4). As Jakes remarks after Ruth introduces them to Jewish sabbath wine:

Figure 4.4 "The Situation of the Situation": Reviving Sophiatown. Patrick Shai as Jakes and Arthur Molepo as Mingus in *Sophiatown* by the Junction Avenue Theatre Company, 1986; directed by Malcolm Purkey. *Photograph and permission*: Ruphin Coudyzer

> God is One and God is Three and the ancestors are many. I speak Zulu and Xhosa and Tswana and English and Afrikaans and Tsotsitaal and if I'm lucky Ruth will teach me Hebrew . . . And this Softown is a brand new generation and we are blessed with a perfect confusion.
>
> (JATC 1995: 180)

This celebration of "perfect confusion" marks a moment suspended in time, caught in the machine of apartheid capitalism that engineered this place and would soon demolish it. Fahfee, numbers-game man and ANC activist (Ramaloa Makhene), reminds the audience of the links between 1955 and 1985: "This year is the year of the Congress of the people. We won't move. What's the number? . . . It's 26. 26 June 1955" (p. 49). As director Malcolm Purkey remarks, the association of moments in the (anti-)apartheid calendar (such as 26 June 1955, the declaration of the Freedom Charter) with the numbers game constitutes a key structuring principle of the play (Purkey 1993: xii). It also implies that the prediction of an imminent ANC victory at that time had something of a magic spell about it. Far from denigrating the Defiance Campaign and the history of struggle, this invocation bears witness to the intensity of the desire for change as well as the difficulty of achieving it.

Sophiatown participates not only in the historical reconstruction of this period but also in contemporary debates about the legacy of the 1950s. The play engages with what might be called the partial postcolonial moment of the Defiance Campaign and the Freedom Charter (1955) in the context of the government declaration of "emergency" in the 1980s. While celebrating the utopian potential of Sophiatown and the "situation's" view that memorialized it in the songs and stories of the period, it also acknowledges that this utopia was at best only partially there. The mass resistance to removals never materialized, in part because Sophiatown's poorer tenants saw the Meadowlands houses as an improvement on their overpriced backyard shacks. Nonetheless, *Sophiatown* emphasizes the value of memory, not merely for healing but for agitation. The songs that punctuate the domestic scenes in this play with comments on the struggle link the self-aware but insufficient urbanity of the *Drum* era and the militant cultural politics of the 1980s. The final song, "Izinyembezi Zabantu" [The Tears of the People], juxtaposes pathos and militancy, as the play concludes with a litany of those, such as Modisane or Matshikiza, who were to die in exile and so links the time of the plot with the time of performance:

> And out of this dust Triomf rises.[43] What triumph is this? Triumph over music? Triumph over meeting? Triumph over the future? . . . I hope that the dust of that triumph . . . covers these purified suburbs with ash. Memory is a weapon. Only a long rain will clean away these tears.
>
> (JATC 1995: 204–5)

Invoking Don Mattera's recollection of the Sophiatown rubble as a prediction of its revival – "Memory is a weapon" (Mattera 1987: 151), the song is a both a lament and a call to arms. A generation after Sophiatown the students of Soweto would hear this call to arms in their struggle against the apartheid state. The drama of this state is the subject of the next chapter.

5

DRY WHITE SEASONS[1]
Domestic drama and the Afrikaner ascendancy

In May 1961, more than a year after the Sharpeville demonstration gave the government the excuse to ban the ANC and the PAC and with them mass resistance to apartheid, Prime Minister Hendrik Verwoerd took white South Africa out of the British Commonwealth as an essentially Afrikaner Republic. Although the all-white referendum on the republic was promoted in terms of national self-determination, the idea appealed hardly at all to English-speaking voters (Moodie 1975: 285) and the Thanksgiving Celebration at the Voortrekker Monument, at which Verwoerd invoked God's will before a crowd decked out in Voortrekker garb (Pelzer 1966: 32), left no doubt as to the priority of Afrikaner interests. The prime minister's invocation of divine authority lent this event the aura of prophecy fulfilled, harking back to the Covenant struck by the Boers on the eve of Blood River (Meyer 1940: 92), while the reprise of Voortrekker themes and theatrics reminded the nation that the *tuiste vir die nageslag* [home for posterity] (Cronjé 1945) was to be a corporatist *volkstaat* rather than a liberal democracy on the British model (Meyer 1942: 29).

In the middle of 1962, the relatively cosmopolitan National Theatre Organization (NTO) was replaced by new provincial Performing Arts Councils (PACs): Performing Arts Council of the Transvaal (PACT), Cape Performing Arts Board (CAPAB), Performing Arts Council of the Orange Free State (PACOFS), and Natal Performing Arts Council (NAPAC). While the mandate of these institutions was to demonstrate the "vitality of the artistic life of the country" and so express its "cultural aspirations" toward the maturity of the European capitals (Dept of Information 1966: 1), the role assigned to them by the Nationalist state reflected its partisan agenda. From the first season, the proportion of Afrikaans-language shows (including translations of European classics as well as local drama) was higher than the English-language equivalents. In the first decade, only CAPAB produced South African English drama, most famously, Fugard's *People Are Living There* (1969), while avoiding the more controversial treatments of race and sex in, for example, Fugard's *Blood Knot* (1961) and *Hello and Goodbye* (1965).[2] In the same period, PACT, CAPAB, and PACOFS produced over a dozen original Afrikaans plays, from N. P. van Wyk Louw's revisionist Anglo-Boer War drama, *Die Pluimsaad waai ver* [The Plumed Seed Blows Far (and Wide)] (PACT, 1966) to P. G. du

Plessis' portrayal of poor whites in *Siener in die Suburbs* [Seer in the Suburbs, PACT, 1971], and Chris Barnard's of a misfit Afrikaner clerk in *Die Rebellie van Lafras Verwey* (PACT 1974), as well as revivals of 1930s plays.

At least as important as the promotion of Afrikaans plays was the institutional role of the PACs in the grand drama of Afrikaner nationalism. The Commission of Inquiry into the Performing Arts reiterated the Nationalist commitment to Afrikanerization, claiming that "national education is the cardinal task of the theatre, to establish language, national sentiment . . . and the entire life of the nation" (Commission of Inquiry 1977: 19). This project was sustained by the establishment of an economic and social base for the promotion of Afrikaners at all levels of employment, from intellectuals and writers producing plays, translations, and criticism for subsidized stages and magazines to technicians working backstage for Afrikaans productions.[3] In this way, cultural institutions made a significant contribution to *volkskapitalisme*, joining institutions like the Land Bank, the Volkskas, and the Afrikaner Handelsinstituut for the financial and social advancement of Afrikaners (O'Meara 1983). So successful were the PACs in promoting Afrikaners in the theatre, that they completely absorbed the private groups that had been in operation since the 1930s (Commission of Inquiry 1977: 6).

Ironically, this very success was cause for concern. Worrying that Afrikaans theatre might be unable to survive without state support (Commission of Inquiry 1977: 20), the PACs appealed to the *ethnic* if not political loyalty of Afrikaner intellectuals. Even plays deemed too provocative for performance were published by subsidized presses. On the other hand, controversial plays by white English-speakers and, even more, by blacks writing in English, could expect no such support. Ethnic attachment to the *volk* was no guarantee of obedience to the state, however. In the late 1960s and 1970s, young Afrikaans intellectuals, among them André Brink, formed the *Sestigers* [Sixties Writers] to criticize their elders, and no less an elder national figure than N. P. van Wyk Louw defied Verwoerd's call for literature to "praise the achievements of Afrikaner patriots" (quoted in O'Meara 1996: 128). Louw's play, *Die Pluimsaad waai ver* (Louw 1972), commissioned for the first Republic Festival in 1966, deviated from the sacred history of the "Second War of Independence" to offer a nuanced account of the Anglo-Boer War. Where Preller and his followers favored the heroic stubbornness of President Paul Kruger (of the then South African Republic) and the *bittereinders* [fighters until the bitter end], Louw focused on the moderate and worldly President Steyn (Orange Free State), acknowledged the lack of discipline and often downright cowardice of the troops, and so earned the play the ire of the prime minister.[4] After Verwoerd's assassination, his followers proposed a Verwoerd prize for "patriotic literature," only to be rebuked by Louw, who compared the proposal to the Stalin Prize (O'Meara 1996: 129). Despite these disputes between *verkrampte* [narrow-minded] and *verligte* [enlightened] members of the *volk*, however, Afrikaans writers were largely exempt from censorship.[5]

Above all, race and sex remained taboo. Where independent English theatres occasionally tackled interracial themes in plays like *The Kimberley Train* by Lewis

Sowden (1958) or Fugard's *Blood Knot*, the PACs rejected the Afrikaans equivalent in Bartho Smit's *Die Verminktes* [The Maimed, 1960]. While ready to produce Louw's controversial treatment of sacred history, they resisted the exposure of Afrikaner hypocrisy in *Putsonderwater* [Well Without Water, 1962], which received an underpublicized production (PACOFS, 1969) seven years after its publication. Moreover, the promotion of the Afrikaans language did not extend to Afrikaans writing by coloureds, despite ongoing debate about those who were after all native speakers of the "mother tongue" (Goldin 1987: 164–68). Although published by an Afrikaans press, *Kanna Hy Kô Hystoe* [Kanna's Coming Home], Adam Small's lyrical evocation of a family's reactions to a native son briefly returned from "white" life in Canada, had to wait seven years for a student production by coloured actors (DRAMSOC, University of the Western Cape [UWC], 1972) and nine for a professional production – by an all-white cast (PACT, 1974). Despite its semantic and historical association with Africa, the moniker "Afrikaner" was exclusively reserved for members of the white *volk*, but the Afrikaans language could not be purged of its hybrid ancestry. Afrikaner ideology attempted to exorcise this troublesome ghost by branding coloured identity as degenerate, while anti-apartheid discourse responded by denying the importance of linguistic and cultural affiliation in favor of the political affiliation of black people of whatever shade (Simone 1994: 161–64). Caught between these claims, coloured identity or, more precisely, the lived experience of in-betweenness that character-ized the lives of the people so designated, resisted reduction to an "artifact of policy" (p. 162).

Although produced within different institutional contexts, the plays mentioned so far have in common the intimate portrayal of people deemed undesirable or simply impossible by apartheid. Originating for the most part outside Johannesburg, in the 1950s the center for bohemian integration, they mark the passing of that era while attempting to deal with its passing. The transgression of racist law takes most blatant form in the drama of miscegenation, but it also animates plays that depict people from a single racial group – *Hello and Goodbye* deals with poor whites who were supposed to disappear with *volkskapitalisme*, while *Kanna* deals with the effects of poverty as well as segregation on a coloured community. By probing the contradictions in the Calvinist precepts of (sexual) self-control and (economic) self-reliance so fundamental to Afrikaner self-representation (De Klerk 1975) and thus exposing the economic and psychological alienation of the Afrikaner in the so-called Afrikaner Republic, plays like Smit's *Putsonderwater* and, in milder form, Du Plessis' *Siener in die Suburbs*, pushed the limits of official tolerance. While these plays, largely ignored by non-Afrikaans scholars, abound in the excessive senti-ment, emphatic moral conflicts, and sudden reversals associated with melodrama on racial themes since *The Octoroon* (1861), they share with this unacknowledged American ancestor an engagement with the racial obsessions of a not-so-master-race, especially the contradiction between the official picture of racial purity and ethnic advancement on the one hand and the twin specters of "poor whites" and "passing whites" shadowing the *volk*, on the other.

Although Fugard's plays from this period, from *The Blood Knot* (1961) to *Boesman and Lena* (1969), produced mainly by independent or university theatres, are not generally associated with Afrikaans drama, produced mainly by the state, his work ought to be considered in this context. In the first place, as Fugard himself noted, many of the characters in these ostensibly English plays would more plausibly be speaking Afrikaans (Fugard and Simon 1982: 48). In the second place, these plays share with their Afrikaans counterparts the sentimental garrulity and the under-dog types of melodrama. Both, it may be argued, encourage feeling from their sympathetic but alienated audiences for the suffering underdogs, without, how-ever, directly indicting the social agents causing that suffering.

In a decade or more of total political repression (from the police state estab-lished in the early 1960s to the rebellion of students and workers in the 1970s), domestic drama – in venues as different as the palaces of national culture, the drama departments of liberal universities, or all-purpose township halls – managed nonetheless to depict the physical and emotional harm of apartheid on South Africans, from members of the inner circle, such as Senator Harmse in *Die Verminktes*, through forgotten cousins of the master race, such as Hester in *Hello and Goodbye* or Tjokkie in *Siener*, to "step-children" like Kanna and the family he left behind. In the African townships, domestic melodrama, such as Sam Mhangwane's long-running *Unfaithful Woman* and Gibson Kente's *Sikhalo* (1966) also focused on the suffering of individuals as well as on the potential of family feeling as a force for survival in if not resistance to apartheid. Portraying maimed individuals in the apartheid home offered a critical foil to the grandiose image of the "home for posterity." But the confines of the naturalist interior may also foreclose the dramatic analysis of this *domestication* of politics in the claustrophobic space of the home, as, for example, in *No-Good Friday*. Using these questions as points of reference, this chapter explores the drama of, in, and against the Afrikaner ascendancy as a drama of blood, sweat, and tears, rather than collective action.

Miscegenation and melodrama

On 3 September 1961, *The Blood Knot* opened at the Rehearsal Room at Dorkay House in Johannesburg before an invited audience of blacks and whites.[6] On 11 November, it reopened at the commercial (and therefore all-white) Intimate Theatre, and, over the next year, played across the country. Directed by the author, who also played the role of Morris, a light-skinned coloured man, against Zakes Mokae, his collaborator from *No-Good Friday* (1958), who played Zachariah, Morris's dark-skinned brother, the play portrays the intimate conflict between two differently black men who act out white obsessions with racial purity on each other's bodies and minds. The conflict comes to a head when Morris assumes the role of a "white gentleman" in imaginary anticipation of a visit from Zach's white penfriend, Ethel, and, after she breaks off the correspondence, turns his frustra-tion onto his brother. Emboldened by the trappings of whiteness as he wears the "gentleman's" suit bought for the occasion, Morris torments Zach with racial insults, while Zach first goads and then threatens to attack his brother. The threat of violence is deflected only by Morris's final appeal to the "bloodknot" binding the brothers. Since Morris and Zach are coloured, this mark of kinship includes not only their immediate family, but also the unmentioned legacy of white sexual exploitation of blacks, rewritten as white fears of miscegenation.

The Blood Knot was not the first South African play to dramatize apartheid society's compulsion to fix the signs of racial difference on individuals and to expose the contradictions of white fears of racial contamination through sexual contact. The predominantly white, English-speaking audience would have known about Lewis Sowden's *Kimberley Train* (Library Theatre, Johannesburg, 1958) and Basil Warner's *Try for White* (Cockpit Players, Cape Town, 1959; dir: Leonard Schach), both of which portray thwarted unions between coloured women and white men.[7] Bilingual spectators may have also read Bartho Smit's play, *Die Verminktes*, which juxtaposes in a savagely critical if contradictory manner the discrepancies between Afrikaners' public condemnation of miscegenation and their secret practice of sexual exploitation. Very few members of this audience may have known about *Ruby and Frank* (1938), Dhlomo's play about doomed love between a coloured woman and an African man, performed two decades earlier.[8]

Although Fugard was not writing in direct response to any of these plays, they made available for dramatic treatment formerly taboo subjects of race and sex. *The Blood Knot* draws on the attempts, already manifest in *The Kimberley Train*, *Try for White*, and *Die Verminktes*, to make the domestic interior and the conflict around family and romantic love accommodate political and social conflicts around racial difference. They share a mode of representation that vacillates between naturalism and melodrama, between a dispassionate exposure of the effects of public policy on individual psychology and a sentimental play for audience sympathy for apparently fateful suffering. One might argue that melodrama furnished the best techniques for dramatizing the consequences of apartheid's most intimate and most melodramatic law, the Population Registration Act of 1950, since the Act not only demanded the social separation of "European," "coloured," "Indian," and "Bantu" groups on a massive scale, but also destroyed families by separating children and spouses in the name of racial purity. Lurid stories of brown children born to white parents or white fiancés exposed as coloured received more public exposure than coloureds who managed to pass or gain official "reclassification," but both kinds of stories had the shape of melodramatic sensation scenes rather than the rational social planning Afrikaner ideologues desired.[9] Melodrama in the state and in the theatre replayed the contradictions of an impossible policy and unmanageable social situation in the domestic setting.

The significance of Fugard's focus on black characters and exclusion of whites from the stage (but emphatically not from the house) can best be seen against the more predictable focus in the other plays on white (mis)perception of racial "others," as well as the legal fictions legitimating those perceptions. Where *The*

Blood Knot probes the contradictions but also the emotional truth of Morris's internalization of white supremacist fictions as he seesaws between attachment to his brother and (self)loathing of his color, *The Kimberley Train* dwells on prevailing white prejudices, even when expressed by coloured characters. Bertha, the mother of Elaine whose marriage with John Powers is thwarted, agrees with John's father (her master), when she states that coloureds are "second" as opposed to "third-class" (Sowden 1976: 27), reinforcing Nationalist propaganda discouraging coloureds from affiliation with Africans (Goldin 1987: 166–75). Performed by a prominent Afrikaans actress, Kita Redelinghuys, this character's acceptance of second-class citizenship appeared natural and convincing.[10] At the end of the play, Elaine appears to submit to the axiom that whiteness is an essential – and therefore inaccessible – birthright: "It is not enough to pretend to be white. You have to know the colour inside you and not give a damn . . . . I wasn't able to do it" (Sowden 1976: 73), echoing a line of white writing about coloureds that descends from Sarah Gertrude Millin's *God's Step-Children* (1925).[11] Millin's essay on *The People of South Africa*, published in 1954, reflects English liberal ambivalence about coloured aspirations in the wake of the Population Registration Act, as it vacillates between the suggestion that "the whites have lost nothing" by "coloureds passing for white" (Millin 1954: 265) and the insistence nonetheless that coloureds constitute a "definite, inferior and static race" whose members may "assert their whiteness" but are doomed to failure (p. 269).

But Elaine's "passing" into white society by way of the "Kimberley train," an underground organization supporting coloureds who "tried for white," suggests that whiteness is a product of socialization and thus that "pretending" may well be "enough" to give the lie to theories of racial difference. Although the melodrama of doomed love may make the lived experience of oppression look like fate or God's will rather than public policy, this conclusion implies that passing is a response to particular historical conditions, in this case the social engineering on the part of the state as well as the effects of indoctrination in the powers of whiteness. Ironically, it is not Elaine, but her white fiancé who ends up "trapped" (p. 75). Like Ashis Nandy's "White Sahib," John is less a "dedicated oppressor" than a "self-destructive co-victim . . . caught in the hinges of history he swears by" (Nandy 1983: xv).

This play between the subject born into and forever marked by racial identity and conflicting individual responses to socialization, public policy, and personal prejudice reaches its high and low points in *Die Verminktes*, written by Bartho Smit, an Afrikaans intellectual deeply engaged with the future of *volkskultuur* and later head of the Afrikaanse Pers's literary division. Where *The Kimberley Train* dwells on the suffering of the powerless, "trapped" by the apartheid system, *Die Verminktes* indicts the powerful, the agents and ideologues of apartheid in the Afrikaner Nationalist state. Where the former focuses on the fate of the country's "stepchildren," the latter confronts the sins of its white fathers: the social bigotry, political ambitions, and personal bad faith of a so-called Christian ruling class. These men are not "co-victims" but "dedicated oppressors"; Afrikaner humiliation at the hands of the British had in the Afrikaner Republic been transformed into Afrikaner hegemony. Smit's assault on the violence of apartheid policy, in the person of the ideologue, Professor Jan Barnard, and exposure of the contradiction between public policy and private hypocrisy, in the person of Senator Bart Harmse, secretly the father of his coloured housekeeper's philosopher son, Frans, made the play unperformable in Verwoerd's Republic. Smit's previous stage successes – *Moeder Hanna* [Mother Hanna; NTO 1958], an Anglo-Boer War drama, and *Don Juan onner die Boere* [Don Juan among the Boers, 1960], a comedy – as well as his vigorous support for subsidized Afrikaans theatre, did not suffice to counteract hostility to the play's attack on the probity of the *volk*. The play was shelved until 1977.[12]

Despite its critique of Afrikaner hypocrisy, *Die Verminktes* is itself maimed by its inherited discourses. It begins bravely, with the sound of the (recently banned) ANC hymn, "Nkosi Sikelel' iAfrika," from the African manservant's off-stage room, and goes on to attack the official defense of apartheid. When Professor Barnard vilifies coloureds as the "hole in the dike" protecting the "little white island" from the "black sea" that threatens to engulf it (Smit 1976: 16), Frans retorts that the "only difference between white and coloured is that the one was lucky enough to be born on the sunny side of the wall and the other unlucky enough to be born on the dark side" (p. 17).[13] He explicitly debunks the "scientific" validity of the "pure race," implying that Afrikaners have denied their hybrid inheritance motivated by racism and the desire for power (p. 18).

But, although the play allows Frans to expose the political expediency behind Barnard's ideological crusade and the personal hypocrisy behind Senator Harmse's objections to his son's marriage to his ward, Elize, it apparently cannot allow the couple to escape the constraints of their society. Rather, it abandons the logic of dramatic conflict and resolution for a retreat into the platitudes of racial determinism. This retreat is prefigured by stereotypes like the *skollie* who blackmails Harmse while assenting to the senator's insulting epithet "swart vuilgoed" ["black trash"] so long as he gets his money (p. 24).[14] Harmse's attempt to deter Elize from marrying Frans echoes not only the language of Afrikaner racial pride but also the racial panic made famous by *The Octoroon*, when he tells her that her blood and "all the generations of your people" ["al die geslagte van jou volk"] will compel her to search Frans's body for signs of racial degeneration (p. 35). Finally, Harmse's castration of his son, while it exposes what Aimé Césaire called the "decivilization" of the colonizer (Césaire 1972: 13), shifts the indictment onto the victim.[15] This act of mutilation provides the occasion, but not the motivation, for Frans to switch from protecting Elize to attacking her in the same language as her foster father, threatening her with the "dark blood of Africa" (p. 56).

At this point, the play's struggle to accommodate the competing ideologies of racial determinism and liberal individualism renders it incoherent. After Frans's words drive Elize to suicide, Smit has Frans suddenly switch roles from articulate hero to coon, as he delivers the final speech in the language of the *skollie*: "Ma' die mêem hoef nie sêd te wies nie oer die castration nie – kôs why, da' wag nou 'n

White Future vi' har [But the madam mustn't be sad 'bout the castration, 'cos why, now there's a White Future waiting for her]" (p. 57). This final sensation scene vacillates between "moral significance and an excess of thrill, sensation, and strong affective attraction" in the manner that Tom Gunning identifies with the melodrama of sensation, which forgoes the moral transparency usually associated with melodrama for the "horror of opacity" (Gunning 1994: 51).[16] Juxtaposed with the crescendo of "Nkosi Sikelel' iAfrika" off-stage, the meaning of this mimicry is hard to decipher. Is Frans fomenting revolution by throwing the "master's" racial projection back in his father's face? Or is he simply reverting to racial type? In the 1977 all-white production by PACT, Don Lamprecht played this scene as a blackface caricature of a man "trying for white." Although the logic of the action thus far suggests that nurture not nature is the key to white identity, the resurgence of ethnic sentiment represses that acknowledgment and the play reverts to racial typing, retreating behind the platitudes of a racially exclusive *volkseie*.[17]

While *Die Verminktes's* struggle to represent the public as well as private drama of apartheid as a national tragedy eventually renders plot and character opaque, *The Blood Knot's* focus on the dreams of an oppressed individual occludes the structural oppression around this individual. This occlusion of the structures of oppression does not, to be sure, erase them. When Zach returns home from work in the opening moments of the play, he grapples with the workings of profit and the impact of labor exploitation on his immediate physical comfort, as he settles into a footbath: "I do the bloody work. . . . It's my stinking feet that's got the hardnesses but he goes and makes my profit" (Fugard 1992: 5).[18] Morrie, in his turn, hopes that they might escape wage slavery altogether by buying a farm in "one of those blank spaces" on the map (p. 10). Although the agents of exploitation, from the ambiguous referent in Zach's complaint (who might be either his boss or the man who sold the footsalts) to the bureaucrats responsible for the "bad water" and open sewers of Korsten, remain unnamed, the description of the fetid ghetto blasted by industry and overcrowding is confirmed by the atmosphere created by Frank Graves's set of exposed brick, chicken-wire, and broken furniture (Figure 5.1). Language and set remind readers and spectators that black settlements like this one were being squeezed as Verwoerd's government intensified mass removals. In a period when 100,000 Africans and several thousand coloureds a year were being displaced (Thompson 1990: 193), the prospect of finding a "blank space" for a farm seemed pathetically unlikely. Images like these resist readings that would elevate Fugard's subject to "the universal human plight of Man's search for warmth, intelligibility and meaning in an alien world" (Vandenbroucke 1986: 262) and thus reduce apartheid's specific exploitation of particular groups of people to an unchanging existential fate of humankind.

Rather than directly represent the agents of apartheid, Fugard shows us in Morrie a character who has internalized apartheid prohibitions on mobility, labor, and sex and, in Zach, one who appears at first to be "better adjusted to the humiliations and pleasures of daily life" (Vandenbroucke 1986: 65) but is finally as

Figure 5.1 "No longer a white gentleman": Fugard as Morrie in *The Blood Knot*, Dorkay House, 1962. *Photograph*: John Cohen; *source*: NELM

confined as Morrie. The final battle, however, has each confronting the other in desperation made more vivid by the battered appearance of the "gentleman's suit" (Figure 5.1). As worn by Fugard at the end of the play, the suit is clearly no longer the disguise that Morrie believed would allow him to pass. As Orkin's reading of this play demonstrates, Morrie filters apartheid prohibitions through conflicting emotions about his own body and those of his brother, Minnie, his brother's erstwhile fun-loving friend, Ethel, the penfriend they never meet, and an imaginary and nameless black woman who appears fleetingly in their "game" at the end of the play. Morrie's ambivalent affection for his brother is constrained by his attempts to sublimate Zach's desire for sex into interest in a penfriend and, more threateningly, by his sense of the risk they take in even thinking of a white woman:

> When they get their hands on a dark-born boy playing with a white idea, you think they don't find out what he's been dreaming at night. They have ways and means, my friend. . . . Like confinement in a cell . . . for days without end. . . . All they need for evidence is a man's dreams. Not so much his hate. . . . It's his dreams that they drag off in judgment.
>
> (Fugard 1992: 58–59)

In Morrie's scenario of surveillance and punishment the power of the all-seeing Calvinist God, whom Morrie has invoked before (p. 46), joins that of the panopticon state – embedded in the individual body and soul. As Orkin argues, following Foucault, characters like Morrie have so internalized the state's prohibition on "immorality" and the idea of the state's omniscience that the actual exercise of police power is rendered unnecessary because "he who is subjected to the field of visibility and knows it, assumes responsibility for the constraints of power; he has them play spontaneously on himself; . . . he becomes the principle of his own subjection" (Foucault 1979: 202–3; Orkin 1991: 102–3).

The pathology of this self-inflicted punishment is nowhere more striking than in the sinister "game" that ends the play. At the start, Morrie rationalizes his initial reluctance to wear the "gentleman's" suit designed to woo Ethel with the by now familiar truism of the innateness of white identity, "[t]he clothes don't maketh the white man. It is that white something inside you, that special meaning and manner of whiteness that I got to find" (Fugard 1992: 73) but, once in costume, he finds that "special meaning" not in himself or in his new clothes, but in the sudden fear in Zach's eyes for this "different sort of man" (p. 79). It is the fearful gaze of his black (br)other, not any inner drive, that makes Morrie act white and that provokes Zach in his turn to threaten violence. As the stage photograph (Figure 5.1) suggests, Morrie draws strength from Zach's expression of fear, but both are finally trapped in the same dreary room. Although they interrupt the game before anyone is physically hurt, the characters are left with the sense that, "without a future," the "bloodknot" that binds them is all they have (p. 96).

Compelling as this final image has been for critics of all sorts of persuasions, there is an invisible figure in this picture that all of them have missed. While some have read this scene as a moving, if ambiguous affirmation of brotherly love (Brown 1982; Orkin 1991: 106), others as a depiction of resignation to oppression (Kavanagh 1982: 171; Nkosi 1983: 139–41), none has acknowledged the unseen scapegoat that makes both the battle and the truce possible. When the final round of their game seems about to flag, Morrie conjures up a "horribly old woman" who resembles their mother (Fugard 1992: 91). Only once they have chased off this imaginary mother with stones and insults, blamed her for "mak[ing] life unbearable" (p. 92), and laughed derisively at her exposed body, are they able to continue their game and reinvigorate their sense of brotherhood. By blaming his black mother rather than his unknown (and plausibly white) father or, by extension, the white paternalist state, Morrie deflects responsibility for his humiliation onto a victim rather than a perpetrator of apartheid. By reducing the brothers' mother to an imaginary intruder and, further, to dismembered female body parts, this play risks being consumed by its final sensation scene, rendering opaque the social and familial relations that both bear the brunt of apartheid brutality and constitute the crucible for survival and resilience if not resistance to it. If *The Blood Knot* is "the most important work of theatre in the history of South Africa up to that point" (Vandenbroucke 1986: 68) or, more plausibly, at least an example of a "more authentic South African drama" (Orkin 1991: 90), then its claim to authenticity seems to rest explicitly on its representation of black men as exemplary South African agents and implicitly on its exclusion of the black woman who gave birth to them.

The Blood Knot's treatment of the effects of white supremacist ideology and apartheid social engineering on two black men captured the attention of (predominantly) white, English-speaking, liberal audiences, who, in Nadine Gordimer's phrase, "sat fascinated, week after week, as if by a snake" (Gordimer 1964: 55). Opening in South Africa a few months after Verwoerd proclaimed South Africa a republic and performed over a year when state action against overt political resistance intensified, the play reminded those audiences of the day to day consequences of racist legislation. It was hailed as a "world-class play" and a "milestone in South African drama," not merely for its probing of the most intimate reverberations of apartheid but also for the performance of a black and a white actor together on the same stage.[19] By 1964, audiences in Britain, Belgium, and the United States, had joined in the chorus of approbation for the play and condemnation of the society that gave birth to it (Read 1991: 43–49). *The Blood Knot* also allowed its liberal spectators to disassociate themselves from the apartheid state acting in the name of all white South Africans and to associate themselves instead with the gesture of protest implied by the casting.

Yet, even as the action of the play challenged South African racial and sexual taboos, the performance of *The Blood Knot* marked the end rather than the beginning of the era of interracial collaboration that had made possible not only *No-Good Friday* (1958) or *King Kong* (1959), but also the communist-affiliated African National Theatre two decades before. Although it made this kind of collaboration more visible to mainstream audiences, *The Blood Knot* presented not the "first multiracial cast" (Orkin 1991: 91), but the *last* for more than a decade. In closing the remaining loopholes for integrated casts and audiences, the Group Areas Act of 1965 did not completely eliminate interracial organization but it made such collaboration difficult. Thus, while Gibson Kente and Sam Mhangwane could make a living in black townships with apolitical melodramas like *Sikhalo* and *Unfaithful Woman* (1966), Zakes Mokae could combine theatre and anti-apartheid activities only in British exile. Moreover, the international acclaim that greeted *The Blood Knot* also encouraged the Anti-Apartheid Movement (AAM) in Britain to intensify efforts against the apartheid state. In June 1963, shortly after the government reinforced cultural apartheid by establishing the PACs, the AAM issued a declaration in which 276 playwrights refused rights to "any theatre where discrimination is made among audiences on grounds of colour" (Vandenbroucke 1986: 78).

"Well without water": race, sex and poverty in the Afrikaner ascendancy

Increased isolation from metropolitan culture encouraged *verligte* as well as *verkrampte* Afrikaners to turn toward the cultural *eie* [identiy]. But this volkish solidarity

110

was undermined by the unresolved discrepancy between the promise of *volksontwik-keling* [people's development] and the reality of Afrikaans-speaking poor whites and "browns" left out of the Afrikaner ascendancy. It was also weakened by the waning influence of Calvinism on Afrikaner sexual and familial relations and by the state's increasingly inapplicable claim, in the face of its systematic brutality, to represent a Christian nation. English-speakers were on the other hand dismayed and demoralized after Sharpeville. As Fugard remarked in 1963: "This country is in the grip of its worst drought – and that drought is in the human heart" (1984: 83).

The "family plays" (Fugard and Simon 1982: 40) of this period – *People Are Living There* and *Hello and Goodbye* – use encounters between family and quasi-family members in run-down domestic settings to dramatize the effects of this drought not only on human hearts parched by alienation but also on poor whites marked by social and economic deprivation. The "second-hand Smits of Valley Road" in *Hello and Goodbye* (Fugard 1991: 115) belong to the class of people left behind by *volksontwikkeling*. To be sure, poor whites had privileges withheld from blacks: in *Hello and Goodbye*, Johnnie Smit's access to his father's disability pension from the railways (an Afrikaner sinecure) allows him the small luxuries of a three-roomed house in the Port Elizabeth inner city, orange squash, beer, and trips to the beach. But, as Johnnie's recollection of his father's work during the Depression vividly conveys, in hard times, these meager privileges brought poor Afrikaners up against the fragile line that separated them from blacks: "The kaffirs sit and watch them work. The white men are hungry . . . And all the time the kaffirs sit and watch the white man doing kaffir work, hungry for the work" (Fugard 1991: 121).

Important as these details are for the local *con-texture* of the play, *Hello and Goodbye* focuses more directly on two individuals abandoned to this environment than on the environment itself. Their struggle is less with each other than with the dead weight of their father and his impoverished material, psychological, and existential legacy. Johnnie pretends almost to the very end that their father is still alive, and his alternately violent and caressing handling of his father's crutches gives material weight to the old man's psychological power, while replaying Morrie's obsession with an omniscient authority that is state, deity, and absent father in one. Hester, on the other hand, has something of Zach's (sexual) "drive" and honest recognition of harsh facts (Fugard and Simon 1982: 44). But, where *The Blood Knot* culminates in the spectacular racist game between brothers, *Hello and Goodbye* ends after Hester discovers *nothing*: no inheritance amid the bric-a-brac of her childhood and no father brooding in the next room. She returns empty-handed to the uncertain life of an aging whore in Johannesburg and Johnnie shifts from pretending his father is still alive to taking on his crutches and his shadow.

The minimal action registers the influence of Beckett, especially *Waiting for Godot*, which Fugard directed at Dorkay House, and of the existentialism of Camus and Sartre, whom Fugard was reading (1984: 62, 61). As a self-aware individual, Hester has abandoned social constraints and faces up to an empty life, while Johnnie embodies the man of bad faith who will not know himself. But the fatalism of Johnnie, who represents the "point of view of the play" (Fugard 1984: 44), has a particular local color. Treating both his father's loss of a leg to dynamite on the job and his own failure to take a railway job as "God's will," Johnnie reflects the fatalistic combination of Afrikaner nationalism and Calvinist dogma which declared, on the occasion of the erection of the Voortrekker Monument, that "disasters, adversity, privation, reversals, and suffering are some of the best means in God's hands to form a people" (*Gedenkboek* 1940: 11). Although Johnnie understands his fate in familial terms, he uses language that echoes Afrikaner nationalist rationalization of collective suffering to justify his own weakness.

Hester, on the other hand, rebels not only against her father's familial manipulation, his "groaning and moaning and what the Bible says" (Fugard 1991: 85–86), but also against Afrikaner Calvinist patriarchy:

> There's no father, no brother, no sister, no Sunday, or sin. There's nothing. The fairy stories is finished. They died in a hundred Jo'burg rooms. There is a man. And I'm a woman. [. . .] You want a sin. Well, there's one. I *Hoer*. I've *hoer*ed all the brothers and fathers and sons [. . .] into one thing . . . Man.
>
> (p. 108)

Like his father, Johnnie tries to blame Hester's rebellion on impure blood, "You weren't a real Afrikaner by nature, he said. Must have been some English blood somewhere, on Mommie's side" (p. 101). Hester's obliteration of family ties and boundaries between kin and strangers not only transgresses Afrikaner and Calvinist custom (Orkin 1991: 137) but also challenges a broader patriarchal regime that separates women into two sharply differentiated classes: mother and whore, guardian of clan or national purity or scapegoat for its contamination. Hester is scandalous not merely because she challenges prevailing prohibitions on sexually and economically independent women, but because she strips her mother of any association with an Afrikaner collectivity and heroic endurance when she describes her – *and her peers* – as a small figure who "fell into her grave the way they all do – tired, *moeg*. Frightened" (Fugard 1991: 126). Her attack on Afrikaner symbols and customs makes her indictment of the family an indictment of the *volk* as well.

At the same time, putting these words in the mouth of a whore defuses the scandal. Like the spectacle of Morrie and Zach's bodies in intimate struggle, which hypnotized white spectators "like a snake," as Gordimer had it, Hester's account of her life risks making the character an object of fascination rather than understanding for spectators largely cut off from white poverty. The circumstances of the original performance reinforced this. Like Fugard's earlier plays, the production of *Hello and Goodbye* was made possible by English-speaking liberals and progressives, who were also its primary audience. It was organized by Phoenix Players, set up by Union Artists' Ian Bernhardt and Barney Simon, who directed the play. Fugard played Johnnie while Molly Seftel, part of the Jewish bohemia associated with Sophiatown, played Hester. After a week's private performances for integrated audiences, the play opened to exclusively white audiences at the Library Theatre, Johannesburg, on 26 October 1965, and later toured Pretoria and Cape Town.[20] The production at the Library Theatre, former home of the Johannesburg Repertory and other liberal ventures, placed Fugard's play within a line of white English dramas including Lewis Sowden's *Red Rand* (1937) and *The Kimberley Train* (1958) and drew predominantly English-speaking affluent audiences rather than poorer or Afrikaans audiences and excluded blacks.[21]

Response to the performance reflected the tension between fascination and empathy that highlighted Hester's ambiguous role. Where director Simon interpreted Fugard's insertion of Afrikaans expletives into a South African English marked already by Afrikanerisms as "love and respect" for his mother's tongue (Fugard and Simon 1982: 48), the reviewers were less sure. Most English-language critics praised the performance, while W. E. G. Louw, brother of the poet, described the play as true to life but talky.[22] Critics from opposite sides of the political spectrum, however, lambasted the play as a "torment" or as "exaggerating and saying nothing"[23]; the latter (in the *Vaderland*) reiterated the sentiments of lower-middle-class Afrikaners too close to poor white life for comfort.

Produced by PACOFS in Bloemfontein, *Putsonderwater* [Well without Water] had greater potential to reach a broader Afrikaner audience. Although written in allegorical language and set in an unnamed town rather than a recognizable environment, Smit's play has several thematic features in common with Fugard's: both depict the sexual repression and social isolation as well as the economic deprivation of small-town Afrikaners and both use the figure of the whore to embody the effects of this repression and the attempt to resist it in a desperate rebellion against a peculiarly Afrikaans version of patriarchy. But neither the abstract location nor the playwright's acknowledgment of a French literary source (Georges Bernanos's novella, *Sous le soleil de Satan* [Under the Sun of Satan]) made *Putsonderwater* safe for state subsidy. First performed abroad, to acclaim in Belgium, it was taken up by PACOFS only after it had been tested in a student production at Rhodes University, the liberal *English*-language institution that hosted the premiere of Fugard's *Boesman and Lena* the same year.[24] After deliberations in parliament, as well as the Censorship Board's closed-door meetings, the PACOFS production was permitted as a short, experimental run in a small house without publicity for invited, non-paying audiences only.[25] Even after this tryout, a mainstage production by CAPAB was quashed until the play received a full production from PACT in 1981.[26]

Presented by the author and the PACOFS dramaturg as an "attempt to depict the West's crisis of belief" (Smit 1962: n.p.) in a "fantastic parable,"[27] *Putsonderwater* indicts the hypocrisy of church and society notables in a *platteland dorpie* [backwoods village]. Following Smit's location of the action in the square of an "imaginary village in the open desert of our country," director/designer Henk Hugo (based at the University of the Orange Free State) used a spare, stylized set in which walls separating public and private space were only hinted at (Figure 5.2)

Figure 5.2 Dry White Seasons in *Well without Water* by Bartho Smit; Rina La Grange-Steyn as Maria, and Neels Coetzee as the "son"; directed by Henk Hugo, PACOFS, 1969. *Source*: State Archive, Pretoria

and without, apart from the well, naturalist clutter that might interfere with the naive and lyrical fancy of the central character, Maria, daughter of Jan Alleman (John Everyman). At the same time, however, he favored naturalistic acting for the quarrels between Maria and her respectable exploiters – doctor, police sergeant, and minister (or, more pointedly, *dominee*) – which made the Afrikaans and Calvinist undertones of *Putsonderwater* inescapable.

When the play opens, one of these men has already impregnated the girl. Although taken in by her own fantasy of the City of Gold that combines the *dominee*'s promise to take her to Johannesburg with his sermons about the Apostle John (in Afrikaans: Johannes), she is nonetheless capable of twisting these self-important old men "around her little finger" by playing up to the desire of each to believe that he is "baas op Putsonderwater" [boss in Putsonderwater] (Smit 1962: 5). In their dealings with Maria, each man, especially the doctor and the *dominee*, plays a sort of Prospero, demanding filial obedience and encouraging her belief in their power as magicians [*toornaars*; p. 7]: the *dominee* uses a ritual incantation of the Song of Solomon to seduce her, while the doctor claims to have power over life and death. In their desire to magnify their "paternal omnipotence" through displays of magic and in their "neurotically touchy" reaction to perceived threats to their authority, these two resemble the Prospero that Octave Mannoni endows with the petulant and arbitrary authority of the colonizer (Mannoni 1964: 105).[28]

Maria is no Miranda, however. In Rita La Grange-Steyn's performance, she

114

resembles a younger Hester Smit, whose rebellion against her Calvinist father also took the form of sex, and whose vulnerability expressed itself in aggressive behavior toward someone made more vulnerable by his racial position. In Hester's case, this would be the Indian hawker whose innocent question, "Girlie, where's your Mommie?" and sympathetic, if awkward, silence in response to her curt "She's dead" provoke her to yell "Voetsek" (an expletive reserved for blacks and animals) (Fugard 1991: 125). In Maria's case, it is the nameless coloured "son," whose interruption of her fantasy earns him an insult to his coloured mother (Smit 1962: 3). After her act of pushing the *dominee* down the well (when he tried to rape her) leads the sergeant to kill her father for the crime, and her attempt to confess, prodded by the undead *dominee*, provokes patronizing disbelief, she comes to resemble her biblical namesakes, both the fallen Magdalena and the virgin (pp. 64–65). But, where Bernanos's Catholic story redeems his heroine by association with an immaculate virgin, Smit's Calvinist drama leaves her closer to animal unconsciousness than divine grace.[29] Treated by her pursuers as a creature – from a bitch in heat (p. 3) to a doe in the Song of Solomon (p. 20) – she takes the position, if not the character, of Caliban: resisting taming, she becomes an object of conquest and discipline. There is no simple allegory here: Maria does not stand for the colonized masses who do not appear in this drama, nor does she simply represent poor whites subject to manipulation by a hypocritical Afrikaner brotherhood. Nonetheless, struggling with the language of her manipulators – biblical, moral, and the lore of poor white migration to the Golden City – she speaks in part for these victims. Maria's incomprehension of the power struggles in the arid heart of Afrikaner country, her utopian vision of paradise in this desert, and her obliviousness to the indigenous people apparently eradicated from this wilderness make her both an innocent and an unwitting participant in Afrikaner hegemony.

The figure of the seer trapped by the social and economic pressures of poor white life, manipulated by shadowy but powerful agents, plays a central role in several Afrikaans plays in the brief period of the early 1970s that might be called the *verligte* moment of Afrikaans culture, after the culture wars of the 1960s and before the eruption of Soweto drew even the most obstinate Afrikaner away from preoccupation with his *eie*. P. G. du Plessis' *Siener in die Suburbs* [Seer in the Suburbs, PACT 1971] and Chris Barnard's *Die Rebellie van Lafras Verwey* [The Rebellion of Lafras Verwey, SABC 1971; PACT 1975] take their cue from the clash between the prosaic reality of alienated Afrikaans proles in the so-called Afrikaner Republic and their dream of transcendence or revolt, which are ultimately shattered by the intrusion of that reality.[30]

The most famous photograph of PACT's production of *Siener in die Suburbs* shows the petty gangster Jakes (Marius Weyers) on his motorbike in full leather regalia, with his girl Tiemie (Sandra Prinsloo), in mini-skirt and make-up, on the pillion behind him. Reproduced in reviews, the PACT Yearbook for 1971, and in publicity for the SABC-TV version several years later, this picture of plebeian vitality – especially Weyers's rough masculine swagger as an Afrikaner prole, which dominated the stage (Figure 5.3) – reflected the Afrikaner establishment's

115

Figure 5.3 Masculine swagger in *Siener van die Suburbs* by P. G. Du Plessis; Marius Weyers as Jakes; directed by Louis van Niekerk, PACT 1971. *Source and permission*: PACT

eventual embrace of these characters as "indigenous" (*inheems*). Where vulgar language and illicit sex – in combination with racial, religious, or political controversy – had provoked censorship of plays such as *Putsonderwater*, these elements on their own made "delightful" (*heerlike*) dramatic material.[31] Although initially ill at ease with the public display of dialogue that "sound[ed] as though it had never been committed to paper" and criminal acts including *dagga* smoking simulated on stage,[32] critics warmed to it enough to imitate its style.[33] This reaction to the previously scorned language of the white working classes bears a certain resemblance to the initial reception and eventual canonization of Michel Tremblay's *Les Belles-Sœurs* [The Sisters-in-Law], the first Québécois play to make of *joual*, the dialect of working-class Montréalais ca.1968, the stuff of legitimate theatre (Tremblay 1972: 113–76). Although Du Plessis and his audience were probably unaware of this play, the historical parallels between "the white niggers of America" and the "white kaffirs" of Africa and their common British imperial enemy, especially in the early years of Afrikaner anti-imperialism, had been noted.[34] Even at the height of the Afrikaner ascendancy, Afrikaans was still caught up in the racial anxieties troubling the white speakers of this creolized language.

Yet, this popular consumption of the play did not make the story of Tjokkie, the seer in the Southern – and white working-class – suburbs of Johannesburg merely a diverting spectacle for the Afrikaner *nouveaux riches*. The naturalist brick-wall-and-backyard set (Figure 5.3) made the poverty and constricting character of this environment clear, while the vehicles on stage – the motorbike and the Buick – do not provide a way out. Jakes's bike, part of the glamorous lure that got Tiemie pregnant, is a thoroughly unstable vehicle for her "to get out of the suburbs" and Tjokkie's old Buick on blocks offers him only temporary refuge from his tormenter, Jakes. By the end of the play, Tjokkie's clairvoyance and Jakes's successful attempt to get him to "see" against his will have broken up this untidy but previously functional family home. Tjokkie's prediction of the outcome of the Friday races allows Giel, his mother's gambling man, to leave with his winnings, abandoning earlier promises to be a father to the family, and his vision of another man in Tiemie's "garden" (perhaps her middle-aged, middle-class employer) provokes Jakes to proprietary violence, smashing up Tiemie's possessions as well as her face. Only Tjokkie's vision of his returning father, long presumed dead in the North African campaign in World War II, appears to be wishful thinking. Weighed down by his sense of responsibility, Tjokkie retreats under the Buick, which becomes his suicide weapon, crushing him as he crawls under it and lowers the jack.

While Du Plessis' reading of his own play in terms of "the great myths of death, exile and love," and the work of Nietzsche and Pirandello (Polley 1973: 83–88) may lend this proletarian tale a metaphysical gloss and a European pedigree, this view risks losing sight of the vividly evoked locality in which Tjokkie and Jakes play out their agon. Tjokkie's vision (and Don Lamprecht's trance-like stumble afterward) may invite speculation about the metaphysical dimension of the text but what comes across most powerfully in performance is the physicality of his world. Under François Swart's direction, the performers, especially Lamprecht, Weyers, and Prinsloo, gave their characters bodily weight as well as dynamic presence lacking or only minimally perceptible in the upright bodies and actors of the heroic drama. Certainly, *Siener* depicts a narrow suburban world that seems even narrower now in the hindsight of the new South Africa, but its performance in 1971 revealed a vital, if minority, truth to that world marginalized by the dominant ideology of Afrikaner probity and prosperity.

Where *Siener* portrays a man who is compelled to clairvoyance, *Die Rebellie van Lafras Verwey* deals with a man who, in author Chris Barnard's program notes, "refuses to believe his eyes, turns reason upside down and rises up against reality."[35] Lafras's refusal wells up from a reservoir of resentment against the "washed out [*bleek* or "pale"] bureaucrats" who dismiss him as a mere "second-grade clerk" (Barnard 1971: 3). It also stems from the desire to translate his resentment into revolutionary action, even if the man he treats as his comrade-in-arms is a drug smuggler using him as an unwitting courier. The original radio-play used musical themes, especially Prokofiev's "Kyrie Eleison", to give Lafras a signature forceful enough to encourage audience identification with him. It further blurred the boundaries between the world inside his head and the outside world he refuses to see by using naturalistic sound for plausible dialogue – between Lafras and his boss or fellow clerks, his "secret agent," or Petra, the hapless pregnant woman he befriends – as well as fantasy – from Lafras bellowing commands to an imaginary revolutionary guard in the bathroom at work at the start of the play, to his reverie of a happy life with Petra as the police break down his door at the end.

In suggesting that neither society nor an individual alienated from social norms can absolutely determine the latter's reality, Barnard draws on R. D. Laing's comments on *elusion* – "a relation in which one pretends oneself away from one's original self; then pretends oneself back from this pretense so as to appear to have arrived at the starting point" (Laing 1969: 30) – and on the socially constructed character of normality, "the state of total immersion in one's social fantasy system" (p. 23). Deriving, like col-lusion and il-lusion, from *ludere* [Latin: "play" or "deceive"], *e-lusion* is the attempt to evade an untenable state of alienation through playing a role.[36] The action of the play and the emotional affect encouraged by the musical signature and naturalistic sound suggest that Lafras's normal (if not healthy) state is the state of refusal to which he returns after pretending to be a civil servant. Though manifested by a retreat into a self-created drama, Lafras's role-playing does not create "a world of his own" so much as a "delusionary significant place for himself in the *world of others*" (Laing 1969: 118). It is an anti-social and thus *social* rather than strictly psychological response to a society that appears to have no place for him.

The staging of *Die Rebellie van Lafras Verwey* brought spectators face to face with the line between invisible and visible worlds and the public consequences of crossing it. On the one hand, the troops that Lafras commands at the start of the play are nowhere to be seen. On the other, at the end, he manages to persuade the police outside his door that he has "fifty-odd" men (p. 49) and a machine-gun (p. 52), until they shoot through the door and find his lone body. In between, he continually collides with objects and people that interrupt his reverie and comes literally crashing to the ground. In combination with Annette Engelbrecht (known for portraying abject women, such as Fé in *Siener* and Kietie in *Kanna*) as Petra, Tobie Cronjé's performance emphasized Lafras's social and physical clumsiness while giving his fantasy world tangible weight. The minimal set and chiaroscuro lighting allowed the audience to glimpse the social and economic dimensions of Lafras's distress, from the drab inadequacy of his kitchen utensils to his mortifying exchange with his boss, while shrouding this world in the semi-darkness of Lafras's imagination.[37] The revival at the People's Space (1979) pushed the confusion of inner and outer realities further. By placing the spectators on revolving chairs in the centre of the space, this staging encouraged them to experience the drama around them without allowing them the comforting illusion of the proscenium view.[38]

Like Billy Liar, another clerkly fibber, Lafras is not exactly lying: his rebellion is both substantial and illusory.[39] He subverts the orderly business of bureaucracy by wasting time and misplacing ledgers, in a manner that the Situationists might approve. He pretends to Petra that he can play the piano, only to be humiliated, in a noisy, crowded scene, when a carnival barker and hangers-on tease him about a piano competition (pp. 34–35). This humiliation provokes his declaration of war against "all the bigwigs [*kokkedore*] who make the laws . . . who tread on ordinary guys and who incubate the world's money under their fat behinds" (p. 37) but, echoed in his final cryptic conversation with the agent, it prefigures the collapse of the boundary between his world and the "empty space in the others' world" (Laing 1969: 119) that he had failed to conquer.

In depicting a misfit's attempt to occupy the "other world" of the powerful, at a historical moment when Afrikaners, rather than the English, were now the powerful other, *Die Rebellie van Lafras Verwey* brings to an end the line of plays about alienated, impoverished Afrikaners, bewildered by capitalism and urban life, which began with Gert, the displaced farmer in *As die Tuig Skawe* (1926). Like Gert, Lafras rails against the fat cats of the world, but, where Grosskopf clearly endorsed his protagonist's indictment of rich and rootless Jews, Barnard makes Lafras a victim of his own misguided rebellion. Though *volksontwikkeling* has made Lafras a clerk with a pension rather than an impoverished farmer, he is still at the mercy of powerful agents with whom he cannot identify, even if they are members of the same *volk*. By making Lafras's enemies his own (*volk*) rather than one of the demons of Afrikaner mythology, Barnard short-circuits the usual Afrikaner alibi of blaming the enemy. He suggests that Afrikaner power is as corrupt as its predecessors and thus exposes the mythic and, at this point, anachronistic character, of appeals to a classless *volkseie*. Lafras's alienation is that of a worker as well as an individual subject. His reification as a "cog in the machine" of the civil service (Barnard 1971: 21) and a tool in the hands of the drug syndicate makes of him a "thing." Unlike the reified worker in the marxist narrative, however, who becomes the vanguard of the revolution, Lafras lives and dies according to someone else's script. This drama of an alienated white clerk, which was performed the year before the Soweto uprising, in a period when black unions were on the rise after decades of enforced silence and white affluence had slumped in the wake of the international "oil crisis," looks back on Afrikaner mythic history as well as forward to the present time, when white misfits, now no longer coddled by the sinecure of an Afrikaner national bureaucracy, wander the streets of the Golden City.

Home languages: *Kanna Hy Kô Hystoe* and Africanizing Afrikaans

When Adam Small's *Kanna Hy Kô Hystoe* [Kanna's Coming Home, 1965] received its first subsidized production at PACT's Breytenbach Theatre in Pretoria in 1974, it had already been hailed by writer and critic André Brink as a "high point in Afrikaans drama" (Brink 1986: 168).[40] Brink's praise of *Kanna* as an *Afrikaans* play invited his Afrikaner readers to revise their sense of Afrikaans as a European language by acknowledging the African and other influences on their mother tongue. Written and performed in *Kaaps*, once the lingua franca of colonial Cape Town and later the mother tongue of a few million people known variously as "coloureds" or "brown people," *Kanna* penetrated Afrikanerdom's innermost defenses, by reminding the audience that the mother tongue of the *volk* was not a purely European language but one creolized by African and Asian influences. While the cultural establishment attempted to deflect this challenge by treating *Kaaps* as a quaint dialect and the suffering of the characters as the pathos of an "unforgettable theatrical experience,"[41] without directly confronting the impact of apartheid on their lives or the peculiar Afrikaner ambivalence about the kinship between white and black speakers of Afrikaans, *Kanna's* claim to exemplary *Afrikaans* expression brought white spectators up against this family history.

Kanna draws on many sources, from the European literary tradition to the radio soap operas broadcast by commercial rather than official Afrikaans radio before the introduction of television (in 1976). As a professor at UWC, Small was well placed to negotiate the tricky relationship between the mass culture permeating the lives of his students and their families and the Afrikaans high culture on the university syllabus. Where Afrikaans literary drama of the period focused on male protagonists, whether public heroes like President Steyn in *Die Pluimsaad waai ver* or private individuals in self-inflicted torment, from Bart Harmse in *Die Verminktes* to Tjokkie in *Siener in die Suburbs*, *Kanna* depicts a household held together, sociologically as well as dramaturgically, by a woman. Kanna, the "welfare kid" who escaped the gangs of District Six for the good life in Canada, may be the play's critical outside eye, but at its center is Makiet, mother to Kanna, his brother Diekie, and his sister Kietie, who – in both Charlyn Wessels's performance in the UWC production in coloured Athlone (Figure 5.4) and Wilna Snyman's in the all-white PACT production in Pretoria – dominates the stage as she moves around in her wheelchair and acts as the inside voice of the drama, bearing witness to the family's distress.

Small uses techniques that recall international dramatists from Bertolt Brecht to Tennessee Williams – scene titles, narrative retrospection, music that alternately draws the audience in and holds them at bay – to juxtapose the play's present line of action, namely Kanna's brief return home for Makiet's funeral, with scenes and voices from the family's history. But he also borrows from radio drama the use of changing voices to mark different moments in time and, from soap opera, the fatefulness that permeates most of the characters' sense of their lot, and the heightened, even melodramatic treatment of emotional trauma: from the move to the city to Kietie's subjection to serial rape and Diekie's trial for the murder of his sister's pimp. As Small recognized, melodrama is a risky medium for this play since it might have encouraged the local audience to treat the story as merely a soap opera, and the white audience to reinforce stereotypes about coloured delinquency wrapped in the picturesque garb of resilient but irresponsible ghetto dwellers.[42]

To counter what he saw as the political liability of excess emotion, Small as director used a simple set of black flats, marked with slogans from District Six, which juxtaposed political aspirations – "Freedom Now" – with quips on local culture – "You are now entering fairyland."[43] He also encouraged understated

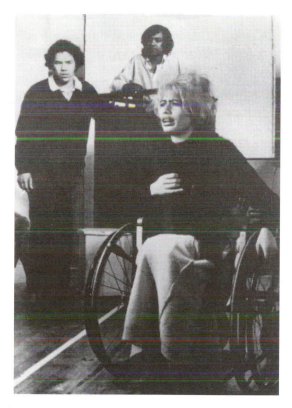

Figure 5.4 Charlyn Wessels center stage in *Kanna Hy Kô Hystoe* by Adam Small; Dramsoc, UWC, December 1972. *Source*: *S'ketsh*, Winter 1973

performances, especially by Norman Thomas as Kanna, to offset the high emotion of characters like Kietie (Lynette Thomas) and Diekie (Jonathan Sam), and alternately separated and fused music and speech to frame the emotional speeches. Juxtaposing the play's inside chronicler, the street preacher, Jakop, and the outsider commentator, Kanna, the opening scene – "O, Wáar is Moses?" – establishes the pervading tension between identification and critique.[44] Reminiscent of the Dixieland and *marabi* fusions of the New Year Cape Carnivals, the guitar music accompanying Jakop's song ironizes his appeal to Moses as a savior and a "murderer" (Small 1965: 7), prefiguring Diekie's vain attempt to restore his family's honor, while at the same time evoking the forgetful affirmation of the carnival. Kanna's prosaic account of his progress from poverty in Cape Town to prosperity in Canada highlights, with each spot on a new character, the sacrifices made on his behalf, as it darkens the irony of the family's hope that Kanna will return to save them.

Instead, the succeeding scenes show Kanna's equivocal attempts to explain himself and his family by exposing their suffering to public view and by redescribing lives lived in *Kaaps* in "high" Afrikaans. In doing so, he faces resistance from the others who don't want him to tell the story because "we are not *that* bad" (p. 32). This tension is played out not only between Kanna's measured narration of Kietie's first rape and Jakop's oracular testifying to her suffering but between Kanna's apparently neutral (but, for these characters, alienating) formal Afrikaans, and Jakop's vernacular reformulation of Dutch Reformed liturgy (pp. 33–34):

Nou vrinne [vriende]	Now friends
Die Here het gebring	The Lord has brought his miracles
an my sy wonnerwerke [wonderwerke] oek [ook]	To me also
Hy het gevra wat's in my hand	He asked what's in my hand
In my hand was my kitaar [gitaar]	In my hand is my guitar
Kô [kom] laat ons sing.	Come let us sing.

Not only the dialect variation that bears witness to the Eastern as well as Western influences on Afrikaans but also the use of the guitar, instrument of secular entertainment, to accompany a hymn, challenges the authority of an Afrikaner Nationalist creed obsessed with the separation of sacred and profane. In the face of the violence of Kietie's second rape, in this case by Poena, the gangbanger who claims her, Jakop, the "oriekel van God," is struck down and the characters deprived of effective speech. The scene ends in cognitive as well as auditory dissonance as Kietie's mad laughter overlaps the music of the hymn and the light shrinks from Jakop's motionless body to the glow of Kanna's cigarette as he looks silently on (pp. 37–38).

Caught in the discrepancy between the lives of the family, experienced in *Kaaps*, and the rationalizing account of that experience in officially "pure" Afrikaans, the characters in this drama are trapped by the apartheid bureaucracy that makes the rules of translation. The next scene, "Goodbye Diekie," dramatizes the impossibility of translation and thus of common humanity in a society whose official ear is deafened by the discourse of racial degeneration. The invisible judge, whose voice responds indifferently to the family's attempt to explain the social causes and personal motivation leading up to Diekie's fatal assault on Poena, hears only dishonesty in the plea, alongside the family's admission of dependence on income from Kietie's prostitution and Poena's drug-dealing. In his absence, Poena is only a shadowy object for Diekie's growing anger and frustration at his own helplessness, directed to a distant Kanna: "Kanna, Poena was a real piece of trash [was 'n regte vylgoed (vuilgoed) gewees] . . . I was beside myself" (p. 41). When Makiet attempts to translate Kietie's death into the reassuring language of sentimental melodrama: "It was a nice funeral. . . . People were very fond of Kietie" (p. 48), Diekie tells Kanna bluntly, "they were just inquisitive [nieskierag (nuuskierig)], and Ma wasn't at the funeral" (p. 41). Diekie's moment as the voice of objectivity is brief, however, as he finds himself in the defendant's box, where he "suddenly stands to attention, his voice stammering" (p. 48) and, over the course of the rest of the scene, is reduced to a fragmentary and panicked defense until condemned to hang.

The judge's remoteness from Makiet and Diekie and from the increasingly desperate emotion of their conflicting narratives of mitigation is matched by Kanna's – in this scene as he comments from the sidelines and intervenes only too late with an appeal to "mitigating circumstances" (p. 53) in the language of the court rather than family feeling, and in the next, when the present action of the play finally brings him face to face with the family gathered at Makiet's funeral. His appeal for mitigation is complicated on the one hand by the impersonation of coloured stereotypes like the inquisitive neighbor who treats the family as a spectacle, "Look at [kiek (kyk) vir] Poena at night [and] the men that Poena sends. Look at Kietie in the room" (p. 54), and, on the other, by his concluding generalization about Diekie's case in the language of the court: "If they allowed mitigating circumstances [versagting] for Diekie, they would have to do the same for thousands" (p. 57). In the final scene, although Kanna finally speaks *Kaaps* to his cousins on the way to Makiet's funeral in the soulless Cape Flats township where they now live, having been "removed" from District Six, his remarks about Canada and their embarrassed comments on their lives appear to be uttered in different languages. Only the encounter with Makiet, apparently dead but vividly present in her wheelchair on stage, pulls Kanna away from his outsider role and into the family room, as he weeps for her death and his loss of family feeling.

In these final moments, the director and the players do not shrink from pathos but neither do they wallow in it. To be sure, response to the local production at the Nico Malan Nursing College (ironically compared to the whites-only Nico Malan State Theatre in Cape Town), included laughing and weeping with the characters, but the public display of identification with soical as well as individual conditions made this reaction more than private affect. Local critics also suggested that, by representing a dysfunctional community as the consequence of segregation and poverty, even without an explicit indictment of the system, the play lit a "fuse" in local black audiences and earned broader support than militant plays directed by and for intellectuals.[45] The pathos of *Kanna Hy Kô Hystoe*, as well as its affinity with radio melodrama, encouraged these audiences to identify the situation and, crucially, the form of representation as their own without, however, blinding them with tears.

Displayed before a white audience at PACT's Breytenbach Theatre in Pretoria, *Kanna Hy Kô Hystoe* had a more ambiguous reception. Asserting the universality of a story of a "people trapped in living conditions that could affect *anyone*," director Louis van Niekerk offered no acknowledgment of the fact that whites in South Africa were protected from such living conditions by the franchise and by job and housing laws.[46] Van Niekerk's appeal to universality evaded the political implications of cultural if not political equality in Brink's call for an integrated Afrikaans and relapsed instead into the racialist commonplaces of apartheid lore, claiming that "their language tells us that they are coloured" and that "this language" is irreducibly "different" from "other ['European'] languages, such as Afrikaans, Italian, Spanish." Afrikaans reviewers identified the play's theme as "Coloureds' problems with communication and adaptation to the city,"[47] forgetting the structurally similar problems of Afrikaners a generation before and the fact that coloureds lived under official discrimination from which Arikaners had benefited. The relatively progressive *Rand Daily Mail* pointedly hailed the production as PACT's first by a *black* playwright, anticipating Small's identification of himself as black, and emphasized his criticism of the inadequate facilities for cultural activities in coloured communities.[48]

Praising the "bruinmens-egheid" ["brown authenticity"] of the white actors,[49] white critics unwittingly reiterated a long tradition of blackface minstrelsy, in which white performers have enacted their love – and theft – of black culture by claiming to re-present it more authentically than blacks themselves. As Eric Lott notes in a comparable American context, this "love and theft" articulated white working-class desire for the vitality of black culture as well as their fear of economic competition from black workers. At the same time, this act of expropriation reinforced the difference between Afrikaans and *Kaaps*, white and coloured. Struggling to exorcize the dreaded desire for kinship that had manifested itself in the miscegenation dramas, the PACT production was caught between melodrama and blackface. While Wilna Snyman gave Makiet emotional depth and social verisimilitude, seconded by Don Lamprecht who replaced Pieter Joubert in the role of Kanna, the overall tone was set rather by Annette Engelbrecht's hysterical Kietie and the chorus of smirking musicians and layabouts in the background (Figure 5.5). This picture evokes the stereotypes of coloured delinquency that Small wished to escape and thus reinforces the habit of white audiences to see coloureds as different from themselves.

In the years after the white production of *Kanna* and before the Soweto uprising in 1976, Afrikaners became belatedly more willing to embrace coloureds as brothers – or at least as step-brothers – in the *taal*. In 1961, Small had spoken as a "voice in the wilderness" calling for brotherhood between white and "brown" speakers of Afrikaans (Small 1961: 23) against the skepticism of Afrikaner and coloured intellectuals who doubted that *Kaaps* could rise to the level of poetry (February 1981: 94–96), and against the objections of political activists working for solidarity between coloureds and Africans (p. 98). In 1974, on the other hand, he spoke to a generation of Afrikaner intellectuals fearful for the future of their language. However willing they were to include *Kaaps* under the rubric of Afrikaans, even liberal Afrikaners like the writer Jan Rabie presumed that black Afrikaans speakers would follow the longstanding Afrikaner crusade against English as an "international whiteman's language" (Rabie 1985: 32), apparently forgetting the likewise longstanding association of English education and emancipation in South Africa and the intense opposition to Afrikaans education among the black majority. Writing in response to Rabie, UWC professor and self-described "Afrikaans-speaking *Afrikaan*" (Gerwel 1985: 43), Jake Gerwel reminded

Figure 5.5 "A chorus of smirks and layabouts" in PACT's all-white production of *Kanna Hy Kô Hystoe*; directed by Louis van Niekerk. *Source and permission*: PACT

him that Afrikaners had alienated other Afrikaans speakers with their attempt to purge the language of its black history. By 1984, when the country was convulsed by civil unrest, Small wrote bluntly as a *black* Afrikaans speaker, arguing that Afrikaaners could not speak of brotherhood in the *taal* while they withheld civil rights from black South Africans, Afrikaans-speaking or otherwise. Some young white Afrikaans writers subjected icons of Afrikanerdom to a much more savage critique than the 1960s generation, as in Koos Kombuis's (André Letoit's) parody of "Die Stem" (1985): ". . . ruis die stem van al die squatters/van ons land Azania (comes the voice of all the squatters/of our land Azania)".[50]

In the wake of the Soweto uprising, in which urban African students decisively rejected the state's attempt to impose Afrikaans-medium instruction on their schools, serious study of the black history of Afrikaans was stymied by the arrogance of its white defenders. Black Afrikaans nonetheless found informal expression in song, carnival, and theatre and institutional support from black intellectuals, such as Small and Gerwel at UWC. Under their guidance, members of UWC-Dramsoc went on to found the Cape Flats Players in the 1970s and the Peninsula Theatre in the 1980s, which performed in *Kaaps* for audiences in the Western Cape. These companies produced socially critical plays, from Small's *What about de Lô?* [Law] (1973) to Melvin Witbooi's *Dit Sal Die Blêrrie Dag Wies* [That'll Be the Bloody Day, performed 1984], about the demolition of District Six (Smith 1990: 30–36). By the mid-1980s, this movement had received a certain legitimacy, marked by UWC's symposia on Black Afrikaans writers and even occasional African writers in Afrikaans, such as Sandile Dikeni, a Xhosa-speaking poet and law student at UWC. This legitimacy was debated in periodicals like *Die Vrye Weekblad* and *Die Suid-Afrikaan*, which examined the question of Afrikaans' hybridity, as well as its uncertain future as one of ten indigenous official languages arrayed against the likewise offical but globally dominant English.[51]

Twilight of the idols: the ends of Afrikanerdom

As this chapter has shown, Afrikaans has been put to many contradictory uses, from racist propaganda to the representation of the disenfranchised, but it is in the intimate drama of family life that the public and private strains *on* and *of* Afrikaans have made themselves most intensely felt. For the most part, these strains have manifested themselves in the tension between the conventions of the naturalist milieu and character and the allegorical tendency of the action that threatens to burst the bounds of this convention. Thirty years after *Putsonderwater* was condemned by the Afrikaner establishment, *Diepe Grond* [Still Waters Run Deep] (first performed 1985; published De Wet 1991), the first of Reza De Wet's Gothic *sprokies* [tales] on Afrikaans themes, took the same stage at Rhodes that had accommodated *Putsonderwater* and raised a similar storm.[52] Only this time, *volkseenheit* had given away to the dissidence of a younger, more worldly and, in some cases, more critical generation of Afrikaners.[53]

Dedicated to Bartho Smit, *Diepe Grond* recalls *Putsonderwater* in its setting – a desolate farm parched by drought and neglect – and in its central female character: Soekie, a "child-woman" whose "naive spontaneity is matched by ripe sensuality" (De Wet 1991: 12). But, where Smit situates his characters in a public village square, De Wet keeps hers inside a squalid, once-wealthy farmhouse, indifferent to the outside, and, where *Putsonderwater* justifies its central murder as the panicked response of a child trapped in a woman's body, *Diepe Grond* revels in its demonic travesty of Afrikaner probity. Soekie and her brother Frikkie inhabit a single, flea-ridden room, protected from the outside by their black nanny, Alina, and occupy their time by punishing and cajoling each other in the roles of their Calvinist parents in a manner (in the performances by Susan Coetzer and Dawid Minaar at the Market Theatre) redolent of Sam Shephard and Flannery O'Connor rather than Cocteau's *enfants terribles*. When their game is interrupted by a lawyer who has come at the bidding of their relatives to find out why the pair have been selling off family heirlooms for "paraffin and toilet paper" (p. 27), brother and sister begin by playing "grown-up," serving tea and mouthing words of concern about the farm, only to turn first to seduction and later to murder by *sjambok* (an Afrikaner "cat o' nine tails") when the lawyer proves unwilling to play along.[54] Like her predecessor, De Wet courts allegory but, where Smith is wedded to the illumination of the Afrikaner condition, De Wet flirts with it, cunningly inviting the Market audience schooled by a decade of political

126

theatre to look for meaning in the still water, only to trouble its surface just as a message seems within reach.

It is ironic that only now, when majority rule has stripped Afrikaans of its hold on power, is it possible to dramatize directly the effect of that power on the nation and the family. Deon Opperman's *Donkerland* (1996), a revisionist dramatization of the rise and fall of Afrikaner nationalism through the eyes and lives of an Afrikaans faimily, the De Witts, and their farm, Donkerland (Dark – and, by implication, rich – Land) from 1838 to 1994, stands on the cusp of this transformation. On the one hand, *Donkerland* may be the last Afrikaans play on this epic scale (five hours) to receive state subsidy. On the other, Opperman broke with Afrikaner "sacred history" that had sustained even mildly critical playwrights like W. A. de Klerk and Louw. Produced by PACT at the Afrikaans-language *Kleinkaroofees* and revived at the English-language Grahamstown Festival, the play reminds members of both privileged groups just how linked their pasts and presents have been and just how intimate have been the consequences of domination of the majority. As David Graver wrote of the Grahamstown performance,

> Opperman transforms the history of his people from a heroic tale of righteous battles and triumphs to a series of . . . conflicts first with an English enemy they cannot conquer and then with black compatriots whose humanity they refuse to recognize.
>
> (Graver 1997: 56)

The fluid scenography and the assignment of multiple roles to each character takes the dramaturgy out of the confines of domestic naturalism and allows for the juxtaposition of familial and national drama. Although accused of "one-sidedness" and of "picking at old wounds," Opperman opens new vistas on Afrikaner history, by portraying rebels from the tribal cause in the person of a proletarianized and radicalized teacher (played by the same actor, André Odendaal, as the original patriarch to make the kinship inescapable), by dramatizing the sexual intimacy with and exploitation of black dependants, which created the black Afrikaner, and by confronting, in the humbling loss of the farm, the fact that the "klein strepie mensdom" [the small trace of humanity] of the Afrikaner will not direct the future of South Africa.[55]

With this history in view, we should not be surprised, returning to the Soweto students' rebellion against Afrikaans, to find a sharp turn away from "brown" or even "black Afrikaans" to black solidarity across ethnic lines. But, while this act of renaming should be recognized as a tactical necessity in a civil war and the struggle for the "historical and ethical *right to signify*" (Bhabha 1992: 49), it cannot, any more than the dismissive term "so-called coloured," simply reduce lived experience and "ordinary" signifying to a mere "artifact of policy" (Simone 1994: 162–63). It is the personal and generalizable history behind the name "Afrikaans-speaking *Afrikaan*" that supersedes "coloured" as well as the name itself that challenges the "teleology of nouns" (Bhabha 1992: 54) and that suggests, perhaps, that the *adjective* rather than the noun is the index of a postcolonial affiliation. Gerwel's childhood experience of Afrikaans as the language of his sharecropper family as against the English landowners in his native Eastern Cape (Gerwel 1985: 45) remind us that affiliations under apartheid did not always answer to black or white only. The hybrid identity that emerges from these affiliations is not a degenerate but a stronger plant generated by multiple strains. While the attempt to strip Afrikaans of its association with white supremacy and to relocate black and white Afrikaans-speakers as the third-largest linguistic group (after isiZulu and isiXhosa) in South Africa may become a minority pursuit in the future, the attempt itself serves as a caution against preemptive insistence on a uniform national character in present-day South Africa. More immediately, however, we should examine the impact of black consciousness and the theatre associated with it in the years leading up to the Soweto uprising. That is the subject of the next chapter.

6

THE DRAMA OF BLACK
CONSCIOUSNESSES

In July 1972, the South African Black Theatre Union (SABTU) was announced during a festival sponsored by the Theatre Council of Natal (TECON) at Orient Hall in Durban. The program included South African drama, such as *The Coat* (1966), devised by the Serpent Players in collaboration with Athol Fugard, *The Lahnee's Pleasure* (first performed 1972; published Govender 1977), by Ronnie Govender of the Shah Theatre in Durban and poetry presented by the Mihloti Group from Alexandra Township near Johannesburg, and Dramsoc of the University of the Western Cape (UWC), as well as significant additions from abroad, such as the University of Natal (Black Section) production of *Encounter*, about the Kenyan Mau Mau, by the Indian/Ugandan writer Kuldip Sondhi and TECON's production of *Requiem for Brother X*, by the African-American playwright William Wellington Mackey. The organizers, the Black Peoples' Convention (BPC) and the black South African Students' Association (SASO) intended the program to highlight the range of cultural production dismissed as "non-white" by the state and to promote political unity of Africans, coloureds, and South Africans of Indian descent under the banner of black identity. They challenged not only apartheid but also the presumption of well-meaning whites, especially students associated with the National Union of South African Students (NUSAS), to lead the struggle against it.

In their insistence on the key role of conscientization in the liberation of black people and on the autonomy of black institutions as an a priori for black emancipation from institutionalized racism before blacks could meet whites on equal terms, SASO and the Black Consciousness Movement (BCM) more generally drew on Frantz Fanon's analysis of the colonized mentality, Paolo Freire's pedagogy of the oppressed, and the arguments for black autonomy in the United States articulated by Stokely Carmichael (Kwame Ture) and Malcolm X, as well as on African leaders, especially Kwame Nkrumah of Ghana. Also significant was the indirect legacy of Africanists in the ANC and the PAC, both banned in 1960. But, where the PAC had stressed the priority of indigenous Africans, SASO's leaders included South Africans of Indian descent and its founding president, Stephen Biko, argued for an inclusive interpretation of black consciousness "not as a matter of pigmentation" but rather as a "reflection of a mental attitude" defying white supremacism (Biko 1978: 48).[1] SASO also argued that establishing black-only institutions was not a surrender to apartheid norms of "separate development" but rather a necessary means of establishing black self-respect (Biko 1978: 71–72).

The BCM's stress on conscientization has led some to criticize the movement for emphasizing the mentality of intellectuals at the expense of the material hardship of ordinary black South Africans (Kavanagh 1985; Frederikse 1990; Sole 1987) and others to argue that the movement's focus on "black manhood" marginalizes the contributions of women (Driver 1990; McClintock 1991). SASO's activities from 1969–74 included rural and urban community programs for literacy, health, building infrastructure and adult education (see *Black Review*, 1972–79). Their cultural activities, however, reflected an intellectual disdain not only for official "tribal culture," but also for black commercial entertainers like Gibson Kente (Kraai 1973: 11). The TECON festival of July 1972 included popular forms that had been sanctioned by political engagement, such as the poetry of lament and resistance by Mihloti (*imihloti* or "tears") and Adam Small's "Ode to the Blackman" (Dramsoc UWC), but most groups offered plays whose dense English dialogue and abstract theory were not immediately accessible to most township dwellers (Kavanagh 1985). Nonetheless, although the conscientization plots of plays like Sondhi's *Encounter* (produced by UNICUS 1972; published Sondhi 1968) and Mthuli Shezi's *Shanti* (produced by the People's Educational Theatre [PET], 1973; published Shezi 1981), spoke primarily to a black student elite, the very fact of their performance constituted defiance of the state and was recognized as such by township audiences in Soweto, (Indian) Lenasia and (coloured) Coronationville. TECON, PET, and other similar groups survived only a few years before their members were tried for treason in 1975, but their "theatre of determination" (Khoapa 1973: 201) would set the tone for much of the theatre in the 1970s and 1980s.

Much has been made in recent debates about South African theatre of the distinction between a theatre of "protest" (associated with the portrayal of suffering and the appeal to humanist commiseration, especially in the work of Fugard) and a more militant successor, variously called the "theatre of resistance," "defiance," or "determination" associated with post-Soweto township activism (Steadman 1991; Mda 1995). Although resistance theatre has usually been associated with the practices of workshop improvisation, direct address, and political statement (see chapter 7), its practitioners were less interested in developing a clearly defined genre or set of performance techniques, than in creating theatre that might challenge the status quo. Thus BCM's "theatre of defiance" could include melodrama alongside agitprop, when either or both served the organization's goals of black self-representation, even though BCM pronouncements tended in theory to dismiss melodrama as reactionary. Although focused primarily on those institutions and performances that adhered explicitly to the Black Consciousness Movement in the 1970s, the discussion here takes into account performances outside its direct orbit that registered its influence, such as Kente's musical melodrama, *Too Late!* (1975) and Ronnie Govender's satirical comedy, *The Lahnee's Pleasure* (1972/77), which conveyed BCM themes of black empowerment through melodramatic or comic scenarios with more popular appeal. Hence the title of this chapter refers not to a clearly demarcated genre or school of drama but rather to the dramatic tensions among different and not always compatible themes, techniques, and institutional structures appropriated by Black Consciousness.

Beats, Black Power, and the rhythm of violence

SABTU members were not the first proponents of a theatre of defiance. But, where the African National Theatre's work like *The Rude Criminal* drew on international communist agitprop, SABTU plays like *Shanti* attempted to combine the theme of anti-colonial rebellion, the rhetoric of black consciousness, and the desire of young intellectuals to see themselves as the vanguard of the armed struggle. This attempt was itself not new. *The Rhythm of Violence* (1964), written by Lewis Nkosi in exile, was banned in South Africa and thus not directly available to SABTU. It is significant in part because it is the first play by a South African to deal with the frustrations of young black intellectuals drawn to political violence and in part because its ironic treatment offers an illuminating contrast to the single-minded militancy of *Shanti* and other plays produced by SABTU affiliates.

The play deals with a group of students anticipating the success of their plan to blow up the Johannesburg City Council and a National Party rally inside the building on the stroke of midnight. Although the first act opens several hours earlier as two policemen trade racist insults about an off-stage demonstration and its chief speaker, the action focuses on the private behavior of that speaker, the charismatic Gama [name], his friends and "his" women, and especially on the conflict between Gama and his younger brother T(h)ula [quiet]. Unlike his militant brother, Tula is moved to try to defuse the bomb by the plight of an Afrikaans woman, Sarie Marais (whose name recalls the romantic patriotism of the song of the same name), whose father is attending the rally to tender his resignation; their interaction provides a sentimental contrast to the ironic banter of the others. At the end, the irony and sentimentality of the second act give way to the display of state power in the third, as the weeping Sarie is torn from Tula's dead body by policemen determined to extract information about the other saboteurs.

Recent South African readings of this unperformed and, in the historical context, unperformable play have argued for its "direct experiential link with life lived under the apartheid regime" (Orkin 1991: 109) and thus for its exemplary status as a "timely index" of a shift from "protest to resistance" (Steadman 1990: 217). While still in South Africa, shortly before Sharpeville, Nkosi had indeed hinted at an imminent political explosion (Nkosi 1965: 8–9). After his departure in 1961 on a one-way exit visa to Harvard University, he remained aware of events in South Africa, including sabotage committed by Umkhonto we

Sizwe [spear of the nation] and Poqo [pure], affiliated, respectively, with the ANC and PAC. Although written and published in the United States, *The Rhythm of Violence* catches the dangerous mix of arrogance and racial panic in the reactions of Afrikaner police to well-spoken black South Africans and also draws on the rhetoric of violent resistance; however, its atmosphere is redolent less of sustained commitment than of the frustration, recklessness, and whimsy of student rebellion, closer perhaps to the African Resistance Movement (ARM) than to the PAC.[2] Gama's speech in the first act, from the opening slogan – "from Cape to Cairo, from Morocco to Mozambique, Africans are shouting Freedom" (Nkosi 1964: 71) – to the taunting critique of ANC inaction, certainly echoes the PAC line.[3] The second act, however, displays the witty but often superficial enthusiasms of the bohemian set. The Hillbrow Club with its "avant-garde pictures [and] strong African motifs," its pictures of student riots and posters proclaiming "INTER-RACIAL SEX IS A HISTORICAL FACT" alongside "FREEDOM IN OUR LIFETIME" (p. 79), suggests less a national liberation front than a party where flirtation alternates with histrionic speeches about "the BOMB" to produce an inconsistent mix of political bravado, casual sexism, and wanton self-parody.

Notwithstanding its South African theme, the language of *The Rhythm of Violence* resonates with American rhythms. While it anticipates the BCM's interest in African-American culture in the 1970s, Nkosi's play dwells less on the politics of Black Power than on the counter-cultural appeal of the cool blackman. All his characters use American idiom, from the students – who might plausibly affect Beat lingo – to the Afrikaans policemen – who definitely would not. This American dimension does not invalidate the significance of the text for South Africa, but it does challenge those critics who see the play as an index of post-Sharpeville activism to look more closely at the urbane irony that complicates the play's engagement with politics. Although undoubtedly moved by the civil rights drama of African-American playwrights like Loften Mitchell, whose *Land Beyond the River* (1957) dramatized the struggle for equal education in the wake of the Supreme Court's *Brown* vs *Board of Education* ruling, Nkosi was a keener observer of the Beat scene, with its interracial bohemia and stylish hipster rebellion (Nkosi 1965: 65). Black Beat poet Ted Joans, whose celebration of sexual conquest Nkosi quotes with pleasure, may echo as persistently in *The Rhythm of Violence* as the voice of Potlako Leballo, firebrand spokesman for the PAC in exile.[4]

More than just exotic flavor, Joans brings to *The Rhythm of Violence* the place and occasion of bohemian rebellion. Joans's poems or, as he preferred to call them, "show-off stunts" for "Bohemian Greenwich Village, USA" (Wilentz 1960: 101), use bebop rhythm and exoticizing stereotypes as a vehicle for sly digs at white would-be bohemians. His most notorious phrase – "White America, my hand is on your thigh" – quoted by Nkosi in *Home and Exile* (1965: 65), conjures up the aggressive "Negro" persona of Norman Mailer's provocative essay, "The White Negro" (1957) (Joans 1961: 33), rather than the militants of the civil rights movement. But where Mailer sees in "the Negro" the "wise primitive in a giant jungle" (Mailer 1992: 593), responding to "life on the margin between totalitarianism and democracy" with instant gratification and spontaneous violence (Mailer 1992: 589), Joans ironically impersonates the stereotype. This strategy shapes the party banter in *Rhythm of Violence*; Gama plays up to the epithet "dark and lascivious Moor" (Nkosi 1964: 82) tossed to him by his white side-kick, Jimmy; Jimmy is in turn mocked when his African girlfriend, Kitty, dismisses his praise for the "mysterious and splendid African woman" as a "myth for sex-starved white men" (p. 83). The irony in the impersonation is inconsistent, however. While Nkosi puts the racial stereotypes in quotation marks, his treatment of the men's propensity for slapping women and the women's "melting" response suggests a casual presupposition of patriarchal domination as natural behavior. On the other hand, the histrionic treatment of the policemen seems merely a "show-off stunt." Inspired perhaps by Joans's call to anarchic mimicry – "Let's play something horrible. You be Hitler . . . you be Strijdom of South Africa" (Joans 1961: 9), Nkosi has Jan, one of the policemen who had bluntly insulted Tula moments before, act out the role of a "Native leader" (Nkosi 1964: 77), whom he calls Lundula ("thoughtless" or "conceited"), to the point where he is apparently "completely identified with the African cause" (p. 79).

These ambiguous impersonations beg the question of the play's implied audience. Where the banter between friends might be seen as "colonial mimicry," in the sense defined by Homi Bhabha, as a "mode of appropriation as well as resistance" (Bhabha 1986: 181), "a strategy of subversion that turns the gaze of the discriminated back upon the eye of power" (p. 173), and thus as a way for hypothetical performers of this play to speak indirectly to South African activists, the policeman possessed by "Lundula" is not so easily brought in line. The irreducibility of this role-playing to a single political line may add to the literary interest of the play, but it is hard to see how it might have mobilized an audience to political action. For all its evocation of post-Sharpeville politics, *The Rhythm of Violence* is closer to the bravado of the Beats. Its mimicry, albeit ironic, of the macho American hipster owes as much to the style of *Drum* as to the masculinist cast of the PAC, but its characters resemble the "situations" more than they do members of a political vanguard. The value of the play thus lies less in any representation of political militancy in the post-Sharpeville period than its dramatization of the dilemmas of intellectuals, only partly prepared for the demands of a potentially revolutionary situation.

Black Theatre Union/white institutional unconscious?

While the text of *The Rhythm of Violence* harked back to the situation of the "situation" and the ambivalent man-in-exile, the performances staged by SABTU reflected its members' understanding of themselves as "organic intellectuals," men (and a few women) who had emerged from the "rising subaltern classes" to act in the interests of the masses rather than traditional alienated intellectuals (Gramsci 1971: 6). SABTU welcomed the industrial and service workers of Serpent Players, but its members were mainly students from the segregated universities established under the auspices of the so-called Extension of Education Act (1959), such as the "Indian" University of Durban-Westville, the "coloured" University of the Western Cape, the University of Zululand and the medical school for black students at the otherwise white University of Natal.[5] SABTU regarded theatre as a "means to assist Blacks to reassert their pride, dignity, group identity and solidarity," (*PET Newsletter*, 2) in part by recovering a history of "black civiliza-tions" from India to South America and in part by offering "positive representa-tions of the needs, aspirations, and goals of Black people as seen by Blacks now" (Kraai 1973: 11). Borrowing from Freire's *Pedagogy of the Oppressed* the concept of conscientization, "the process of learning to perceive social and political and economic contradictions and to take action against the oppressive elements of reality" (Freire 1972: 16), they hoped, as Stephen Biko put it, to transform "Blacks' ability to assess and improve their own influence on themselves and their environment" (Woods 1986: 145).

The positions espoused by SASO and other BCM groups were not always consistent, however. Their desire to present positive images of black solidarity and precolonial society did not always match their claim to train blacks to perceive contradictions in their actions and aspirations to emancipation and modernity. Critics, especially those associated with Marxism, have argued that the BCM's emphasis on racism as the fundamental determinant of oppression in South Africa and on solidarity among people of color as the primary means of combating this oppression, misrepresents the structural hegemony of capitalism (Kavanagh 1985: 160) and ignores differences between different groups identified as "Black" as well as differences between classes, even among Africans, the least privileged South Africans (Sole 1984: 72). More contentiously, one Marxist critic has claimed that the BCM represented an *antimodern* tendency and that its leaders, such as Biko, were by virtue of rural origins and intellectual status cut off from a newly insurgent industrial proletariat (Kavanagh 1985: 159).

This critique overshoots its mark in the claim that Black Consciousness intel-lectuals like Biko had no meaningful contact with a black working class.[6] Biko and his colleagues in the Black Community Programs, which published *Black Review* (1972–79), worked to build educational and social organizations among rural as well as urban Africans and also endorsed the efforts of the Institute for Industrial Education, founded – in part by NUSAS's Wage Commission – to give legal and strategic advice to black unions (Gwala 1974: 173–74).[7] They matched this practice with an analysis of the racial inflection of class structure in South Africa: "white workers cannot be regarded as genuine workers so long as they hide behind job reservation, discriminating wages, discriminating trade unions and the general pool of privileges open to whites in South Africa" (Khoapa 1973: 45). This analysis pointed out that most South Africans experienced economic power as white power. As Fanon wrote (and SASO undoubtedly read):

> In the colonies, the economic substructure is also a superstructure. . .
> you are rich because you are white; you are white because you are rich.

This is why Marxist analysis should always be slightly stretched every time we have to do with the colonial problem.

(Fanon 1968: 29).

Fanon's reminder that even the meanest white person in a colony enjoys ruling class privilege as a white echoes in Biko's retort to white radicals: "They tell us that the situation is a class struggle rather than a racial one. Let them go to Van Tonder in the Free State and tell him this" (Biko 1978: 89). Biko's critique of the piecemeal and individualistic advancement of token blacks (1978: 89–92) drew on the arguments of African-American activists, especially Malcolm X and Stokely Carmichael. The latter argued in 1966 that the "integration of individual 'acceptable Negroes' did not change the structure of institutional racism" (Carmichael 1968: 125–26).[8] In Biko's writing, at least, the primary focus on racism as the source and vehicle of oppression is less a matter of principle than a matter of strategy, a means of unifying and mobilizing different disenfranchised groups against the apartheid state (Steadman 1985a: 172).

BCM's cultural work also aspired to reach black people of all classes but reflected the tastes of SABTU's university-educated leaders. If we follow the repertoire of TECON, SABTU's longest-lasting affiliate, from its founding in 1969 to its banning in 1973, we can see a shift from literary interpretation toward political performances, but this shift is not as singular as its proponents would have it. Rather, tensions between the conscientization and entertainment remain unresolved. This is not to deny the political impact of these performances, but rather to suggest that this impact is best understood in the context of multiple and not always compatible influences. In the first instance, TECON, founded by Srini and Sumboornam (Sam) Moodley and other students at the University of Durban-Westville, benefited from the example of Indic theatre groups (of Indian origin) such as the Shah Academy (founded 1965) and the Avon Theatre Group (1966) and the relative social and economic stability of the Indian middle classes. Indians were disenfranchised and denied full educational, social and economic mobility, as were all black South Africans, but their exemption from the pass laws and from the punitive fiction of "tribal" identity, their education in English, and their greater access to capital made a certain identification with metropolitan English culture more plausible. The Shah Theatre Academy was founded under the aegis of Krisha Shah, the Indian-born New York director who brought his production of *The King of the Dark Chamber* by Rabindranath Tagore to South Africa in 1961 and returned in 1963 to conduct workshops on predominantly Western theatre techniques (Naidoo 1997: 39). Under the "shadow of the Shah," Academy members favored realist drama rather than the Indian epics that had entertained their parents (Schauffer 1994: 8–18), although they also produced satirical revues in a format familiar to general Indian audiences.

It is therefore not surprising that TECON's first production was *Look Back in Anger*, John Osborne's portrait of a would-be rebel as angry young man. Their next production, *In the Heart of Negritude* (1970), featured the poetry of Aimé Césaire and

Léopold Senghor, poets who had been formed as much by the avant-garde in Paris as by their origins in Martinique and Senegal, respectively, and thus drew on a thoroughly metropolitan variant of Black Consciousness.[9] Nonetheless, TECON's contribution to the 1972 festival, *Requiem for Brother X*, William Wellington Mackey's "dramatic dialogue about black people trapped in the [American] ghetto" (Mackey 1986: 325), suggests a closer engagement with a black vernacular idiom, albeit American, while their best-known production, *Antigone in '71*, a South African adaptation of Jean Anouilh's modern version of Sophocles' *Antigone*, introduced, albeit under classical cover, the theme of militant opposition to an oppressive state. In the early 1970s, black intellectual interest in this theme was sharpened by the civil war in Mozambique, where Frelimo, the Front for the Liberation of Mozambique, was gaining ground against the Portuguese colonists. The domestic political atmosphere was also heating up as the white, state-appointed administrators of the black universities responded to student protests against apartheid in general and discriminatory educational policy in particular by closing down the universities and detaining student leaders.[10]

The festival as a whole registered the impact of these events and the desire of its participants to conscientize their audience through dramatizing militant resistance. The project of conscientization clearly informed the work of most groups, from Serpent Players' adaptation of Camus' *The Just* (also known as *The Terrorists*) to the poetry of Mihloti,[11] but only Kuldip Sondhi's *Encounter*, directed by Sam Moodley (who was also active in TECON), for the University of Natal–Black Section (UNICUS) dealt directly with anticolonial insurrection in Africa. It dramatized an encounter between British colonial soldiers and Mau Mau guerrillas that ends in the guerrillas' favor, and inspired the best-known play of the movement, Mthuli Shezi's *Shanti*, which was produced by PET and later by TECON in 1973. *Encounter* was a significant choice because it was written by a playwright of Indian origin who identified with the cause of African national liberation. Its naturalistic dramaturgy, which focused on the private hopes and fears of the protagonists, and the use of extended dialogue to move the plot along – from the English Lt. Dewey arguing with his settler subordinate Paddy to the fatal encounter between Dewey and his guerrilla captor General Nyati – reflected the literary training of the author as well as the audience of black students and their associates. However, the direct performance style of this non-professional, all-black cast worked against the naturalist nuances of the text's portrayal of fallible men to emphasize the play's message as a "Black view of white-labelled terrorism."[12]

Encounter was considered inflammatory enough to be banned by the time SABTU organized its second and last festival in Cape Town in December 1972, which otherwise included *The Coat*, *The Lahnee's Pleasure*, and *Requiem for Brother X*, from the Durban program. SABTU was effectively dismantled a few months later in March 1973 by the banning of its president, Srini Moodley, and its director, Sathasivan (Saths) Cooper, both officers in TECON (Gwala 1974: 94–97).[13] Before being banned, however, Saths Cooper attended a black arts event sponsored by Mihloti at Mofolo Hall, in Soweto. The proceedings included a speech written by Cooper and presented by Sipho Buthelezi, entitled "What is Black Theatre?," which called for a "new and relevant Black theatre . . . by artists who have self-love and love of all Black people." It ended with a short sketch called "Before and After the Revolution," in which a white interrogator is interrogated by his former prisoners.[14] This sketch shared with *Encounter* an explicit defense of revolutionary violence, but, unlike *Encounter*, was delivered in terse agitprop style, using choral chants and direct audience address, in the manner of Mihloti's poetry. Apart from cementing the connection between groups in Durban and in Johannesburg, this event signaled a growing interest in agitprop methods of political mobilization: short, sharp performances of material that could be quickly memorized and performed, the better to avoid the confiscation of a crucial text or the arrest of a cast member. It also highlighted the political charge of the occasion of performance over the content of the show.

This event confirms the link between SABTU, mostly based in Durban, and MDALI (*umDali* or "Creator") – the Music, Drama and Literature Institute, the umbrella organization for several groups, including Mihloti, in the Johannesburg area – but, for strategic reasons, deflects the question of their differences. While the commitment to inclusive black emancipation animated both groups, their institutional structures were inevitably shaped by the state's differential treatment of Africans and Indians. SABTU was able to draw on the relative mobility of its Indian members and on connections to an Indian middle class, and so gain access to venues such as Orient Hall, without immediate state interference. It could also count on coverage in the Indian-oriented press in Durban, which offered favorable accounts not only of the Indian-oriented comedy, *The Lahnee's Pleasure*, but even of explicitly political drama such as *Requiem for Brother X* and *The Just*.[15] MDALI's predominantly African members in Soweto, Alexandra, and other townships had to deal with direct interference from state officials ready to deport Africans to the bantustans, as well as indirect pressure, such as the dearth of capital and suitable venues, and the black press's unwillingness to cover such events. One consequence of this increased state pressure was a greater insistence on the goal of black autonomy. Where SABTU members functioned independently of white organizations or facilitators and thus had no need to assert their autonomy, MDALI leader Molefe Pheto emphatically rejected any affiliation with white facilitators or would-be integrated organizations, such as Phoenix Players (Khoapa 1973: 204–205).

BCM members were most emphatically critical of white "management" of black talent in such shows as *Ipi Tombi* (1974, roughly translated as "Girls! Where?!"), which used a sketchy "Jim comes to Jo-burg" scenario as an alibi for scantily clad women dancing to canned *mbaqanga* to the greater profit of impresario Bertha Egnos (Kruger 1995b: 47–48), but they were also sceptical of interracial collaborations such as that between Elizabeth Sneddon and Welcome Msomi, who produced *Umabatha*, "the Zulu *Macbeth*" (Coplan 1985: 78–82), or between Cornelius [Corney] Mabaso and Phoenix Players, who produced the variety show, *Isuntu*, which toured Japan as *Meropa* and London as *KwaZulu* (Coplan 1985: 220). Founded by Union Artists' Ian Bernhardt and director Barney Simon initially to produce Athol Fugard's *Hello and Goodbye* in 1965, Phoenix Players continued the Union tradition of sponsoring black cast shows such as the Soweto Ensemble's *Shaka* (directed by Mabaso in 1968) and *Phiri*, a local – and much celebrated – adaptation of Ben Jonson's *Volpone*, directed by Simon in 1972. Phoenix's white members, especially Simon, were committed to developing a non-racial South African theatre and furthering the work of black performers and producers such as Mabaso and Stanley "Fats" Dibeco, who had worked with Fugard and Simon at Dorkay House,[16] but their personal commitment did not in itself alter the apartheid structures which excluded most blacks from formal training in all areas from performance to management. The division of labor for *Phiri*, for example, was not structurally different from that of *King Kong*, produced thirteen years earlier.[17] As the biographical sketches in the program indicate, the mostly white production team had access to capital, formal training, and informal connections in London as well as Johannesburg; the black performers had access mostly only to informal training and limited capital. The exception, Corney Mabaso, who had studied directing in London, proved the rule of apartheid restrictions on performance education in South Africa. This ongoing division of labor suggests the persistence of what might be called a *white institutional unconscious*, the assumption that whites were better disposed to exercise organizational skills and access to capital. It is this white institutional unconscious, over and above the conscious intentions of white facilitators, that Pheto censured when he criticized the "concept" of "multiracial organizations" (Khoapa 1973: 204).

In keeping with this critique, SABTU emphasized black participants sometimes to the exclusion of white collaborators: the Serpent Players appear, for example, under the names of the actors John Kani and Winston Ntshona without their long-time collaborator, Fugard. Founded in 1963, the group performed local adaptations of European classics, such as Büchner's *Woyzeck*, Brecht's *Caucasian Chalk Circle*, and Sophocles' *Antigone*, before turning to improvisation on the daily lives of participants.[18] This turn came with *The Coat*, which was devised as an "acting exercise" in response to the trial of key members of the group in 1966 and revived for the SABTU festival. The action was based on an incident at one of the trials: a man who had just been sentenced gave his coat to the wife of another prisoner, telling her to "give this to my wife. Tell her to use it" (see Walder 1993: xxiv–xxvi). Although performed initially for a white "theatre appreciation group" in Port Elizabeth, the play's performance under the name of Serpent Players in the New Brighton township (where most company members lived) and its publication in 1967 in *The Classic*, a magazine read by black intellectuals, secured its identification with black theatre and its performance at the SABTU festival in Cape Town. However, it received less critical attention than the more militant plays on the SABTU program, possibly because it favored the subtle representation of everyday social gests – from the exchange of clothing to the interaction of members of a community – estranged under the pressure of political trials that disrupted this community – rather than the direct call for action.

Multiracial organizations were not the only targets of BCM critique. Spurred on by SASO's condemnation of escapism, Black Consciousness intellectuals dismissed township shows as cheap entertainment, even when produced and financed by blacks such as Kente and Sam Mhangwane. They were particularly critical of Mhangwane, partly because his long-running melodramas *Unfaithful Woman* (1966) and *Blame Yourself* (1970) preached Christian resignation rather than resistance, and partly because Mhangwane insisted on remaining affiliated with the white-run South African Theatre Organization (SATO), on the grounds that white professionals had much to teach black practitioners.[19] This was a clear case of the white institutional unconscious and thus an easy target for BCM ire.

A much more versatile showman, Kente was not so easy to dismiss. Like his predecessors in African variety from Motsieloa to Matshikiza, Kente learned choral music at mission school. After a stint at the Jan Hofmeyr School for Social Work in Johannesburg, he worked as a talent scout for Gallo like Motsieloa before him, writing music for singers such as Miriam Makeba, and, like Matshikiza, weaving loose plots around virtuoso performance numbers, as in *Manana, the Jazz Prophet* (1963), or stellar performers, such as Kenny Majozi as the eponymous hero of *Sikhalo* or Zuluboy, the protagonist of *Lifa* (Figure 6.1).[20] *Sikhalo* ["Isikhalo" or "Lament"; 1966] ran from Mafikeng in the northwest to Kente's home territory in the Eastern Cape before reaching the Witwatersrand University Great Hall, under the auspices of Union Artists. The show secured a place in black township memory as a match for *King Kong* with its "good solid jazz and heart-rendering [*sic?*] Xhosa hymns."[21] The plots of the long-running shows from the 1960s – *Sikhalo*, *Lifa* (1967), and *Zwi* [Alone, 1970] – had sympathetic characters (often women) fall victim to the pressures of township life or the wiles of township toughs (mostly men), but ended with releases from prison or the reconciliation of estranged families, accompanied by explicit moral comment.[22] The spectacular display of African talent, no less than the last-minute reprieves, functioned as recompense for the unmanageable pressures of the apartheid state and its local agents, from the white pass officers to the black policemen, without confronting the state directly. Audiences responded with vocal enthusiasm to the moralizing and to the music.[23]

Above all, Kente's glamour as a successful black entrepreneur and his professional prestige reflected in the shows impressed his audience. Although *Sikhalo* was sponsored by Union Artists, it was sustained by a combination of ticket sales and Kente's commission on cosmetics and other items sold at the shows. Despite apartheid restrictions on where he could perform and for whom, Kente was in 1970 earning enough to pay his regular actors four times what they would have received in the manufacturing sector (Kavanagh 1983: 93). Financially independent, Kente could thus cater to African urban tastes without pressure from white taste-makers or from African intellectuals such as the Soweto Ensemble, who staged Anouilh's *Antigone* and Sartre's *Huis Clos* alongside *Shaka*, a play by Indian

139

Figure 6.1 In the tradition of African vaudeville: Kenny Majozi in *Lifa* by Gibson Kente, 1972. *Source*: *S'ketsh*

South Africa, Sam Gorey.[24] As an entrepreneur supporting a retinue of actors and as a purveyor of moralistic entertainment, Kente's contribution resembles what Karin Barber has called the "radical conservatism" of Yoruba popular theatre. Although produced under very different political conditions, Kente's township melodrama, especially in the 1960s, shares with popular Yoruba theatre at the same time a conservative populist thematic and an entrepreneurial production structure. Both respond to the precarious social and economic circumstances of entrepreneur/producer and audiences alike by celebrating individual virtue and satirizing the pretensions of social status seekers and economic predators. Although concluding on a reconciliatory note, they "reveal in heightened and concentrated form the anxieties, preoccupations and convictions that underpin ordinary people's daily experience" (Barber 1986: 6).[25]

It was this manifest power that Kente exercised as role model of individual black advancement as well as his production of light entertainment and his relatively conservative politics that provoked criticism from Black Consciousness intellectuals. Mafika Gwala, one of the editors of *Black Review 1973*, called for a national theatre whose "true representation" of the nation would be "far more serious than entertainment" (Gwala 1973: 132). More pointedly, Mihloti attacked the sensationalism of township melodrama:

> Mihloti will not . . . produce plays that tell you how unfaithful our women are. We do not present plays of our broken families, of how Black people fight and murder each other . . . this kind of theatre leaves the people broken and despaired. We tell the people to stop moaning and to wake up and start doing something about their valuable and beautiful black lives.
>
> (Gwala 1974: 113)

While this article does not explicitly attack the black-oriented press, it implicates in the critique black critics' celebrations of Kente's "thrilling new ventures" and even of black audience's enthusiasm for *Ipi Tombi*, which was staged in the townships only after it had played for a year in metropolitan venues forbidden to blacks and left no room for the possibility that black response to this show might include an appreciation of measurable black contributions, such as the hit song "Mama Tembu's wedding" attributed to Margaret Singana.[26] By contrast, MDALI's Black Arts Festival at the Donaldson Orlando Cultural Club (DOCC) in Soweto in March 1973 provoked mixed reactions. It followed SABTU's example by offering a program of metropolitan drama and writing from Africa and the African diaspora, as well as local poetry, juxtaposing James Baldwin and Frantz Fanon with Mongane Serote and uJebe Masokoane (later president of PET).

S'ketsh, an independent black arts magazine whose writers included white activists such as Robert McLaren (Kavanagh) as well as Soweto poet and later editor, Sipho Sepamla, and veteran journalist and now *Sowetan* editor, Aggrey Klaaste, endorsed the principle of black theatre and acknowledged the educational value of Mihloti's program but regretted that the festival chose as its dramatic centerpiece Peter Weiss's *Marat/Sade*, whose subject – the French Revolution staged by the Marquis de Sade at the Charenton asylum outside Paris – was remote from most spectators in Soweto. He also claimed that Baldwin's American English was hard to follow. Concluding that there was very little "South African blackness in this black festival" (*S'ketsh* 1973: 43), the reviewer (Sipho Sepamla) drew attention to the unresolved tension between Black Consciousness intellectuals' interest in the African diaspora and the tastes of most Soweto residents for musicals and melodrama. Notwithstanding the emphatic rejection of melodrama by BCM intellectuals, the repertoire of SABTU affiliates included a number of plays whose portrayal of heightened emotion – whether love, frustration, or defiance – drew on the conventions of melodrama.

Manhood, martyrdom, and melodrama

Melodrama, which portrays social conflict as family drama using broad moralistic strokes against the backdrop of a cruel or indifferent society, may seem an unlikely vehicle for representing political action, since it has tended – from its nineteenth-century heyday in the work of playwrights like Dion Boucicault (*The Poor of New York* and *The Colleen Bawn*) to its twentieth-century manifestation as in soap opera – to focus on the suffering of families rather than the social or political causes of their condition. Kente's *Sikhalo* (1966) shares with domestic dramas like *Hello and Goodbye* or *Kanna Hy Kô Hystoe* the picture of an unmanageable society against which ordinary people have no power. *Requiem for Brother X* indicts the social and economic consequences of racism more explicitly. It was written by William Wellington Mackey in 1966 in homage to Malcolm X (assassinated 1965) and produced across the United States by black, university, and community theatres. It reached SABTU by way of the *Black Drama Anthology* (1971), which included plays such as Amiri Baraka's *Junkies Are Full of SHIT* (1971). This play, which denounced white capital's role in pushing drugs to blacks, was produced by Mihloti in February 1975. A "dialogue of confrontation," Mackey's characterization of his play and those of his associates (Mackey 1986: 327) became the signature term for Black Consciousness theatre in South Africa, quoted by many SABTU members. More generally, the development of African-American theatre since the Black Arts movement in the 1960s, and the rejection of white charity by activists such as Baraka, offered a model for institutional autonomy.

Requiem was performed by TECON at the SABTU festivals in June and December 1972 and by PET in late 1973. TECON's focus on *Requiem for Brother X*'s emphatic indictment of white government and what their program note calls "dirty white politics," highlights the play's agitational dimension rather than its affiliation to African-American social drama in a domestic setting, represented most forcefully by Lorraine Hansberry's *Raisin in the Sun* (1959). While the agitational dimension of Mackey's play and the characters help to concentrate its dramatic effect, the complex dynamics of family interaction and the role of

142

women in Hansberry's play suggest a more flexible way of en/gendering agency. The desire for upward mobility in *Raisin in the Sun* and African-American society of the 1950s has, in the 1960s world of *Requiem*, given way to entrenched ghettoization. If the conditions portrayed by the latter play are more desperate, so too are the reactions of the characters. In *Raisin*, Walter Lee gambles and loses his family's savings on a friend's fraudulent business deal; in *Requiem*, Nate abandons his formal education for Malcolm X's call to resist white supremacy, but he still chases after white women, unaware that his child is about to be born to a forgotten white girlfriend who has sought refuge with his family. Despite his vehement defense of Malcolm's principle of black self-defense, Nate's rebellion is essentially rhetorical: he plays out a scenario in which he makes himself over into the bum he imagines he appears to be in the eyes of prospective employers: "And when I go for that white man's examination, I'm gonna wear clothes that I'd have left in the alley for another week" (Mackey 1986: 344).

Where Nate's rebellion ends in self-parody and Matt's ends in resignation, the women in the family make do. Martha, Matt's wife, plays housewife to the men and midwife to the "little white girl" (Mackey 1986: 328). Bonita, Nate's and Matt's sister, resembles in name and sharply critical attitude Beneatha Younger, the daughter of the house in *Raisin in the Sun*, and shares with her predecessor a critique of her elders' aspirations for stable if subaltern lives. She also exposes the bad faith of white social workers who interpret the lives of individual blacks in terms of the demeaning abstractions of the "War on Poverty" – "WE ARE THE DEPRIVED, THE SOCIALLY DISADVANTAGED, THE HELPLESS" – while remarking ironically that the off-stage "white girl" has stolen her role, "I'm supposed to be in there, screaming and carrying on with a baby in my belly. WE'RE SUPPOSED TO BE THE ONES WHO MAKE MISTAKES, NOT THEM!" (p. 332). At the end Bonita and Martha, rather than the hapless men, deliver the baby and, with it, the rather fragile possibility of a new life. Despite their action, the last moments of the play are dominated by the complaints of the men, from father Jude's ambiguous laughter over his own chanting of the sorrow song, "There is trouble all over this world" (p. 345), to Matt's attack on his brother as an "ANIMAL" (p. 346), to Nate's defiant despair – "My soul will rot in hell" – and, finally, back to their father's laughter which overlaps with the baby's cry as the lights fade. Although Bonita demonstrates the capacity for decisive action, the play as a whole is a complaint rather than an act of defiance. The complaint of that would-be revolutionary, Jimmy Porter, master whiner protagonist of *Look Back in Anger*, TECON's first production, haunts this dialogue of confrontation. The impotent self-pity that characterizes this most notorious "male complaint" does not dominate *Requiem* to the extent that it does *Look Back in Anger*.[27] But it does draw attention away from the portrayal of defiant young blacks and its denunciation of legal discrimination and the institutional unconscious of white benevolence. The performance of this text thus brings into play the company's attack on the institutionalized discrimination of apartheid structures as well as the representation of fictional characters grappling with comparable conditions in

America. The appearance of known SASO leaders in key roles, such as Saths Cooper as Nate and Asha Rambally (later editor of *Black Review*) as Bonita, and the political risks for both performers and spectators would have offset the melodramatic tenor of the male complaint enough to confirm its place as prime exhibit – at least in 1972 – of a "theatre of determination . . . self-reliance and . . . new awareness" (Khoapa 1973: 201) and its role as a "gleaming weapon . . . in the cause of liberation."[28]

But the status of the performance as an act of political defiance does not obliterate the problem of gender relations in the play or in the movement that produced it. The melodramatic moment in this "theatre of determination" returns in the best-known play in the Black Consciousness repertoire – *Shanti*. The retrospective reputation of *Shanti* as the signature play of the People's Educational Theatre (PET) and of the Black Consciousness Movement more generally is due in part to its publication in Kavanagh's influential anthology, *South African People's Plays* (1981), at a time when other BCM texts had been confiscated or destroyed, and in part to the posthumous role of its author, Mthuli Shezi, as Black Consciousness martyr. Shezi attended the SABTU festival in Durban in June 1972 as vice-president of the BPC, after which he was expelled from the University of Zululand. While on his way to the SABTU festival in Cape Town, he was pushed in front of a train by a white official whom Shezi had challenged for insulting a black woman (Khoapa 1973: 100; Steadman 1985: 324). Shezi's death, along with the banning of the SASO and TECON executive in Natal, prompted the founding of PET in March 1973. The organization responsible for mounting *Shanti* was a fusion of a mainly Indian PET based in Lenasia and Shiqomo [spear] based in Soweto. The officers of the combined organization included Nomsisi Kraai, who played Shanti and published "What Is Black Theatre?" in *PET Newsletter*,[29] uJebe Masokoane, who played Thabo, Shanti's companion and martyr to the struggle, with Solly Ismail as director and Sadecque Variava as organizer and editor of the newsletter (Steadman 1985: 168). PET members treated Shezi's death as a "heroic act" *(PET Newsletter* 3). They argued that his play "portray[ed] the true meaning of Black Consciousness, the evils and oppression that face the Blackman today" and called on their audience and one another to "clench our fists even higher in determination" (*PET Newsletter*, 2). In this light, Masokoane's performance of Thabo can be seen as a re-embodiment of Shezi, the absent martyr and author of the play.

Shanti deals in part with the love between Shanti [Hindi: "peace"], and Thabo [isiZulu: "happy one"], but it uses the trope of interracial love chiefly to frame Thabo's coming to manhood. Thabo achieves manhood by way of imprisonment for alleged pass violation, escape to Mozambique, and death at the hands of a Frelimo guerrilla whose group he had hoped to join. Although Thabo's encounter with this group takes place only in scene eight (of eleven), it is on this revolutionary meeting, like that in *Encounter*, that the drama turns. But, where the pivotal confrontation in Suldip's play shows a British officer meeting his death at the hands of the Mau Mau, the scene in *Shanti* emphasizes Thabo's conversion from doubt to commitment to the armed struggle, but celebrates that commitment as Thabo dies at the hand of a guerrilla suspicious of his attempt to contact Shanti. The rest of the action frames this encounter. The play opens with a Zulu lament, "Zixolise" ["We have suffered"], sung off-stage as Shanti weeps for the dead Thabo. This song and another sung later by Thabo's fellow-prisoners, "Senzani na sihlutshwana?" ["What have we done to be punished so?"] powerfully recalls the long tradition of African protest hymns as well as the contemporary poetry of defiance, sung at the funerals of activists by groups like Mihloti. However, the dialogue spoken by Shanti and her fellow students, Thabo and Koos (who functions as a spokesman for coloured defiance of racial classification), is in an academic English (Shezi's second language) that vacillates between sentimental expressions of love or pain and emphatic denunciations of apartheid's abuses. At its best, the terse presentation brings home the arbitrariness of apartheid power; the perfunctory language of the police who arrest Thabo in his friend's house and who frame him for robbery is all too plausible, for instance. Likewise, the value of the blunt exchange between Thabo and General Mobu and the comments of his suspicious cohort, Mangaya, lies not in an attempt to give the characters depth or interiority as individuals, but rather to harness the encounter to a lesson. The play endorses the armed struggle and thus publicizes a taboo topic, but its lesson also includes the reminder that its agents are not uniformly heroic.

Whatever the shortcomings of the text, it is in performance for black audiences that the political impact of the play as an instrument of conscientization can be seen. *Shanti* opened in Lenasia in September 1973; it played in Soweto and neighboring Coronationville from 22–28 November and then on 15 December in Hamanskraal, near Pretoria (Kavanagh 1985: 170). These few appearances were enough to provoke police harassment of spectators as well as performers. The police also confiscated equipment and copies of the script (Kavanagh 1985: 171). The play, the *PET Newsletter*, and the pamphlet praising Shezi as a Black Consciousness martyr, were cited as evidence in the charges against Variava and Ismail, as well as Cooper, Moodley, and other SASO and BPC leaders (Mbanjwa 1975: 81–83). These charges, under the broad provisions of the 1967 Terrorism Act, initially included the conspiracy to "stage, present, produce and/or participate in anti-white, racialistic, subversive and/or revolutionary plays and/or dramas."[30] Notwithstanding its academic English and its insular student milieu, *Shanti* gained legitimacy as a "means toward Black Liberation" (*PET Newsletter*, 2) or, to use the later normative phrase, a "cultural weapon," by virtue of its display as a key element in the initial indictment (Steadman 1985: 186). To be sure, one police operative with literary pretensions found the indictment of apartheid laws by Thabo and the other prisoners to be "too ambiguous" and even argued, in notes in the margins of the text, that it "had too little to do with the development of plot" and could not "by the same token have any effect on stimulating strong terroristic action" (Steadman 1985: 166). Furthermore most of the detainees, including TECON officers Cooper and Moodley, were eventually convicted for allegedly plotting actual rather than virtual "terroristic action" or the "violent overthrow of the state" as members of political organizations, SASO and BPC.[31] Nonetheless, the public articulation of the initial charge before a gallery packed with black observers on 7 February and 12 March, and the reappearance of the text at the later trial of Variava, charged with "compiling and producing the PET newsletter and producing the play *Shanti*," brought the political implications of the play to the attention of a larger proportion of its target audience than the initial stage performances had been able to do.[32]

Shanti's place in an arsenal of cultural weapons rests on a battery of assumptions about who should handle those weapons. Despite its critique of township musicals, especially their sensationalist portrayal of women, BCM discourse kept women in the conventional role of home-maker disseminating national values to the youth. In the *Black Review 1974/75*, which was edited by a woman, Thoko Mbanjwa, women were urged to take part in the work of "nutrition, childcare, basic skills such as knitting, sewing . . . cooking" (Mbanjwa 1975: 121); the following issue argued that women were "basically responsible for the survival and maintenance of their families, the socialization of the youth, and the transmission of the Black Consciousness Heritage" (Rambally 1977: 109). While many African women *were* largely responsible for their families in an apartheid environment where men were absent migrant workers, others, such as Mamphele Ramphele, were politically active in their own right. It is therefore hard to defend BCM arguments that a "man's wife and children" were primarily responsible for building up the man's self-esteem, to counter his "feeling of being emasculated under apartheid" (Manganyi 1973: 10–11), even though some women have endorsed this view (Driver 1990: 235–36). In the TECON arena, Vino Cooper and Sam Moodley, interviewed after their husbands, Saths Cooper and Srini Moodley, were banned, advocated struggle in the name of "strong black men," despite their own evident activism.[33] The presumed primacy of black manhood permeates the very definition of Black Consciousness, which calls on the "Black *man*" to "reject all value-systems that . . . reduce *his* human dignity," "to build up *his* own value-systems," and "to see *himself* as self-defined" (Khoapa 1973: 41; emphasis added). This a priori emphasis on the masculine pronoun *in combination* with the positing of manhood as the telos of liberation, assigns to women the role of recipient of or auxiliary to the liberation struggle, rather than its agent. Women may confirm the ideals of Black Consciousness by adhering to a predetermined set of behavioral norms (especially sexual norms) deemed appropriately black or by inculcating these norms in the youth, but they may not act as co-creators of those norms. This relegation of women to the passive function of spectator waiting for liberation or a sort of national litmus-paper, whose social and sexual behavior is monitored as a test for authenticity, is not of course peculiar to South Africa, but, as several critics have noted, it is remarkably prevalent in discourses of national liberation (McClintock 1991; Yuval-Davis 1993) and continues to be controversial in South Africa (Ramphela 1995; Mosala 1995; Madikizela 1995).

Despite the presence of women, such as Nomsisi Kraai and Sam Moodley, in PET, TECON, and their affiliates in SABTU, the roles assigned to women largely reflected the masculinist habitus not only of BCM but of South African society at large. This masculinism, if not outright misogyny, surfaces at moments in the play, such as Koos' reprimand to Shanti: "it is not good for a lady to imitate Hamlet [by thinking too much]" (Shezi 1981: 69). It also drives the play's equation of agency and manhood. This equation of agency with manhood leaves Shanti little more than the conventional feminine gestures of waiting and weeping for her fallen hero. Ending with the image of the weeping woman, with which it began, *Shanti* returns to the drama of protest as lament, which its producers hoped to replace with a more militant representation of decisive action in the "theatre of determination." Shanti, the character, may be more politically aware than the women in township melodrama, such as Thando, the girlfriend of the hero in *Sikhalo*, who falls in with *tsotsis*, but *Shanti*, the play, leaves its eponymous character in a similar position: waiting for her man. By treating suffering as a female matter and as a natural foil to male agency and by representing that agency as martyrdom, *Shanti* replicates the melodramatic dramaturgy that PET and its associates had so vigorously attacked.

Beyond BCM: drama and Black Consciousness

Although it was a courageous response to an impossible situation, the talky format of BCM theatre separated its participants from a wider black audience. Disdaining popular forms of comedy and melodrama, the producers of *Shanti* missed an opportunity to refunction local entertainments to critical ends. It is noteworthy that plays produced on the margins of the movement responded more generously to popular tastes and proved more able to move local – and differently black – audiences to reflection, as well as laughter and tears. Although ignored or mentioned only in passing by standard accounts of black theatre (e.g. Orkin 1991: 201) possibly because they portrayed Indians and coloureds rather than blacks in general or because they used politically ambiguous popular forms, *The Lahnee's Pleasure* and *Kanna Hy Kô Hystoe* outlasted their initial appearances under the aegis of SABTU. Although more satirical and more explicitly political than *Kanna*, *The Lahnee's Pleasure* shared much with the earlier play. Both drew from the peculiar conditions of these minority communities and their style of performance from genres patronized by these audiences. While Shezi relied on English to convey abstract political ideas to a multilingual audience, Small and Govender used the native idiom of their communities, *Kaaps* and "Indian" English, to engage their immediate public as well as black-identified intellectuals.

The Lahnee's Pleasure succeeded on several apparently incompatible fronts. It exposed Indian class prejudice to public view yet granted legitimate space to "Indian" English. It made local and national audiences laugh at the small world of Sunny, the bartender, the Indian customers, and the "lahnee" [white] owner in a segregated "backbar" in a provincial Natal town yet managed to grant stage time to an advocate of black power in the person of the unnamed Stranger.[34] Provoked by Sunny's subservience to his lahnee and the lahnee's patronizing treatment of the customers, especially Mothie, a sugarmill worker driven to drink and distraction by his daughter's elopement, the Stranger argues that Indians, like other blacks, should stand up for their rights.

Notwithstanding the force of this message, the Stranger's authority was compromised by the stage action. While the contradiction between his call for self-assertion against white tyranny and his endorsement of authoritarian paternal discipline, especially of wayward daughters – "girls are too free these days" (R. Govender 1977: 30) – may have escaped critical attention, the comic characters stole the show. The improvisation of Mohammed Alli as Sunny and Kessie Govender and later Essop Kahn as Mothie, which was incorporated into the published text (R. Govender 1977: ii), gave audiences an ambiguous mix of satire and ingratiation. Although the force of the satire, as a challenge to Indian class prejudice as well as the invisibility of Indian concerns, was noted in initial reviews,[35] the differences between the performances of Kessie Govender and Essop Kahn highlighted the ambiguity of the play. While Kahn played up the absurd aspects of Mothie's plight and used the role to launch a lucrative but apolitical comic career (Naidoo 1997: 36), Kessie Govender challenged white as well as Indian spectators' prejudices by punctuating the comedy with such lines as "What you think we dirty people, what? . . . We don't eat beef and pork. . . . We don't smell like white people" (R. Govender 1977: 21) and he went on to write his own critiques of Indian/African relations in such plays as *Working Class Hero* (1979). Created at the Stable Theatre in Durban and performed in Cape Town and Johannesburg, this play tackled the tense labor relations between Indian contractors and African wage-workers.

Although *Lahnee*'s signal combination of comedy and politics was eclipsed during the 1970s and 1980s, several Indian writers have recently returned to this material. Ronnie Govender's work includes one-man dramatizations of his short stories (performed by Charles Pillai), collected as *At the Edge* (1991) and *1949* (1996). The latter included hilarious impersonations of types from meddlesome aunts to self-important bartenders, while the title story dealt with one Zulu man's failed attempt to protect his Indian employer from the mob during the 1949 anti-Indian riots.[36] The satiric potential of Indian/amaZulu encounters continues to stimulate playwrights in the region of KwaZulu/Natal. Kriben Pillay's *Looking for Muruga* (first performed 1991; published 1995) for instance, portrayed a Zulu student training for the classical Indian role of the god Muruga under the critical eye of his friend, an Indian bartender, also called Muruga, who makes fun of Sherwin, a Europhile intellectual who wants to write about the bartender he misremembers as an abject comic (Figure 6.2).

The fact that *The Lahnee's Pleasure* could be played in several different ways does not disable its political impact but it does point to the pitfalls as well as the possibilities of wrapping politics in popular packages. These ambiguities are nowhere more apparent than in the shows of Gibson Kente, black capitalist, Christian, and the most popular purveyor of township melodrama. Kente's combination of sentimental tears, laughter, singing, and dancing had provoked BCM's

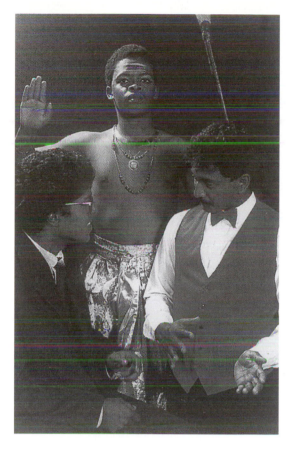

Figure 6.2 A "Zulu-Indian" god (Dante Mashile) and his Indian interlocutors (Sherwin Christopher and Satchu Annamalai) in *Looking for Muruga* by Kriben Pillai, Asoka Theatre, Durban, 1991. *Photograph*: Fiona Clyde; *source and permission*: Kriben Pillai

ire, but he took up the challenge represented, on the one hand, by *Shanti* and, on the other, by the collaborative experiments of the Serpent Players. In response to the conscientization efforts of BPC and SASO, Kente incorporated politics into the formerly apolitical township musical. He did so not by giving his township personalities political speeches, but by adding characters, such as the black policeman, whose harassment of sympathetic characters would draw the audience's attention, however indirectly, to the state behind him.

In Kente's *How Long?* and *Too Late!* (first performed in 1974 and 1975 respectively), the plot treats the deaths of sympathetic, if helpless, women (Khulu, the grandmother, in the former, and Ntanana, the crippled daughter, in the latter), as the indirect result of apartheid bureaucracy and direct police brutality, even though the stage performance continued to rely on pathos and broad gestural acting to keep the audience's attention, as the funeral scene at the end of *How Long?* suggests (Figure 6.3).[37] This indictment, however implicit, brought Kente to the attention of the political police, who had hitherto tolerated him, and provoked the multiple bannings of these plays and ultimately Kente's detention. Kente responded to this harassment by retreating from explicit protest to family conflict in *Can You Take It?* (first performed 1977), "a township love story in the presentational style of the Broadway musical" (Coplan 1985: 211). In *La Duma* [Thunder; 1978], political strife took the form of conflict between a policeman and his activist son but also took the blame for the fragmentation of African communities. At the height of the "emergency" in the 1980s, Kente produced *Bad Times Mzala*, an anti-sanctions play, and *Sekunjalo* [Now Is the Time; 1985], which pitted a harsh post-independence "African socialist" state against the capitalist hero, Sechaba [nation], to protest what he saw as the anti-capitalist and anti-Christian tendencies of a future South Africa proposed by the ANC and its allies.[38]

While the general thrust of Kente's plays has been conservative, in the sense that the sentimental plots close with the pathos of reconciliation rather than resistance, however indirect, *Too Late!* registers the impact of the BCM call for a "theatre of determination." Although the play does not portray organized defiance of the state, it shows characters engaged in small acts of resistance to

Figure 6.3 In the tradition of African vaudeville II: funeral finale of *How Long?* by Gibson Kente, 1974. *Source and permission*: Baileys African History Archive

the arbitrariness of state power, represented indirectly by the pink gloves and Afrikaans insults of the faceless bureaucrat at the pass office, or directly by the brutality of a stupid but dangerous black policeman, Pelepele [Hot Pepper]. Where BCM intellectuals favored plays like *Shanti*, which portrayed individual acts of resistance, Kente's audiences relished the anarchic dodging of the comic Offside, who, in Ronnie Mokoena's performance, was both clown and *imbongi*. Where *Shanti* showed characters with only an abstract connection to community life, *Too Late!* revolves around a family, centered on Madinto, who runs a shebeen to support her crippled daughter Ntanana and her orphaned nephew Saduva. Madinto's traffic in illegal liquor, like the petty theft of the *majitas* [township toughs], is depicted as the consequence of unjust restrictions on legitimate employment for urban Africans. The transformation of Saduva from a "God-loving boy" into a "*majita*" during his prison term for carrying an invalid pass, is likewise shown to be a regrettable but unavoidable result of apartheid. Even Pelepele's most brutal act, killing Ntanana as she tries to protect Saduva, is partly the effect of his job and is offset by her final act of – uncharacteristic – violence, as she kicks her assailant in the balls. As Dr. Phuza [Drink] asks: "Can't something be done to curb the bitterness in both young and old, before it's TOO LATE?" (Kente 1981: 122).[39]

The style of performance in *Too Late!* follows Kente's usual mix of sentimental dialogue and formulaic declarations alongside comic gags and group mime in which performers' bodily and facial mimicry of, say, panicked response to a pass raid, makes a more vivid impression on the audience than verbal comment lost in the noise. Kente's direction takes account of African audience's documented tendency to laugh at stage violence (Routh 1950b) as well as their fluid response to sudden shifts in mood: he invites laughter in response to Pelepele's clownish brutality *and* to Ntanana's retaliation, only to switch to sentimental mode as Ntanana's musical signature announces her death.[40] On the one hand, the music provides the professional singing and musicianship that, in the words of one critic, "make up for the flaws of articulation" (*S'ketsh* 1975b: 9) that are due, for the most part, to Kente's insistence that his vernacular-speaking cast memorize lines in English, so as to reach a broad audience. On the other, borrowing and transforming the model of *King Kong*, Kente uses key songs and phrases and signatures to mark particular characters or shifts in mood. Thus, for example, the familiar Xhosa hymn, "Ngabayini lisoni sam'?" ["What could it be, my sin?"], first appears in a church scene, after Mfundisi has criticized the abuse of church teachings to defend unjust law and before he shames the policemen who invade the church looking for *majitas*. In this context, it reinforces the moral authority of the church but, when the opening phrase, "What's my sin?," reappears, it is to ironic effect, as Saduva curtly dismisses his girlfriend's shock at his tough prison behavior. The song "Ndilahlekile" ["I am lost"], which is first heard as a sentimental background to the scene in which Ntanana is discovered scavenging orange peels for food while Madinto is in prison for running a shebeen, resurfaces at the end to soften Saduva's previously tough behavior at the moment at which he admits his debt to his family and thus also to moderate his bitterness, which might otherwise have appeared as defiance.

Despite the moralizing gloss on Saduva's bitterness, younger and more dis-affected members of the audience responded more readily to his anger. Provoked by their rowdy sentiments, the Publications Control Board banned the play a month after its opening in February 1975. Released for performance in Soweto after Kente had agreed to modify the script, *Too Late!* was still subject to the whim of local authorities elsewhere. While this censorship indicates the state's anxiety about the play's potential for agitation, it does not in itself prove that the performance radicalized its spectators. Robert Kavanagh, who argues retrospec-tively for "radical elements in the audience," nonetheless concedes that Kente did not "intend his play to mobilize the revolutionary energies of the black working class and youth" (1985: 134–35), but rather to capitalize on growing interest in protest, while still satisfying audience desire for "pathos" and "bawdy hilarity" (*S'ketsh*, 1975b: 8–9). While critics like Klaaste regretted the "spurious bubble of happiness" buoyed up by the musical format, despite the overlay of protest rhetoric, *Too Late!* succeeded in "making everybody happy" (*S'ketsh* 1975b: 8) and in moving the "old people in the audience" who "moaned during a scene when a mother [Madinto] . . . comes back from jail to find her invalid child killed by a policeman" (Kavanagh 1981: 86), and in rousing the disaffected youth. Elliot Makhaya, reviewing for the *World*, also registered audience response as mostly a combination of enthusiasm for the "pure entertainment" of Ronnie Mokoena and vocal sympathy for the family's plight, expressed in cries of "Shame" as well as enthusiastic participation in singing familiar hymns. This participation in the event can be contrasted with European-affiliated (usually but not always white) audiences' silent identification with an actor's convincing (or otherwise) simulation of feeling.[41]

While the text of *Too Late!* lacked the militancy of *Shanti* or the critical gest of *The Coat* and, in any case, represented a politically risky detour from Kente's usual conciliatory mode, its performance on the eve of the Soweto uprising captured the contradictory mix of anxiety and anticipation of this transformative moment for South Africa's urban black majority. This mix animated the drama – in stage and house – around other plays in this period which attempted to infuse the musical or melodramatic forms with Black Consciousness content. For instance, Rev. Mzwandile Maqina's *Give Us This Day* (1974) attempted to dramatize the "true story of the Tiro killing," the life and death of O. R. Tiro, student representative council president of the University of the North, who died in detention after having been imprisoned for allegedly fomenting student unrest. In Klaaste's assessment, the play used a "Kentesian format," including "exhibitionistic" comic acting and emphatic depiction of the "political tragedy" (*S'ketsh* [1975c]: 26–27). The results may have been "uneven" but the play was considered dangerous enough to be banned in 1975 (Steadman 1985: 469).

Theatre in the next decade, labeled variously and not always consistently "political," "protest," or "resistance" theatre, would continue to grapple with the tension between popular entertainment and intellectual aspiration, and between the lavish spectacles of township musicals promoted by Kente and the spare concreteness of the workshop theatre devised by Fugard, Simon, and their associates. In this decade, the struggle for economic, political, and human rights escalated, especially in the wake of the Soweto uprising of 1976 and the banning of key anti-apartheid organizations in the following year. In the vacuum created by the state's suppression of political speech and organization, theatre constituted a counter public sphere. Bolstered by the cultural capital of elite education as well as the finance capital of powerful corporations like Anglo-American and inhabited by relatively integrated groups of performers and audiences, the Space (1971–79), the Market (1976–) and other lesser-known venues provided a space for social assembly as well as cultural production. Protected by capital and international visibility from state violence to a far greater degree than black institutions, these theatres were able to accommodate Africanist groups such as the Dhlomo Theatre or the Soyikwa Institute, who saw themselves as inheritors of the Black Consciousness Movement and regarded their patrons in the Market and elsewhere with some ambivalence. The emergence of a Marketable South African theatre and competing institutions is the subject of the next chapter.

7

SPACES AND MARKETS

The place of theatre as testimony

In October 1972, *Sizwe Banzi Is Dead* (by Athol Fugard, John Kani, and Winston Ntshona) played for a single Sunday night performance for a members-only audience at the Space Theatre in Cape Town. Before embarking on an overseas tour, it visited local venues as different as Johannesburg and New Brighton (Kani's and Ntshona's home township) before being banned in Cape Town. In October 1981, *Woza Albert!* (by Percy Mtwa, Mbongeni Ngema, and Barney Simon) opened, after a short run upstairs, on the main stage of the Market Theatre in Johannesburg, then – as now – South Africa's most famous theatre. The intervening nine years saw the resurgence of mass opposition to apartheid and the growth of theatre as a key witness in the anti-apartheid struggle. This theatre of testimony is distinguished by the dramatic interpretation of individual and collective narratives, and of politically provocative topics, such as the pass laws, prison conditions, workers' rights, and, to a lesser degree, the condition of women. Its presentation combines physical and verbal comedy, impersonation of multiple roles with minimal props, and direct address to the audience by performers representing themselves and their own convictions as well as those of fictional characters. Its practitioners have drawn on different models from township musicals and variety to European experiments, such as Grotowski's "poor theatre" and Brecht's "social gest." At its initial stages, this theatre had its institutional basis in groups who used scripts generated through improvisation or workshops rather than private composition.

What distinguishes the testimonial theatre of the 1970s and 1980s from the political theatre that had surfaced sporadically since the 1930s was not its engagement with dangerous subjects nor even its experiments with form but its institutional stability, sustained by liberal capital, and the emergence of an audience that was large enough and legitimate enough – at home and abroad – to deflect overt suppression by the state. At a time when mass dissent was on the rise, and when liberal capitalist associations, from the Anglo-American Corporation to its philanthropic affiliate, the Urban Foundation, were looking for ways to manage dissent, the Space and the Market gained political and economic advantages, denied their predecessors from the African National Theatre to the Serpent Players (1963–1970s). The Space and the Market were able to use their national and later international visibility to evade censorship in the turbulent 1970s at a time when the violence of the apartheid state became well known worldwide. These institutions attempted to provide a place and occasion for social assembly as well as dissident culture, by staging theatre that defied apartheid structures and by attempting, albeit unevenly, to open the doors of the house, the workshop, and the office to all. On the stage and in the house, they attempted to translate the subjunctive mood of the virtual public sphere into the future indicative of a new South Africa. After the demise of the Space in 1981, the Market dominated the field; it had capital to support its own company's productions, to host productions by black-run institutions, such as the Dhlomo Theatre in Johannesburg, Soyikwa Institute and the FUNDA ("Learning") Centre in Soweto, or the Stable Theatre in Durban, as well as groups formed around writer/directors, such as Bahumutsi (Maishe Maponya), or Committed Artists (Mbongeni Ngema), who were more likely to get state surveillance than support, and to disseminate South African theatre at home and abroad.

This accommodation was not always a happy one. Groups associated with FUNDA and Soyikwa argued that the Market's greater access to capital and the social and political mobility of its (mostly) white executive made it a powerful institution that absorbed the work of black groups but did not substantially alter their conditions of production, plagued by poverty and invisibility as well as state violence in townships far from the prestige and security of the city center (Maponya 1984; Kavanagh 1989). This history of structural discrimination has led more recent commentators such as Zakes Mda, who preferred to see his plays premiere at township venues, to insist on differentiating the "protest theatre," identified with Fugard and his principal sponsor, the Market, which "depicts a situation of oppression . . . to the oppressor, with a view of appealing to his or her conscience," from a "theatre for resistance [performed] with the overt aims of rallying and mobilizing the oppressed to fight against oppression" (Mda 1995: 40–41), associated with playwrights like Maponya.

Yet despite this assertion of a clear-cut difference between protest and resistance, it is difficult, as Ian Steadman notes in "Theatre beyond Apartheid," to draw a precise line between a theatre of resistance located in the people's venues in the townships and a protest theatre presumably catering to an elite audience's appetite for indulging in sympathy with oppression (Steadman 1991: 82). Some theatres intent on "mobiliz[ing] the masses" were met with indifference by township audiences but welcomed by audiences at the Market and similar venues. The Market functioned both as a site for resistance to apartheid and a bulwark of liberal capital against the threat of civic violence implied by this resistance. Its repertoire straddled the border between protest and resistance, lament and defiance, accommodating, for instance, Elsa Joubert's sentimental treatment of people displaced by apartheid capitalism in *Die Swerfjare van Poppie Nongena* [The Long Years of Suffering of Poppie Nongena], the stage adaptation (1979) of the novel by Joubert and director Sandra Kotzé, alongside Mda's utterly unsentimental treatment in *The Hill* (first performed 1980; published in Mda 1990), or juxtaposing, in the season of the "emergency" (1985–86), the Company's terse documentary drama of resistance and betrayal, *Born in the RSA*, with Junction Avenue Theatre Company's *Sophiatown*, a revival of an era at once nostalgic and defiant. Where *Sarafina* (1986), a Broadway-style musical loosely based on the 1976 uprising that gave its creator, Ngema, celebrity status, was preferred by township audiences and aspirant black performers, Maponya's plays, from the agitprop of *The Hungry Earth* (1979) to the indictment of *Gangsters* (1984), found a readier response among metropolitan audiences than among township residents.

While this irony does not invalidate all formal, institutional, or political distinctions among theatre events accommodated by the Market and related ventures, they remind us that these distinctions are complex. This chapter attempts to account for the formation and institution of testimonial theatre as *the* expression of South Africa by offering a critical account of key productions and performers in the context of the institutions (visible structures and organizations), formations (associated participants, whether described as a "company" or "cultural workers"), as well as the prevailing forms and conventions of testimony, resistance, and restoration on stage.[1]

Occupying space

The Space/*Die Ruimte* opened on 28 May 1972 with Fugard's *Statements after an Arrest under the Immorality Act*. Fugard played Errol Philander, a coloured teacher, with Yvonne Bryceland as Frieda Joubert, his white lover, caught in the act by a policeman's flashlight. But the theatre work that was to lead to the Space's most compelling productions, *Sizwe Banzi Is Dead* (October 1972) and *The Island* (July 1973) really began with *The Coat* (1966), and other "acting exercises" by the Serpent Players. Although the arresting staging of *Statements* – combining physical and emotional exposure and terse report – owed much to Peter Brook and the London Academy of Music and Dramatic Art (LAMDA), Charles Marowitz's Open Space, and 1960s experiments (Astbury 1979: n.p.), the action also harked back to the melodramas of racial transgression of the very different South African 1960s.[2] *The Coat*, on the other hand, combined the life-narratives of African performers with the gestic techniques honed by Brecht to show the social attitudes and interaction of characters in speech and gesture (Brecht 1992: 198), so as to produce a new kind of South African theatre.

The Serpent Players harnessed Brechtian techniques such as acting in the third person and the juxtaposition of discrete scenes to highlight the social gest rather than the individual feeling in an action and so also the collective implications of individual behavior in the lives of performers and their families. Whereas the group had hitherto worked with Fugard's adaptations of European plays from Machiavelli's *La Mandragola* (performed as *The Cure*, with a township setting) to *The Caucasian Chalk Circle*, *The Coat* dealt with actual township life; it was based on an incident at the trial of one of the players: a man who had just been sentenced gave his coat to the wife of another prisoner, telling her to "Give this to my wife. Tell her to use it" (Walder 1993: xxiv–xxvi). The group used the object of the coat (in both senses) as the "mandate" (Fugard's term for the instigation of an improvised action) for a series of encounters, such as between the woman bearing the convict's message and his waiting wife or between the latter and the rent board official threatening to evict her. Fugard acted less as author than as provocateur, scribe, and overall organizer (Fugard 1984: 124–26, 135–43).

The performance drew on Brecht both in its technique and in its critical engagement with the pressing contradictions between private aspiration and public repression but it also spoke directly of and to the lives of urban Africans. The actors, among them Kani and Nomhle Nkonyeni, introduced themselves using the names of characters they had played in previous Serpent productions (Kani as Haemon in *Antigone* and Nkonyeni as Aniko in *The Caucasian Chalk Circle*). This gesture directed audience attention to the implications of the actions rather than the personal motivations of the characters, while also hiding the identity of the actors from the security police. While the coolness of Brecht might at first glance seem foreign to performers and audiences accustomed to the sentiment of township melodrama, the matter-of-fact acting favored by Brecht apparently suited the Serpent Players who, unlike the "situations" that frequented Dorkay House, were disciplined industrial workers and participants in the most politically active black community in the country (Fugard 1984: 96).

This discipline shaped the performances of *Sizwe Banzi* and *The Island*, devised by Kani, Ntshona, and Fugard. The latter, performed initially (July 1973) as *Die Hodoshe Span* [Hodoshe's Work-team], distilled the essential elements of two men's lives in prison from the actual experience of ex-political prisoner Norman Ntshinga in Robben Island Prison. The reenactment of *Antigone* derived from a performance on Robben Island, with Nelson Mandela as Creon (Mandela 1995: 456).[3] The classical allusion as well as the resonance of its theme earned *The Island* more international attention.[4] But *Sizwe Banzi* offers a richer synthesis of performance forms and a more compelling engagement with the experience of South African audiences. The story of Sizwe Banzi [the nation is strong], a man from the country who came to the city in search of work and gets it only once he acquires the identity and the valid passbook of a dead man, Robert Zwelinzima [weighty feeling], with the help of Buntu [humanity], was prompted by a photograph of a man in his Sunday best, posing with a cigarette in one hand and a pipe in the other, and a broad smile on his face. A man with such a smile, reasoned Kani and Ntshona, had to have his pass in order. This "celebratory image of a man, affirmative, full of life" and the ambiguous tale of survival behind the picture provided the mandate of the drama.[5] The action was generated by the contradiction between this "dream picture" (Figure 7.1) and the reality of discrimination represented by the official passbook photograph and "native identification" numbers. The Space program, which listed the participants (including Fugard) by I.D. numbers only, emphasized this alienation as well as the collaborative creation of the play, while shielding Kani and Ntshona (temporarily) from police interference.[6]

Figure 7.1 "The Dream Picture": The man with his pass in order; Winston Ntshona as "Robert Zwelinzima" in *Sizwe Banzi Is Dead* by Fugard, Ntshona, and John Kani (1972); photograph from the revival at the Royal Court, London, 1974. *Photograph and permission*: Donald Cooper

While the play emerged out of the contradiction between an affirmative image and a sober representation of apartheid, it also negotiated the tension between different modes of performance. The balancing act between Grotowskian "poor theatre" and exuberant impersonation, Brechtian coolness and the engaging, even ingratiating variety act, corresponded to the tension, in the lives of actors and characters alike, between the matter-of-fact negotiation of absurd but painful conflicts caused by apartheid law and the energetic mockery of that absurdity. The dramatization of this tension using props like the passbook and the social gests involved in handling them drew on Brecht by way of *The Coat*. The pace and tone of the performance was, however, shaped by the actors' life-histories, especially Kani's seven years with Ford. Kani's expansive impersonation of different characters, set off by Ntshona's straight-man portrayal of Sizwe, also suggests the variety sketches that toured the townships.[7] Kani's virtuoso performance as Styles and his antagonists, from his boss to a horde of cheeky cockroaches, was not really a monologue, as it is often described, but a satirical variety turn. Kani's impersonation of "Baas Bradley" and his own former self at the Ford assembly plant in anticipation of the visit of Henry Ford Jr. is typical:

"Tell the boys in your language, that this is a very big day . . ."
"Gentlemen, the old fool says this is a hell of a big day . . ."

"Tell the boys that Mr. Henry Ford the Second is the big baas . . . the Makhulu baas . . ."

"Mr Baas Bradley says . . . Mr. Ford is the grandmother baas of them all"

(Fugard 1993: 153)

Although more subtle than the clownish commentators in Kente's plays from Kenny Majozi's Zuluboy in *Lifa* to Ronnie Mokoena's Offside in *Too Late!*, Kani's comic mimicry of his boss's efforts to speak to his "boys," enhanced by direct engagement of the audience, recalls the performance style of township shows.

This affinity did not please everybody. Sipho Sepamla criticized the ingratiating aspect of the impersonation for making black spectators "laugh too hard at the white man to see beyond that" (*S'ketsh* 1973: 24); his skepticism was echoed in New York, where Kani's performance was compared to that staple of minstrelsy, Stephin Fetchit.[8] In St. Stephen's Hall in New Brighton, however, audiences proved able to combine heartfelt laughter at situations they knew all too well with strategic intervention:

> At the end of the Ford Factory story a man . . . entered the acting area and then, as if he was a referee at a boxing match, held up John's arm and announced that "Kani has knocked out Henry Ford the Junior."
>
> (Fugard 1993: 30)

Fugard calls this intervention Brechtian and, while it corresponds to Brecht's idea of the active spectator, it is also thoroughly African. As Fugard had already noted of *The Coat*, there was a significant difference between the white audience's emotional but alienated response of "horror and fascination" (1984: 143) and the cast members' dispassionate comment on the handling of the coat and associated objects, like the *umuti* [medicine] in the pocket that allegedly lightened the convict's sentence (p. 137). The difference between the fascination with staged suffering favored by audiences accustomed to the illusionistic Anglo-American stage and an African preference for interacting with the action rather than silently watching may have been new to Fugard, but African interest in social relations on stage was noted in the 1940s (Routh 1950b: 23), as well as in accounts of present-day African producers and audiences.[9]

While Kani's opening act reproduces some of the flavor of township comedy, Kani and Ntshona together kept more closely to plot and argument than Kente. The invisible pass in Kani's hands (and Nkosi's meaningful stare at the object) conveyed the real power of this document (Figure 7.2). Sizwe hesitates to give up his name to acquire another man's passbook, and is persuaded only when Buntu draws him into dramatizing a series of encounters – with a policeman and a prospective employer – to bring home the urgency of the decision. If the mostly white audience in Cape Town was touched by the bitter comedy of this predicament and if some blacks in Johannesburg found the play too talky,[10] those in New Brighton were moved to interrupt the debate:

Figure 7.2 Winston, John, and the passbook in *Sizwe Banzi Is Dead*. *Source*: NELM

After watching the first few seconds of the operation [putting Sizwe's photograph into Zwelinzima's pass] in stunned silence . . . a voice shouted out from the audience: "Don't do it brother . . ." Another voice responded . . . "Go ahead and try. They haven't caught me yet." That was the cue for the most amazing and spontaneous debate I have ever heard. As I stood . . . listening to it all, I realized I was watching a very special example of one of theatre's major responsibilities in an oppressive society: to break . . . the conspiracy of silence. . . . The action of our play was being matched . . . by the action of the audience. . . . A performance on stage had provoked a political event in the auditorium.

(Fugard 1993: 31–32)

What is noteworthy about this audience's participation in the remaking of *Sizwe Banzi* is not simply the urgent engagement with the subject matter; Fugard's stress on the "urgent and real" desire to "speak and be heard" oddly implies that this audience has never discussed the matter before. In contrast to the European-affiliated audience's emotional response of (silent) "horror and fascination," this audience's response demonstrates the remarkable convergence of Brechtian analysis and African vocal reaction to the dramatized situation.

This intervention is powerful not because it "breaks the silence" but because it acknowledges the symbolic character of the action. The audience's debate, like the show it interrupts, is a *performance*; its enactment here – in the liminal space between the familiar ground of the township outside and the occasional, unlikely character of the show inside the hall – is significant precisely because it is impossible outside. When Buntu and "Robert" in *Sizwe Banzi* simulate likely encounters with potential power brokers like the boss or the police or when prisoner John (Kani) mimes "calling home" from *The Island* – recalling the symbolic acts of Robben Island prisoners deprived of family contact – this performance reenacts ordinary acts in extraordinary circumstances. By intervening in the play, the members of the audience do not abandon the fiction; they *use* it. Their participation in a public performance reenacts the symbolic action of reclaiming and occupying public space and so entertains the possibility of a future public culture.

Engendered environments

The collaboration that produced *Sizwe Banzi Is Dead* set important formal and institutional precedents – the collective composition of scripts, only later recorded by an individual, the tricky negotiation of the different knowledge and experience of black or white participants, the primarily masculine cast of the enterprise – but did not encompass all the activity at the Space. Following the lead of the London theatre clubs as well as Dorkay House, the Space management (led by Brian Astbury, Yvonne Bryceland's husband) used the theatre's club status to evade censorship and produce theatre that was sexually as well as politically provocative, such as a local adaptation of *The Maids* by Jean Genet, which displayed the camp talents of Bill Curry and Vincent Ebrahim as the (coloured) maids, and of Pieter-Dirk Uys as the white Madam, in an early incarnation of the imperious diva that would become his alter ego: Evita Bezuidenhout. It also launched Uys as a satiric playwright with *Selle ou Storie* [Same Old Story] (first perfromed 1975; published Uys 1983), about the loves of gay and straight urban whites. While plays like this may have been common in New York or London, this play offended the local censors by not only the portrayal of gay characters but also the playful scrambling of English and Afrikaans. A cultural climate shaped by prurient censors on the one hand and revolutionary puritans on the other had little room for dramatizations of gay life.[11]

If Uys's theatre sustained the Space's aspirations to ironic urbanity, the plays of Fatima Dike, "an independent, sarky black woman" (Amato 1977: 14), depicted the ravages of black urban life with decidedly unironic urgency. Born in Langa, near Cape Town, Dike had an urban upbringing denied by apartheid law to many blacks. The range of themes and styles of her plays – from *The Sacrifice of Kreli* (Space Theatre, 1976; published Dike 1978), in English and isiXhosa, about the clash between British and amaGcakela in 1885, to *So What's New?* (Market Theatre, 1991; published Dike 1996), about four independent Soweto women, draws on education from Cape Town, via the Iowa Writers' Workshop, to New York. Where Kani and Ntshona had turned to Fugard as a scribe, Dike was one of the first black playwrights to be commissioned by a theatre and her second play, *The First South African* (The Space, 1977), was the first by a woman to be published in Ravan Press's pioneering series.[12]

Despite Dike's interest in women, *The First South African* (Dike 1977) gives the title of national protagonist to a male character and, in fusing manhood and nationhood, comes closer to BCM drama than to the women's theatre of the 1980s. The eponymous hero "was a man who looked like a white man, who had the heart of a black man, and was a 'coloured'" (Dike 1977: 46). Raised not by his white father, but by his Xhosa mother and her husband, Ruben Zwelinzima Jama is called Rooi, ostensibly because of his red hair; the name also alludes to the red ochre that the initiates wear after the Xhosa circumcision ceremony and to the term used historically to distinguish between traditionalist ("red") and Christianized amaXhosa. Caught in the contradiction between white and black demands on his identity, Zwelinzima (whose name recalls the protagonist of *Sizwe Banzi*) abuses Xhosa custom when he sleeps with his neighbor's daughter without paternal consent, hangs out with *tsotsis*, and abandons his family to work as a white on the railroad.

Though composed primarily of naturalistic dialogue in English, isiXhosa, *tsotsitaal*, and Afrikaans, the play harnesses several performance styles to the representation of ghetto life. It opens with a series of monologues: Joe Harzenberg, the actor playing Rooi, declaims a poem that begins with the creation and ends with the question: "Am I a man?" in the style of BCM performance poetry; Nomhle Nkonyeni, as his mother, answers questions posed by an unseen bureaucrat in a Brechtian way reminiscent of *The Coat*, and Max, Rooi's conman friend, treats spectators as suckers about to buy his stolen goods, in the flamboyant manner of Kente's *tsotsis*. The protagonist is introduced not with words, however, but in the play's most compelling image. Initially indistinguishable from the other blanketed youths at the circumcision ceremony, Rooi reveals himself when his white arm reaches out to the symbolic gifts left by the elders. In this image is distilled the unbearable tension between the "brotherhood of man" invoked by the ritual and the tragic implications of Rooi's "so-striking physical difference" (Amato 1977: 16). The community of men that might have sustained Rooi is vividly present here, but so is the reminder of the racial discrimination that is suffocating this community and distorting the youths' idea of manhood into *tsotsi* bravado. The stick that the elders give Rooi when he comes of age returns to beat him in the final scene. Driven from his family home, he performs his self-hatred for an imaginary *baas* in the familiar stereotype of the coloured *skollie*, "Nee, my baas. I'm quiet . . . I'm listening (*He stands to attention*)," while wrestling with the remaining symbol of paternal authority: "Leave me alone. . . . I'm tired of you (*He takes the stick and puts it across his shoulders and breaks it*)" (Dike 1977: 43).

Although this play deals mostly with the barriers faced by a man whose society will not acknowledge him, it also depicts the lives of women. Rooi's girlfriend

Thembi and his mother Freda are defined in relation to the male protagonist, to be sure, but the scenes of conflict between men and women suggest the limits of traditionalist *and* nationalist subjection of women. Although the subjugation of women is integral to the initiation ceremony, as the elder intones "with this stick, beat your mother when she forgets that she's a woman" (p. 6), Nkonyeni's performance gave Freda stage presence and moral authority more subtly dramatized than the suffering mother of the text might suggest. Her first appearance, in which Freda responds to the demands of an unseen white bureaucrat to give up her child, used the sober directness gleaned from her work on *The Coat* to draw out the social gest of the bureaucrat's instructions as well as the mother's response. In a later scene, Freda calls into question Rooi's understanding of manhood – he is willing to fight a *tsotsi* who insulted his girl but not to pay *lobola* [bride-price] to her father – with high emotion: "Why should I listen to you? You feel that you're a man now. . . . Do it outside these four walls" (p. 17). Nkonyeni's histrionics represented not only maternal feeling but also a black woman's defiance of a white (seeming) man. Shifting to the vernacular for the punchline, "Ungubani yena lo unqoqoza kakubi kangaka?" ["Who are you to shout at me like this?"], Nkonyeni and Dike direct the question to the character but also to the actor on stage and the men in the house and beyond.

Several other plays at the Space foregrounded women's voices. While *Imfuduso* (1978) brought women from Crossroads, the informal settlement that was established largely by women from the Transkei and Ciskei bantustans, and the immediate drama of their lives to the Space, Geraldine Aron's *Bar and Ger* (1978) recreated the inner life of white children insulated from the world. Dike's *Glasshouse* (1979, the last production by the Astbury management) used the lives of children to rather more pointed effect; in this semi-autobiographical play, a white girl and a black girl (the child of the former's servant) grow up in the same household but in different worlds. When Astbury and Bryceland left for London, the Space became the People's Space (*Volksruimte/ Indawo Yezizwe*, 1979–81), run by Rob Amato. It produced plays by and about black working people in the cities, such as Matsamela Manaka's *Egoli*, and in the rural areas, such as Zakes Mda's *Dark Voices Ring* (1979) and *The Hill* (1980; both in Mda 1990) and hosted others, such Kessie Govender's *Working Class Hero* (Stable Theatre, Durban, 1979).[13]

With the establishment of the Market Theatre, as well as institutions like the Federated Union of Black Artists (FUBA, 1978) and the FUNDA Centre in Soweto (1984), the engine of production began to shift to Johannesburg. The financial and cultural capital of the Market would shape theatre production nationwide, not only in the Witwatersrand, but also in the metropolitan centers of Cape Town and Durban, through hosting guest productions. The Market Theatre Laboratory would (from 1989) offer training to black students and community theatres. After the demise of the People's Space, the only substantial counterweight to the Market was the Grahamstown Festival. Beginning in 1974 as the exclusively white Anglophone affair of the 1820 Settlers Memorial Foundation, the festival was by 1984 ready to include black companies and performances in the fringe, subject to boycotts and protests by black groups who noted that invitations without financial aid did not amount to much. Only in the 1990s, with the emergence of other festivals such as the Afrikaans Kleinkaroofees and community theatre festivals organized by the Market Lab and the Windybrow (directed for PACT by Walter Chakela), did the renamed Grahamstown Foundation fund the work of selected community groups at the festival.[14]

Before the opening of the Market in 1976, however, a key production commissioned by the Space helped to cement links between Cape Town and Johannesburg and to establish the generic features of what came to be called theatre of resistance. Workshop '71's *Survival*, which opened at the Space in May 1976 and played in townships on the Witwatersrand in the wake of the Soweto uprising, was received by audiences and the police as part of that uprising. Like *Sizwe Banzi*, this play grew out of the life narratives of black male workers. But, where *Sizwe Banzi* favored intimate talk leavened with comedy, *Survival* used dialogue chiefly to provide a functional frame for individual narratives delivered directly to the audience. This direct address in English, punctuated by song, usually in the vernacular, and the masculine testimony that would provide the format for theatre in the wake of the Soweto uprising and in the shadow of the "emergency" in the 1980s, for plays like *Egoli* (YMCA, Soweto; then Space, 1979), *The Hungry Earth* by Maishe Maponya (DOCC, Soweto, 1979), and *Asinamali* (Ngema, 1985).

Before *Survival*, Workshop '71 had progressed from a workshop directed by Witwatersrand (Wits) University lecturer, Robert (Mshengu) McLaren (Kavanagh) into a professional theatre company, whose *Uhlanga* [The Reed, 1975] by James Mthoba, a one-man *Everyman*, toured the country. Performed at the Space and at Cape township venues before the uprising and then in Soweto and environs and at the Wits Box in the midst of the unrest, *Survival* was also the last production of the group, who went into exile when they took the show to the United States.[15] However brief its South African run, the performance of this play participated in a "revolutionary situation" partly by conscientizing white spectators but also by assembling township audiences as participants in defiance of laws against "riotous assembly" and "seditious speech" (Kavanagh 1981: 127).

Rather than a single plotline, *Survival* is structured around a place – prison – which is also an occasion for four prisoners to reenact their politicization in response to everyday life in apartheid society. Using a mixture of direct angry address and poignant introspection reminiscent of *The Island*, each actor delivered a "report" in his own name, in which he reenacted, with other actors playing roles from family members to court interpreters, the events that led to the arrest of his character. This matter-of-fact presentation, coupled with the fluid movement from one role to another, highlighted the collective character of the action. In Themba's report, for instance, Themba Ntinga, who plays the intellectual Leroi Williams whose chosen American name reflects his interest in international black liberation, alternates with the other characters, allowing the actors to draw from the individual stories the common social gests of oppression and resistance. As Williams comments, "suddenly, at obstinate moments, these circumstances come

together and trap a human being so tightly that for one moment the parts become a whole" (Workshop '71 1981: 160). Arising out of particular circumstances – Edward Nkosi kills one of his mother's clients in a revolt against the conditions that pushed her into prostitution; Vusi Mabandla kills a black policeman trying to prevent him from driving his father to hospital without a license; Slaksa Mphahlele is jailed for striking and Williams for agitation – this generalization has greater analytic clarity than the abstract statements in plays like *Shanti*, but the final scene nonetheless echoes the militant tone of the earlier play. As the prisoners go on hunger strike, they shout (p. 167):

Phela, phela, phela [a]malanga	Enough, enough, enough of these days
Azophela, azophela [a]malanga	There will be an end to these days

Despite the (mimed) beating of the prisoners at the end of the play, the actors survive to "go forward" (p. 168).

The reports may have seemed "strong and ugly" to some white reviewers (Kavanagh 1981: 126), but the final note of anticipation of liberation struck home with whites as well as blacks.[16] In the townships, it provoked police raids as well as applause. While the relative isolation of New Brighton and the relative quiescence of 1973 had allowed the audience to play with the performance of *Sizwe Banzi Is Dead*, the explosion in Soweto and the national crisis it provoked gave *Survival* an impact that was more direct but also short-lived. Facing police at township venues such as the Dube YMCA, the players incorporated them into the show, by opening with a comic impersonation of a policeman looking for "agitators" and by encouraging audience reaction, especially in the finale, "we go for(ward) . . . ". Rather than displaying politics as a theme, the players turned threats of state violence into politically enabling performance. However brief its run, *Survival* participated in the *enactment* of counter-publicity generated not only by the student rebellion in black schools and universities but also by church organizations and resurgent industrial unions (Brickill and Brooks 1980; Lodge 1985).

The performance made visible a public more diverse than the audience for BCM drama, and more vocally dissident than the audience for "Western" theatrical experiments. This is the public – or rather, the overlapping publics from liberal professionals through students at universities (black and white) to organic intellectuals and workers (mostly black) – that would sustain anti-apartheid theatre until 1990. Producers and engaged critics hailed this theatre as "majority theatre" and its audience as a vanguard for a future democratic South Africa (Kavanagh 1985: 214–15).[17] The summoning of a majority or even a vanguard through theatre was certainly no easy task. However, the Space had opened up an arena for integrated performance and social assembly that had long seemed impossible or undesirable, and the Market would build on its example. Galvanized by the events of 1976 and sustained by the political and cultural formations that grew up in its wake to establish the United Democratic Front (1983–90), progressives, intellectuals, and aspiring theatre practitioners from quite different classes would manage, despite internal and external criticism, to find common ground in this institution.

Marketplace or resistance

For many South Africans, June 1976 signals not merely the rebellion of black high school students against apartheid education but *the* turning point of the anti-apartheid struggle and thus the beginning of the end of white minority rule. Although students and industrial workers had been on the move since the founding of SASO in 1969 and the strikes of the early 1970s, the rebellion that exploded in Soweto on 16 June ignited not only government schools and beerhalls – torched as symbols of the state – but also the popular imagination, as tens of thousands across the country marched in support of the students. The nationwide impact of the Soweto uprising was temporarily slowed by the arrest and murder of leaders like Biko, and by the blanket suppression of anti-apartheid organizations in 1977 under the Internal Security Act (1976), which allowed for indefinite detention, and was reinforced by the state's military and propaganda machines. But, despite this repression, the force of the rebellion would redouble in the 1980s, guided by community groups that reemerged under the umbrella of the UDF, aided and eventually superseded by a resurgent ANC-in-exile, and would eventually force the apartheid state to negotiate its own demise.

The Market opened a few days after the uprising. As the army invaded Soweto, the company rehearsed *The Seagull*, Chekhov's ironic portrait of the pre-revolutionary Russian gentry. While this play should not be read simply as an allegory of South African whites on the eve of revolution, the ambiguities of the place and occasion of its performance should be noted. Located in Newtown, on the border between the central business district and Fordsburg, a mixed neighborhood that had housed migrants of all colors since the 1890s, the Market Theatre occupied a building that was once an Indian fruit market until the Group Areas Act whitewashed the city center (Graver and Kruger 1989: 273).[18] Simon's vision of the theatre as a "meeting place for all South Africans . . . as enriching and relevant as the market it . . . replaced" (Graver and Kruger 1989: 273) acknowledged this history of dispossession but did not directly contest the acquiescence of Johannesburg's capitalist elite to the urban planning of the apartheid state, from the first Urban Areas Acts of the 1920s through the demolition of Sophiatown in the 1950s to the Pageview removals of the 1970s, protested but not prevented by the Johannesburg City Council.

The refurbished Market was sponsored – as *King Kong* had been – by South Africa's major private companies.[19] It stood rather awkwardly between the historical displacement of black commerce by the combined forces of apartheid and capital and the present aspiration to become, in the words of a management committee member, "an oasis in a society of total chaos . . . where people could talk together and we could put on theatre that . . . said things about South Africa" (Schwartz 1988: 37).[20] By concentrating capital in the central building, especially in the first decade, the board expressed the desire of its primary audience for metropolitan prestige, reinforced by comparisons with institutions like Covent Garden in London (Graver and Kruger 1989: 275). However well intentioned, the Market's emphasis on a building, in which "black people can watch theatre in a decent way," in the words of manager, Mannie Manim (Graver and Kruger 1989: 274) betrayed a certain disdain for township theatre, while failing to change the laws that made funding for "decent theatre" in the townships precarious. This conflation of social propriety with cultural standing is not merely a product of apartheid; the unintended snobbery here recalls the British Arts Council's dismissal of non-traditional, out-of-the-way venues as "unprofessional" in the name of "standards" and "proper theatre" (Kruger 1992: 11–17).

This discrimination between cultivated centers and neglected peripheries marks many cities, although it took on particular force under apartheid. The cultural prestige of legitimate theatre has often been marked by the physical prominence of the building located on an urban hub (Carlson 1989: 61–97) or, less obviously, by the location of the building in a *liminoid* space (Carlson 1989: 110) on the border between the legitimate city of commerce, prosperity, and modernity and the illegitimate city of crime, poverty, and backwardness. In Johannesburg in 1976, this faultline had become a battleline formerly marked by the barrier between the permanent white city and the apparently impermanent black "location." By 1986, Johannesburg's centennial year, the theatre was no longer an outpost of gentrification but the hub of development including a fleamarket, a gallery, and a cluster of boutiques and restaurants, frequented mostly by affluent whites, as well as a new Stock Exchange building in nearby Diagonal Street, once the spine of Indian trade. It was also backed if not always supported by adjoining black organizations like FUBA and the Afrika Cultural Centre, whose members boycotted the centennial celebrations but received funding from some of the same liberal patrons as the Market. In the years between the centennial and the post-apartheid reorganization of the city government and the cultural budget, tensions in the image of what one promoter called the "island of sanity. . . cushioning the shock of South Africa's collision with the future" (Graver and Kruger 1989: 275) – between liberal amelioration of impossible conditions and radical transformation of those conditions – manifested themselves in battles over the legitimate occupancy of stage and house, as well as the political relevance of the repertoire.

As an icon of national reconciliation and cultural prestige in one of Africa's most developed and most fragmented urban centers, the Market Theatre occupied – and still occupies – uncertain terrain. The institution of political theatre and its concretization in the buildings on the threshold between liberal promises of progress and the brutal regression of apartheid represented the condition of *geopathology*, the "problem of place and place *as problem*" (Chaudhuri 1995: 55). If Chaudhuri sees geopathology as the condition of metropolitan realist drama, I use it to highlight the way in which the Market marked the deformation of urban space by the apartheid imagination and attempted to counter removals and banishment in the decade and a half between the Soweto uprising and the release of Nelson Mandela in 1990 by enacting drama not only of struggle but also of restoration.

To understand the range and limits of the Market's impact on South African theatre, we should consider the institutional models available to its founders. Apart from the commercial theatres producing imports from American and those British playwrights who ignored the boycott, the dominant institution in Johannesburg was PACT, where Manim worked for a decade. Strictly segregated by the state and largely confined to a mixture of canonical drama and inoffensive comedy by the pressures of censorship and the school curriculum, PACT was no "non-racial meeting place" but its well-appointed houses and professional train-ing gave Manim a model of sorts for the "decent theatre" which he hoped to extend to general audiences. Barney Simon's intermittent association with PACT included access to its experimental studio in the 1970s to produce plays such as Büchner's *Woyzeck* (Arena 1973) and to assemble the professional (white) actors, such as Aletta Bezuidenhout, Vanessa Cooke, and Marius Weyers (from PACT) and Paul Slabolepszy (from the Space), who would form the nucleus of his company. As the Company (before the Market), this group performed classical adaptations, such as the perennially relevant *Antigone* (with Bezuidenhout, 1975), and local material, such as *Hey Listen!* (1974), monologues adapted from Simon's *Jo'burg, Sis!* stories, with Weyers as an urban misfit, Slabolepszy as a handyman choked up by the fate of a young girl attacked by dogs meant for blacks, and Cooke, as a would-be Miss South Africa.

Less visible but equally important were the institutions that provided Simon with his theatrical education. Working backstage at the Theatre Workshop in London's East End in 1959, Simon witnessed Joan Littlewood's transformation of texts from *Macbeth* to Brendan Behan's *The Hostage* through workshops with actors and designers into a democratic theatre event.[21] Simon's work in the 1960s with Union Artists on shows like *Phiri* reflects the influence of Littlewood's methods but also the limits of their application in a society that made democracy impossible. Exposure to independent theatre of color during his stay in the United States, while directing plays by Fugard (1968–70), and to black nurses and other profes-sionals in the Transkei and KwaZulu (quasi-independent bantustans), with whom he developed health education sketches in 1973–74 (Simon 1974), gave him alternative institutional models to the paternalism of Union Artists, which would move the Market beyond minority culture to an oppositional but ultimately majority public sphere.

While the Market Company performances in the first season focused on inter-national modern drama, the season as a whole represented a small but significant shift toward black producers as well as actors. The main theatre opened in October with Peter Weiss's *Marat/Sade* (dir.: Simon), whose dramatization of sex, madness, and revolution was to become the mainstay of university drama programs, and continued with Trevor Griffiths' *Comedians* (dir.: Leonard Schach), whose portrayal of a socially critical even hostile comedian received critical acclaim but grumbling from the censors. The mainstage also accommodated revivals of *The Sacrifice of Kreli* (from the Space) and Fugard standards, *The Island* and *People Are Living There*. The Upstairs studio featured *Vroue van Troje* [Trojan Women, adapted from Euripides by Simon and a cast that included PACT stalwarts Weyers and Wilna Snyman], satirical revues, by Robert Kirby (*How Now, Sacred Cow?*) and Pieter-Dirk Uys (*Strike up the Banned*), the latter's *God's Forgotten* (Uys 1981), on Afrikaner women under siege in a future civil war, and revivals of *The Blood Knot* and *Waiting for Godot*, developed with black casts in Durban and Soweto by Benjy Francis, who had been involved with TECON.

This season showed the Market's capacity to absorb personnel from its rival institutions and to accommodate black directors (initially of Indian descent, such as Francis and Alan Joseph) as well as performers (such as James Mthoba of Workshop '71 and Sam Williams of Phoenix, both in Francis's productions). Joseph would go on to head the Johannesburg Civic Theatre and PACT itself. Francis later directed Mda's *Dead End* and *We Shall Sing for the Fatherland* in Soweto (1979), founded the Dhlomo Theatre in honor of the pioneer playwright, and set up the Afrika Cultural Centre, which he still heads. While the Market's accommodation of black players and producers did not immediately dissolve decades of discrimination, it should not be dismissed as tokenism. The signal contribution of artists like Mthoba and Williams should not be treated merely as the "continuation of the old United [*sic*] Artists tradition of black collaboration" (Fuchs 1990: 41) nor should the work of directors like Francis be slighted. Rather their presence drew the attention of a new generation of spectators to a submerged intercultural tradition that had survived in the interstices between paternalism and resistance, and thus suggested the possibility of harnessing that tradition to the transformation of the institution.

These institutional shifts not only reintroduced an older generation of black actors schooled in literary drama and intercultural collaboration to a wider audience, but it also established links with a new generation of actors whose theatre experience was shaped first by township musicals and melodramas and second by BCM performance poetry and agitprop. Soweto plays in this vein, like Mtsaka's *Not His Pride* (1973), Khayalethu Mqayisa's *Confused Mhlaba* (1974), or Shimane Mekgoe's *Lindiwe* (1975), grafted explicit political content onto emphatic, high-volume presentation of township melodramas. Those such as *The Hungry Earth* (1978) and *Egoli* (1979), which were mediated by facilitators like Simon, Amato, and Francis, followed the example of *The Island* and *Survival*, using the rhythm of alternating restrained and explosive gestural expression to create harsh and lyrical testimony to the struggle with apartheid brutality. To be sure, not all theatre at the Market should be called testimonial. In the fifteen odd years between the Soweto uprising and the unbanning of the ANC, the Market produced European classics and modern iconoclasts from Shakespeare and Brecht to Dario Fo and Sam Shephard, as well as local history plays, such as *The Native Who Caused All the Trouble* (Vanessa Cooke, Fink Haysom, and Danny Keogh, 1983). Based on an incident in the 1930s in which a Sotho claimed ownership of land in Cape Town to the consternation of the white authorities, this play bore a striking if unintended resemblance to the story dramatized in *Tau* forty years earlier. Nonetheless, it was the dialectic between testimony and spectacle that was to drive the theatre of, in, and through the Market to represent South Africa at home and abroad.

Bearing witness / overbearing spectacle

While bearing witness on stage may not have led to immediate "mobilization of the oppressed" (to recall Mda's prescription for resistance), the enactment of testimony should not be dismissed as merely "protest" or "lament." Honed by precise body techniques, voiced in whispers as well as shouts, this enactment went beyond display to the clarifying re-presentation of South African lives. Some protest plays replicated the formulas established by *Survival*. *Asinamali*, for instance, combined the rousing testimony of black men in prison with a rather blunt ridicule of white bureaucrats and black and white women that reduced differentiated testimony to a generalized call to arms. At its most effective, however, in plays like *Egoli, Born in the RSA* (1985), or *Have You Seen Zandile?* (1986), it drew on intimate as well as public acts and, especially in the latter two, also highlighted tensions as well as connections between men and women.

Egoli offered an exemplary case of the pitfalls and power of testimonial theatre. It was workshopped by author Matsamela Manaka and actors John Moalusi Ledwaba and Hamilton Mahonga Silwane under the auspices of Soyikwa Theatre in mid-1979. Founded by Manaka, Soyikwa (after Wole Soyinka) attempted to operate independently but benefited from Urban Foundation support for Soweto venues such as the YMCA and later the FUNDA Centre, headed by Manaka from 1984 (Fuchs 1990: 87). *Egoli* [isiZulu: "place of gold" and an alternative name for Johannesburg] was not the first play to deal with the lives of black miners, at the literal and figurative base of apartheid in the Witwatersrand goldfields; Maponya's *Hungry Earth* used the lives of three miners as the basis for an epic meditation on migrant labor in rural as well as urban settings.[22] But, where Maponya portrays typical characters in speech that remain relatively abstract, albeit enlivened by "spectacular action" (Steadman 1995: xvi), Manaka depicts the effects of drink, dangerous work, and the confinement of the single-sex hostels by focusing on a particular miner (John) and his more level-headed room-mate (Hamilton). The initial performance at the YMCA relied too much, in Benjy Francis's view, on sketches of John's various encounters with employers on the mines and elsewhere – and not enough on "economy of gesture and thought" – to concentrate the actors' and the audience's attention (*S'ketsh* 1979: 16). Reshaped at the People's Space, *Egoli* revived the dramaturgy of *The Island* – two black men struggling with each other as well as their confinement – while pushing beyond that play's abstract representation to the visceral *embodiment* of brutalization. Although the action included mine scenes and a dream sequence in which the men reenact their flight from prison, it always returned to the hostel room, furnished with little more than bunks, cleaning equipment, and a precious radio. The climax comes after a narrow escape from a mine accident – dramatized by the two men groping through a black-out lit only by their headlamps; John reacts by drinking and dancing with concentrated intensity until he vomits and collapses.[23] Roused by Hamilton who berates him first in his own voice and then in the voice of an impersonal official reporting the death in the accident of the son John thought was safe at home, John is restored by his friend's "gentle[, a]lmost ceremonial" cleansing of his face and torso (Manaka 1980: 27).

The play ends with the actors singing of "sweat turned into blood" in the mines and the hope of "justice, freedom and peace . . . in the country of our forefathers" (Manaka 1980: 28), but it is the embodiment of degradation and restoration that concentrates the power of the performance. By vomiting on stage, Ledwaba not only assailed his own body, but also arrested the flow of meaning from performer to audience. His act of self-inflicted violence compelled the audience's attention to the actor's testimony against violence done his character by degrading work conditions one mile underground, but its excess also confounded the audience's attempt to render it a transparent sign.[24] The performance at the Market (December 1979) provoked gasps and nervous laughter from the predominantly white audience, but it was a *black* writer, the poet Oswald Mtshali, rather than the more reticent white reviewers, who came closest to commenting directly on this scene, arguing that the play was "deliberately honed to cut to the bone and expose the raw nerve, letting the salt of suffering run into the empty wound. It will make the smug and complacent very uncomfortable."[25]

However powerful its effect on spectators, Ledwaba's action raises an important question about the function of spectacular violence in anti-apartheid theatre and, more generally, about what Njabulo Ndebele called the formulaic "exhibition-ism" (1986: 143) of protest. Although this question became the subject of intense public debate only later (Ndebele 1986; De Kok and Press 1990; Steadman 1991; Mda 1995), it had already emerged as a potential problem. When Fugard distinguished between the "horror and fascination" of white audiences and the engaged but matter-of-fact interaction of black audiences with the stage represen-tation of their daily life, he drew attention to the risk of turning protest into a spectacle. As several critics were to argue, the display of apartheid before metro-politan spectators at home and abroad, who were separated by race or class privilege from the oppression portrayed on stage, may have nourished those spectators' sense of moral outrage while allowing them to forget their implication in apartheid. This nourishment resembles what Frantz Fanon called the "catharsis" afforded the colonizer by the spectacle of the colonized's "stinging denunciations of distressing conditions," the "violent, resounding, florid writing," which "on the whole serves to reassure the occupying power" (Fanon 1968: 239). While metropolitan audiences in Johannesburg or Cape Town or, for that matter, New York, did not literally constitute an "occupying power," their desire for catharsis was evinced in respectful reviews for the "strong and ugly" scenes of apartheid suffering and anti-apartheid defiance.

But answering the question about spectacular violence might be more complicated than reiterating the different tendencies of black and white audiences. To be sure, *Egoli* confirms the separation between metropolitan and indigenous audiences in that it received more vocal interest in Johannesburg, Cape Town, and various European festivals than among township audiences.[26] While it is likely that the Soweto script treated John's degradation as one among many instances of brutalization superseded by the rousing chorus on freedom at the end[27] and that the vomiting and cleansing "ceremony" became the climax during the rehearsals at the Space, this reshaping was endorsed by Francis, a self-identified black activist. The organic connection between gesture and thought that Francis called for emerges in the precise enactment of brutality and its redress, which in turn provides the ground for the call to solidarity at the end.

While testimonial theatre did not completely escape the perils of exhibitionism, its most compelling work avoided the temptation to make a spectacle of unspeakable brutality. Especially during the "state of emergency" proclaimed in the mid-1980s, police intimidation and censorship pushed militant playwrights like Manaka and Maponya out of township venues and into the Market, whose prestige gave it a certain immunity. Even agitprop designed for black audiences, such as Maponya's *Umongikazi* [Nurse] (first performed 1983; published Maponya 1995), were tested at the Market before moving to the townships. In *Umongikazi* black nurses confront arrogant doctors and hostile administrators, who were usually white, whether in the white hospitals that grudgingly employed black nurses, or in black hospitals, where they worked in overcrowded and underfunded wards. The play, which ended with a call for unionization, was well received by nurses at Baragwanath Hospital in Soweto, but booed by township audiences disappointed because the show was too short and too austere.[28] Notwithstanding this reception, the police found the performance provocative enough to summon Maponya for a not-so "friendly chat" about his connection to the Health Workers' Association (Maponya 1995: ix–x). His next project, *Gangsters* and *Dirty Work*, a diptych on the security state and its agents, was planned and performed at the Market and, while it was tolerated there, *Gangsters* was restricted to "experimental" or "avantgard[e]" venues by order of the Publication Control Board (Steadman 1995: xx–xxi).

While *Gangsters* and *Dirty Work* were produced under the aegis of Maponya's Bahumutsi Players, both plays were shaped by European theatre as well as by the company's political intent. *Dirty Work*, a solo piece shaped by John Maythan, who played the security expert giving a lecture to a nervous white audience, bears comparison with Robert Kirby's impersonations of funny but frightening Afrikaner bureaucrats, and, as Maponya acknowledges, *Gangsters* drew liberally from Beckett's *Catastrophe* (1982), which Maponya had been invited to direct in 1984 (Maponya 1995: x). Beckett's spare depiction of an enigmatic scene, in which a director (D) employs the services of an assistant (A) to manipulate a silent protagonist (P), apparently cowed by some unnamed torment, and an unseen audience whose taped applause seems to mock as much as ratify the director's work, may have appeared remote from the actual torture in South African prisons but *Catastrophe*'s refusal to name the catastrophe or its agents and therefore to give the action a single referent informs Maponya's play.

Even though *Gangsters* pours a particular content into *Catastrophe*'s abstract form, as the pointed title implies and the dialogue and setting in a South African prison explicate, it retains the latter's resistance to the "violent, florid" spectacle of violence that Fanon associated with a cheap catharsis tossed to (neo)colonial spectators. This resistance works in part through the refusal to indulge the audience with a suspense- and emotion-laden story about a heroic protagonist – the play opens with the police "discovering" the dead man whom they then have to "cover up" – and, in part, by the almost total absence of references to a specific model, such as Biko, whose death from headwounds inflicted in detention was likewise covered up before the inquest.[29] The play was performed at the Market in July 1984, with John Maythan as Major Whitebeard, Union Artists veteran Sol Rachilo as his lackey, Jonathan, and with Maponya himself as the poet, Rasechaba [father of the nation].[30] The performance opens with the silent, dead poet covered in black and draped as if on a cross (Figure 7.3, see over), with the perpetrators posed on either side. By presenting the evidence and the complicity of Whitebeard and Jonathan at the outset, the play avoids a spectacle of torture. This scene of a crime covered up returns at intervals, punctuating the unfolding conflict between Rasechaba and his antagonists, the white policeman and the black stooge, and thus reminding the audience of the absent force of state violence. At the same time, the confrontations between the poet and his jailers provide an occasion for Maponya to include nationalist poetry that would otherwise be banned. Although the final image returns to Beckett's directions – the spot on the poet's head (Maponya 1986: 87) – the last scene displays the stupidity as well as the brutality of his antagonists and grants that image the effect of a silent prophecy that magnifies the power of the voice on tape.[31]

If *Gangsters* offers an eloquent witness against those indicted in the title, its companion piece, *Dirty Work*, portrays a garrulous front man whose lecture never quite manages to cover up the disturbing noises-off. Maythan's impersonation of a paranoid but plausible security expert clearly entertained its predominantly white audiences but also reminded them of their assent to the increasingly draconian "emergency" state. *Dirty Work* was not just a "humorous prelude" to the "more serious" treatment of *Gangsters* (Steadman 1995: xi); it was also an opportunity to refunction the spectacular tendency in protest drama by compelling its habitual audience to look in a distorted but recognizable self-image. While resistance theatre by Maponya and others had targeted black audiences, even when pressed by political and financial constraints to perform far from that target audience, this play turns those constraints to advantage. By directing a white actor in a performance whose ambiguous character entertained but also discomforted its liberal spectators, allowing them a catharsis of sorts through laughing at this paranoid bureaucrat, Maponya confronts these spectators with their own paranoia. This sort of theatre may be more ironic than the agitprop of *Umongikazi*, but its irony

173

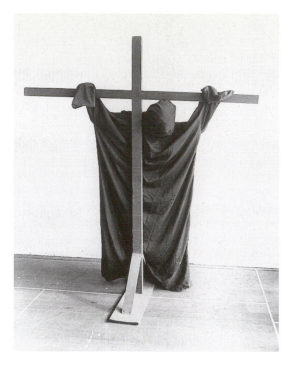

Figure 7.3 The "silent, dead poet" in *Gangsters* by Maishe Maponya, Market Theatre 1984. *Photograph and permission*: Ruphin Coudyzer

also enables *Dirty Work*, its white protagonists and its black author to turn the gaze of power back on itself.

Woza Albert! [Albert, Arise! 1981] anticipated *Dirty Work*'s strategy of insinuating satiric images of white power figures into a comic act to confront the laughing white audience with a spectacle of their kin, although its weapons were slapstick, burlesque, and broad mimicry rather than the irony of *Dirty Work* and its satire broad, even generous, rather than corrosive. One of the most widely performed plays to originate at the Market, *Woza Albert!* differs from much protest theatre not so much in its use of humorous moments, which are present in most plays from *Sizwe* through *Survival* to *Asinamali*, but in its explicit appropriation of a plot structured less by the testimonial of the anti-apartheid agent than by vaudeville gags of the underdog. Although both Mtwa and Ngema acknowledged the impact of Grotowski and Brook on their technique, and the contribution of Simon to organizing the material (Mtwa, Ngema, and Simon 1983: i), the influence of Kente – with whom they worked on *Mama and the Load* (Market mainstage, 1980) – is clear in the variety sketches and physical comedy loosely attached to the main idea, the Second Coming of Christ to South Africa – and in the sly approach to political topics.[32] The picture of Mtwa and Ngema in whiteface – or rather, "pink

Figure 7.4 "Pink-nose" mimicry in *Woza Albert!* by Mbongeni Ngema, Percy Mtwa (pictured), and Barney Simon (director), Market Theatre, 1981. *Photograph and permission*: Ruphin Coudyzer

nose" – imitation of white bosses (Figure 7.4) recalls Kente stalwarts like Kenny Majozi; the ping-pong balls perform a similar function to the plastic gloves worn by the otherwise unseen bureaucrat in *Too Late!*

But the creators of *Woza Albert!* went beyond comedy to discomfort their audiences. Despite attempts to reclaim it as an authentic Soweto product (Ndlovu 1986: xxiii), the play targets (in both senses) a metropolitan audience.[33] Taking its location at the Market as its point of departure, *Woza Albert!* eschews a transparent representation of black struggle. Under general camouflage of the myth of Christ's return as *Morena* [Sesotho for Lord] and the particular camouflage of pink noses, police helmets, and other accoutrements of apartheid authority, they disturb the mimetic stability of the black/white dichotomy. Mimicking white bureaucrats and foremen, Mtwa and Ngema turn their bodies into distorting mirrors parodying their audience. In so doing, they shift the parameters of anti-apartheid representation by unsettling rather than confirming the sympathetic spectator's presumption of solidarity. They also point to what might be called post-apartheid satire, in which savvy urbane blacks shepherd hapless whites lost in an environment now beyond their control, as in Paul Slabolepszy's *Mooi Street*

Moves (1992) or, in gentler slapstick version in Simon's *Silent Movie* (1992), both featuring Seputla Sebogodi (Figure 7.5).

The impersonation of authority figures in *Woza Albert!* may be compared to what Bhabha has called the colonial subject's mimicry of domination. For Bhabha, colonial mimicry is "a strategy of subversion that turn[s] the gaze of the discriminated back upon the eye of power" (Bhabha 1986: 173). *Woza Albert!* turns the equivocation of colonial mimicry into a strategy of critique. In performance, Mtwa and Ngema tease metropolitan audiences in Johannesburg – or New York (Kruger 1991) – by inviting them to share their jokes at the impersonated "whites" only to remind them that they are themselves the butt of the joke. In the opening scene, Mtwa impersonates a white policeman who harasses an abject Ngema while offering conspiratorial racist asides to the audience about the alleged depravity of blacks; in the second scene, both actors play prisoners to an invisible but irascible warden. The prisoners' submission to a body inspection becomes an occasion for mooning the audience: the actors' *imitation* of submission thus turns into an act of defiance directed at the complicity of the audience rather than the cruelty of the invisible warden. Unlike the imitation of defiance in *Asinamali*, which allows a metropolitan audience to have it both ways, to pity the victim and share the sense of outrage, the mimicry in this scene *implicates* the metropolitan audience as spectators of the display of apartheid and so brings them up short against their desire for a cathartic spectacle of outrage and their reluctance fully to confront their implication in the oppression on display.

But the effectiveness of *Woza Albert!* is not limited to confronting metropolitan spectators with their complicity. The opening scenes may offer a "mimicry of colonial domination" whose subversion depends on its being seen by the privileged metropolitan spectator, "the eye of power," but the final scene in the graveyard where Morena raises fallen heroes from the dead addresses a majority audience. The invocation of an anti-apartheid pantheon – "Woza [Arise] Albert [Luthuli]," "Woza Lilian [Ngoyi] . . . Woza Bram Fischer, woza Ruth First" (Mtwa, Ngema and Simon: 73, 78–80) – is not simply a rousing conclusion; it is significant because it makes full sense only to those who know these names and the history of resistance they represent. The end of the play points beyond the mere display of apartheid by acknowledging, indeed enacting, the tensions between the testimonial address of the performance and the audience's as yet uncertain mastery of the role of critical witness.[34]

Where activists such as Maponya framed their doubts about the Market's role in the radical transformation of South African society in terms of doubts about the substitution of the Market's metropolitan audience for the desired majority audience outside, Simon responded to the challenge by producing theatre to re-form this audience from bystanders into witnesses of apartheid. In a series of plays from *Cincinatti* [*sic*] (1979) to *Born in the RSA* (1985), Simon and Company actors used narratives based on their research into individual lives as well as current events to create performances that attempted critically to reflect and refract contemporary South African experiences. These experiments tacitly acknowledged other plays in

Figure 7.5 The white country bumpkin and the black city dude in *Silent Movie*, by Barney
Simon, with Seputla Sebogodi and Lionel Newton (pictured). *Photograph and
permission*: Ruphin Coudyzer

the Market repertoire. They drew on the portrayal of defiant black men in plays like *Survival* and *Egoli* as well as the representation of random but inexorable white violence: the violence of a white prole who attacks his friend but blames a black man, as in Paul Slabolepszy's *Saturday Night at the Palace* (1982), or between white men conscripted to fight them in such plays as *Môre is 'n Lang Dag* [Tomorrow Is a Long Day; Deon Opperman, 1984], or between men and women at home, as in *This Is for Keeps* (Vanessa Cooke, Danny Keogh, and Janice Honeyman, 1983). But they went beyond depictions of alienation to represent solidarity as the basis of liberation. While acknowledging the "separate development" of black, white, and those caught between, the Company hoped to confound simple oppositions between black struggle and white introspection by linking private selves and public agents, testimony and action.

Born in the RSA, a dramatic response to the state violence of the mid-1980s, tops this experimentation with the collective re-presentation of personal and public material. *Call Me Woman* (1979), inspired in part by Ntosake Shange's *For Colored Girls Who Have Considered Suicide When the Rainbow Is Enuf* (1971), depicted women's experience, while *Black Dog/Injemnyana* (Market Theatre, 1984; published Simon *et al.* 1997) drew on the model of *Survival* to juxtapose the lives of unrelated individuals during the Soweto uprising and to foster reflection on the unrest.[35] The monologues in *Call Me Woman* – including a black woman's first sexual encounter in the back of a car (a township status symbol), and an Indian woman's shame at being denied access to a white family's phone after Indian men had chased her car on the highway – seemed too trivial for some male critics, although its directness moved others.[36] The narratives in *Black Dog* – from an account of the eponymous leader (John Ledwaba) to comments by township dwellers in the thick of the action and whites on the sidelines, including an ex-serviceman from an anti-terrorist unit – remained too disconnected on the level of plot or argument to *represent* the connection between black and white lives that it *displayed* on stage (Figure 7.6).

While these experiments never quite integrated black and white spaces or public and private action nor fully deployed the tension between monologue and dialogue, speech and song, *Born in the RSA* combined these elements to portray characters as protagonists of national as well as personal dramas of contact and conflict. While all three drew on immediate experience and research on actual people, only *Born in the RSA* combined the display of these testimonies with their collective and individual enactment, by working the gaps as well as links between nationhood and selfhood, agitation and restoration, agency and being. As the title suggests, the authors of these testimonies share a common birthplace; as its ironic iteration implies, however, they are separated by acts of public disenfranchisement as well as private disavowal. On a stage empty but for chairs, microphones, and newspapers, against a backdrop of images from the day-to-day struggle during the "emergency," this "docudrama" (in the program) used the format of courtroom testimony stripped of the naturalistic box that might hem it in.

From the first monologue, the performers explored the critical and creative

Figure 7.6 Displaying the Struggle in *Black Dog/Injemnyana* by Barney Simon and the cast; Marie Human, Gcina Mhlophe, John Ledwaba, Neil McCarthy, and Kurt Egelhof at the Market Theatre 1984. *Photograph and permission*: Ruphin Coudyzer

tension between (Brechtian) report *on* and (Aristotelian) embodiment *of* action. The opening speech of Mia Steinman – Afrikaner by birth, Jewish by marriage, and anti-apartheid lawyer by family inheritance as well as personal commitment – begins not with biography, but with the paragraphs in the Internal Security Act (1976, amended 1984) that prohibited legal redress against the state or its agents and that justified the "emergency," declared in July 1985 just before the play opened (Simon *et al.* 1986: 134).[37] By juxtaposing the current crisis with the history of Treason Trials since the 1950s and by embedding both in the memory of an Afrikaans woman (played by English-speaking actress, Fiona Ramsay), the play challenges the iconic dominance of the male activist, black or white. By making this activist a snappily dressed, chain-smoking talker with a personal, family, and political history, Ramsay gives this national protagonist the substantial dimensions of what is commonly called a "rounded character," but also the critical eye of a commentator who introduces the other characters as clients and witnesses. By juxtaposing the political Mia with the apolitical Nicky (Terry Norton), a woman seeking a divorce from Glen (Neil McCarthy), later exposed as a police spy, the company hoped to engage the attention of "ordinary South

Africans" (Simon *et al*. 1994: 12). It sought to do this by suggesting the "endless spiral of connections" (Simon *et al*. 1986: 136) that entangle not only the police spy, disguised (as so many were) as a campus radical, and his targets – art teacher Susan (Vanessa Cooke) and union organizer Thenjiwe (Thoko Ntshinga) – but also the unwilling witnesses – Thenjiwe's sister Sindiswa (Gcina Mhlophe), whose son is arrested on a bogus charge, and her tenant, Zach, the gentle musician (Timmy Kwebulana). Reflecting on her performance of Sindiswe, based on a woman who was searching for a child imprisoned during a random police sweep, Mhlophe highlighted the experience of inadvertently as well as actively political people and emphasized the ethical responsibility of the performer to tell this story.[38] By linking political agents with those in retreat from politics, the play plots the interplay between commitment and betrayal, agency and quietism, which complicates the overall conflict between oppressor and oppressed, while at the same time reminding its audience that the state did not allow black South Africans to evade politics.

The most explicitly political character in the play, Thenjiwe, whom Mia introduces – half in jest – as the "first woman president of South Africa" (Simon *et al*. 1986: 142), is also the one who does not introduce herself. Preceded by her reputation (expressed in Mia's characterization, Zach's praise for her commitment, and Sindiswa's more ambivalent mix of awe and exasperation), Ntshinga takes on her role almost casually, as she begins singing underneath Zach's account of his rapport with her nephew. What is striking here is not just the play of voices but also the embodiment and the demonstration of character, between the vivid recounting of torture – Thenjiwe is forced to stand for days on end – and the cool *Verfremdung* of the scene in which it occurs (pp. 160–61):

Cop (Glen): It's not fair, the captain is at home sleeping with his wife and I have to sit here staring at this fucken *kaffermeid*.

Thenjiwe: It was a very young white cop. . . . *ag*, shame, for a moment I pitied him. At least I was doing something I believed in. But what was his life locked up in a cell with a swaying swelling *kaffermeid* with rolling eyes? He took money out of his pocket and sent the black cop to buy him a cool drink. He watched me. [. . .]

Thenjiwe: He moved toward me. . . . I wanted to tell him: "Listen man, it's no use. It'll take you an hour to get me to lie down and I'm no good . . . standing." . . . His gun was on the table. If I could just fall that way I could land on it. . . . I saw it happen (*she mimes shooting poses*), kazoom, kazoom, . . . like a crazy cowboy movie . . . the black cop arrived with the cool drink. . . . I think we were both disappointed.

Significantly, the torture does not appear in this scene. In *Egoli*, Ledwaba embodied his character by inflicting pain on himself and so risked making a spectacle rather than an example of his body, but here Ntshinga and McCarthy keep their distance from each other and from their respective characters. Although her account of Thenjiwe's pain is certainly vivid, as well as an accurate picture of documented torture techniques, Ntshinga does not swell up. She remains, as Brecht would have it, *sovereign* over her character's experience, presenting its various aspects – suffering, tenacity, irony – to the audience for analysis as well as inviting them to share her pleasure in the imagined retribution in the idiom of the gangster picture, much loved by urban African audiences.[39]

Songs of resistance and restoration

This theatre of resistance is also a theatre of restoration. The restorative dimension of the action emerges especially at the moments when the performers break from their characters' witness "boxes" and join each other in song. The first song – Thenjiwe's solo introduction – pulls on several strands of history: "Likashona iLanga" [The Setting Sun] was a hit by *King Kong* bandleader Mackey Davashe; it was also associated with the ANC – and was later used as the signature for a television documentary about the organization, *Ulibambe likashona iLanga* [Hold up the Setting Sun, 1993]. Most are the songs of the Soweto uprising, such as "Alala amabhunu," sung by Mhlophe and Kwebulana, along with Ntshinga, after Thenjiwe has survived torture and contacted the outside:

Alala nezimbamu amabhunu ekhaya	The Boers sleep with guns
Adubula abantwana . . .	They shoot children . . .
Ayabesaba abantwana	They are afraid of the children.

(Simon et al. 1986: 170; translation modified)

This song and the final victory song, sung by Ntshinga and the other women – "Thina sizwe esimnyama sizofela izwe" [We the Black Nation will die for our land . . .] (p. 176) – speak of martyrdom as well as solidarity, lament as well as struggle, and thus take their place in a lineage that stretches from Caluza's "Sixotshwa emsebenzini" [We are being expelled from work] via Kente's musicals to the present. Performed at activist funerals, songs like "Thina sizwe" highlighted the sacrifice of (mostly male) martyrs. Performed here by the women in the play, it bears witness to women's contribution to resistance and restoration. *Born in the RSA* looks back to the most famous uprising of women under the ANC banner, the march on Pretoria on 9 August 1956 (now officially Women's Day), and its signature song, "Wathint' Abafazi, Wathint' Imbokodo" [You Strike the Women, You Strike a Rock] (Vusisizwe Players 1996), and forward to the play by that name, performed by the Vusisizwe Players at various Cape Town venues and at the Market in 1986, the thirtieth anniversary of the march on Pretoria.[40] This play portrays three market women at Crossroads, who quarrel and commiserate about their problems with their husbands (with whom they may not legally live) and their children, as well as the police, borrowing the testimonial form established by *Survival*. However, it focuses on the struggles of women against African as well as apartheid patriarchy, challenging the masculine bias of many of *Survival*'s heirs.

If the final song of *Born in the RSA* recapitulates the historical as well as current role of women in the anti-apartheid struggle, another song in the middle of the play prefigures a future beyond that struggle. At a party before they are arrested Thenjiwe, Susan, and Sindiswa serenade Mia as the *Andries Susters* in "I never loved a man – the way that – I love you" (Simon *et al.* 1994: 21). Although this is an irreverent moment, it is also a moving expression of female solidarity as well as a testament to the difficult necessity of non-racial collaboration. The cheeky appropriation of the white American trio, the Andrews Sisters, by two black women and one white one points to a new South African urbanity on the other side of the struggle. While many local appropriations of American popular culture have favored the masculine bravado of the gangster or of BCM, this song and stage picture (Figure 7.7) offer an image of female independence that recalls a different lineage – from Emily Motsieloa (leader of the Dangerous Blues before she arranged music for her husband, Griffiths) in the 1930s and after, to Miriam Makeba and Letta Mbuli from the 1950s, to Jennifer Ferguson (singer-songwriter and ex-ANC MP) and Gcina Mhlophe today.

The use of American popular culture to figure female independence recurs in other plays at the Market. *So What's New?* (1991), Fatima Dike's play about four independent women making their way legally and otherwise in the chaotic

Figure 7.7 The *Andries Susters* in *Born in the RSA* by Barney Simon and the cast; Thoko Ntshinga, Vanessa Cooke, and Gcina Mphlophe at the Market Theatre, 1985. *Photograph and permission*: Ruphin Coudyzer

environment of 1990 Soweto, also uses American music as a touchstone for independence and urbanity.[41] With irony as well as nostalgia, the three older women compare their days as the Chattanooga Sisters (Figure 7.8) with their present trouble with wayward men, rebellious children (including a daughter, Mercedes, struggling with a confusing mix of political idealism and adolescent love), and rising crime at their doorstep, and seek a whimsical escape in the impossible plots of *The Bold and the Beautiful* (Dike 1996). These women are not heroes; Mercedes's mother, Big Dee (Doris Sihula, left), runs a (then still illegal) shebeen, and one of her friends is a drug dealer, whose wares are available at Mercedes' school. Nor are they outright cynics. Despite the title, which reflects wryly on ongoing lawlessness, the characters and the actors that play them speak of and to a new class of self-employed black women whose lives are shaped by global culture as well as local attachments. *Have You Seen Zandile?* (1986), Gcina Mhlophe's autobiographical play, does not display the American-style consumer durables of Big Dee's house, but American music provides the young rural protagonist with a point of reference for a life other than that of the rural wife whose marriage into a leading village family will bring prestige and *lobola* to her mother. Zandile hopes that she might live up to her storyteller grandmother's

Figure 7.8 The Chattanooga Sisters in *So What's New?* by Fatima Dike. Doris Sihula, Maphiki Maboe, Nomsa Xaba, Matshabi Tyelele at the Market Theatre, 1991; directed by Barney Simon. *Photograph and permission*: Ruphin Coudyzer

example by educating herself and escaping to Johannesburg, the quintessentially modern South African city. Despite her desire to escape from rural bondage, Zandile carries the best of the country with her. Her last performance at her Transkei school, isiXhosa praises for an admired teacher, is followed by a scene in which Letta Mbuli's version of "I'll Never Be the Same" accompanies her friend's departure for Johannesburg (Mhlophe 1988: 57). Her own odyssey is accompanied by urban and rural music; Zandile's independence will depend on a synthesis of modernity and tradition. Mhlophe's focus in *Zandile* on the aspirations of young rural women and on the intimate secrets (from menstruation to anxieties about sex) shared by girls across the world, earned her praise from audiences but criticism from the ANC-affiliated Cultural Desk for straying from the "correct" line on the struggle defined by public (masculine) action.[42]

The representation of mature women as national players, in the characters of *Born in the RSA* or *So What's New?* as well as in the persons of Ntshinga, Mhlophe, and Sihula, provides an instructive contrast to the South African stage's most famous activist, Sarafina. Written by Ngema and based loosely on the students at Morris Isaacson High School who led the Soweto uprising, *Sarafina!* (1986) is closer to Kente than to testimonial theatre. Rather than probing the complex drama of the uprising, it celebrates the unequivocal triumph of youth over adversity. The enduring appeal of the play, along with the performance of Leleti Khumalo, later the second Mrs. Ngema, from Johannesburg to Broadway, has led to claims that the play empowers women (Orkin 1991: 232–33) or at least "inspir[es them] through recognition" (Chapman 1996: 365). While the script gave a significant role not only to the students' defiance but also to the teacher who inspired the students to make their own history (even if her name, "Mistress 'It's a Pity'," echoed the caricatures in Kente's repertoire), the production focused on the spectacle of youthful vitality. The play ends with Sarafina borne aloft by her singing comrades, not as an agent but rather as an icon of struggle, an object of male desire and female envy (Guldimann 1996).[43] More principled black practitioners and critics have decried Ngema's commercial exploitation of his cast as well as the story of the struggle (Nyatsumba 1990; J. Mofokeng 1996), but the strongest indictment of the play's "inspiration" is the spectacle of young black women in community workshops across the country, lipsynching to the musical in the hope that they too would make it to the Great White Way.[44] In this poignant but telling image, the aura of the Soweto uprising and the struggle that toppled the apartheid regime congeal into the commodity fetish of fame, obscuring rather than illuminating the history of struggle.

Bearing witness to the future

Sarafina may be an extreme example of the commodification of the struggle but it is also a revealing one, since it shows us how mobilization might come to mean mostly getting the audience on its feet to applaud the display. In its corruption of the promise of liberation in the easy slogan of "liberation theatre" (Ngema 1995), it also casts in relief the testimonial theatre that inhabits the subjunctive place and time between the act of defiance and the future of a new society. Despite his emphatic distinction between protest and resistance, lament and mobilization, Zakes Mda's own drama dwells in this subjunctive space, while also exposing the future *im*perfect of postcolonial Africa. Living in exile in Lesotho, a country completely surrounded by South Africa, from adolescence until his return to South Africa in 1994, Mda had a critical perspective on the region. Plays like *We Shall Sing for the Fatherland* (FUBA 1979), *And the Girls in Their Sunday Dresses* (Meso Theatre, Edinburgh Festival, 1988), and *The Nun's Romantic Story* (Civic Theatre, Johannesburg, 1995) cast a critical eye on the pretensions of African postcolonies, where, beset by corruption and historical amnesia, as well as international capital and the World Bank, the dream of postcolonialism has run aground on the reality of *postcolonization*. Produced by institutions from FUBA and the People's Space to the Edinburgh Festival, these plays also demonstrate not only the potential value of alternative international connections for local theatres but also the tensions between foreign prestige and local neglect.

Mda's postcolonial plays provide a bridge between the anti-apartheid testimonial theatre that dominated the last two decades of SA theatre and the emergent drama of a tentatively post-apartheid society. But even those plays by Mda that deal directly with apartheid, *Dark Voices Ring* (1979) and *The Hill* (1980), challenge the conventions of testimonial theatre by dramatizing the actions, thoughts, and dreams of rural people on the margins of apartheid capitalism and, indeed, of anti-apartheid theatre. Originating at the People's Space, directed by Amato and Nkonyeni in a rare collaboration between a white man and a black woman, they focus on apparently apolitical people on the rural margins of an industrial South Africa and on the destruction of their lives by apartheid capitalism – whether on the grand scale of the gold mining industry or the smaller, but no less insidious one of hard labor on white farms. These plays challenge the bias toward urban setting and overt action in the theatre of resistance favored by Mda. Partly because it takes up the themes of migrant labor and emasculation in the mines treated in such plays as *Egoli*, and partly because its skillful combination of the probing of interiority of European social drama, and the devastating critique of migrant labor grounded in documentary research invites close analysis, *The Hill* has received the most scholarly attention.[45] Nonetheless, *Dark Voices Ring*, with its rural context, domestic female-centered space, and the unfolding of interior states and social history in dialogue, represents the more significant testimonial and theatrical development.[46]

Dark Voices Ring was written to expose the "ill-treatment of farm laborers in the Republic [of South Africa]," and to this end drew on accounts ranging from Henry Nxumalo's 1952 article in *Drum* to the documentation of the South African Institute of Race Relations (Horn 1990: xx). Although white exploitation of black farm laborers, whether working as tenants or prisoners leased by the state, is not enacted, it sets the stage for the drama of a nameless old couple, driven from the farm where the man had been *baas*-boy [overseer] when prisoners rebelled and burnt down his hut and his baby daughter before setting fire to the *huis* [(big) house]. Rather than indulging in a spectacle of degradation, Mda pares down the action to the intimate encounter between the fearful woman and her apparently catatonic husband, and a young man, buoyed by his imminent departure for guerrilla activity "in the north," whom the old woman insists is her son-in-law. The old woman is at the center of this drama, trapped by her obsessive mourning for her daughter (whose death she denies) and for her lost status as *baas*-boy's wife, as well as by fear that her neighbors on the reserve will repeat the attack that left her destitute. The cognitive dissonance that disables this character was, in Nkonyeni's performance, embodied in the tension between her tight reserve and her sudden gestures against unnameable outside threats. Out of the contrast between the old woman's matter-of-fact account of the birth of her daughter – begun out in the fields and finished in the *huis* – which she interprets as a vindication of her family's special status, and her gradually more panicked confrontation with her traumatic loss, Nkonyeni concretized Mda's indictment of the conditions that led the overseer to turn on his fellow blacks. Rather than the young man's lecture about the old man's misguided sense of duty, it is the woman's reenactment of her husband's enforced brutality and the young man's impersonation of a prisoner that shows the depth of the old man's degradation: "*She flogs his back with an imaginary whip . . .*" (Mda 1990: 62). Likewise, it is their duo impersonation of the prisoners' song – "Senzenina Ma-Afrika?" [What Have We Done for You, Mother Africa?] (p. 63) – that gives dramatic weight to the otherwise abstract commitment to a "just war" (p. 64) and prepares the audience for the old man's sudden animation at the young man's departure and thus also for the promise of freedom.

Written in 1973, *We Shall Sing for the Fatherland* has been Mda's most visible play. First performed at FUBA in 1979 (dir.: Francis) and at the Market (dir.: Nicholas Ellenbogen), it was revived in Lesotho the following year and became something of a set text in the 1980s, performed by Soyikwa Institute students in 1988 and 1989 (dir.: Walter Chakela), and revived at the Windybrow in 1995. Its reputation in South Africa is noteworthy because it deals not with the familiar themes of struggle against apartheid oppression but with oppression in a postcolonial society marked by the corruption of a new African business elite beholden to multinational corporate interests and by the deprivation of the majority, including peasant veterans of the "Wars of Freedom" (Mda 1990: 30). Like Fanon, Mda emphasizes the persistence of inequity despite the rhetoric of black empowerment. While the published text blames "white" interests (p. 35) for the collusion between international Banker and local Businessman, the stage text was amended to "multinational" and the punchline added to the Banker's speech: "We must teach them that the only colour that matters is the colour of money" (Horn 1990: xvii).[47]

The veterans in this play, the Sergeant and his subordinate, Janabari, survive by scavenging the houses, yards, and trashcans of the new rich and by bribing Ofisiri, the local policeman, to allow them to sleep in the city park. Compared to Beckett's tramps (although Mda had not read Beckett when he was writing the play [Holloway 1988: 83]), the soldiers – especially Janabari played by Workshop '71 veteran James Mthoba – had more in common with the distracted Professor and his retinue left behind by Nigerian independence in Soyinka's 1965 play, *The Road*. Like the actors of the Yoruba popular theatre, on which Soyinka's satire draws, the performers here, especially Mthoba and Eddie Nhlapo, perform on a functionally rather than naturalistically decorated stage and rely on a combination of buffoonery and pointed comment to get the satire across (Figure 7.9). Like Soyinka's scavengers, the Sergeant and Janabari try to accumulate not only food and shelter but also a measure of dignity in a society that has betrayed them. Snubbed by the African businessman Mafutha and shunned by the government that their fight helped to create, the veterans can take pride only in national achievements that exclude them:

Janabari: Proud to see our young men and women in positions which used to be held only by our colonial masters.

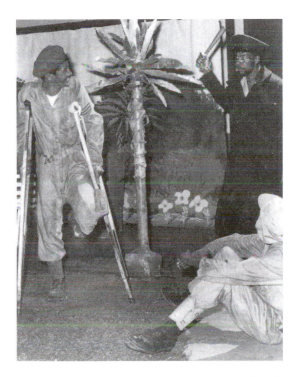

Figure 7.9 The ironies of postcolonization in *We Shall Sing for the Fatherland* by Zakes Mda. Edward Soutien, Eddie Nhlapho, and James Mthoba at the Federated Union of Black Artists, directed by Benjy Francis. *Source*: *The Plays of Zakes Mda* (Johannesburg: Ravan, 1984)

Sergeant: Yes Janabari, proud to see Ofisiri in his neat uniform, Mr. Mafutha and his money-bags, and all the rest of them who hold the reins of power . . .

(Mda 1990: 39)

Even as they freeze to death in the park, they attempt to "sing for the fatherland" (p. 44). Their "voices . . . gone" (p. 44), their corpses rifled, the ghosts of the Sergeant and Janabari can only haunt their unmarked graves, while a local bigwig, perhaps Mr. Mafutha, who might have died of a "new-fangled disease like gastric ulcers" (p. 35), receives a grand funeral off-stage. By juxtaposing death by starvation with death by "gastric ulcer" (and, by implication, overconsumption), Mda does more then merely contrast the poor with the rich. Rather he invokes long-standing Basotho lore that warns against the insatiable appetites of the powerful, including those leaders, "voracious man-eaters" who "expropriate the labor and sustenance" of their own people (Coplan 1994: 37).

The presence of the policeman supervising the prisoners digging the paupers' graves in the final tableau – after the Sergeant's and Janabari's ironic laughter leaves the stage – recalls the numerous prisoners in anti-apartheid theatre; this discomforting parallel led critics to comment on the play's "brave look at the darker side of independence."[48] The exact location of this dark postcolonial comedy is left unsaid, although the park bears comparison with Uhuru [Freedom] Park in Nairobi and the Businessman and his ilk with the rapacious capitalists of 1970s Kenya (Horn 1990: xiii), while the dialogue alludes to the currency of South Africa and the food of Lesotho. This combination of a general state of uneven development and the details of different local environments did not undermine the play's effect but rather invited audiences to ponder its relevance for a post-colonial South Africa. This relevance was confirmed, if only indirectly, by the banning of the published text in South Africa in 1981 and by its near absence from stages in Lesotho, ruled by dictatorial cliques from the civil war of 1970 until the relatively fair and free election of 1993 and once again (in 1998) torn by civil war.[49] The 1997 showdown between veterans of the Zimbabwe wars of independence and a government unwilling to grant land and equal treatment to veterans of minority groups confirms the ongoing relevance of this drama of national betrayal. Less overt but more wide-reaching, the tension between South Africa's new black managerial class and the organized working class suggests that the discrepancy between postcolonial rhetoric and postcolonized inequity remains unresolved.[50]

And the Girls in Their Sunday Dresses (1988) distills the themes and structure of *We Shall Sing for the Fatherland*, returning to the interlocking motifs of the consumption of power and the power of consumption. Where the earlier play juxtaposed the veterans waiting in vain for the Cabinet to "take an interest in them" (Mda 1990: 37) with the objects of their envy and ironic amusement, the Policeman who bullies them and the Banker, the Businessman, and the pretty Civil Servant who pass them by, *And the Girls* dispenses with all but the two protagonists waiting in a long line to buy subsidized rice from an unnamed agency that appears to be siphoning off food and profits. The Woman has returned from South Africa, after being abandoned by her Italian lover, while the Lady is an aging courtesan who may or may not have had the same lover; both have no apparent resources other than those being dispensed with the rice. The office "girls" of the title appear only fleetingly in the dialogue and not at all on stage, yet their affluent remoteness highlights the gap between those waiting in line for food and the invisible bureau-crats who continually postpone delivery. Where the personal interaction or pointed aloofness of the characters in *We Shall Sing* clearly distinguished between haves and have-nots and invited sympathy for the latter, the absence of any character embodying power in *And the Girls* highlights the impersonal nature of that power. Further, the reduction of the Lady over the course of the play from a high-class courtesan proud of her fine clothing and other commodities to one more disheveled petitioner in line suggests that distinctions between haves and have-nots in a postcolonial society dependent on outside aid are unstable and beyond the protagonists' control.

Setting this play in Lesotho, Mda returns to the environment of *The Hill*, the landscape of endemic poverty, caused historically by white appropriation of Basotho land and reinforced in the present by the scarcity of income which forces the majority of able-bodied men and many women to earn their living in South Africa.[51] The earlier play depicted the experience of dislocation through the eyes of male migrants waiting for the call to the mines and used the female characters – all sex workers – essentially as foils for the men; they thwart the men's attempts to survive and play upon their alienation from their families by robbing them (although the oldest woman – played by Nkonyeni in the Space production – anonymously offers money to bribe the recruiters to take the young, naive migrant who turns out to be her nephew). *And the Girls*, on the other hand, depicts the world through the eyes of a woman who has herself made the crossing into South Africa. Thus the play registers a shift in gender roles in and around Lesotho: after a major strike (1987) and retrenchment of "foreign" workers in South African mines through the 1990s, the pattern of migration was reversed, with more men compelled to stay home on the land, while women sought out domestic work and informal commerce in the border areas or in South Africa (Coplan 1994: 174–77). Although the Woman and the Lady appear to be dependent on the bureaucrats manning offices like the rice depot and are willing to submit to the preposterous questions (about sexual habits and the like) apparently required before they can receive the rice, at the end they reclaim a defiant if precarious independence.

Despite its female cast and its critique of sexual and economic dependency, this play is not primarily about the "subservient role of women in the social hierarchy of Lesotho" (Marx 1994: 20). Rather Mda uses the initial difference between the Lady's willingness to submit to the whims of others, whether her former clients or the bureaucrats at the depot, and the Woman's defiance to dramatize the differ-ence between an aspiring African elite dependent on global consumer goods and the mass of working people. While one could argue that this allegory has its place in a theatre designed to mobilize audiences out of postcolonial complacency, it strains under the abstractness of the Woman's indictments, such as "We are all victims of a social order" (Mda 1993b: 20). Moreover, as Bhekizizwe Peterson argues in his introduction, "such typifications allow for insights into the experience of the lower classes, of which women form a significant proportion, but they rarely highlight the specific predicaments facing women as a gendered constituency" (Peterson 1993: xxi–xxii). Although much more vividly rendered, the conflict between the whore and the national activist in *And the Girls* recapitulates the allegorical trajectory of plays like *Shanti*, in which women come to stand for the nation. The force of this allegory depends on a familiar but problematic split between the pure national agent and the prostitute, without, however, delving into the complex social and sexual pressures that might lead Basotho women to work away from their male kin, including sex work (Coplan 1994: 150–200).

And the Girls complicates this allegorical turn insofar as it undoes the simple opposition between saint and sinner, showing the Woman's weakness and, finally, the Lady's refusal to submit to the bureaucrat's intrusive questions: "To hell with the rice! I am going home and I know that never again will I need the food-aid rice and my chair of patience. Are you coming or not?" (Mda 1993b: 37). This line appears to confirm the allegorical emphasis on the mobilization of marginalized people against the local representatives of central power. Although the play actually ends with a moment of sisterly commiseration about men – "They are all children of one person" – it is the invitation, rather than the resolution, that more effectively concludes the drama by staging the conditions of solidarity without assuming the easy enactment of empowerment.

This dramatization of conditions of empowerment as well as the persistence of inequality in postcolonial society should grant *And the Girls* a place in the South African repertoire but thus far, despite its merits, the play has yet to be produced in South Africa. The cause for this neglect is not censorship, although the portrayal of the haughty "office girls" might rile some government bureaucrats accused of lack of accountability, and the critique of the gap between the newly powerful and the still oppressed may strike some directors of subsidized theatres as an outdated preoccupation with anti-apartheid paradigms. Community theatres, which have no guaranteed sources of funding, tend to prefer work written locally or in house by authors tolerant of improvised modifications to plays by authors expecting royalty payments and strict adherence to the text. While these hypotheses do not fully explain the neglect of the play, they do help to sketch a new configuration of theatre in South Africa, which will be explored in the next chapter.

8

THEATRE IN THE
INTERREGNUM AND BEYOND

1994 brought a new political dispensation to South Africa, but shifts in the organization, management, and subsidy of cultural institutions had been underway for some time. Already in 1990, the release of long-term political prisoners and the relegitimation of banned organizations such as the ANC compelled extraparty movements, the civic groups that had grown up in the absence of legitimate structures, and the cultural groups linked with them, to reevaluate their roles in the political culture and cultural politics of nation and community. The conviction that sustained several generations of theatre activists and cultural workers and that produced such memorable events as *Sizwe Banzi Is Dead*, *Woza Albert!*, and *Born in the RSA*, gave way to a variety of not quite compatible political persuasions and cultural practices. Without the binding force of a common enemy, discrepancies in economic and social conditions opened too wide to permit easy appeals to a united national culture. The loss of political unity also represented a potential gain, however, since it cleared space for theatre to address issues and audiences – social problems arising from displacement, accelerated urbanization, and poverty, and the lives of women and sexual and ethnic minorities – using forms, from naturalism to forum theatre, other than the testimonial and agitprop that dominated the anti-apartheid stage. Uncertainty about the future has been exacerbated by social instability and outright violence, political or criminal, especially in Gauteng and KwaZulu/Natal, which has disrupted theatre-going and other evening entertainments.

Theatre and society in South Africa at the end of the twentieth century are not yet *post*-apartheid but rather tentatively post-*anti*-apartheid. This interregnum properly began not with the election in 1994 but with Mandela's liberation in 1990 and may end with his retirement in 1999. It has been shaped by the sense, shared by Mandela and his generation of international activists, of history as well as the problems of redress and reconciliation, reconstruction and development, which demand an eye on the past as well as the future. Leaving summations to those writing in the next millennium, this chapter will explore plays and performances that grapple with the difficulties of transformation and that redefine the form, content, and/or institutional framework of theatre. This redefinition has not taken place at all levels at once and is unlikely to produce an orderly master-narrative of the new South Africa. Instead, an account of theatre practice in the 1990s should include practices ranging from the internationally inspired and acclaimed *Faustus in Africa* (1995) and other collaborations between Handspring Puppets and director/designer/animator William Kentridge, to the functional skits performed in clinics, schools, and bus depots by health workers or voter organizers as well as by trained actors, to the role-playing at the heart of *Heart to Heart* (1991–96), a graphic romance-in-progress, many of which have originated outside the usual theatre venues or outside theatres altogether.

At the start of the decade, however, the Market Theatre and, to a degree, the Grahamstown Festival still provided the most visible venues for new plays dealing with the social, cultural, and economic upheavals of transition. These transitional plays depicted not only white anxieties about black aspirations, such as Neil McCarthy's *Rainshark* (Market Theatre, 1991) and Fugard's *Playland* (Market Theatre, 1992), but also the lure of fool's gold for blacks and whites in the erstwhile Golden City, such as Susan Pam-Grant's *Curl Up and Dye* (Black Sun nightclub; Market Theatre, 1989), Slabolepszy's *Mooi Street Moves* (Grahamstown Festival; Market Theatre 1992), Ledwaba's *Jozi, Jozi* (Market Theatre, 1994), and adaptations like *The Suit* (Market Theatre, 1993) and *The Good Woman of Sharkville* (1996). These "Johannesburg" plays, especially *Mooi Street Moves* and *Jozi, Jozi*, restored an old South African figure: the rural na(t)ive in the big city.[1] But, where earlier incarnations, such as the displaced Afrikaner in *As die Tuig Skawe* (1926), the displaced African in *No-Good Friday* (1958) or in the film that gave the genre its name, *Jim Comes to Jo'burg* (dir.: Donald Swanson, 1949), blame their displacement on discrimination (whether by the English or the apartheid state), the 1990s plays depict a world of lawlessness and robber capitalism, in which race no longer determines power and a sense of community remains elusive.[2]

Whatever their differences, *Mooi Street Moves* and *Jozi, Jozi* both dwell on and in the pathology of Johannesburg. The status of the city as the country's criminal as well as economic center is simultaneously the milieu and subject of this drama and the ongoing concern of theatre administrators. Slabolepszy dramatizes the encounter between a white naif, Henry Stone, lost in Hillbrow, a dense and dangerous area, and a black city dude, Stix Letsebe, who lives in the flat once occupied by Henry's brother. In more or less naturalistic fashion, he situates the encounter in the sparsely furnished but vividly realized setting of the flat, and establishes the narrative that has led Henry to the city seeking – if not his fortune – enough money to buy the dream machine: a rig for extracting water from dry (rural) land. While the plot does not provide similarly complex motivation for Stix, the action measures each character's ability to survive in this milieu; Stix's skill in salesmanship and conmanship in the informal market along Mooi (Pretty) Street dominates the action and the stage in Sebogodi's performance, until Stix's murder by an (off-stage) agent of the protection racket running the building abruptly ends the play.[3] Ledwaba, on the other hand, does not pretend to naturalism, favoring instead comic vignettes of black residents and would-be residents of the city. Mining the vein opened by African variety and disseminated by *Woza Albert!*,

Jozi, Jozi presents a corrupt policeman demanding bribes from the homeless people living in central Park Station, as well as the plight of undocumented migrants, including a naive Malawian, whose formal attire and language recall the late Malawian president and self-styled "Black Englishman" but do not prevent his being fleeced by more wily locals. Updating the *Jim Comes to Jo'burg* scenario, Ledwaba's newcomer is still a comical foreigner, the butt of jokes for savvy city-dwellers, on-stage and in the house.

Where *Jozi, Jozi* essentially updates the *Jim Comes to Jo'burg* scenario (including jokes about city women – in malicious drag), and *Mooi Street Moves*, for all its sharp repartee and social critique, basically inverts the *Jim* paradigm with a white rural idiot and a black city dude, *Curl Up and Dye* offers a more complex portrayal of transitional Johannesburg through the interaction of women at a salon in the decaying neighborhood of Joubert Park (near Park Station). Its alternately ironic and poignant dialogue charts the shifting loyalties that link Rolene (Pam-Grant), the working-class white manager, to the other women: her underpaid and long-suffering black assistant, Miriam (played by TV casting agent, Lillian Dube), her "best friend," drug-addict Charmaine, her "best customer," the crudely racist Mrs. Dubois (Val Donald-Bell), and her newest customer, Dudu Dhlamini (Nandi Nyembe, in the first of several roles in theatre and TV), who, as a nurse at a private hospital and a single woman supporting her children in defiance of customary African deference to male relatives, is the only one able to manage her life in the city.[4]

Curl Up and Dye uses stereotyping associated with hairstyles to establish the dramaturgy of racial conflict. Mrs. Dubois, a "poor white" caretaker, is happy to have her *bouffant* compared to that of "Mrs. P. W. Botha" (wife of the hard-line president) (Pam-Grant 1993: 132), even if Miriam's compliment turns to exasperation when Mrs. Dubois dismisses her complaints about lack of money: "I ask her how her child is and then I got to listen to this political nonsense. Who does she think she is . . . expect[ing] wage increases all the time?" (p. 133). On the other hand, Dudu, who wears braids, refuses Rolene's attempt to sell her a "Whitney Touch," while insisting – to Miriam – that she knows more about the woman Rolene calls "that famous black negro in America" (p. 116): "Of course I've heard of her. . . . *Ucabanga ukuthi ngingu lomlungu?* [Who does this white (girl) think I am?]" (p. 116; trans. modified).[5] As the play unfolds, these stereotypes come unstuck; Rolene is caught between habitual affiliation with Mrs. Dubois and new admiration for Dudu's independence, as she has been between an ingrained bossy attitude to Miriam and an inconsistent, if genuine, appreciation of her loyalty.

The contradictions between apparently unmediated emotion and an apartheid structure of feeling play themselves out in the languages of ethnicity (English, isiZulu, Afrikaans) and class, as well as private feeling.[6] Intimacy and publicity interpenetrate each other on stage; the "private lives" of these women are irreducibly social, in that they are subject to institutional intrusion but also in that their problems require social as well as personal solutions.[7] The interplay of language and affiliation is vividly dramatized in the climax, when Dudu and Rolene realize that they are neighbors in a hitherto "white" building and that this revelation is bound to explode their uneasy intimacy. Dudu realizes that Rolene is the woman whose husband threatens to shoot black passers-by and beats his wife "night after night" (p. 135), while Rolene realizes that Dudu knows what she has been desperately trying to hide (p. 138). When Dudu shifts from indirect expression of fellow-feeling, speaking in Zulu to Miriam about *inje lendoda* [the dog of a man], to advice that sounds official though meant to be friendly – "Rolene, you must report your husband to the police or welfare. It's enough . . . I just packed my things" – Mrs. Dubois attempts to reimpose white fellow-feeling: "Now are you a bladdy *kafferboetie* [nigger-lover] or are you a white woman?" (p. 139). Faced with this choice, Rolene succumbs to a form of race pride that only heightens her abjectness, as she calls Dudu a "black bitch" (p. 140), chases Miriam out, and remains to answer a threatening call from her husband.

While this ending leaves Rolene alone and alienated, it exposes the contradictions in the roles the characters would like to play and those that the drama compels them to enact. If Rolene remains attached to the impossible comedy of a happy marriage and Miriam to the melodrama of an unhappy one, Dudu creates a new script around her declaration of independence. This declaration may seem out of place in the "salon [that] has fallen behind the times" (p. 83) or, indeed, in a city that has seen reported rape rates climb in recent years, but its performance bears witness, as does *So What's New?* (which opened in 1991, in the wake of *Curl Up and Dye*'s revival) to the perseverance of women, especially black women, in this ferocious urban environment.

This testimony is all the more striking in comparison with those plays, especially Sophiatown revivals, that treat urban women ambiguously. Jerry Mofokeng's revival of *Nongogo* (Civic Theatre, 1994), in which Dambise Kente gave the eponymous whore a depth and resilience not immediately evident in Fugard's melodrama, but Corney Mabaso's and Mothobi Mutloatse's riff on Themba's photonovella of female flirtation and betrayal, *Baby, Come Duze* (1991), seems, like *Bloke*, Mutloatse's musical adaptation of Modisane's self-lacerating autobiography (Windybrow 1994), both nostalgic and casually misogynist. Against this Sophiatown that never quite was, the Market's adaptation of *The Suit*, a story by Themba, Sophiatown wit and, in his own echo of Dostoyevsky, South Africa's Underground Man, conveyed precisely the tension between high melodrama and sharp irony that animated Themba and his subjects – lively, self-aware, and sometimes self-destructive ghetto denizens. The story is simple – and peculiar. A man discovers his wife with another man who escapes, leaving behind his suit. To punish his wife, the husband insists that she treat the suit as an honored guest, but his irrational elaborations on this torment lead to her death. Under Simon's direction, the shifting third person narration (from Themba's story) juxtaposed with dialogue (additions by Mutloatse and the cast), highlighted different views of the action, not only that of the husband and wife, but also the interventions of friends and passers-by. The high melodramatic color of Themba's aggrieved and later grieving husband was complicated by the actors' delivery: Sello Maake kaNcube and Stella Khumalo were angry, ironic, and pathetic by turns. Their performances suggested the allure but also the limits of gender typing in this ghetto melodrama, while the narrative reminded the 1990s audience of the decidedly unglamorous social environment that was the precondition for this story. In *The Suit*, as in the sharper moments of *Sophiatown* (1986; revived in 1994), the past offers neither the definitive explanation for the present nor a refuge from it. Instead, it acts on the corrosive edge of the interregnum, tracing the acid effects of habits of violence and disorder on past and present in the postcolonial city.

These occasional successes have not prevented a certain confusion in post-anti-apartheid theatre institutions.[8] The transfer of the management of state institutions to erstwhile outsiders (such as Walter Chakela at PACT's Windybrow and Mbongeni Ngema at the Playhouse in Durban) and the subsidy of the Market (from 1995, the year of Simon's death) have, as it were, legitimated resistance but this legitimation has led ironically not so much to innovation as to variations on the struggle formula, in plays like *Gauteng* [Sesotho: place of gold; also the province whose capital is now Johannesburg], Manaka's recapitulation of his earlier plays, *Egoli* and *Ekhaya* (1995), or *Maria, Maria*, Ngema's musical mix of the Christ story and the life of Steve Biko (1997). While occasional directors such as Mofokeng have sought to create a repertoire through the principled revival of South African classics such as *Nongogo* or Kente's *Lifa* (1970), or of African-American playwrights, such as August Wilson, others have followed Kente's example with musical melodramas such as *Sheila's Day* (first performed 1993; published in Perkins 1999) and *The Game* (by Duma Ndlovu, first performed 1997; with Nomhle Nkonyeni) or evenings of loosely linked celebrations, such as *Woza* (a mix of numbers from *King Kong*, *Ipi Tombi*, and recent hits).

The production of new work and new ways of doing theatre for new audiences has in the 1990s more often happened on the festival circuit or outside theatre altogether, than on the mainstages of the subsidized theatre. Some of the best recent work hosted by the Market, such as the collaborations between Adrian Kohler's and Basil Jones' Handspring Puppet Company and director/designer/animator William Kentridge, was created outside its purview. The vivid and intelligent – and expensive – puppet/actor/animation pieces, *Woyzeck on the High-veld* (1993), *Faustus in Africa* (1995), and *Ubu and the Truth Commission* (1997), were sponsored by outside sources such as the German government and have toured more widely in Europe and North America than in South Africa. This was in part due to the costs of mounting them, but also in part to limited local audience interest (despite critical enthusiasm) for their subtle, allusive, and perhaps therefore *elusive* productions. Drawing on the experience of practitioners trained in fine art, professional theatre, culture for development, and agitprop, these productions combine classic texts of European drama, (South) African themes (schematically: urbanization in *Woyzeck*; the legacy of European colonization in *Faustus*; and the challenge of reconciliation with the perpetrators of state violence in *Ubu*), and dazzling experimentation with puppetry, animation, and live performance to explore the historical and contemporary implications of these stories as well as to push the limits of their representation (Figure 8.1).[9]

While *Woyzeck*'s animated backdrop of urban desolation and the expansive highveld dwarfing performers and puppets has perhaps the greater visual impact, *Faustus* entwines the European tradition's most powerful and ambiguous legend of modernization with the iconography of advertising in and loot from Africa, and the representation of the pact with the devil as imperial adventuring and capitalist exploitation (Faustus's proverbial long spoon turns into a drill penetrating a hellish mine). Despite the title, the rather cramped set evoking an imperial Victorian counting house, and some rhetorical flourishes from Marlowe (Faustus signs the devil's pact in blood), this *Faustus* plays more with Goethe's text, from Lesego Rampholokeng's dub/rap version of *Knittelvers*, to the projections of *fraktur* script to the allusion (in an image of Faust flying over Victoria Falls) to Faust's grandiose attempt to tame the sea, which culminates *Faust II*. Perhaps because Goethe's text offers too many opportunities for even this multi-media production, such as Faust's exploitation of thousands in a vain attempt to master nature, an effort that Goethe's Mephisto calls colonization, which might have transformed the fleeting image of the Falls into an analysis of the spectacular fusion of modernization and colonization in that episode, the textual pastiche seems more patchwork than effective synthesis.[10] But the animation, acting, and puppetry offer a

Figure 8.1 Apartheid medicine in *Woyzeck on the Highveld;* directed and designed by William Kentridge, puppets by Handspring Puppet Company, 1993. *Photograph and permission*: Ruphin Coudyzer

compelling picture of the formidably abstract forces of capitalism, imperialism, racism, and sexism, fighting through the bodies of Africans. Surrounded by the commodities of imperial capitalism (from a typewriter framed by wild animals to Pear's soap in the hands of picannins), magic lantern images show Faust on safari, shooting at animals and Africans already framed for his hunting pleasure. The heads of the Africans in turn metamorphose into sculpture on pedestals with auction-lot numbers.

In front of these images, Faust and his side-kick, Mr. Johnson (after Joyce Carey's sad exemplar of colonized consciousness) perform with the black and white puppeteers (Kohler and Louis Sebeko) who animate them both and whose presence creates one more layer of commentary on the tension between human beings and technology (Figure 8.2). Apart from God (the voice of Busi Zokufa, who also plays Gretchen), master of ceremonies Mephisto (Leslie Fong) is the only puppet-less character on stage, but he has a puppet shadow, a finely-jointed hyena (animated by Jones) who seduces Johnson with promises of (post)imperial glory, turning him into a puppet ruler (with the trademark leopard-skin hat of the erstwhile Zairean dictator, Mobutu) backed by global capital. The hyena adds an ironic twist to the canine icons of His Master's Voice on the screen, reconnecting this European folktale to imperial capitalism as well as to a pan-African trickster-figure. On the sound-track, the jazz-*marabi* fusions of the Motsieloas mix with Congolese and Tanzanian music to plot Faust's African journey while also tracing elements in the history of a distinctly South African modernity.

Figure 8.2 Faust, Mr. Johnson, and their puppet-masters (Adrian Kohler and Louis Sebeko) in *Faustus in Africa*; director Kentridge; Handspring, 1995. *Photograph and permission*: Ruphin Coudyzer

Although most theatre in South Africa lacks the international capital to mount this ambitious critique of capitalism, much of the most socially engaged and theatrically focused performances have been low-tech but high-skill depictions of local stories. The techniques of so-called "physical theatre," including the mimicry of animals and humans, the creation of location through gesture, and knock-about comedy, have proven particularly effective for crossing barriers of language, culture, and age. Theatre for Africa (directed by Nicholas Ellenbogen) uses mime, sound, beautifully crafted costumes and masks, and the appeal of the South African wilds to create evocative eco-parables such as *Horn of Sorrow* (1989), *Elephant of Africa* (1992), and *The Guardians of Africa* (1996), which attempt to address the conflict between the environmentalism of affluent but often sentimental city-dwellers and local people accustomed to harvesting rare flora and fauna, as well as that between apparently traditional and apparently modern modes of interaction with the environment. The texts of these parables do not always match their visual power, but the group's example has led two members, Ellis Pearson and Bheki Mkhwane, to apply their techniques to urban stories. In *Boy Called Rubbish* (Grahamstown Festival, 1996), Pearson plays a boy in a shantytown whose confrontations with a cruel foster-mother, a drunken foster-father, a sadistic teacher, and other assorted abusive and abused neighbors (all played by Mkhwane) vividly convey the hazards of shantytown life, even as they send them up.[11] Thanks to the performers' acute sense of timing as well as their mimicry skill, the audience is treated to a story that combines juvenile idiocy (from water splashed on the front-row seats to ketchup blood) with somber social analysis – at one point Mkhwane drops out of character to shake his head at the morbidity of Pearson's splattered "blood"; at another, one of several false endings, Pearson intones, "and so he went to bed without supper, and his life never got better, the end," only to reassure the hesitantly clapping audience that the second act will – perhaps – make things all right again.

While the regional festivals (in Hermanus, Oudtshoorn, Natal Midlands, and Bloemfontein, as well as Grahamstown) have hosted the occasional large-cast community show, such as Brett Bailey's *Zombie* (1996) and *iMumbo Jumbo* (1997: about Chief Gcaleka and his search for the Xhosa king Hintsa's head in a Scottish museum), which featured *izinsangoma* [diviners] and church choirs from Rini (Grahamstown's poorer twin city) as well as trained actors, they have also provided space for intimate explorations of South African life, especially the struggles of women. In Vivian Moodley's *Got Green Chillies, Makoti* (Natal Technikon, 1993; Grahamstown Festival 1994), Petunia Ramaphala plays a poor but enterprising vegetable hawker, grappling with her past as an activist and wife to a wandering husband, as well as her present dealings with Indian as well as white madams (all of whom she impersonates). Thulani Mtshali's *Weemen* (premiere Bachaki Theatre, Grahamstown Festival 1996; published Mtshali 1999), a three-hander dealing not only with the suffering and resistance of an abused woman, but also with the husband's uneven contrition and his dealings with the female boss and *isangoma* who expose his failings, had an analytic and psychological discernment lacking in more graphic and more publicized plays on this topic – such as Aubrey Sekhabi's *On My Birthday* (Northwest Arts Council, 1996). Similarly, *Purdah* by Creative Arts Workshop (CAW) director Ismael Mahomed (1993), wove together a portrait of an Indian South African woman and a broader indictment of Muslim fundamentalism. While the places, occasions, forms, and budgets of these productions differ sharply from the Handspring productions, they share a sceptical relationship to the subsidized houses.

After (anti)apartheid: action and activism in the community

If the Market and other subsidized houses have seemed somewhat adrift in the interregnum, the itinerant theatres and organizations under the community theatre umbrella seem more rooted. Groups with limited resources but remarkable staying power have taken up the challenges of the new (and not so new) South Africa. Community theatre in South Africa has grown out of issue-oriented theatre by social activists for audiences who may be potential if not actual activists themselves. The Cape Flats Players (1971–), CAW (1987–), Cape Arts Project (1988–), Bachaki (1988–), and many others use topical scripts written for performance by people with multiple skills, using functional, portable sets and props, for audiences whose engagement with the subject and occasion of the performance plays at least as great a role in the production of the event's meaning as the text. This engagement with particular communities emerged locally before the 1990s but the spurt of local and international funding that led to the establishment of the Community Theatre for Development Trust (1992) supplemented the training and production at the Market Lab and the community theatre instruction offered by universities, especially historically black institutions such as UWC and the University of Zululand.[12] This combination of funding and training encouraged the growth of community theatres and the festivals supporting them, including the regional festivals as well as the Market Lab's Community Theatre and Zwakala Festivals, the Windybrow's New Plays series, and the Ikwezi Community Theatre Festival at the Baxter Theatre in Cape Town.

While many participants in these festivals suffer from the discrepancy between their professional ambitions and their incomplete technical training, others have demonstrated that theatrical skill and compelling drama need not come from the major stages.[13] From the point of view of community theatre activists, drama, even socially critical drama on the mainstage of the Market and other established institutions, is by virtue of its place and occasion, its status as drama (as an autonomous written work), and its participants' expectations of professional production as well as specialized spectatorship, primarily involved in the production of artistic work and careers, rather than in the process of developing social agents out of performers and spectators (Mahomed 1993; Mda 1997: 293). Rather than accept the term "amateur" (which invokes the affluent leisure of neocolonial times) or "non-professional" (which implies dubious competence), community theatre practitioners prefer to be called activists or, simply, theatre practitioners, arguing that the distinction between professional and non-professional perpetuates the legacy of unequal distribution of resources on what I have called *post-anti*-apartheid theatre.[14] They have also suggested that the emphasis on product rather than process obscures the social functions of theatre not immediately visible under the lens of art, including, in the language of the *White Paper on Arts, Culture, and Heritage*, contributing to "potential employment and wealth creation" in specific communities (*White Paper* 1996: 4). Sibikwa Community Theatre in Benoni, for instance, has organized its plays around the links between the 1950s, heyday of Sophiatown, and the present – such as *Kwela Bafana* (1994) and *Uhambo* (1997) – around veteran performers from that era, who might otherwise be unemployed.

With these experiences in mind, community theatre activists have argued that the common distinction between "art theatre" and "community theatre" implies that the latter has no art (Mda 1993a: 48–49). While the term "art theatre" might usefully characterize theatre that has the means to institutionalize *as art* the production of polished works, including works of social criticism, theatre art should not be the exclusive property of the art theatre. The most effective community theatre necessarily engages in the art of the theatre, in the sense of artful and mindful theatre work. Community theatre workers also contest the privilege habitually accorded the tastes of "professional spectators," those schooled in the silent viewing and polite applause of Western decorum, arguing that the active (but often subtle) responses of audiences not beholden to this decorum reflect a serious engagement with the occasion and effect of the performed action.

The working out of these tensions in the forms, places, and occasions of community theatre can best be seen if we compare the ways in which different plays tackle a common topic. *Purdah* (Mahomed 1999a), *Weemen* (Mtshali 1999), *On My Birthday*, and *Teacher, Stop Abuse* (Border Youth Theatre at Grahamstown, 1994) all portray women struggling against abusive men. *Teacher, Stop Abuse* undermines its critique of the eponymous teacher with a series of dances that show off the sexiness of the student and her friends as do other uneasy mixes of female solidarity and the chorus line (Kruger 1995b: 46–50) and *On My Birthday*'s graphic stage violence risks making a spectacle of the subject for non-community audiences (at the Market and, in 1997, at the Lincoln Center). *Purdah*, *Weemen*, and more recent plays like *Gap-Toothed Sisters* (Women Unite, Ikwezi Festival, 1998) on the other hand, contextualize spectacle within a narrative that clarifies not only the individual woman's plight but also the social constraints and opportunities faced by women in similar situations.

In *Purdah* (Grahamstown Festival, 1993), Aasifah Omar begins and ends her performance with the naturalistic embodiment of a particular individual: Ayesha is an 18-year-old Muslim awaiting trial for killing her abusive husband. But Omar's performance also encompasses the voices that command Ayesha to occupy the prescribed roles of Muslim daughter and wife – her abject mother,

her sinister and occasionally comic aunt, and, by implication, her father and her husband – and the voice of her legal counsel that argues against them. Although legal discourse sounds unrealistic from a young woman compelled to leave school at 13, it serves what Brecht would certainly call a realistic purpose – reminding the (predominantly Indian) audience of the consequences of the institution of purdah. The analytic aspect of the action rejoins the naturalistic aspect in the dramatic tableaux created by Omar's interaction with objects on stage. The impact of a fundamentalist Islam on her body is vividly realized in her clothing (from the white *hejab* that covers her body at the start of the play, to the discarded jeans and T-shirt of her pre-pubescent life, to the bridal veil, and back to the *hejab*, which is stained red at the end as she mimes killing her husband) as well as in her handling of other objects (a used sanitary napkin, crushed photographs of her husband and father, scattered sugar placed in her mouth at the betrothal). In her hands, the mundane as well as the ritual objects concretize and incorporate the effects of ideology on everyday life (Figure 8.3).[15]

Inspired in part by the work of Women Against Violence and Exploitation (WAVE), whose offices were next to CAW's in Lenasia and in part by the story of Amina Begun, a 13-year-old Indian girl sold as a bride to a 56-year-old Saudi Arabian, *Purdah* was first performed at Wits University Orientation (February 1993) at the request of the Islamic Students' Association.[16] Welcomed by WAVE, whose volunteers facilitated private performances in the homes of Muslim women, the play provoked praise from liberal Muslims but insults and death threats as well as condemnation by imams in the Johannesburg-area Muslim hierarchy. Despite this response, several conservative clerics who saw the play after denouncing it came to acknowledge the justice of its indictment of domestic abuse in the community, although they were ambivalent about its public display. Revived in Grahamstown in 1993, 1994, and 1995 for a more general audience alongside new plays by Mahomed and other CAW writers, the play still drew full houses, suggesting its ongoing relevance as well as theatrical power.[17]

Like *Purdah*, *Weemen* portrays the social as well as personal conditions of abuse and a woman's attempt to wrest control over those conditions from her abuser. But, where *Purdah* begins and ends with a single performer's embodiment and explication of her character, *Weemen* uses the interaction of three actors – and at least five characters – to focus on the shifting social roles they represent and thus draw the audience's attention to the analysis, at once nuanced and didactic, of this interaction.[18] Like Bachaki's first play, *Top Down* (1988), which deals in part with the Soweto uprising, *Weemen* represents violence only indirectly. The action ironically invokes the conventions of melodrama: the man (Thabo Mabe) chases his wife (Zandile Tlali) with a (visibly fake) ax, which she later seizes when she contemplates killing him as he lies in a drunken stupor. But the significance of the drama emerges more forcefully in the clash between her attempt to earn a living selling sweets to local children and his attempt to thwart her, first by stealing her money and, later, as a born-again Christian, by manipulating her sense of duty. The conflict between these two individuals is complicated not only by the nuanced

Figure 8.3 The imprint of ideology on everyday life: the *hejab* (around Aasifah Omar) in *Purdah* by Ismael Mahomed, Creative Arts Workshop, Lenasia, 1993. *Source and permission*: Ismael Mahomed

performance of their changing social roles, but also by the other *weemen* in this drama. The husband may be a tyrant at home but outside he is caught between a better-educated female boss and an assertive *sangoma* (both played by the same actor who plays the children buying sweets) whose various challenges expose his bad faith.

By downplaying the spectacle of suffering in favor of the demonstration of different forms of abuse and resistance, *Weemen* preempts the laughter that has often been African audiences' response to stage violence; "it plays expertly to African sensibilities by highlighting the ethics and rationality [in addition to rationalization] of behavior, rather than the pity and terror of suffering" (Graver 1997: 59).[19] Members of the (overwhelmingly black) audience at the Grahamstown performance in 1996, especially women, offered comment in the form of advice to the woman on stage, urging her to "leave him. He'll never change" and critically comparing the situation on stage with others of their acquaintance. This active response did not come from naive or unschooled spectators (these same women had discussed the Wimbledon scores before the show); rather it suggests both an appreciation of the actors' skill in dramatizing this situation and a keen appreciation of the social issues at stake on stage and off.

While the abuse of individual women by their husbands is not the central subject of *Zombie* (premiere Grahamstown Festival 1996; published Bailey 1999), the social upheaval that has exacerbated the scapegoating of women is certainly part of its subtext. Where *Purdah* and *Weemen* had turned away from the public sphere of the struggle into the intimate sphere and enclosed space of the home and the bed, *Zombie*'s large-scale performance of the Rini/Grahamstown community response to the witchhunt in the Bhongweni/Kokstad area of the Eastern Cape in 1995 throws the domestic space into turmoil, exposing it to unresolved secular and spiritual conflicts (see cover picture). The witchhunt took place after twelve school boys were killed in a taxi crash and rumors circulated that witches had stolen the boys' souls. The Christian community's attempts to bury the boys were twice interrupted by young comrades who claimed that the coffins contained witchmeat. At the instigation of these comrades, whose zeal was in part a response to their own disempowerment as their political authority gained by direct action during the 1980s passed back to older and better educated people in the communities in the 1990s, two old women were killed before elders could intervene. The tensions in the community – between Christian and animist, adolescent comrades and their elders, tightly knit, women-run rural households and "urban," "male" violence – remain unresolved. As one character notes, "in the old days, a sacrifice would have washed away the ominous feelings in the air, but today, nothing is finished."[20]

The regional and, indeed, national engagement with this sort of unfinished business was reflected in the willingness of Rini's elders, the Masakhene Church Choir, and school children to join local and metropolitan actors in reenacting the events. The reenactment, in its turn, suggests that dramatizing reactions to "ominous feelings in the air" requires more than either naturalism or anti-apartheid agitprop could offer. To dramatize this story, director and writer Brett Bailey filled a series of stylized tableaux with performances that ranged from finely realized individual embodiments, through the choral enactment of singers or *izinsangoma*, to the silent presence of boys representing the souls of the dead with "skittish bird-like hoppings" that alternate with "long creepy stares" behind their birdmasks (Graver 1997: 59; see cover). Both the grandmother killed as a witch and her frightened 6-year-old granddaughter were played by young men, whose gestic precision highlighted the uncanny quality of the action, while also alluding to the comrades' perception of community power as female. This power is vividly rendered when the five *izinsangoma* and the drums behind them are in full swing but the quiet moments are also breathtaking:

Near the end, a rousing cleansing ritual suddenly stops when a comrade straddles a coffin and hacks at a corpse made of wool and feathers. All we hear are the chorus's umbrellas opening and closing like exhausted birds' wings, the blows of his ax, and his growing sobs.

(Graver 1997: 59)

At this moment, the motivation of the comrade as well as that of the baffled elders are equally in play. The reprise of the cleansing dance that ends the play and envelops the audience is stirring indeed, but the ominous and enigmatic sounds in the air still haunt the space after the dancers have gone.

If community theatre of this kind intersects aesthetically and institutionally with theatre at places like the Market, it also overlaps with the pedagogical theatre (aka theatre for development) sponsored by non-theatre professionals in institutions like the Johannesburg City Health Dept. or the Institute for Applied English Language Studies (AELS). Community theatre thus crosses and recrosses the border between experimental theatre (performed at festivals or in the studio spaces of the stationary houses) and theatre for development. Its conceptual and practical fluidity brings together apparently incompatible places, occasions, and practices – performances for the Market's "professional audiences" alongside those in community halls in Soweto or Lenasia for people directly engaged by the action; drama that focuses primarily on the appreciation of character alongside more explicitly issue-oriented plays that allow participants to face hidden problems in the community – but it is also this very fluidity that makes possible the revision of the axioms of anti-apartheid theatre and the renegotiation of the relationship between aesthetics and politics, form and function, subjunctive enactment in the theatre, and indicative action in streets and houses. At the present moment, however, as community activists take up positions in public arts administration, and as NGO funding dwindles, the future of independent community theatre is uncertain.

Pedagogy, performance, and spect-action for development

Like the term "community theatre," "theatre for development" has been used to describe related but not always identical practices. As prominent theorist-practitioners have noted (Mlama 1991; Mda 1993a; Kerr 1995), the term has covered a range of activities. At one extreme, it refers to the use of theatre techniques (actors presenting a script for an audience) to communicate the development policy of national or international agencies or to implement technical solutions to immediate problems (such as the use of condoms by people at risk of AIDS). At the other, it includes performances devised by locals as well as visitors, which are intended to facilitate analysis of long-term causes and thus also to develop the social agency as well as dramatic skills of the performers.[21] This opposition, often summarized as that between a "domesticating top-down" and a "participatory bottom-up" approach (Kerr 1995: 149) draws on the work of

Augusto Boal and his mentor, Paulo Freire, especially the distinction between "banking education," in which the teacher/expert reinforces the passivity of student/recipient in the guise of giving information, and "problem-*posing* education" (better known as conscientization), in which teacher/catalyst and students together explore the contradiction in the ideology of education that reproduces social hierarchies, and so to expose their own participation in it as a problem before they can act to change it (Freire 1972: 45–59).

While Freire's image of the teacher who gives up the role of expert for that of collaborator engaged in a collective struggle has inspired educators to use their training to articulate the aspirations of oppressed communities, and while Boal's call to transform spectators into spect-actors (1992: 2) has motivated theatre for development workers to encourage dramatic actors to move to social action (Mda 1993a: 22), this exhortation leaves unresolved the practical tensions between visiting experts and local participants. Development workers in Southern Africa are usually urbanized, specialized employees of national or international agencies (such as UNESCO or WHO) or clients of private agencies like the Ford Foundation (Mda 1993a: 23). In some cases, locally trained experts identifying with the technical solutions of modernization regard the recalcitrance of rural clients as mere backwardness; as Kerr documents, *Laedza Banani* [roughly: the sun is up; let us work together] in Botswana, for instance, was shaped less by the populist aspirations of participants or expatriates like Kerr than by the "large contingent of government health staff on the . . . board" (Kerr 1995: 159).

Other projects have tried to escape dependency on outside agencies. Although Lesotho-based Maratholi Travelling Theatre had to contend with government suspicion of rural agitation and with local expectations that the group would behave like experts bearing hand-outs, their success in the 1980s was noteworthy. Supported by Roma University and funds generated by its own instructional videos, Maratholi attempted to move from top-down instruction – dramatizing specific problems (such as agricultural unproductivity) along with expert solutions (food aid or farming instruction) – to a participatory theatre, in which locals redefined problems to take fuller account of social tensions and the disruption of production through hand-outs (Mda 1993a: 132), and beyond to a conscientizing theatre, in which participants create a forum for enacting not only specific problems but also for questioning the benevolence of development agencies or even of activist organizations like trade unions.[22] In *The Trade Union Play*, for instance, the catalysts performing the roles of migrant miners enlisted the participation of a migrant miner and ex-member of NUM, the (South African) National Union of Mineworkers, who argued that the union was more interested in anti-apartheid politics than in Basotho miners and their Lesotho-based families, provoking debate among the participants about the relevance of the industrial union to rural Lesotho. This debate was complicated by the gender imbalance between the male miners and the predominantly female inhabitants of villages deprived of male wage-earners by the mines, which generated a more sceptical view of NUM than would be expected in an anti-apartheid South African public (Mda 1993: 145–56).

If the heuristic distinction between top-down and bottom-up intervention is thus complicated in practice by the multiple identifications of its practitioners, so too is the distinction between elite and popular forms. While some critics posit a clear opposition between the imported "well-made play" and indigenous folk forms such as comic improvisation (Kamlongera 1989; Kerr 1995: 105–51), they have had to acknowledge that popular theatre, even for rural audiences, means the urban commercial theatre of impresarios like Kente (touring in Botswana and Lesotho), whose enterprise has been characterized by social conservatism and the reinforcement of urban consumerism through the sale of commodities – including skin-lightening cream – before performances. While such practices may exacerbate the culture of dependence in impoverished rural areas (Horn 1985), they also encourage participants to acknowledge the impact of urban life on rural people. These complexities suggest that the task of forging links between pedagogy and performance, and between performance and social change, is not one that can be quickly executed or evaluated on the basis of immediate efficiency.

Theatre for development projects in South Africa have received little attention, partly because they were until recently officially denied the funding and documentation of international agencies and partly because they were almost totally eclipsed at home by the more visible theatre of the anti-apartheid movements. Nonetheless, despite the claim that theatre for development did not exist in South Africa under apartheid (Mda 1997: 289), small-scale projects began at least in the 1970s and were well underway before 1994, the year of the election and the return of exiles such as Mda. Although operating on the margins of an apartheid government engaged in the *under*-development of the African population, these projects reflected many of the aspirations and problems of theatre for development in neighboring countries, in the relationships among catalysts, local experts, and target audiences, and in the tensions between different kinds of performance, between development as instruction or as conscientization.

These tensions manifest themselves in the Health Education (HE) theatre project developed under Ford Foundation auspices by Barney Simon and black nurses at mission hospitals in the Transkei and KwaZulu in 1973, and continue to surface in more recent projects, such as theatre against AIDS. Whereas the hospital report identified theatre in technical terms, as a "means of conveying HE messages" – to specific problems such as literacy or suspicion of health professionals in isolation from the social and economic deprivation causing these problems – Simon and the nurse-performers came to evaluate their performance (in the sense of action and achievement) in the communities they visited as a process of education through self-education. Listening to patients the better to enact their concerns, they came to understand the "ends of a person" as one nurse put it, the impact of apartheid on physical and psychic health, and the value of traditional medicine and other "non-scientific" practices in alleviating the plight of their audiences (Simon 1974: 85).[23] In 1987, Clive Evian, a doctor specializing in community medicine and associated with the non-governmental Progressive Primary Care Network, established health education role-playing at the Wits Rural Facility in the Mhala Mhala district (then in Gazankulu bantustan close to the Kruger National Park; now part of Mpumalanga province). Set up with the initial purpose of educating *nurses* away from their attachment to hard-won expertise and associated social status, which tended to be expressed in impatience if not outright hostility toward rural patients, this theatrical activity eventually included lay as well as professional health and community workers. It served not only to convey HE messages but also to provide for interaction between WRF, its clients, and other communities in the area.[24]

Theatre, AIDS, and the reformance of social actors

Confronted with an HIV+ population in the inner city that has exceeded 10 per cent of the sexually active population and a national rate of infection of over 1,000 a day, AIDS prevention programs in South Africa have been using all possible methods, including theatre, to engage the attention of people unwilling or unable to see themselves at risk of the disease. These projects owe a debt to the pioneering work of WRF as well as the Johannesburg City Health Department whose AIDS Prevention Program has since the late 1980s emphasized the importance of dismantling barriers between experts and clients, if the latter are to learn not only about the disease but also about the social and economic pressures exacerbating its spread.[25] This AIDS theatre program has assembled acting groups from lay health workers and trainee actors in the community-oriented programs at the Market Lab and FUBA. They perform skits which promote caution about multiple sex partners as well as the use of condoms, and direct the audience to sources of information in the clinics and elsewhere, while encouraging users of such services to ask questions of each other as well as the performers. The basic plot depicts the conflict between Cindy, a young urban African woman, and Ray, who meets her at a party but refuses, rather violently, to use a condom. It resolves the conflict by having Ray and Cindy discuss the matter with close friends, who persuade them to use condoms – and tact – with each other (Evian 1992: 35–37). The script treats resistance to AIDS in a matter-of-fact, even technical manner but also gives performers space to probe the social constraints underpinning resistance (male unwillingness to compromise "manhood" or female unwillingness to appear too demanding). This probing worked best, in the performances I observed in 1994, with audiences who talked back to performers as well as characters. While white-collar clerks and managers (schooled in professional decorum and in the decorous spectatorship of the well-made play) clapped politely and dispersed after an all-English performance at a Midrand bank, and some male workers watching a performance in isiZulu in a migrant hostel near Alexandra called AIDS a white disease and made disparaging comments about the women, students at Orlando High School (in their teens and twenties) mixed jokes in English, isiZulu, and other vernaculars about the party action with arguments about condom use, in which the subject of AIDS transmission and prevention was supplemented by comments on pregnancy, violence between partners, and the independence of women. They also expressed interest in the performers' backgrounds and access to training for themselves.[26]

The degree to which question time enables the dismantling of the expertise barrier – or, more contentiously, transformation of spectators into spect-actors and agents of change in themselves and society – is not simply judged by question-naires. Gary Friedman, director of African Research and Educational Puppetry Program (AREPP) (since 1987), Puppets Against Aids, which provided training in making puppets as well as AIDS education, cautions against the premature equation of the audience's acknowledgment of information or even of models of behavior in performance with the transformation of behavior in the long-term. He argues that performances about AIDS should aim not merely to convey information but to encourage spectators who might be unwilling to talk to health professionals to discuss their anxieties to and through the characters as well as the actors (Friedman 1992: 39). The reaction of the Soweto student audience reflected, on the one hand, anxieties about AIDS and rapidly changing gender norms, often expressed as advice to the characters and, on the other, a willingness to explore social agency, expressed as interest in performance and health educa-tion training. The tentative character of the response also suggests that conscientization, outside the relatively homogeneous group of the village or the union – the sites for Boal's Forum Theatre – is less likely to happen in a sudden conversion than in fits and starts provoked by the performance and subsequent experiences of the participants. At the same time, the intersection of attempts to reform social and personal behavior on the part of producers and of explorations of social and performance roles on the part of spectators (and potential actors) like the Soweto students suggests the potential power of the synthesis – or syncresis – of reform and performance, of what Shannon Jackson has elsewhere called *reformance*: the attempt to re-create individuals by reforming behaviors and environments along alternative lines (Jackson 1996: 339).

Friedman's caution seems prescient in the wake of the spectacular misappro-priation of R14.27 million out of the Health Ministry's annual total of ca. R90 million AIDS funding for Mbongeni Ngema's production of *Sarafina II*, an "AIDS musical," in January 1996. The plot deals with a young woman diagnosed HIV+ who dies after prayer and traditional medicine fail to cure her. In township melodrama style, the play culminated in a spectacular funeral which favored elaborate song and dance numbers rather than a critique of myths about AIDS (including: rapid decline and death after diagnosis, the blaming of women, indifference to contraception). Supposed to tour the country in a R1 million bus (more than the annual budget for urban-based AIDS theatre groups such as AREPP and several times that of groups in rural provinces), the production performed only briefly in the Durban Playhouse and the specially refitted Eyethu Cinema in Soweto. Whereas most theatre against AIDS is performed free, the better to reach people unable or unwilling to attend formal theatre performances,

Ngema charged R20 admission. Apart from questions of accountability, the effect of patronage on government contracts, and the morality of cashing in on the AIDS crisis, what is striking is the apparent willingness of ministry officials (including the director of the AIDS program) to believe that others might believe that this single expensive display of conspicuous consumption could, even if its message had been clinically sound, change the behavior of audiences seduced by the spectacle and its producer's boasts of sexual conquest.[27]

In retrospect, the case of *Sarafina II* is instructive if only because its exploitation of the AIDS crisis for profit, its exacerbation of the gulf between producer and consumers, and its contempt for its audience's needs disguised as a response to their desires, provide a spectacular foil for the virtues of more modest projects of *reformance*, which have at their best used mobile and effective technology to engage audiences. The *Broken Dreams* project (Market Lab, 1995–) offers an illuminating contrast to *Sarafina II* not only because the former cost less than 1 per cent of the latter to produce but also because it reverses Ngema's exploitation of AIDS for his own publicity: while the Market Lab may have relied initially on the reputation of its principal author, Zakes Mda, to publicize performances, this publicity has not overshadowed the primary purposes of those performances: to dramatize the consequences of sexual abuse for children, particularly those abused by HIV+ relatives. Performed by five professional actors and the children at each of several hundred schools since 1995, and assisted on site by professional and lay community counselors, *Broken Dreams* offers children an opportunity to speak about their experiences in the first or third person, in person or in character. This occasion for reenactment and redress may not do away with the problems exacerbating abuse (from overcrowding to the fragmentation of families to the much-discussed rage of the unemployable young men of the "lost generation" of the 1980s – such as those driving the action of *Zombie*).[28] However, it has provided children and their families with a forum for restoration and drawn more public attention and private funding to the treatment of survivors and, to a lesser degree, their abusers.[29]

Heart to Heart: performance, publication, and alternative publicity

The programmatic AIDS theatre run by the Johannesburg and other health departments remains primarily an instructional rather than a conscientizing practice. Audience response to the social agency of the *performers*, over and above their comments on the script's messages about AIDS and sexual behavior, suggests its conscientizing potential, but also the difficulty of realizing that potential with a standardized script designed to encourage reproducible, if limited, changes of behavior. As the *Broken Dreams* project suggests, standardization and an instructional (and in this case, therapeutic) emphasis have the virtues of efficiency and mass communication, but they do not give their participants the time and space to develop agency outside the frame of performance. Conscientization requires time and sustained social interaction if visiting facilitators are to get beyond the role of experts, if the host community is to get beyond passive reception, and if both are to work toward the transformation not merely of the immediate performance and its script but also of entrenched scripts of thought and behavior. I would like to conclude by looking at a particular project of reformance that attempted to combine the pleasures of performance with the enactment of new modes of social behavior in the production of a graphic record of that enactment. Although the *Heart to Heart* project took place at a particular site, WRF, and a school in the neighboring Mhala Mhala region, it offers an exemplary place and occasion for examining not only the uses of theatre in society but also – because it takes theatre practice out of the theatre institution – for breaching the disciplinary boundaries around theatre as such, and thus for challenging presumptions about the proper object of theatre research that still influence the study of theatre in South Africa. Rather than taking us away from theatre to "social engineering," as one South African writes (Hauptfleisch 1997: 105), it may be that, as French theatre-activist Armand Gatti put it, "in order to create theatre, it is necessary to leave it behind" (1982: 71).

The *Heart to Heart* project combined workshops with students (ca.14- to 24-year-olds) with the production of a graphic story ("comic") that expressed student concerns about sexuality as well as the influence of gender socialization, economic imperatives, and the gaps between urban and rural youth. The workshops were led by Patricia Watson – in a dual role as workshop facilitator (for the Storyteller Group) and researcher (AELS, Wits) – and included students at Magwagwaza High School in the Mhalav Mhala region, whose poverty under apartheid and the Gazankulu administration had been offset somewhat by the services and employment offered by WRF and Tintswalo Hospital.[30] Published (1994; revised 1996) by the Storyteller Group, this project is illuminating on several fronts:

1 It combined performance modeled on Boal's Forum Theatre with critical literacy pedagogy: students and facilitators produced *Heart to Heart*, a rural love story for local and in time (inter)national readers.

2 The published text includes not only two versions of a romance – the sentimental *Dream Love* (1991) and its revision in *True Love* (produced with the same students in 1993) – but also the linking "*students' story*" which re-presents the students' input in dramatized conflict about changes to *Dream Love*.

3 It combined the production with longer-term exploration of habits of gender socialization and so raised important questions not only about apartheid but also practices identified as "traditional." Questions about tensions between patriarchal social authority and the growing economic autonomy of women, between individual rights and community cohesion, or between local legitimacy and institutions like WRF, underlay the workshops even if participants were not always able to tackle them directly.[31]

To appreciate the originality and the exemplarity of this project, we should establish its affiliation, not only with theatre for development but also with the pedagogical graphic fiction ("comics") produced by anti-apartheid organizations since the 1970s. Under the auspices of the South African Council on Higher Education (SACHED), magazines like *Learn and Teach* and *Upbeat* used comic strips or graphic versions of literary texts like Mphahlele's *Down Second Avenue* to counter official propaganda in subjects like English or South African history. Their popularity with high school students and their peers demonstrated the potential for developing literacy as a means of social action rather than merely the acquisition of discrete skills.[32] More recently, organizations such as the Storyteller Group (Johannesburg), in consultation with public institutions such as Wits and the Medical Research Council (MRC), have produced full-length (32 pages, A4) graphic stories. Although they incorporate guidance on topics such as AIDS and gender socialization, they do so within a narrative framework and visual style borrowed from the familiar and appealing photonovella and "action comic" formats. The visual style combines the realism of local scenes with the cartoon character of exaggerated gestures and facial expressions, off-kilter framing, and printed sound effects. This strategy seeks not only to grant social space to taboo topics, but also to make them part of the pleasure of recognizing the everyday and the local as legitimately "storied" (Esterhuysen 1991: 276). For instance, *99 Sharp Street* deals with young Africans attempting to further their education (Esterhuysen 1991: 275–78). The title alludes to "sharp, sharp," response to the greeting "Heyta Ngwenya?" [roughly "Yo! What's happenin'?"]. The stories were situated in Hillbrow, and the language combined school English in the text-blocks with city slang in the bubbles (by Nanhlala Sicelo, a playwright trained at CAW). Distributed as inserts in a Sales House catalogue, whose clients include white-collar workers as well as students, *99 Sharp Street* targeted Johannesburg youth but also appealed to students in rural areas.

The popularity of graphic stories like *99 Sharp Street* provided the occasion for *Heart to Heart*, as well as the point of departure for investigating – by means of performance – the ways in which rural youth negotiate popular culture and social scripts that they perceive as urban; students' evident enjoyment of *99 Sharp Street* was colored by their sense of its association with Egoli (Johannesburg's vernacular name more aptly captures its association with gold, glamour, and other metropolitan attractions). It was in response to the students' skepticism that their own environment, characterized by rural poverty as well as pockets of wealth represented either by remote-controlled institutions like WRF or by a few local big-wigs associated with the Gazankulu administration, could be "storied" or their own lives "performed" that Watson proposed workshops to produce a local graphic story.

The first version of this story, *Dream Love*, was "driven by the youth" in that the student participants generated the romance plot, in which a young woman (Tintswalo) is swept off her feet by an older, wealthier man (Magezi), who owns a chain of stores in the district. The conclusion – the birth of a baby followed by a spectacular wedding – endorses Tintswalo's willingness to abandon school for marriage but leaves unresolved Magezi's relationship with another girlfriend (Mafresh) and the tension between the young wife and her mother-in-law. This plot reflects local awareness of the importance of (relative) wealth in a "good match" as well as local tensions between the "traditional" family structure, exemplified by the mother-in-law's suspicion of the *xitlakati* [xiTsonga: discardable rag] daughter-in-law, and the "modern," exemplified by her daughter-in-law's desire for autonomy. But it also articulates a local variant of transnational cultural product: the soap opera romance. The lavish weddings featured on American soap-operas, such as *Days of Our Lives* and *Santa Barbara* (shown in South Africa since the 1980s), shadow the wedding in *Dream Love*; what the latter lacks in first world prestige, it makes up for in an equivalent emphasis on conspicuous consumption and community preeminence.[33] The gender politics of this romance are, however, more complicated than suggested either by American or local examples. Soap opera's primary audience is generally understood to be women, who, like the *Bold and Beautiful* fans in Dike's *So What's New?*, derive pleasure from its focus on emotion and interpersonal relationships as well as on glamorous protagonists' manipulation of their rivals. By contrast, the romance plot of *Dream Love* articulated the preferences of the male participants, who did most of the talking and who appeared to take pleasure not only in the image of an alluring but passive female but also in the action of a male protagonist whose economic and sexual power contrasted sharply with their own prospects. Even though they inhabited a society in which masculine authority was undermined by the loss of "traditional" male jobs in mining and manufacture and by the growing autonomy of working women, the male students resisted proposals to make Magezi's status more closely resemble their own reality.[34] In other words, their subjunctive enactment reinforced rather than challenged the ideology of patriarchy.

Although they prepared a storyboard based on the romance scenario, the Storyteller Group acknowledged that the story articulated in fantasy form a patriarchal script that foreclosed the conscientizing potential of the workshops (Watson 1998: 5.4, 6.3). Nonetheless, the occasion of this foreclosure, the performance of the male participants that silenced the women in the group, was also the site where conscientization might take place. Before working dramatizing alternative scenarios to key moments of *Dream Love* in the second set of workshops (1993), Watson reconfigured the place and thus the occasion of the performance with a more explicit negotiation and acknowledgment of the dialectic between agency and dependence, urban capital and expertise and rural know-how, white and black. The 1991 workshops had reproduced the asymmetrical relationship between metropolis and periphery by taking place at WRF, which functioned as a local *Egoli* by virtue of its institutional prestige, employment prospects, and literal and figurative connection to Johannesburg. By moving the location of the workshops from WRF to a local, albeit unfinished school hall, and by offering English exam preparation to the students in return for participation, she offered students a more direct bargain than they had received in 1991. Separating the workshops from the constraints of the formal classroom allowed students to speak Tsonga as well as English and mitigated against the authoritarian instruction prevailing in South African schools.

To this reconfiguration of place and occasion, Watson added the reorganization of the immediate space to help participants revise the conventions and conditions of subjunctive and indicative enactment that had marginalized the women in the 1991 workshops. To this end, Watson took on a more interventionist role than Boal's Forum Theatre formula implies:

1   she seated the women apart from the men to provide the former with physical as well as moral support to speak up individually or in chorus;

2   she withheld this privilege from the men, requiring instead that each speak from a "hot seat" unaided by his peers;

3   she broke the convention of the facilitator as disinterested "joker" (Boal 1992: 21) at moments of deadlocked conflict by posing questions which highlighted her position of authority and the feminist critique of patriarchy underlying her procedure (Watson 1998: 6.3, 6.4.3), while "rupturing the homogenization of the students' voices" (6.1).

As the "students' story" linking the two romances shows, this revision of the space and the action within it did not automatically transform the gender imbalance of the performance or that of the students' interaction, but it did produce new alignments. The women as a group gained the space to challenge the prevailing view of female subordination which they had previously tolerated. Some male participants turned away from the adamant defense of patriarchal prerogatives to acknowledge the claims of women, as citizens of a "new" South Africa, to equal treatment in the domestic as well as the public sphere and to grant that this accommodation would involve relinquishing male privilege.

The result of the second set of workshops was not only *True Love* but also the re-presentation of the workshops themselves in the "students' story." *True Love* begins with the same first page and apparent preparations for the wedding, only to deconstruct this idyll as a daydream. Thereafter, it juxtaposes elements of the "dream" script with Tintswalo's skepticism, where previously she had been swept away. Far from resigning herself to Magezi's womanizing, this Tintswalo objects angrily when she finds him with Mafresh and gives him an ultimatum. The end leaves Tintswalo and her friend Lindi debating the relative merits of sex, marriage, and education, and finally, in a virtuoso representation of the disjunction between romantic expectations and uncertain outcome, has the angular and ironic figures from the "student's story" literally roll up the lush landscape, as the creators inspect their handiwork.

The students' story's angular images and jumpy narrative captured on paper the multi-dimensionality of the workshops in the clash of scripts, places, and occasions of social as well as dramatic representation. It also provided opportunity for reenactment and intervention. The students did not seize upon this opportunity immediately, however. When asked to reenact Tintswalo's discovery of Magezi and Mafresh in Club Mauritius, "most . . . acted . . . the *Dream Love* story" (Storyteller Group 1994: 15) but one pair chose to reverse the roles, having Magezi confront Tintswalo with another boyfriend. Where the conventional reenactment endorsed the double standard that reinforced the characters' and the actors' acceptance that Magezi's money and social prestige would grant him access to several women, the revision provoked arguments that ranged from (stereo-) typical reactions, such as "Beat her" and "A man needs more than one woman" to more critical responses, such as "It's unfair of you to expect your girlfriend to be faithful when you're not" (p. 16) (Figure 8.4). In addition to a gender gap, the graphic also highlights the age-range of the students; while younger boys, who were more likely to be subject to beating themselves (p. 17), strongly defended Magezi's authority as "head of the family" (p. 16), older students argued for reasonable conflict resolution. The response of students at other schools who read the comic as members of focus groups registered gender conflict but also suggested that male readers could identify with the female protagonist's desire for autonomy: "it doesn't have advice for women only but also for me" (Watson 1994: 4).

The reenactment of this scene present an instance – and a critique – of "simultaneous dramaturgy" (Boal 1979: 132), the enactment of alternatives to crucial decisions. Boal argues that the participants' grasp of the conflict is sharpened if they change only the decision and not the agents, but this scene undoes the authority of the existing script (an authority otherwise reinforced by the presence of the workshop facilitator) and thus goes further toward transforming the student spectator/readers of that script into spect-actors (Boal 1992: 2) of their own script, even if it cannot ensure that they will translate this into social action beyond the liminal space of the workshop. The scene also highlights the ambiguity of the facilitator's role. Although the facilitator did not give instruction in the manner of more programmatic theatre for development, she did ask leading questions, such as "Which girls would like their boyfriends to love them without having sex?" At the same time, the students' story acknowledged the difficulty of ongoing revision, by drawing their reader into the crisis of the "students' story" – "After the workshops, we were all very tired" (Storyteller Group 1994: 17) – and by inviting readers to think of alternatives: "This publication shows that there is no one story that can speak for everyone" (Storyteller Group 1994: ii). The scene reinforces the credibility of the action by locating it in the everyday world. The bare concrete floor, the sparse furniture, and the unfinished wall open to the outside illuminate the facts of poverty as well as the community's matter-of-fact attitude to these facts.

What sets *Heart to Heart* apart from many other culture-for-development projects is its acknowledgment of the appeal of the transnational culture industry and its success in refunctioning mass-cultural forms, like soap operas and comics. The

Figure 8.4 Spect-action and social action in *Heart to Heart*. *Source*: *Heart to Heart* (Johannesburg: Storyteller Group, 1994); *permission*: Neil Napper, director: Storyteller Group

facilitators argued (and student and teacher responses confirmed) the importance of acknowledging students' ambivalent response to the appeal of mass culture (Watson 1994: 7). The mixture of seduction and instruction is reflected in student responses, for instance:

> The *Dream Love* is so nice. That's how I dream. When I first read the comic I didn't finish the Student's Story, but after I read *True Love* I was really confused. I went back and finished the *Students' Story* . . . Shoo, this book makes me [to] think.
>
> (Watson 1994: 1)

While some Africanists, such as theatre director Mofokeng, who protested the commercialization of African culture *Sarafina*, argued that *Heart to Heart*'s images were too sexual to reflect "traditional" African mores, student responses overwhelmingly confirmed an analytic interest in the story over and above the appeal of the images.

More than most rural culture for development projects, *Heart to Heart*'s resonance is potentially national – even international – in scope, not only because the publication has been distributed as a teaching tool in "francophone" as well as "anglophone" Africa,[35] but because its exuberant and emancipatory depiction of a rural story mediated by a narrative repertoire generally understood as urban acknowledges the impact of mass cultural commodities that remind rural South Africans of their alienation from development, while also allowing for the possibility that the fantasy generated in response to these commodities might, as Negt and Kluge suggest, constitute an "unconscious practical critique of alienation" (Negt and Kluge 1993: 33). This local refunctioning of a globalized culture industry in *Heart to Heart* in the graphic story and the different accounts of its performance makes visible the tension between manipulation and communication, critical intervention and outside imposition, that troubles – and animates – not only this particular project, but the staging of conscientization more generally. Operating within several media, this process demonstrates the central role of performance in enacting the dialectic between fiction and daily practice or between "subjunctive" and "indicative" action (Williams 1979: 219, 224). However, it also reminds theatre practitioners and scholars that the place and occasion of theatre as a counter public sphere, as a discursive and social field within which representations of alternative action can be entertained to challenge the status quo in post-*anti*-apartheid South Africa, can be fully located only in relation to other institutions of social and cultural representation. Even if, as Scottish-based theatre activist John McGrath wrote in another context, "theatre cannot cause a social change," it "can articulate the pressures toward one" by providing the means whereby "people can find their voice, their solidarity and their collective determination" (McGrath 1981: vii). Whereas theatre practitioners in the anti-apartheid era could dismiss schools and broadcast media as the irredeemable agents of a repressive state, those working in and on the present moment, feel called upon to participate in the transformation of these institutions – by means of performance.

NOTES

1 INTRODUCTION: THE DRAMA OF SOUTH AFRICA

1 Comments based on live coverage by the South African Broadcasting Corporation as well as commentary in the *Mail and Guardian* (13–19 May 1994), *Sowetan* (10 May 1994), and *Sunday Nation* (15 May 1994), the more conservative *Johannesburg Star* (10 May 1994), and the Afrikaner flagship, *Die Burger* (10 May 1994).

2 For the conception of performance as *subjunctive*, hypothetical but not, at its most powerful, a mere illusion, see Williams (1979: 218–19) and Kruger (1993a).

3 isiNguni is the language-group that comprises the mutually intelligible languages, isiZulu, isiXhosa, siSwati, and isiNdebele, that together comprise about 18 million speakers out of ca. 39 million people.

4 As Hobsbawm and Ranger famously propose, "invented tradition" is "a set of practices . . . of a ritual or symbolic nature, which seek to inculcate certain values and norms of behavior by repetition [and] . . . attempt to establish continuity with . . . a suitable historical past" (1982: 1). The invention of tradition is a modern practice in that the attempt to establish an apparently invariant past tradition in the present depends on the work of rewriting the difference between past and present *as* the invariance of tradition.

5 For Mandela's speech, see the *Sunday Nation: Inauguration Special* (15 May 1994).

6 Turner's characterization of "liminoid phenomena" as "ludic offerings placed for sale on the 'free market'" (1982: 54) is apt enough, but his conclusion – that such phenomena are idiosyncratic and "personal-psychological" – would have to be tested against the mass production of objects of sale, such as Madiba T-shirts, as well as the more general commodification of the "rainbow nation" in such spectacles as the Rugby World Cup (1995).

7 There is no firm separation between traditional and modern, precolonial and post-colonial, deferential and critical *izibongo*; *izimbongi* have used their skills to challenge as well as support traditional authority. As Vail and White note: "At its best, praise poetry is lively, mischievous, dense with history . . . and capable of redefining authority and the qualities of a nation in a manner that can . . . make the prevailing ruler 'pensive'" (1991: 56).

8 Choreographer Suria Govender borrows the idea of the "ambivalent ethics of cross-cultural borrowings" (1996: 2) from Rustom Bharucha's critique of big-budget inter-culturalism like Peter Brook's version of the *Mahabharata* (Bharucha 1991: 1–10) but

217

does not discuss the ambivalent position of South Africans of Indian descent (see Naidoo 1997 and chapter 6).

9 In the language of 1910, the Cape (British since 1806) and Natal (since 1845) ceased to be colonies when they joined the old Boer polities, the South African Republic and the Orange Free State in the new, independent and in this sense, postcolonial, Union of South Africa. In the language of current historiography, the Union (1910–61) was neocolonial both in its economic dependence on British manufacture and in its oppression of the black majority, although this oppression was then endorsed in Europe and North America. While economically more self-sufficient and politically distant from postwar Europe in the throes of decolonization, the apartheid Republic (1961–94) persisted in neocolonial economic underdevelopment, political repression, and cultural tutelage.

10 Although the term "hybridity" highlights the persistence of racial categories in South Africa, its biological derivation is unhelpful in discussing *practices, conventions, scripts*, and *behaviors*, whose association with a particular ethnicity or other identity is subject to continual revision; see Balme (1995: 16–37).

11 Recent work on national pageants challenges the boundaries between social anthropology and theatre history; see Rassool and Witz (1993), Merrington (1997), Maingard (1997a), and chapter 2 of this volume.

12 For the Rugby World Cup ceremony's recapitulation of the Tricentenary, see Coetzee (1995) and Maingard (1997a).

13 For an analysis of the connections between theatre criticism and English politics of the period, see Bate (1989); for its implications for South Africa, see David Johnson (1996).

14 My use of "publicity" in the sense of "publicness" draws on Habermas's theory of the public sphere as a realm of Enlightenment self-representation rather than the commodification implied in "publicity" today (Habermas 1989 [1962]), and on Negt and Kluge's (1993) critique of the ideal-typical status of a bourgeois public sphere, in the name of counter-publics of those excluded from legitimate publicity. While the latter focuses on advanced capitalist societies, my interest is in the ways in which a relatively under-capitalized theatre under apartheid capitalism constituted a virtual public sphere when the overt counter-publicity of mass political opposition was under threat, and the ways in which the subjunctive character of dramatic representation retained relative autonomy from direct political retaliation (see also Kruger 1992: 3–21).

15 This opposition between urban and rural cultural practice was never clear-cut, even in the early days of urbanization ca. 1920, since African variety toured the hinterland and migrant workers carried modes of performance and spectatorship from city to country and back. Despite this qualification, urbanizing South Africa has since the early twentieth century been the site for the most dizzying form of cultural fusion and confusion.

16 Minstrelsy has a long history in South Africa. See Erlmann (1991) and chapter 2.

17 Shakespeare featured more prominently in the curriculum than on the commercial or amateur stages. While arguments have been made that "Shakespeare" functioned as an instrument of acculturation, as well as resistance – see Orkin (1989) and Johnson (1996) – the evidence in the archives of the mission schools, as well as organizations like the Bantu Men's Social Centre, suggests that non-professionals tended to prefer the "new drama," loosely defined, from Galsworthy's drama of "social concern" to Drinkwater's Schillerian history plays.

18 As O'Meara's (1983) definitive study of the promotion of Afrikaner enterprises though state contracts and of Afrikaner culture through direct or indirect subsidy shows, *volkskapitalisme* was neither strictly popular nor strictly capitalist.

19 The place of Afrikaans on a "creole continuum" between written Dutch and the pidgins spoken by non-native speakers in the Cape colony is still contested, but most commentators agree that Afrikaans has creolized features such as the loss of gender and number markers and simplified tense, as well as lexical input from indigenous (mostly Khoisan) and other sources, such as Malayu used by Asian slaves; see Roberge (1995) and Davids (1994).

20 Credo Mutwa's home was burnt during the Soweto uprising by activists who considered him an apartheid stooge (Kavanagh's introduction to *South African People's Plays*, 1981: 2); he has since joined the ranks of entrepreneurs marketing authentic Africa to tourists.

21 Debates about English in South Africa have moved from defending the custodianship of English-speaking whites (Butler 1986) to a variety of arguments for democratization: furthering standard English as a means of pan-African unity (Omotoso 1991), as well as the cultural value of diverse englishes (Ndebele 1987). ANC policy has fluctuated between acknowledging the legitimacy of indigenous languages and defending the practicability of the priority of English (Heugh 1995). The Report of the Language Task Action Group (LANGTAG) attacks the hegemony of English but its practical projects seem more directed toward undoing the hegemony of Afrikaans by redirecting funds to develop indigenous language dictionaries, media programing, and education; see Alexander (1996). Local content mandates for television have more impact on current affairs and documentary programing than on drama, since the local mandate for general entertainment programing (including drama) is only 20 per cent.

2 THE PROGRESS OF THE NATIONAL PAGEANT

1 For the program, see the records of the South African Institute for Race Relations (hereafter: SAIRR), Cullen Library, University of the Witwatersrand: AD843/B47.2.

2 "Africans Celebrate Emancipation Centenary," *Bantu World* (*BW*), 9 June 1934, 4 and "The Emancipation Centenary Celebration," *Umteteli wa Bantu* (*UwB*), 9 June 1934, 2. The lead articles in these papers were written in English by Africans, but were published by white capital.

3 Couzens (1985: 99–101) suggests that the Dhlomo brothers were also influenced by *Abraham Lincoln* by the English playwright, John Drinkwater, but newspaper accounts suggest the pathos of Harriet Beecher Stowe rather than the heroic agency of Drinkwater's protagonists.

4 Kavanagh (1985) distinguishes firmly between the state and its intermediaries on the one hand, and the "fundamentally oppressed masses" on the other; Orkin (1991) allows for the ambivalence of figures like Dhlomo.

5 [R. V. Selope Thema,] "Honor the Great Emancipators," *BW* (2 June 1934), 1.

6 "This Day of Freedom," *UwB*, 5 August 1933, 2.

7 Mazrui and Tidy coin this term (1984: 282) to describe a tactical appeal to tradition made by modern African leaders; Mudimbe redeploys the term (1988: 169) to reflect on the irony of invoking tradition in the service of modernization.

8 While separate development appealed to chiefs keen to maintain their ebbing authority, there can be no doubt that the government's interest in segregation, although

rationalized by contradictory assertions about African self-determination and the vulnerability of the "child race," was firmly grounded in "European interests," in the desire for a labor reserve uncontaminated by the "usual antagonism of class war" (Dubow 1987). Marks (1989: 217) notes that ethnic consciousness "has been the product of intense ideological labour by the black intelligentsia and white ideologues," as the ties between the Zulu Cultural Society and the Dept. of Native Affairs confirm.

9 R. V. Selope Thema, "Before the Advent of the White Man, the Dead Ruled the Living with a Rod of Iron in Bantu Society," *BW,* 12 May 1934, 8–9.

10 Class distinctions between elite and popular were solidifying in this period, but there were no "class cultures" as such (Bozzoli 1983: 40). While those present at the BMSC for the Emancipation Celebration, for instance, were appalled by the alleged immorality of slumyard culture but may have gone to minstrel shows, the audience at the Eastern Native Township was more likely to go to a *marabi* dance than to *She Stoops to Conquer.*

11 Couzens' definition of the New African as "detribalised, 'progressive,' adapted and adaptor of the modern South Africa" (1985: 110) highlights the ambiguous class position of this group. New Africans' scorn for the *abaphakathi* was not without irony, since they too had come up through assimilation (pp. 36–37).

12 For the influence of Du Bois and Washington, see Couzens (1985: 86, 98). *Souls of Black Folk* and *Up from Slavery* were two of many African-American texts in the BMSC branch of the Carnegie Non-European Library.

13 Musician and critic Mark Radebe used a Garveyite term, "Africans in America," to pay homage to African-American music and to "the enormous influence of Bantu rhythms on the world's music." See Musicus, "The All-African Music Festival," *UwB,* 29 October 1932, 2; "The Coming of Paul Robeson," *UwB,* 1 June 1933, 2.

14 Apart from Orpheus MacAdoo's Virginia Jubilee Singers, whose repertoire of jubilee and minstrelsy impressed black as well as white South Africans in the 1890s (Erlmann 1991: 21–53), there were few professional black troupes in South Africa. Influence tended to be via sheet music and recordings, although appropriations of African-American shows by white impresarios – such as Ziegfeld's purchase of the rights to Lubrie Hill's *Darktown Follies* in 1913 (Johnson 1991: 174) – might have come to the notice of black South Africans abroad – among them the composer, Reuben Caluza, in New York in the 1930s, and Motsieloa, in London in the 1920s.

15 As with the amaCele, the amaMthethwa claim to Zuluness was offset by a certain historical irony. Although represented in the tradition as Shaka's benefactor, the Mthethwa chieftain, Dingiswayo, was praised for bringing the Mthethwa under European influence by one of the most influential of colonial experts, Theophilus Shepstone, Secretary of Native Affairs in colonial Natal and chief ideologue of "separate development" (Hamilton 1985: 104).

16 Centenary of Natal History and the American Board Mission, Adams College papers, KC70, MS 62a/11.2; Killie Campbell African Library (hereafter KCAL), University of Natal.

17 *BW,* 11 April 1936, 17, and 30 May 1936, 17.

18 "Johannesburg's Jubilee and Empire Exhibition Next Year. Exclusive Interview with B. M. Bellasis [executive director of the Exhibition]," *African World,* 2 March 1935, 227–29.

19 "South Africa's Forthcoming Empire Exhibition," *South African Mining and Engineering Journal,* 18 May 1935, 72.

20 *Official Guide Celebrating the Golden Jubilee of Johannesburg at the Empire Exhibition*, 1. The organizers of the Johannesburg event were probably aware of the White City Exhibitions in London (1908–14), which borrowed the format of the Columbian Exposition (Greenhalgh 1988: 40–41, 90–95).

21 See *Chicago's World Fair* (Chicago: Chicago Historical Society, 1993). Despite the reassurances of the exhibition manager, B. M. Bellasis, that there would be "no restrictions on Native visitors" (Letter to J. D. Rheinhallt Jones, secretary of the SAIRR, 27 June 1936; SAIRR Records, AD843/B66.3), African access was in fact restricted by price and lack of suitable accommodation; see "The Empire Exhibition," *BW*, 24 August 1936, 17 and 14 November 1936, 17.

22 See Johannesburg Public Library (hereafter, JPL) Press Cutting Collection on the Empire Exhibition, Cullen Library: A1092, boxes 37–43, 93–97, 113–14.

23 *Rand Daily Mail*, 10 July 1935.

24 "The Pageant of the Provinces," *Outspan*, May 1936.

25 Compare "Mr. Gyseghem, Pageant Master" in the *Johannesburg Star*, 5 March 1936, with an article in the *Uganda Herald* (26 February 1936), which discusses Van Gyseghem's work in the Soviet Union and the United States (where he worked on Living Newspapers).

26 "The Pageant," *Pretoria News*, 8 May 1936. Preller's work included *Piet Retief* (1906), an account of the Voortrekker encounter with the Zulu king Dingane, whose treatment of the Boer invaders as undeserving victims of Zulu aggression was to set the tone of later official histories, as well as the scenario for the film *De Voortrekkers* (1916) (Hofmeyr 1988: 521–34).

27 "Grand Pageant. Central Committee's Decision," *East London Daily Dispatch*, 10 July 1936. The provinces were: Transvaal, Orange Free State, Natal, Cape Province, "Griqualand," and "Borders" (Eastern Cape).

28 Farewell's agreement with Shaka in 1824 did no more than secure a land grant for trading; it did not imply a desire for British intervention in Natal (Hamilton 1998: 38–43).

29 For Preller, see note 26. For Neethling-Pohl's enthusiasm for Nazi cultural politics (and for information about her husband's wartime internment for pro-Nazi activity in the *Ossewa-Brandwag*, see the Neethling-Pohl files (SA). The film was released to applause by the Afrikaner Nationalist audience at the centenary celebrations but its slighting treatment of the English (to say nothing of blacks) and its fascist overtones led to protests among English South Africans (Davis 1996: 148).

30 See D. G. Grobbelaar's letter to E. S. Sachs, secretary of the Garment Workers' Union, on the subject of his "communist accomplices" and Sachs's "Reply to a Hitlerite," *Garment Worker*, November 1938, 9–10, and the reply by Hester Cornelius, "Ons en die Voortrekkereeufees," *Klerewerker*, October 1938, 4, and her response to Afrikaner Nationalist hostility to socialists, "Aan die Transvaler," *Klerewerker*, October 1938, 5.

31 "Brilliant Pageant of South African History," *RDM*, 17 December 1936, 12; "The South African Pageant," *Star*, 17 December 1936, 26.

32 *Star*, 18 December 1936, 21.

33 "The Empire Exhibition," *BW*, 24 August, 17, and 26 September 1936, 20; "The City Thanks Africans," *BW*, 7 November 1936, 20.

34 A Reader, "A Day at the Empire Exhibition," *BW*, 21 November 1936, 11.

35 "Four Cameos," *Natal Advertiser*, 4 August 1936.

36 "The Empire Exhibition," *Sunday Express*, 4 October 1936.

37 See E. Ntombela, "On Indlamu," in *Native Teachers' Journal* 28, 2 (1949), 97.

38 S. Ncongo, *Native Teachers' Journal*, 28, 2 (1949), 98. For further analysis, see Marks (1989: 230–32).

39 *BW*, 7 May 1932, 17; 28 September 1935, 4; 14 March 1936.

40 W. Mbali, "The Darktown Strutters and Merry Blackbirds play in Queenstown," *BW*, 24 April 1937, 17.

41 Critic at Large [Walter Nhlapo], "De Pitch Black Follies at the BMSC," *BW*, 12 February 1938, 18. See also the program in the SAIRR records, AD843/Kb28.2.2.

42 John Matheus (1887–1983) published "The 'Cruter," in 1926, after the Great Migration had brought close to a million African-Americans to the Northern cities. The play vividly portrays an encounter between a share-cropping family and an unnamed white recruiter, distinguished by his formal wear (hat and gloves) as well as formal speech, as opposed to the sharecroppers' dialect (Matheus 1975).

43 "African Theatrical Syndicate Show," *BW*, 24 February 1940, 20.

44 "The Nu-Zonk Revue," *Ilanga lase Natal*, 18 May 1946, 8.

45 The legacy of this fusion of apartheid law and neocolonial taste recurs in such shows as *Ipi Tombi* (1973; roughly, "Girls?! Where?"), a tribal vaudeville act that used a sketchy version of the familiar "Jim comes to Jo'burg" scenario and canned *mbaqanga* music as backdrop for bare-breasted dancers in short grass skirts. At the same time, however, shows such as Matsamela Manaka's *Goree* (1988), which traces the odyssey of a South African dancer via the "Great White Way" to the island of Goree, show that the syncretism pioneered by Motsieloa can move contemporary African audiences.

46 [W. Nhlapo], "Drama vs. Jazz," *BW*, 24 February 1940, 20.

47 Dhlomo, "Drama and the African" (1977 [1936]: 7).

3 NEW AFRICANS, NEOCOLONIAL THEATRE, AND "AN AFRICAN NATIONAL DRAMATIC MOVEMENT"

1 H. I. E. Dhlomo, "The Importance of African Drama," *Bantu World*, 21 October 1933, 17.

2 Johannesburg Public Library, Strange Theatre Collection (hereafter JPL/STC).

3 Stephen Black, editor's comment on the Johannesburg Rep's production of *The Red Robe* in *The Sjambok*, 14 November 1930, 18.

4 Library Theatre, 2 December 1937, *Red Rand* was directed by Elsie Salomon, who also directed *Lady Windermere's Fan* for the Bantu Dramatic Society in 1935.

5 Like its South African counterpart, the Australian neocolonial stage was dominated by British tours in the 1930s and 1940s under the practical monopoly of one company, J. C. Williamson & Co. Only in the postwar period did subsidy for local work help literary and nationalist groups to break this commercial monopoly; see Love (1984). In Canada, talk about a National Theatre began earlier but, as Alan Filewod writes of the "first self-declared National Theatre in 1915" (1990: 5), such talk emphasized the British aspirations of the "English" Canadians.

6 On the relationship between cultural and other forms of capital, see Bourdieu (1993); on the ambiguous negotiation of critique and affirmation in dissenting fractions of the ruling class, see Williams (1980).

7 The original poem, "On Some South African Novelists," reads like an indictment of
critics as well as writers:

> You praise the firm restraint with which they write,
> I'm with you there, of course.
> They use the snaffle and the curb, all right,
> But where's the bloody horse?
>
> (Campbell 1949: 171)

8 African Consolidated Theatres, who usually booked overseas touring groups for His
Majesty's, had offered the theatre to the Rep on this occasion. In all probability, Dan
Twala was present at the Rep's dress rehearsal (Hoffman and Hoffman 1980: 39).
Hoernlé's error is significant if only because it confirms the force of metropolitan
prestige.

9 "The Africans Invade the Stage," *BW,* 15 April 1933, 1; "Unique Gathering at the
BMSC," *BW,* 6 May 1933, 1; "The Bantu Dramatic Society Stage their First Show,"
UwB, 15 April 1933, 4.

10 Letter to C. Bullock, 20 November 1935; SAIRR: AD843/RJ/ Kb28.2.2.

11 "African Art Forcing Its Way to Realisation," *BW,* 2 March 1935, 1. Sybil Thorndike,
together with her husband, Lewis Casson, both left-leaning veterans of the Old Vic
Theatre in London, were performing Shaw under the auspices of African Consolidated Theatres. They also took an interest in the Johannesburg Rep and the BDS.

12 In a front-page article on "The Growth of African Literature," *BW,* 4 March 1933, 1,
Dhlomo insisted that Africans not be pressurized into writing in indigenous languages
rather than English, citing as an exemplar, Sol Plaatje, author of *Native Life in South
Africa* (1916) as well as Setswana translations of Shakespeare. Rheinhallt Jones's
mistaken attribution of this *uNongqause* to a Xhosa rather than an English author is
only a more explicit expression of the belief shared by his fellow philanthropists, that
"Europeans" had a greater command of "dramatic knowledge" than the Africans
under their tutelage (SAIRR: AD843/RJ/Kb28.2.2).

13 The reference to *Masses and Man* [*Masse-Mensch*] is in an anonymous review of *The Girl
Who Killed to Save* in the *Sunday Times,* 8 November 1936. Drinkwater's history plays
and Galsworthy's social problem plays figured in the curricula of the mission schools
and were available in the BMSC and associated libraries, as were plays by Ibsen,
Brieux, and Dumas. Their emphasis on social concern appealed more to Africans and
their teachers than the subtle ironies of contemporary Granville-Barker, despite claims
in his favor (Steadman 1990: 214).

14 See Dhlomo, "Nongqause – or, The Girl Who Killed to Save," and accompanying
songs in tonic-solfa notation; Rhodes University, Cory Library, Lovedale Collection:
16/309.

15 Although there is no record of performance, the preface stresses the author's intent to
make the play available without cost for educational performances and also laid out
costs for film rights (Lovedale Collection: 16/309).

16 The reason for the change in venue was a 1936 Johannesburg by-law that forbade
African men from performing at venues at which white women were present, even if
the venue – in this case, the BMSC – was supposedly run by and for Africans. BMSC
Annual Report 1937, SAIRR: AD843/B.73.1.

17 Bantu People's Theatre, letter to Rheinhallt Jones, 31 July 1937; SAIRR: AD843/RJ/ Kb28.2.2.
18 Bantu People's Theatre, Draft Constitution, SAIRR: AD843 /RJ/Kb.14.
19 [R. V. Selope Thema,] Editorial, *BW,* 18 January 1936, 4.
20 Dhlomo, "Tshaka – a Reevaluation," *UwB,* 18 June 1932, 4.
21 *Izibongelo* appears to be derived from the verb *-bongela* [roughly: praise for or directly to someone] and suggests a performance for a target audience. The target, in this context, appears to be not so much an individual object of praise as the nation as a whole (at once audience and subject of the representation).
22 Rider Haggard's account, as well as other colonial accounts, such as Colenso's *History of the Anglo-Zulu War* and Sullivan's *The Native Policy of Theophilus Shepstone* (1928), which Dhlomo owned and annotated (Couzens 1985: 138), are likely sources for Dhlomo.
23 At issue here is not whether Dhlomo's portrayal of Shepstone is accurate or not, but rather the dramatic potential of a historical figure who excited controversy among white as well as black commentators and whose ideas continue to provoke debate today (Hamilton 1998: 73–129).
24 While Dhlomo portrays Dunn as an opportunist playing off British against Zulu, his descendants in the 1930s were treated with a certain respect by the African press. Even in 1994, the display at the Zulu Historical Museum at Fort Nongqai in KwaZulu/Natal placed Dunn alongside the Zulu kings as a powerful landowner, who secured power by marrying (over twenty) wives from prominent Zulu families.
25 The play's political character made it an unlikely choice for Lovedale Press, which had published *The Girl Who Killed to Save.* In his letter to R. W. H. Shepherd, director of the press (on 16 April 1938), Dhlomo listed groups eager to stage his plays (including one led by Motsieloa and sponsored by Sowden). Although Shepherd's rejection of Dhlomo's plays was ostensibly based on their weak verse (19 May 1938), a letter rejecting Dhlomo's novella, *An Experiment in Colour,* for its "strident tone" and alleged hostility to whites (3 March 1939), suggests that Dhlomo upset Shepherd's missionary decorum. See Lovedale Collection, 16/309(h), and Midgley (1993: 110–50).
26 Coplan (1994: 34–35) notes that the consultative role of the *pitso* persisted even though the destabilizing conditions of the Lifacane required Moshoeshoe to rule more auto-cratically than his predecessors.
27 Celebrated in the Basutoland Protectorate on 12 March in honor of Moshoeshoe's treaty with Britain in 1862, commemoration dates varied in South Africa, perhaps because celebrations here responded to contemporary debates about local sovereignty. The same day that *Moshoeshoe* opened, a celebration praised the Basotho leader as an "embodiment of democracy" in an "undemocratic South Africa" ("Moshoeshoe Day Celebrations in Kroonstad," *UwB,* 6 May 1939, 7).
28 Shepherd to Dhlomo, 19 May 1938, in which he argued that "This is Africa" was promising but not yet publishable; Lovedale Collection: 16/309.
29 "*Moshoeshoe.* Play Produced by Africans," *BW,* 6 May 1939, 20.
30 After this production, Khutlang became physical director at the BMSC, organizing sports as well as dance performances. Salome Masoleng was the wife of Johannes Masoleng, choreographer for the Darktown Strutters.
31 "Moshoeshoe," *UwB,* 6 May 1939, 4.
32 See Dhlomo's reiteration of the case for English as a means of transcending tribalism in "Reflections on a Literary Competition," *Ilanga lase Natal,* 31 October 1953, 3.

33 Couzens (1985: 161–62) speculates on the link between Thaba Bosiu (in Lesotho) at the end of the play and its Soweto namesake. The publicity surrounding Basotho chief Joel Molapo's speech at Western Native Township on Moshoeshoe Day 1937 confirms the contemporary resonance of the occasion.

34 "The meaning of our name" plays on the link between the singular *isibongo* [clan name] and the plural *izibongo* [either clan names or praises, by implication of the clan and its leaders].

4 COUNTRY COUNTER CITY: URBANIZATION, TRIBALIZATION, AND PERFORMANCE UNDER APARTHEID

1 The 1946 census (Thompson 1990: 178, 244) indicates 24% of Africans lived in the cities, as against 76% whites, 70% Indians, and 62% coloureds. The significance of the African figure is best gauged by comparison with 1936 (17 per cent). This is also the first census in which Africans outnumber whites in the urban areas.

2 Connections between the ANC and dispossessed Africans, such as the 90,000 squatters on vacant land near what is now Soweto in 1946–48, were tenuous; the ANC had only about 6,000 members nationwide (Lodge 1985: 16).

3 Although coloureds and Indians had freehold rights in neighboring suburbs, such as Fietas (Vrededorp), Pageview and Mayfair, these too would be expropriated in the coming decade.

4 Bantu People's Theatre. Drama Festival (25–27 July 1940), 10; (JPL/ STC). Further references in the body of the text.

5 *The Dreamy Kid* (1919) was one of O'Neill's first plays on "Negro subjects"; it was praised by black intellectuals like James Weldon Johnson (1991: 183). Guy Routh worked for the Garment Workers' Union but was also active in experimental theatre in Johannesburg and influenced by the biomechanical acting and constructivist staging of the Soviet director, Vsevolod Meyerhold (Routh 1950a: 26).

6 "The African National Theatre," *Inkululeko*, June 1941, 5, 7.

7 Modikwe Dikobe's story, "We Shall Walk," (Dikobe 1979: 104–108), gives an account of Radebe's activism. Mandela also acknowledges Radebe's influence (Mandela 1995).

8 "Three Good Plays," *Inkululeko*, September 1941, 5. The incident was a court case in 1931 in which a sharecropper, "Kas Tau," was fined for refusing to pay for a dog license (Van Onselen 1996: 3). Van Onselen does not mention the play, his biography of the sharecropper shows how African peasants managed to resist attempts to reduce them to wage-laborers.

9 H. I. E. Dhlomo, "Tshaka – a Reevaluation," *UwB*, 18 June 1932, 4.

10 See program for the City Hall performances (16 and 17 August 1954), H. I. E. Dhlomo papers: KCAL, 8282.

11 The 1937 version of *Dingane*, part of Dhlomo's "This is Africa" series including songs and characters peripheral to the main threads of the action (Dhlomo 1985: 69–113). The stage version, *Dingana*," is shorter but includes additions that may have been the work of Branford (Couzens 1985: 344).

12 "African" cannot be translated into Afrikaans, since its place is already occupied by "Afrikaner" and official substitutes from "naturelle" ("natives") to "Bantu" denied Africans the rightful occupation of the continent.

13 These included *Die Pad van Suid-Afrika* [The Road of South Africa, 1913], an anti-imperialist play on the Anglo-Boer War (1899–1902) by the writer of "Die Stem van

Suid-Afrika," C. J. Langenhoven, and *Magdalena Retief* by the poet Uys Krige (1939), which dealt with the martyrdom of Retief and his family, whose death at Zulu hands spurred Afrikaner revenge. The plays were performed by amateurs and academics in companies like the Pretoria Volksteater (dir.: Neethling-Pohl) (Naudé 1950: 9). Despite the claim that the Afrikaans repertoire was more serious than the English (Bosman 1969: 11), it included farces and sentimental melodrama as well as European classics.

14 See the Jeffreys Collection, Cape Archive: A1637/ 322.

15 Page references are to Gerhard Beukes, *Langs die Steiltjies*, Jeffreys Collection, A1637.

16 For the ideological blueprints of this plan, see Cronje (1945) and Meyer (1940).

17 "Aims and Objects of a National Theatre," printed in the 1948 program, in the Sagan collection: A855/D.

18 See "Aims and Objectives of a National Theatre" for a contradictory assertion of "firm establishment" and "underdevelopment."

19 Page references are to the first (1952) edition of *Die Jaar van die Vuuros*. Translations are mine.

20 Although the sentence could be translated colloquially as "you know that the first Van Niekerks came to clean things up around here," the tone of the general's assertion of divine right calls for the more elevated (or bombastic?) turn of phrase.

21 It appears in such apparently unlikely contexts as the reflections of Edmund Husserl, who wished to extend the *geistige Gestalt* [spiritual form] of Europe to the outposts of European conquest, while dismissing the indigenous inhabitants of these dominions as well as "non-Europeans" in the heart of Europe as interlopers. Husserl (1954: 318–19; 1970: 273–74) excises from the territory of Europe those "races" (especially Romany) who appear merely to wander over [*herumvagabundieren*] rather than naturally arise out of the land. It is certainly noteworthy that, as a Jewish intellectual in exile in Vienna in 1935, he does not mention the Jews.

22 The second (1989) edition replaces early apartheid crudities (like "Native [*Naturelle*] Trust") with late apartheid euphemisms (like "Homeland [*Tuisland*] Trust") and makes the time and place (1950s in South West Africa) more explicit but does not acknowledge international debates on South Africa's treatment of this territory, the International Court's declaration (1971) that South Africa's mandate was illegal, or the 1988 peace accord that ended South African military involvement and set Namibia on the road to independence (1990).

23 Translations are mine.

24 Coplan (1985: 162) suggests that *tsotsi* is a township rendering of "zoot-suit," describing the American suits favored by locals imitating American gangsters (or Hollywood versions of them).

25 Commentary on Sophiatown varies from systematic analysis to unabashed retro-tourism. After accounts written by exiles (such as Modisane, Nkosi, and Matshikiza) were banned, little was written until the revival of the 1980s, which led to the re-publication of writers such as these and Can Themba (1981), photographic essays (Schadeberg 1987), memoirs (Mattera 1987), interviews (Stein and Jacobsen 1986), critical analysis (Visser 1976; Sole 1979; Coplan 1985; Kavanagh 1985; Chapman 1989; Maughan-Brown 1989; Gready 1990; Nixon 1994), films such as *Freedom Square and the Back of the Moon* (dir.: Kentridge 1988), museum displays, and several plays.

26 Sophiatown is not the only lost integrated enclave to suffer this fate. Equally famous is District Six, the coloured neighborhood in central Cape Town cleared for white occupation in the 1960s, and the subject of nostalgia in such plays as *District Six –*

the Musical (music: Dawid Kramer; unpublished script: Taliep Pieterson, 1991) and somewhat more critical reverie in Richard Rive's *Buckingham Palace, District Six* (dir.: Peter Abrahamse, 1989), as well as the still unofficial District Six Museum.

27 Modisane notes that, although Africans were barred from seeing the touring production of *Look Back in Anger* at His Majesty's, he was able to see it because "Alan Dobie, the British actor invited to play Jimmy Porter . . . negotiated an arrangement for me to watch the play through a hole in the back of the auditorium" (Modisane 1986: 172).

28 *Tsotsitaal* is an urban black creole, which is based on Afrikaans but incorporates vocabulary and syntactical variation from African vernaculars.

29 The chair of Union Artists was advertising executive Ian Bernhardt; its members included Solomon Linda, who wrote the hit song, "Mbube" [aka "The Lion Sleeps Tonight"], later rearranged by the Weavers and by Mackey Davashe, bop saxophonist and leader of the *King Kong* band (Coplan 1985: 172–73). Although Coplan, Orkin (1991: 72), and Kavanagh (1985: 47) claim that trade unionist Guy Routh initially held the chair, Routh had left for London by 1950 (Routh 1950a).

30 As recent accounts of *Drum* (Nicol 1991) and Union Artists (Kavanagh 1985) suggest, these organizations functioned under a paternalist dispensation that was no less pervasive for being unspoken.

31 Fugard may have had little knowledge of the matter, but his collaborators, Nkosi and Nat Nakasa, journalists for African papers, would surely have been aware of Henry Nxumalo's exposé in *Drum* (1952).

32 "Situations" were overwhelmingly men. While the mission education of the 1920s and 1930s had produced a small number of female New Africans, distinguished by their work as cultural directors, such as Emily Motsieloa, women in 1950s entertainment tended, like Miriam Makeba, to be managed by men.

33 Anti-semitism in South Africa is usually associated with Afrikaner admirers of the Nazis but Eastern European Jewish immigrants during the British colonial period were subject to the same restrictions as Indians and other Asians until pressure from Anglicized Jews led to the "white" classification of "Eastern" Jews as well; see Krut (1984).

34 Schadeberg (1987: 177) mentions *West Side Story*, as does Irene Menell (in interview). Bloom notes that *King Kong* was proposed partly because Union Artists was unable to secure the rights for *The Threepenny Opera*; see program for *King Kong* (February 1959), JPL/ STC.

35 "Negro Shows Sweep the World," *Drum*, August 1953, 7. For Langston Hughes, however, *Porgy and Bess* was "not a Negro opera but Gershwin's idea of what a Negro opera should look like" (Hughes 1976: 699). Even if it became the "biggest breadbasket for blacks in the history of the American theatre," "whites got the caviar and blacks only the porgies" (p. 698). Although this essay appeared only in 1966, Hughes was well known among black South Africans. His poetry and essays were available in the BMSC library from the 1930s.

36 Despite Bloom's claim to sole authorship, Menell's outline of the plot and lyrics as well as later corroboration (Schadeberg 1987: 177) suggest a collaborative writing process: after Bloom and Matshikiza sketched out a series of numbers based on the boxer's life, Bloom moved to Cape Town, leaving the rest of the team to produce a plot, which he fleshed out on a subsequent visit to Johannesburg. Despite Bloom's claim to know *tsotsitaal* (Glasser 1960: 18), Menell has also suggested that the *tsotsitaal* in the play

should be attributed to Matshikiza, whose own variation, "Matshikese," flavored his *Drum* columns.

37 Bloom glosses the text as "The fault of these men/ Lies in their ignorance"; Kavanagh corrects the Xhosa orthography and translates the named figures but not the key topic sentence (Kavanagh 1985: 111). More recently, John Matshikiza, son of Todd, has claimed that Mandela read the line as a covert expression of support for himself and other ANC members on trial in 1959. See J. Matshikiza, "An Incomplete Masterpiece," *Mail and Guardian*, 4 February 1999.

38 The libretto was based on a story by an Indian South African, G. Naidoo, who had lived in Cato Manor. Unlike *King Kong*, which ran for over a year without trouble, *Mkhumbane* closed a few months after opening in Durban (March 1960), because of police harassment. See "Mkhumbane," *Drum*, July 1950, 72.

39 Coplan (1985: 207) claims that Union Artists refused to support Masinga but the program (JPL/ STC) is headed "Union Artists Presents . . .".

40 Their first play, *Fantastical History of A Useless Man* (September 1976) began with a witty vaudevillian deconstruction of official history, which treated the Afrikaner icon Van Riebeeck as a Dutch imperial bureaucrat and the British icon, Rhodes, as a megalomaniac queen serving Victoria's empire, but its second act was limited by the anxieties of its white dissident cast and audience, who wondered, in the aftermath of the Soweto uprising, whether, in the words of the protagonist "the most I [could] do [was] to be the least obstruction" (JATC 1995: 60).

41 The film and audio versions of *Oh What a Lovely War!* reached South Africa shortly after their London releases. Barney Simon, who worked with Littlewood in 1959, directed *Mother Courage* at the Market Theatre in 1976, and JATC members were avid readers of Brecht's theatrical and theoretical writings.

42 In the 1989 revival, director Purkey cast women in some of the satirical male roles (Orkin 1995: 78). While this may have drawn attention to the performativity of gender, it did not alter the masculinist analysis of history underlying the representation.

43 Triomf [Afrikaans for triumph] was the name of the suburb that replaced Sophiatown.

5 DRY WHITE SEASONS: DOMESTIC DRAMA AND THE AFRIKANER ASCENDANCY

1 This alludes to the title of André Brink's novel, *'n Droë wit Seisoen* (1979) [*A Dry White Season*, 1979], but not to its content, which deals with the wake of the Soweto uprising.

2 Fugard had refused to allow PACT to produce *People* in 1967, because of his "distaste for Government sponsored theatre" (1984: 149), but gave it to CAPAB in 1969 because Yvonne Bryceland was engaged there. CAPAB also restaged *Boesman and Lena* in 1970, after its performance at Rhodes University.

3 The same Commission notes that, by 1976, the SABC employed 250 Afrikaans actors for 2,000 roles (not including dubbing) as opposed to 143 English language actors for 934 roles. The PACs, which produced seven Afrikaans- for five English-language plays followed similar proportions; see *Commission of Inquiry*, Appendix G.

4 The play ran for only a few weeks in Pretoria, an Afrikaner stronghold; see Breytenbach papers (SA 261/1099).

5 Under the Publications and Entertainment Act (1963), the Publications Control Board banned everything from Fanon's *Black Skin, White Masks* to *Black Beauty* (Cope 1983: 74), as well as the work of Sophiatown writers like Modisane and Nkosi. It was not

until 1973 that the Board banned an Afrikaans novel, Brink's *Kennis van die Aand* (1973) [*Looking into Darkness*, 1974], for depicting interracial sex.

6 3 September, rather than 22 October (Orkin 1991: 91) appears to be the opening date; see the NELM bibliography (Read 1991: 41).

7 For accounts of *Try for White* and its director, Schach, who had begun directing at the Little Theatre and went onto the NTO, the Market Theatre and the Cameri in Tel Aviv, see Inskip (1977: 62–64) and Schach (1996: 88–90, 110). For further analysis of *The Kimberley Train*, see Orkin (1991: 86–89).

8 *Ruby and Frank* played at the BMSC in October and November 1939 before going on tour. It was directed by Dhlomo with music by Salome Masoleng, who had composed music for Dhlomo's *Moshoeshoe* (1938); see KCAL 8267. The play's representation of prejudice between coloureds and Africans as well as political groups – from the ANC to the Non-European Unity Movement (NEUM), to the aspiring coloured bourgeoisie – contrasts the domestic preoccupations of the "white" plays.

9 See Orkin (1991: 82–84) for sample cases.

10 Redelinghuys was married to Smit, whose play, *Die Verminktes*, draws on *The Kimberley Train*. Bernard Sachs criticized the play for being talky, but praised Redelinghuys's portrayal of Bertha; see B.S., "A South African Play That Impresses," *South African Jewish Times*, 19 September 1958, and Library Theatre program (SA 459/115).

11 Millin's novel is steeped in the ideological preoccupations of her day, in particular in the contradictory supposition that coloureds were superior to Africans because of their white blood and European socialization but degenerate because their mixed blood allegedly diluted the "pure" European or "pure" African. For the ideology of degeneration and biological theories of race, see Stepan (1985); for the implications for South Africa, see Dubow (1987).

12 See Smit, "Toneelkrisis is Volkskrisis," *Dagbreek en Sontagnuus*, 30 July 1961, 32.

13 Barnard's speech echoes classic Nationalist propaganda, here, *Tuiste vir die Nageslag*: "the more consistent the policy of apartheid . . . the greater the security for the purity of our blood . . . our unadulterated European racial survival" (Cronjé 1945: 79). Once Frans's challenge to his father moves from politics to claiming the Senator's ward as his wife, the elder Harmse drops his liberal language and reverts to the language of the *volk* (Smit 1976: 35).

14 *Skollie* ranges in meaning from the general "rogue" [Dutch: *schoelje*] to the pointed "coloured street hoodlum." Its uncertain derivation, with possible sources including *schuol* [Yiddish: jackal], reflects the hybrid character of the personage; see *Dictionary of South African English on Historical Principles*, s.v. *skolly*.

15 While not physically castrated in the 1977 production, Frans is still cut down by his father's racial invective. Refigured as the suggestion of the Zulu servant, castration appears to be a barbaric act shunned by the "civilized" senator.

16 Gunning is contesting Peter Brook's argument that melodrama is driven by the "moral occult" (Brook 1976: 5), the hidden power of virtue, the revelation of which provides the reversal of fortune that restores the wronged hero(ine) to his/her rightful place. The difference between the melodrama of sensation and the melodrama of virtue redeemed can be seen in the difference between the opaque sensation scene that ends *Die Verminktes* and the conclusions of plays like *Money* (1840), by the English writer, Edward Bulwer-Lytton, or *Helena's Hope Ltd.* (1910), by Stephen Black, which end with the impoverished heroine rescued by her rightful inheritance.

17 Even though Smit later noted that, under apartheid conditions, Frans "had to" [*moes*]

play white (1985: 225), his formulation suggests the issue is an individual deception rather than a reflection on the society that promoted such behavior.

18 Citations refer to the original, *The Blood Knot* (performed in 1961; published in 1964; 1992 edition), as opposed to *Bloodknot*, the revision produced for the 25th anniversary revival in 1988 (Fugard 1991).

19 P. Blakeney, "*The Blood Knot* Is Milestone in S. African Drama," *Johannesburg Sunday Express*, 12 November 1961; I. Jones, "SA Play Regarded as World Class," *Cape Times*, 11 February 1962 (Read 1991: 43–45).

20 This production has been eclipsed by the production at the Space in Cape Town (1974), where Fugard directed Bill Flynn and Yvonne Bryceland, who was to create most of his major female roles from Lena in *Boesman and Lena* (1969) to Helen Martins in *Road to Mecca* (1984).

21 When Fugard agreed to the run, black intellectuals like Dennis Brutus accused him of contributing to the "erosion of human decency" (Fugard 1984: 128–29). Despite this compromise with apartheid institutions, Fugard continued to work with Africans in the Serpent Players despite persistent police harassment.

22 W. E. G. Louw, "Ervaring wat kan skud," *Die Burger*, 23 November 1965, and "Spelers roep met hul gepraat 'n hele lewe op," *Die Beeld*, 24 November 1965. For reviews in the English-language press, see Read (1991: 60–61).

23 L. Sowden, "A Torment of Poor Whites in the Library Theatre's *Hello and Goodbye*," *Rand Daily Mail*, 20 October 1965, and L. Greyling, "*Hello* oordryf en nikssegend," *Die Vaderland*, 24 October 1965.

24 *Putsonderwater* was first produced by Volksteater Vertical in Ghent in 1968 and toured Belgium for a year. At Rhodes, it was directed by Abraham de Vries, whose program notes challenged the establishment to explain why the play had not received a professional production in South Africa; see Smit files; (SA 459/48. *Boesman and Lena* was directed by Fugard, who played Boesman, with Bryceland as Lena and Glynn Day, also a white actor, as the unnamed African. It opened at Rhodes on 10 July 1969).

25 "Putsonderwater Maar – Onderdiekombers" [Well-without-water, but – under-the-blanket], *Die Burger*, 20 July 1969).

26 On CAPAB's canceled plans, see T. Herbst, "Why Was Bartho Smit's *Putsonderwater* Axed at the Last Minute?" *Cape Times*, 10 August 1970.

27 F. Engelen, Program Note for *Putsonderwater* (PACOFS 1969), Smit files, (SA 459/43).

28 Shakespeare's protagonist does not seduce his daughter, but his testy response to Miranda's defense of Ferdinand, who appears to charm her: "one word more/ Shall make me chide thee, if not hate thee" (*Tempest*, I, 2, ll. 478–79), certainly allows for a reading that teases out the entwined strands of sexual and colonial power.

29 Calvinist theology allows for the virgin birth of Jesus (through divine begetting) but not for the immaculate conception of Mary, free from sin (*Encyclopaedia Britannica*, s.v. virgin birth). This distinction between the Catholic doctrine informing *Sous le soleil de Satan* and the Calvinist underpinning of *Putsonderwater* makes of this Mary a fallen woman. *Die Teken*, written and directed by Deon Opperman, produced almost two decades after *Putsonderwater* (PACOFS 1985), returns to the theme, portraying a father who is so scandalized by his unmarried daughter's belief that she bears the Messiah that he murders the child as the Antichrist (Opperman 1986).

30 By focusing on plays about poor whites, I am excluding others: *Die Verhoor* (PACT 1973) (Brink 1970), offers a trenchant, but even-handed dramatization of the 1830s rebellion of trekboers in the Eastern Cape against the British Colonial administration in

distant Cape Town. *Christine* (PACT 1973), is Smit's most ambitious play (Hauptfleisch and Steadman 1984: 16). Like *Putsonderwater*, it deals with individual bad faith within a corrupt society; the sculptor, Paul Harmse, abandons his Jewish lover to the Nazis and is haunted by his betrayal and self-pity. Despite its notoriety (for showing an unmarried couple in their underwear) and later canonization – also in English translation (Hauptfleisch and Steadman 1984) – the play struggles to balance a garrulous male with the figures of the older and younger woman within a belabored historical frame (Brink 1986: 145–48; 229–31).

31 Barnard, reviewing the play in *Rapport*, 20 August 1971 (cited on the back of the published text).

32 The Afrikaans expression, "asof dit [n]ooit papier geruik het nie," translates literally as "as though it had never sniffed paper" capturing the slangy quality of Du Plessis' dialogue and the illicit activities of his characters.

33 "Sien dan 'n slag, toe ou Tjokkie, jong: wie gaan vanjaar die Herzogprys kry . . . ? . . . Wag, wag, manne, hy gaat sien orrait ["Have a quick vision, come on, Tjokkie: who's going to win the Herzog Prize this year? . . . Hang on, guys, he's gonna have a vision"] (Rykie van Reenen, "Herzogprys lê vanjaar tussen *Siener en Christine*," *Rapport*, 23 April 1972).

34 For "white nigger," see the autobiography of "Québécois terrorist" Pierre Vaillante; for British colonial labeling of Afrikaners as "white kaffirs" and Afrikaner interest in Québécois nationalism, see Hofmeyr (1987).

35 Barnard, Program Notes for *Die Rebellie van Lafras Verwey* (PACT 1975), n.p.

36 The Afrikaans translation of "elusion" as "*ontwyking*," loses the al-lusion to self-deception and self-creation through play and thus also the public, social dimension of Lafras's delusion.

37 Reviews of the PACT production noted that the staging gave Lafras's "petit bourgeois" character more concrete definition; see P. Breytenbach, "Doemprofete verkeerd met Lafras," *Die Transvaler*, 17 April 1975, 4.

38 See "New Plays at the People's Space," *Cape Times*, 15 November 1979.

39 Brink faults *Lafras* for borrowing from *Billy Liar* (1986: 145) while praising Barnard's earlier play, *Pa, maak vir my 'n vlieër, pa* (CAPAB 1964). But the latter is a derivative variation on its source (Pinter's *Birthday Party*), whereas the former offers a more complex portrait of delusion than Keith Waterhouse's social-climbing con-man.

40 Thomas's review of the Cape Flats Players' production cites Brink's verdict – "the best play in Afrikaans" (*S'ketsh* 1972: 26). My translation does not replicate the KHKH pattern of the title, but it restores the idiomatic fluency of the *Kaaps*, lost in the published translation, *Kanna – He Is Coming Home* (Small 1990). Quotations cite *Kaaps* first, followed by official Afrikaans.

41 W. E. G. Louw, "Kanna, 'n onvergeetlike toneelervaring," *Die Burger*, 20 November 1974.

42 Small remarks that "there is a very real danger of a play like this becoming melodramatic" (*S'ketsh* 1972: 33). His aversion to melodrama is not surprising, given its association with the delinquent behavior attributed by whites to urban blacks, but he also insists that the emotion of the drama and its audience should not be dismissed as a "failure of consciousness" but rather as the path to self-understanding.

43 Coloured inhabitants of Cape Town have for various reasons – cosmopolitan contact in the port city and the disassociation with the patriarchal nationalism of African and Afrikaner persuasion – tended to be more tolerant of homosexuals than other sectors of South African society (Gevisser 1994b: 28).

44 The dialogue for the 1972 and 1974 productions remained substantially the same as the 1965 text though only PACT could afford to reproduce the stage-directions for a naturalistic portrayal of District Six.

45 See review by Thomas (*S'ketsh* 972: 26) and the anonymous comments on the "Cape Town crowd's passionate response" in *Johannesburg Post*, 25 February 1972, 4; for the revival at the South African Black Theatre Union (SABTU) festival in December, by C. Ebrahim (*S'ketsh* 1973: 44).

46 Citations of Van Niekerk from the program notes for *Kanna Hy Kô Hystoee* (PACT 1974).

47 P. Breytenbach, "Kanna is ontroerend en aangrypend," *Die Transvaler*, 28 June 1974.

48 R. Daniel, "A Terrible Affinity," *RDM*, 31 May 1974.

49 See, for example, "Díe Kanna is beslis Louis se Triomf," *Pretoria Oggendblad*, 5 July 1974.

50 Quoted in O'Meara (1996: 369–70). The parody attacks Afrikanerdom's most sacred text on several fronts: (a) it calls the country Azania, the choice of the Black Consciousness Movement and, in 1985, a banned word; (b) it mixes languages in a manner associated by the defenders of "pure" Afrikaans with racial miscegenation; (c) it attributes the national voice to disenfranchised squatters rather than the exclusive "we" of the *volk*.

51 See, "Elke Tong het sy Afrikaans," a series of articles in *Die Vrye Weekblad*, 29 September 1993, 13–21. "Strategie om die Tonge te laat leef," *Die Suid-Afrikaan* 48 (1994), 21–24 and the report on the Second Black Afrikaans Writers Symposium in *Die Suid-Afrikaan* 55 (1995/96), 25–27.

52 The literal translation, "deep ground," misses the proverbial allusion, "stille water, diepe grond; onder draai die duiwel rond." The English equivalent, "still waters run deep," only hints at the devil turning beneath the surface.

53 *Diepe Grond* was directed at Rhodes by Denys Webb for the Afrikaanse Toneel- en Kultuurverbond series and at the Market by Lucille Gillward. It was published in the *Vrystaat-Trilogie* (De Wet 1991), together with *Op Dees Aarde* [On this Earth; PACT, 1986], a Gothic tale about a blithe spirit (dead in "illicit" childbirth) visiting her Calvinist "ugly" sisters, and *Nag General* [Goodnight, General; Market, 1988], an indictment of mythic Anglo-Boer war herosim in the name of the survivng women (both directed by Gillward).

54 The arid farm and its stunted inhabitants as allegory for national decline is not a purely Afrikaans trope. Paul Slabolepszy returns to this figure in *Smallholding* (1989), in which a demented paterfamilias, Pa, a "Boere-Rambo," and his crazy son JJ, torment Christiaan, a "God-fearing" postal worker looking for petrol for his car (Slabolepszy 1994: 163).

55 See the objections by Dr. J. Botha, arts editor for *Die Burger*, and Opperman's response, in *Vuka SA* (formerly *Lantern*, a government publication) 1, 6 (1996), 60–62.

6 THE DRAMA OF BLACK CONSCIOUSNESSES

1 "The Definition of Black Consciousness," was one of the exhibits in the Treason Trial of 1975/76; Cullen Library: Black People's Convention (BPC A2217).

2 ARM was founded after the banning of the ANC and PAC, and consisted mostly of white university students whose amateurish attempts at sabotage led quickly to their downfall (Friedrikse 1990: 94–95, 102).

3 The Africanists' Manifesto of April 1959, which heralded their breakaway as the PAC, reads: "The African people of South Africa . . . recognize themselves as part of one

African nation from Cape to Cairo, Madagascar to Morocco" (Karis and Carter 1977, vol. 3: 517). The manifesto also drew on the speech made by Kwame Nkrumah at the Pan-African convention in Accra, December 1958.

4 After Robert Sobukwe, the elected PAC leader, was sentenced to Robben Island, Leballo moved headquarters to Lesotho but his boasts about the Poqo sabotage campaign endangered operatives inside the country (Gerhart 1978: 252–53).

5 Although the student population of South African universities is far less restricted now, social, cultural, and economic distinctions remain significant not only as the legacy of apartheid but also as felt experience.

6 The argument in the following paragraphs draws on Steadman (1985). Note that McLaren is the person behind the author Kavanagh.

7 Since the articles in *Black Review* were for security reasons largely anonymous, citations refer to the editors.

8 Although the condition of African-Americans as a minority was structurally different from that of the majority of black South Africans, Carmichael's critique of piecemeal tinkering rather than the fundamental transformation of institutional structures is relevant here: SASO's separatism was provoked by the members' experience as an impotent minority in NUSAS, a predominantly white institution at that time.

9 Recent African critics have noted negritude's application of "anthropology, existentialism and French poetics" (Mudimbe 1988: 85) and its promulgation of an "Africa mystique" (Irele 1990: 84).

10 The incident that ignited national unrest was a graduation address at the University of the North by the student representative council president, O. R. Tiro, in which he denounced apartheid education (Khoapa 1973: 21–24).

11 SABTU program (BPC: A2177: 6.1.2).

12 SABTU program (A2177: 6.1.2).

13 The 1962 Criminal Law ("No Trial") Amendment allowed the state to detain individuals without trial or to "ban" them by putting them under house-arrest, forbidding visits by more than one person, and by prohibiting any public or published quotations of their positions.

14 "What is Black Theatre?", delivered at the Art Exhibition at Mofolo Hall, Sunday 21 January 1973; Black People's Convention, A2177: 6.1.4. The typescript of the speech and the dramatic sketch were used as evidence in his trial under the Terrorism Act in 1975.

15 See D. Moodley, "All-Race Theatre Ahead," *Durban Post*, 2 July 1972, 17.

16 See program for *Shaka* (JPL/STC).

17 The program for *Phiri* (JPL/STC) lists a black technical director and several stage hands as well as Mackey Davashe (of the *King Kong* band) as musical director of the band, but the director (Barney Simon), designer (Axel Peterson), and overall musical director (Ann Feldman) were white.

18 Fugard remembers the establishment of Serpent Players as the result of a request from Norman Ntshinga who asked Fugard for help setting up a theatre group (Fugard 1984: 81). John Kani claims that he and Winston Ntshona joined the group with the production of *Antigone* in 1965 but that Fugard found an already formed group (Kani and Ntshona 1976: 15–17).

19 See E. Makhaya, "Sam Mhangwane Says: Black Theatre Must Wake Up," *World*, 4 April 1975: "the white man is experienced in theatre and will guide you on how to do it . . . within your own culture."

233

20 See interview with M. Tshabangu, in *S'ketsh* (1972): 8–11. The comparison with Motsieloa is my own.

21 A. Klaaste, "Gibson Kente has a thrilling new venture for the stage. It's very much like *King Kong,*" *The World*, 3 February 1966.

22 See plot summary in Kavanagh (1985: 114–22) and "Gibson Kente '74" in *S'ketsh* (1975a: 24–25).

23 See A. Klaaste, "Gibson Kente has a thrilling new venture for the stage. It's very much like *King Kong,*" *The World*, 3 February 1966, 9.

24 See *Shaka* program (JPL/STC).

25 Black businessmen like Kente faced state restrictions far more systematically repressive than the pressures experienced by Nigerian entrepreneurs from Hubert Ogunde to Baba Sala. Nonetheless, their melodramatic and comic representation of precarious lives and their audience's approval are similar, not least due to the glamour that surrounds successful entrepreneurs in an otherwise struggling community.

26 For comment on *Ipi Tombi*, see Makhaya's articles in *The World*, 25 November, 11; 30 November 1975, 9. For comment on Singana, see *The World*, 4 February 1975, 5.

27 As with Jimmy Porter, the male complaint expresses *ressentiment* against female family members, while masquerading as a rebellion against injustice. Though they differ racially, Nate and Jimmy both find refuge from failed petit bourgeois rebellion against a world ruled by powerful men in the comforts of misogyny at home. If the female complaint serves "to . . . manage the social contradictions that arise from women's sexual and affective allegiance to a phallocentric ideology that has . . . denied women power, privilege, and presence" (Berlant 1988: 243), the male complaint attempts to manage the contradiction between the presumption of male power and the actual subordination of lower-class men by blaming this on women's domination of the domestic sphere.

28 Ebrahim, reviewing the SABTU festival in Cape Town for the *Cape Herald* and *S'ketsh*, described the performance as an "explosion . . . shattering . . . complacency forever" (*S'ketsh* [1973], 44), but argued that the conscientizing character of the event was more important for the black audience than the uneven performances.

29 The *PET Newsletter* appeared only once, in September 1973, before being banned. The text of Kraai's article reproduces several paragraphs from Cooper's January speech of the same title. This reflects the prevailing use of collective and/or anonymous authorship to evade the censors.

30 Charge Sheet, Attorney General's Report, 12 March 1975, 5 (Cullen: NIC, AL2421: N5). Cooper and Srini Moodley were sentenced to Robben Island. Kraai and Pheto were also detained and later went into exile.

31 Compare the charge sheet of 12 March 1975, which included the indictment for "staging . . . revolutionary plays and/or dramas" and the charge sheet for 18 August 1975, which did not (Northwestern University: SASO Trial).

32 "The Trial of SASO/BPC Detainees" (NU: SASO/BPC), 7–8.

33 "Saso Leaders Banned," *Durban Post*, 11 March 1972, 3. The writer expressed sympathy for the women in conventional masculinist terms, pitying them facing "the prospect of being the breadwinner" while their husbands were banned from working.

34 A backbar was a bar attached to a whites-only establishment for the use of Indians. The *lahnee* here is the white boss, but can also refer to a pretentious person with "white" airs. Performed in one act at the SABTU festivals, *The Lahnee's Pleasure* was expanded to two acts at Shah Theatre Academy in Durban in 1977. This version was

revived at the Market Theatre in Johannesburg in 1978 (directed by the author) and again in Durban in 1979 (directed by B. Francis).

35 See reviews of the SABTU festivals by Moodley and Ibrahim in notes 16 and 28.

36 These riots were provoked when an Indian merchant punished an African child for allegedly stealing. Although Zulus attacked the homes, businesses, and persons of Indians in and around Durban, the ammunition for the arson was allegedly supplied by whites who resented Indian competition. This event left Indians in South Africa with a profound sense of their precarious position caught between black and white, which persists today.

37 For *How Long?*, see the scene synopsis in the program (JPL/STC); for *Too Late!*, see the extracts in *S'ketsh* (1975b) and Kente (1981).

38 Recent attempts by other directors to restage his plays have been hampered by the loss of Kente's scripts and recordings in a 1989 fire. Jerry Mofokeng's revival of *Lifa* (1997) relied on a reconstruction based on information from Kente and the 1970s cast.

39 The performance text in *S'ketsh* (1975b: 17–28) ends with Saduva's fate in the balance. The text published in 1981 resolves this ambiguity in favor of Saduva's reconciliation with Pelepele under the eye of Mfundisi, who emphasizes Saduva's essential goodness as a victim rather than an agent of politics: "politics was forced on him" (Kente 1981: 123) and suggests that Saduva's problems can be ameliorated by community support.

40 Ntanana's reaction corresponds to the logic of the action of the moment rather than any received notion of consistent character. In addition to Routh, stage and film director Leontine Sagan, who taught at the Hofmeyr School before Kente studied there, observed that African students found Polonius's social maneuvering more interesting than Hamlet's interiority; in general, they responded more to the "social" rather than the "emotional" element of the drama (Sagan 1996: 211).

41 Makhaya, "New Life and Lustre in Kente's *Too Late!*," *The World*, 2 June 1975, 8–9.

7 SPACES AND MARKETS: THE PLACE OF THEATRE AS TESTIMONY

1 For the distinction among the categories institution, formation, and forms or conventions, see Williams (1995).

2 Even more reminiscent of Brook and LAMDA was *Orestes*, a piece generated from the "image of a man with a . . . suitcase . . . in the Johannesburg Station concourse" (Fugard 1978: 84). This performance, which combined the case of John Harris, member of ARM (chapter 6, n. 2), whose bomb killed a child and maimed an old woman, with the legend of Orestes, led to the formation of the Space (Astbury 1979: 81–93 and Fugard Collection at NELM).

3 In addition to the Serpent Players' production in 1965 and the version on Robben Island in 1970, Sophocles' play was performed by the Company (forerunner of the Market Theatre) in 1974. In 1988, Peter Se-Puma directed an adaptation called *Igazi Lam* [My Blood], which transposed the story into a hypothetical post-civil war South Africa.

4 *Sizwe Banzi* was performed in tandem with *The Island* in Cape Town, Johannesburg, London, New York, Washington, Australia, and West Germany and revived often in South Africa, but *The Island* was also revived on its own in Paris, Dublin, East Germany, and the United States (Read 1991: 91–117).

5 Vandenbroucke (1986: 158). Although Bansi has been the usual spelling, readers

should note that current isiXhosa dictionaries list only "banzi," meaning "broad" or, by extension, "strong." On the historical ironies of black photographic portraiture, see Santu Mofokeng (1996: 81).

6 The program (Fugard Collection, NELM) does not corroborate Kani's more recent claim that the Space program read "devised by Serpent Players, assisted in directing by Athol Fugard" (Vandenbroucke 1986: 158).

7 Sepamla notes the influence of Motsieloa's variety on Kente and, indirectly, on political theatre (1981).

8 See M. Feingold, "Son of Stepinfetchit and a Vigorous Bolshevik," *New York Village Voice*, 5 May 1975, 98.

9 My observation of the audience response to urban problem plays confirms this tendency. I am not claiming that there is any innate African or European way, but pointing out the historical and present-day dynamic between performances and audiences schooled informally or otherwise in certain modes of audience response.

10 For the first reaction, see J. Marquard, "Sizwe Bansi Is Alive and Well," *To the Point*, 23 December 1972; for the second, Sepamla (*S'ketsh* 1973: 24).

11 On the censorship of the play, see Uys (1983: 76–80). Uys's cabaret in the 1980s combined South African political satire with the possibilities of female impersonation, such as Barry Humphries' Dame Edna, rather than exploring a gay sensibility directly. More explicit gay liberation theatre would have to wait until the 1990s.

12 *Not His Pride* (first performed at Wits in 1973) by Makwedini Mtsaka, was the first in this series, though Ravan had previously published *Confused Mhlaba* by Khayalethu Mqayisa (performed at Wits in 1974).

13 Amato directed the Imita Players in East London, including local adaptations of *Oedipus* (1971) and Molière's *The Miser* (1975). At the People's Space, he presided over South African premieres of Sam Shephard's *Cowboy Mouth* and David Hare's *Fanshen* as well as local revivals such as *Lafras Verwey*.

14 Comments on the politics of the National Arts Festival (its official title) are drawn from Grundy (1993), interviews with the Media Officer (then Shelagh Blackman), and personal observation (1979ff.).

15 In 1990, the South African director Jerry Mofokeng revived the play in New York with the same actors, Fana Kekana, Dan Selaelo Maredi, Themba Ntinga, and Seth Sibanda, who had followed careers in teaching, broadcasting, and acting in the United States (Kruger 1991).

16 Roy Christie's positive review of the "note of anticipation," in the *Star* (12 August 1976), contradicts Kavanagh's generalization about a hostile white response.

17 Kavanagh's concept of majority theatre describes the practice of collaboration between black and white practitioners committed to democracy but also prescribes collaboration rather than an exclusively black theatre.

18 The general argument here follows Graver and Kruger (1989: 272–75). Comments on productions are based on the author's observations since 1976; for summary information, see Graver and Kruger (1989), Schwartz (1988: 210–80), and the Market Theatre's Annual Reports.

19 Many corporate sponsors from the Anglo-American Corporation down drew their revenue directly or indirectly from mining, and thus from the exploitation of black migrant workers and the apartheid apparatus that facilitated this exploitation. Nonetheless, individuals in these companies donated money and labor of their own to make the institution independent of government interference.

20 The inclusion of blacks such as Kani on the Management Committee (Schwartz 1988: 278) was likewise ambiguous: on the one hand, it demonstrated a liberal desire to open doors; on the other, it confirmed the ongoing structural discrimination that kept qualified blacks in the minority.

21 Simon's recollection are drawn from personal interviews September–November 1994.

22 Performed at the Wits University Box after its Soweto premiere and directed by Steadman for its overseas tour (Maponya 1995: viii), *The Hungry Earth* was well received by intellectual audiences locally and abroad (though, as its author acknowledged, less so by township audiences). Although justly praised for its "political demystification" of migrant labor (Steadman 1995: xvii), the play favors generality rather than the gestic precision and vivid concreteness of *Egoli*.

23 Ledwaba induced vomiting by rapidly swallowing water during the black-out just before the scene in question (Steadman in conversation, August 1994).

24 The lives of black miners working underground at temperatures above 90°F and surviving above ground in a hierarchical organization dominated by "boss-boys" and their overseers test the limits of representation. The heroic recuperation of this work in post-apartheid museums cannot erase the fact that deep-level mining is still extremely dangerous, claiming hundreds of lives a year (Coplan 1994: 129–30).

25 Quoted in Fuchs (1990: 109). Critics reviewing the performance at the Space (*Cape Times*, 7 August 1979) and the Market (*Star*, 27 December 1979 and *Rand Daily Mail*, 28 December 1979) praised the immediacy and intensity of the play.

26 Ledwaba complained that "these audiences [at, for instance, the Sebokeng performance of *Egoli*] do not know what theatre is about" because they wanted to see "girls' thighs"; E. Makhaya, *Johannesburg Post*, 19 May 1980. Maponya also argued that the black press favored Kente's blockbusters rather than politically and formally challenging work (1984: 24–25), although veterans like Makhaya reviewed both kinds of theatre.

27 Selaneng Kgomongwe voiced local preference for narrative and song rather than the body techniques used in Ledwaba's portrayal of the drunkard (*S'ketsh* 1979: 15).

28 In interview (April 1995), Maponya noted that some disappointed patrons even demanded an extra performance on the same evening to bring the entertainment to the expected two hours or more. He argued that "the oppressed prefer entertainment to redirection" (*Star*, 19 July 1985), attributing this to false consciousness.

29 By stating that *Gangsters* is "Maponya's play on the death of Steve Biko in detention" (O'Brien 1994: 46), Antony O'Brien takes for granted the promotional claim of the organizer of the tour to Lincoln Center (New York), Duma Ndlovu (1986: 59), and thus reduces the play's political as well as theatrical resonance, since the point in the first instance was that any activist could and did receive the same punishment and, in the second, that the body on stage was literally the playwright's as well as the multiple figures he represented. Maponya himself has not identified the protagonist as Biko, even in the 1995 publication when censorship was no longer an issue.

30 The play was revived in February 1985 with a different cast who also performed in New York. The double bill was praised by black as well as white critics; see Kaizer Ngwenya, "Maponya's Sparkler," *Sowetan*, 17 July 1984, and Beatrice Hollyer, "Two Plays to Savour," *Star*, 12 July 1984.

31 By scrapping the alternation between scenes of confrontation between Rasechaba and the police and scenes in which the police plan their cover-up, in favor of a linear

unfolding of confrontation, the revision abandons a productive (Brechtian?) tension between the image of state violence and the vocal resistance of the poet in favor of a predictable narrative of martyrdom. By replacing Rasechaba with Masechaba [Mother of the Nation] and the clothed body with a naked female body – which Jonathan at least appears to covet (Maponya 1995: 110) – the Lincoln Center show made a spectacle of martyrdom. To read this as "feminist" (O'Brien 1994: 59) is problematic not only because it begs the question of the woman displayed as sacrificial victim, but also because it ignores the reinscription of the male gaze on the stripped female body.

32 *Woza Albert!* opened in October 1981, but was published only after the London tour, in 1983. *Mama and the Load* was the first of Kente's plays to receive attention from the non-black press.

33 Makhaya (*Sowetan*, 3 March 1981) noted the influence of Kente as well as the use of comedy to "present explosive political material in a compassionate and humorous way."

34 The last two names were added only in the overseas tour (Benson 1997: 120). Bram Fischer, scion of a leading Afrikaner family, died a life-term prisoner as a member of the SACP. Ruth First, writer and activist, was assassinated in Mozambique by a South African letterbomb.

35 Although the government did not declare a state of emergency until July 1985, unrest during 1984 culminated in industrial and school strikes and the ANC's call, in January 1985, to make the country "ungovernable." Both *Black Dog* and *Born in the RSA* (August 1985) respond to the escalation of police violence, especially against children.

36 Ian Gray's equation of personal, female, and trivial in his review in *The Star* (28 November 1979) is typical; for a defense of the play, see Simon's interview and the letter by R. Morrell (11 December), who noted the interest in the play expressed by both black and white women in the audience, also Simon Collection, NELM. For comments on *Cincinatti* [*sic*], which deserves credit as the first Market play created collectively in workshop but not, despite critical enthusiasm, for its rather dated script about patrons and workers at a sort-of integrated nightclub, see the introduction to the text in Hauptfleisch and Steadman (1984).

37 Citations are from the production script (Simon *et al.* 1986), except where the performance corresponds to the later version (Simon *et al.* 1994). Although rougher, the earlier version maintains South African idiom (in English, Afrikaans, and Zulu) and provides more complete (if not always accurate) translation.

38 Taped interview, January 1995. A black critic (T. Leshoai, "Born in the RSA – United by Boerehaat," *Sowetan*, 30 September, 1985) voiced skepticism about the group's commitment to this responsibility, despite the work of progressive whites in the UDF, many of whom had been harassed by the police. But even this critic acknowledged the value of the play's "introspective questioning" and its representation of the overt violence of the state as well as of the suppressed violence in peaceable individuals, such as Zach, who expresses his frustration with the wanton cruelty of the police into a tersely narrated but terrifying fantasy of smashing up white children in a schoolyard.

39 Ntshinga's apprenticeship at the Space exposed her to a range of styles and genres, from the Africanist history play, *Sacrifice of Kreli*, through a series of comedies, to the title role in the revival of Fugard's *Nongogo*.

40 For the march, see Helen Josephs. The title of the play is often mistranslated as "You Strike the Woman" but "*abafazi*" means "women" and the song emphasizes women's collective

action. The play was written by the cast, Thobeka Maqutyana, Nomvula Qosha, and Poppy Tsira, as well as director Phyllis Klotz. Although published as a "Market play" (Kani 1996), it was produced by the Community Arts Project in Cape Town.

41 The play opened at the Market in September 1991 (dir.: Simon). It was revived in a longer version directed by Mavis Taylor under the auspices of CAPAB in mid-1994.

42 *Have You Seen Zandile?* appeared under the names of Mhlophe, who played Zandile, director Maralin Vanrenen, and co-performer Thembi Mtshali. Mhlophe noted in interview that this pressure on playwrights was partly responsible for her decision to focus primarily on story-telling. She now heads Zanendaba [Tell me a story], a group of women and men who tell traditional and modern stories to children and adults.

43 Like his mentor, Kente, Ngema pays more attention to performance than to producing a definitive text, but where Kente's spectacles are leavened by a moral lesson, Ngema's promoted exuberant singing and dancing over plot. Despite claims that audiences were mostly white (e.g. Mda 1996: xx), *Sarafina* had a formidable reputation among blacks, even those who knew the performance by hearsay or the film version (dir.: Daryl Roodt, 1992).

44 In November 1994, one such lipsynching spectacle appeared at the Market Lab. On a visit to Mohlakeng, a township west of Johannesburg, in the company of Lab facilitators, Mncedi Dayi and Phumudzo Nephawe, I was struck by the hope expressed by both teacher and students at the local school that contact with visiting Americans would lead them to "another *Sarafina.*" The story becomes even more poignant when one remembers the charges of abuse that dogged Ngema's trail during the tour of *Sarafina*; see Erika Munk, "Cultural Difference and the Double Standard," *Village Voice*, 21 June 1988.

45 See Holloway (1988, 1992) and Horn (1990). *The Hill* appeared at the Space, the Market, and some township venues in 1980 and was revived with a student cast at the Soyikwa Institute (and the Windybrow, 1995).

46 Directed at the People's Space by Amato and Nkonyeni, *Dark Voices Ring* introduced the first African woman director of literary drama. Unlike the Market, which concentrated its community outreach on bringing the people to the theatre (buses from Soweto and the like), the People's Space took this and other productions out to community halls in the townships near Cape Town.

47 This change can in part be explained by the casting; in the FUBA production, the black actor, Union Artists veteran Eddie Nhlapo, played the banker (Figure 7.10).

48 "Brave Look at the Darker Side of Independence," *New Nation*, 5–11 April 1989, reviewed the Soyikwa production, as did Victor Metsoamere, "Soyikwa Students Excel," *Sowetan*, 5 April 1979. For the People's Space production, see "Mda's Latest Offering Fills up the Space," *The Voice* 1, 44 (28 October 1979).

49 *We Shall Sing for the Fatherland and Other Plays* was banned in South Africa in 1981 and available only clandestinely until the expanded edition (Mda 1990) appeared.

50 On the trials of Zimbabwe's veterans, see F. Murape, "Too Little, Too Late for Veterans," *Mail and Guardian*, 15 August 1997. On the tensions created by the ANC's shift from a policy of social and economic equity to one of capital growth and economic rationalization, see A. Adelzadeh and M. Lethali, "Is South Africa GEARED for Development?" *Mail and Guardian* (Electronic Edition), 2 May 1997. GEAR is the Growth Employment and Redistribution program intended to replace the Reconstruction and Development Ministry dissolved in 1996.

51 Murray (1981: 4–20) noted that most Basotho men worked in South Africa at some time in their lives, many leaving their families to survive with the handouts of international agencies or by informal labor from crafts to sex work. Coplan (1994: 140–44; 164–79) shows how Basotho migrants have attempted to manage their dislocation and dispossession in oral narratives.

8 THEATRE IN THE INTERREGNUM AND BEYOND

1 *Mooi Street Moves* premiered as a one-act play at the Grahamstown Festival in 1992 and was developed into its final two-act form by the author in collaboration with actors Martin Le Maitre and Seputla Sebogodi at the Market Theatre in 1993. *Jozi, Jozi* was written and directed by Ledwaba and ran for several months in mid-1994 at the Market.

2 Swanson's sentimental story contrasts with the critical treatment in Lionel Rogosin's film, *Come Back Africa!* (1961), whose title alluded to the then-banned ANC slogan – *Mayibuye, iAfrika!* More recent films, such as *Wheels and Deals* (dir.: Michael Hamon, 1992) or *Jump the Gun* (dir.: Les Blair, 1997), depict lawlessness and brutality only hinted at on stage.

3 Slabolepszy's *Fordsburg's Finest* (Market Theatre 1998), returns to the encounter between Johannesburg and an unknowing newcomer, but reverses the roles: Thandi (played by the American Dorcas Johnson), returns to a Johannesburg she left as a baby, to find in place of her parents' house in Fordsburg a used-car lot run by Freddie Volschenk (Marius Weyers), an ex-policeman who resigned when his only son was killed on township duty.

4 *Curl Up and Dye* (dir.: Gillwald) captured audience attention at the Market Theatre for three seasons. The play was shaped in rehearsal by improvisation, especially by Dube and Nyembe.

5 Unlike the isiZulu songs and jokes in much anti-apartheid theatre, the isiZulu dialogue here is essential to the interpersonal dynamics of the play. The alienation of (white) spectators who cannot understand it might encourage them to identify with Rolene's alienation from an environment that is less and less her own, but it also reminds them that they cannot assume to be the primary audience or actors of the drama of South Africa.

6 The structure of feeling "is as firm and definite as 'structure' implies, yet operates in the most delicate parts of our activity" (Williams 1979: 106). The term highlights both the pervasiveness and the intimate operation of apartheid norms, which dictate gender as well as racial hierarchies; as Albie Sachs has written, "one of the few non-racial institutions in South Africa is patriarchy [but] gender takes on a specifically apartheid character . . . some are more unequal than others" (Sachs 1990: 53).

7 As Nancy Fraser notes, "the theoretical separation of intimate and public spheres is predicated on the conventional assumption of their separation in fact." This assumption in turn depends on a mystification of the intimate sphere as a presocial "lifeworld" which obscures the ways in which social borders around the intimate sphere mitigate against women's attempts to change their lot in the public arena (Fraser 1989: 113–43)

8 Despite the White Paper proclaiming redistribution (1996) and the foundation of the National Arts Council (September 1997), with an annual budget of R11.5 million (less than US$3 million) out of R4,000 million of the Dept. of Arts, Culture, Science, and

Technology (DACST) budget for arts and culture, the largest single sum for the performing arts (ca. R100 million) in 1997 still went to the apartheid era PACs. By 1999, the situation had changed somewhat: the NAC received R25 million and the PACS R93 million. The NAC's impartiality as an "independent statutory board" administering funding at "arm's length" from the state is incomplete, however, since its members include directors of theatres competing for funding; chair John Kani is also director of the Market Theatre, and chair of the board of PACT (the NAC's largest petitioner). See *White Paper* (1996), the documents and comment in *The Cultural Weapon* (published bimonthly by the independent arts policy organization Article 27 [after the article in the UN charter promoting artistic expression as a human right].

9 Kentridge has exhibited as a painter, graphic artist, and animator, as well as acting and designing for Junction Avenue Theatre Company. Adrian Kohler, co-founder of Handspring, trained in fine art, but also worked with the theatre for development group, Laedza Banani, in Botswana. Lesego Rampholokeng (who collaborated on the adaptation of *Faustus)* has published and performed as a dub/rap poet.

10 Criticizing the "much hallowed Goethe text" for alleged "verbiage," Mark Gevisser overlooks the production's failure to grasp this and other opportunities that Goethe's text offers for anticolonial rhetoric. See Gevisser, "Empire in all its delirium," *Mail and Guardian*, 21 July 1995.

11 Mkhwane and Pearson had teamed up earlier under the direction of Ellenbogen. In *iKisimus Box (Christmas Box* – the gift given to employees at Christmas) in 1990, Pearson plays Napoleon, a French cellist who wants to marry Abigail Chilli, a Zulu, but has to face the tricks of her brothers (including Mkhwane) and pay *ilobola* (bride-price) before he is accepted by the family.

12 The Market Lab was established by a grant from the Rockefeller Foundation and directed by Vanessa Cooke. Although it receives some of the Market Theatre's now R7 million (ca. US$1.5 million) state subsidy, it depends largely on foundation and commercial support for its two-year training program for fieldworkers who have facilitated community theatre in five provinces, as well as Botswana, Lesotho, and Mozambique.

13 See Mda's criticism of the rough scripts he read as dramaturg for the Market (*Annual Reports*, 1996–97).

14 Comment on the legacy of unequal distribution drawn from Maponya (interview 1995), Mahomed (1993), Mda (1995) and Mtshali (interview, 1996).

15 *Hejab* refers not only to the garment but also to the prescription, under *Shari'a* (Muslim law), which makes women responsible for retreating from the male gaze; see Göle (1997: 62).

16 Information from interviews with Mahomed in Grahamstown (July 1994), in New York (May 1995), and in Johannesburg (March 1998).

17 Mahomed's more recent plays, such as *Leather Boykies* (1994) and *Cheaper than Roses* (1995), tackle controversial social issues – the place of gay men in the Afrikaans hinterland or the dilemma of coloured people, especially women, who previously tried to pass for white and now face an uncertain future – through the medium of comedy and satire rather than through direct indictment. Mahomed now directs the Witbank Civic Theatre whose audiences were previously predominantly Afrikaans.

18 Mtshali drew on his experience with Bachaki since the company's inaugural play, *Top Down* (dir.: Muntu wa Bachaki, 1988) which exposed the corruption of school princi-pals, their lackeys and their white superiors in the Bantu Education system. In that

play Sifeni played the sycophantic vice-principal as well as the rebellious mathematics teacher who encourages student activism (Graver and Kruger 1989). His other plays also focus on conflicts within black communities: *Golden Gloves* (1993 – about the lure of boxing among Soweto youth) and *Devil's Den* (1995 – about the debate on traditional medicine).

19 Kerr (1995: 137) interprets African audience's laughter at violence as self-protective rather derisive.

20 Comment based on observation of the premiere at the Grahamstown Festival (1996) rather than the revised *Ipi Zombi?* (1998).

21 My comments do not claim to offer a full analysis of the debates raised by these projects, but to sketch briefly the issues as a preamble to discussing comparable work in South Africa.

22 Despite Mda (1993a: 50–51), I would call the first of these categories "instructional theatre" rather than "agitprop." Agitprop has historically been associated less with state propaganda than with anti-government cultural workers targeting industrial workers to educate and mobilize them to strike or otherwise challenge their employers and the state (in Europe and America since the 1920s), and more closely resembles the workers' theatre by South African unions in the 1980s than theatre for development initiatives (see von Kotzé 1988, 1989).

23 For the hospitals' comment, see *Health Education Tour* (Simon collection, NELM).

24 As head of the AIDS prevention program from 1989 to 1994, Evian developed this play (interview, 1994; corroborated by Shirley Ngwenya at WRF and Dr. Helene Schneider, head of the Centre for Health Policy at Wits).

25 Statistics from the *Draft White Paper on Population Policy* (Pretoria: Dept of Welfare and Population, 1997); http://www.polity.org.za/govdocs/white_papers/population.html.

26 Comments based on observation and interviews with Evian and the current AIDS theatre director at the Johannesburg Health Dept, Mhlalabesi Vundla.

27 For *Sarafina*'s mismanagement of funds and misleading representation of AIDS, see the Public Protector's Report (Bacqa 1997). For a description of the performance, see Mda (1997: 295–99). Those interested in the etiology of the scandal can consult articles available through the *Mail and Guardian:* http://www.mg.co.za.

28 15,000 reported rapes a year are perpetrated on pre-pubescent children. As in other societies in turmoil, many rapes are perpetrated by young men with no prospects who wish to "punish" women doing better than they (Marilyn Donaldson, clinical psychologist, Tara Alex Clinic). Some HIV+ rapists appear to believe that sex with a child will cure them (Sr. Rexina Maruping, Baragwanath Hospital). Citations from A. Johnson, "Hunting in the Dark for Abusers," *Mail and Guardian*, 27 February– 5 March 1998, 8.

29 An initial grant of R72,000 from the multinational pharmaceutical company, Glaxo-Wellcome as well as aid from the Community Theatre Development Trust enabled the company to reach over 100,000 students in 1995 alone. By 1998, interest among school and community leaders had led to several local affiliates who have performed across the country; see Annual Reports of the Market Theatre Foundation (1995–), and G. O'Hara, "Watering the Grassroots" (interview with Vanessa Cooke), *Mail and Guardian*, 25 September 1996.

30 This region is now on the disputed border between Mpumalanga and Northern province; WRF has been closed.

31 Observations draw on the published text *Heart to Heart* (Storyteller Group 1996),

Watson's thesis (1998), interviews by the author, and a more detailed article (Kruger and Watson, forthcoming), which focuses more on the comic's place in literacy education.

32 The 1997 Draft White Paper on Population Policy estimates overall adult mother-tongue literacy at 82% (76% African, 99.5% white) but leaves the reader to infer that a quarter of the adult population (more than 10 million) remains illiterate, and those able to read in their home languages would not necessarily be able to read signs and documents in urban areas, such as Gauteng, South Africa's biggest metropolitan area, where official – as opposed to commercial – signs in languages other than English or Afrikaans are still rare.

33 The popular appeal of American shows can be gauged in their ratings, as well as those of local soap operas. *Soul City*, a series (1994–) that combines the emotional register and cliff-hanger dramaturgy of soap operas with the pedagogic directness of health education theatre, is now in its fourth year and rates among the top three shows on SATV. The Independent Broadcasting Authority's mandate to increase local drama programing from 9.2 per cent (in 1994) to 20 per cent has been hampered by limited funds for production and training (Maingard 1997b: 263) and the dumping of the American product: US producers can sell reruns up to 400 times more cheaply than the cost of producing a local series; see G. O'Hara, "Local is not yet lekker," *Mail and Guardian*, 28 November 1997. Since TV sets are rare (ca. 4 million to a population of 39 million) and reception is weak in rural areas, rural viewers rely on satellite dishes, usually the property of state-subsidized enterprises or community centers.

34 Apartheid political economy favored a migrant male workforce, dislocated from both bantustan and city. Although the asymmetry between white city and black rural slum left most women and children in desperate poverty, the bantustan bureaucracies employed educated women (almost all as teachers, nurses, or clerks) rather than men, many of whom regarded this as "women's work," preferring work as miners or, failing that, as security guards. In a community which still expects *ilobola* (owed by a suitor to his wife's male relatives), the underemployment of young men makes formal marriage and the attendant prestige remote (Stadler 1993).

35 *Heart to Heart* has been translated into isiZulu and Sesotho, and circulates in English in Southern Africa and in French translation in West Africa (published by the multi-national company Bayard).

GLOSSARY

ama-: Nguni prefix for people
amaCele: clan in South Natal
amaGcakela: clan in Eastern Cape
amakwaya (isiZulu): Anglo/American choir melodies
amaMthethwa: large clan affiliated with amaZulu
amaXhosa: large clan in Eastern Cape
amaZulu: clan that dominated South-Eastern Africa in the nineteenth century
Anglo-Boer War: 1899–1902
baas (Afrikaans): boss (associated with apartheid)
(a)Bantu (isiNguni = "people"): used by apartheid state for segregated black institutions
bantustans: so-called autonomous black states within South African borders (until 1994)
Basotho: people of Lesotho
Bharata Natyam: a classical dance form from Tamil Nadu, South India. The great-grandparents of many South Africans of Indian descent came from this area
Boer: Afrikaner
boerekommando and *kappiekommando* (Afrikaans: lit. farmer and bonnet commandos): refers to the groups of men and women in Voortrekker garb accompanying the wagons leading the Voortrekker Centenary celebrations
bywoners (Afrikaans): land tenants, "poor whites"
Cetshwayo (d. 1884): last autonomous Zulu king (1873–79)
Colour Bar: law preserving certain kinds of skilled employment for whites
coloured: apartheid classification for mixed-race people
dagga (Khoi): cannabis
dominee (Afrikaans): minister
Eisteddfodau: originally Welsh (later British) music and poetry festivals
Gauteng (Sesotho): place of gold; South Africa's richest and densest province; includes Johannesburg and surrounding industrial belts (formerly: Pretoria, Witwatersrand, Vereeniging triangle)

244

Gazankulu: "self-governing" bantustan in northeast South Africa (absorbed 1994 into Northern Province)

Great Trek of 1838: migration of Voortrekkers (see Voortrekkers)

ilobola (isiNguni): bride-price

imbongi (pl. *izimbongi*; isiZulu): praise poet

indaba (isiZulu): Zulu court council; by extension, public debate or issue of public concern

ingoma (isiZulu): music

ingoma ebusuku: night (i.e. urban, commercial) music

inyanga (isiZulu): healer

isangoma: diviner

isicathamiya: dance form of Zulu migration (lit.: "walking like a cat")

isiNguni/isiXhosa/isiZulu: Nguni, Xhosa, Zulu language

izibongo (isiZulu): praises

izinganekwane (isiZulu): folktales

Kaaps: dialect of Afrikaans, spoken by mixed-race people in the Cape

kappiekommando (Afrikaans): see boerekommando

KhoiSan: Khoikhoi & San, herder and hunter-gatherer, original inhabitants of South Africa

KwaZulu: "self-governing" bantustan (until 1994)

KwaZulu/Natal: province in South Africa (since 1994)

kwela: 1950s urban music associated with the penny-whistle

Land Act (1913): the Act which forced the black majority onto 13 per cent of the land

Lenasia: "Indian" township near Soweto

lithoko (Sesotho): chronicle songs

marabi: urban dance music, 1920s–1950s

mbaqanga: applied variously to dance music styles from 1950s to disco-influenced music in 1970s and beyond

mfecane (isiZulu)/*lifecane* (Sesotho): scattering or violent dispersal of amaNguni and other tribes disrupted by Zulu expansion and colonial incursion in the mid-nineteenth century

Moshoeshoe I (1786–1870): King of the Basotho; famous for securing the future of Lesotho by negotiating with the British against the Boers and for offering shelter to a range of tribes displaced by the *mfecane*

Natal: one of four South African provinces (1910–94)

"Nkosi sikelel' iAfrika": ANC and now national anthem

ntsomi (isiXhosa): folktales

Orange Free State: former Boer Republic (1854–1902), and later province (1910–)

pitso (Sesotho): assembly

Republic of South Africa (1961–1994): apartheid state ruled by Afrikaner National Party

Second Great Trek: mass pilgrimage from Cape to Pretoria in 1938 to commemorate Voortrekker Centenary.

Sesotho: Sotho language

Setswana: Tswana language

Shaka (1781–1828): king of amaZulu (1816–28) and ruler of a substantial empire in South-Eastern Africa; blamed for the *mfecane*, the upheaval and dispersal of neighboring tribes who moved as far as present-day Zimbabwe (aMatabele) and Kenya (amaNgoni); murdered by his half-brother Dingane

skollie (Afrikaans): street-smart, devious, but obsequious scoundrel

suiwer (Afrikaans): pure

taal (Afrikaans): language

tiekiedraai: Afrikaans folk-dance; couples turn on a tight circle, by analogy with *tiekie* (archaic threepenny piece)

Transkei: "independent" bantustan (1976–94)

Transvaal: former province (1910–94)

triomf (Afrikaans): triumph. Apartheid name for the white suburb that replaced Sophiatown.

tsotsis (and *tsotsitaal*): gangsters and their language

tuis (Afrikaans): at home; by extension homeland

Umkhonto we Sizwe: Spear of the Nation

umlinganiso (isiZulu): imitation

Union of South Africa (1910–60)

van Riebeeck, Jan (1619–77): official of the Dutch East India Company, responsible for setting up a "refreshment station" at the Cape in 1652; mythologized as the first white settler

Verwoerd, Henrik Frensch (1901–66): minister for Bantu Affairs (1953–58) and later prime minister (1958–66); chief ideologue and architect of "grand apartheid" (from 1950)

volkseenheit (Afrikaans): ethnic unity

volkseie (Afrikaans): ethnic identity

volkskapitalisme (Afrikaans): ethnically based economic development

volksmoeder (Afrikaans): mother of the (Afrikaner) volk

volksontwikkelling (Afrikaans): Afrikaner self-development

volksstaat (Afrikaans): Afrikaner state

Voortrekker: honorific for disgruntled Boers who left the Dutch Cape colony in the 1830s and 1840s

xiTsonga: Tsonga language

Zululand: British colonial name for KwaZulu

REFERENCES

Scripts

NB: Dates in the reference list are those of publication, except in the case of unpublished scripts, where the date refers to the first performance. For plays mentioned in this volume, the date given in parentheses after the title represents the year the play was first performed. Where a play has also been published, a cross-reference to the relevant publication has also been given at its first citation.

Anon. (1973) "Before and After the Revolution," unpublished agitprop sketch, BCM files (A2171), Witwatersrand University Library.

Bachaki Theatre. (1989) "Top Down," synopsis in *Maske und Kothurn* 35, 1: 81–85.

Bailey, B. (1999) "Zombie," in D. Graver (ed.) *Plays for a New South Africa*, Bloomington: Indiana University Press.

Barnard, C. (1971) *Die Rebellie van Lafras Verwey*, Cape Town: Tafelberg.

Black, S. (1984) *Three Plays*, S. Gray (ed.), Johannesburg: Ad Donker (includes: "Love and the Hyphen" [1902/1910] and "Helena's Hope Ltd." [1910]).

Bloom, H., Matshikiza, T., and Williams, P. (1961) *King Kong – An African Jazz Opera*, London: Collins.

Brecht, B. (1967) *Gesammelte Werke*, 20 vols, Frankfurt: Suhrkamp.

Brink, A. P. (1970) *Die Verhoor*, Cape Town: Human & Rousseau.

Butler, G. (1953) *The Dam*, Cape Town: A. A. Balkema.

De Klerk, W. A. (1947) *Drie Dramas*, Cape Town: Nasionale Pers.

—— (1952) *Die Jaar van die Vuuros*, Cape Town: Tafelberg.

—— (1989) *Die Jaar van die Vuuros*, second edition, Cape Town: Tafelberg.

De Wet, R. (1991) *Vrystaat-Trilogie*, Pretoria: HAUM-Literêr.

—— (1994) *Trits*, Pretoria: HAUM-Literêr (includes "Diepe Grond").

Dhlomo, H. I. E. (1939) "Ruby and Frank," unpublished playscript, KCM 8267, Campbell Collection, University of Natal.

—— (1954) *Dingana*, stage version, Durban: University of Natal.

—— (1985) *Collected Works*, T. Couzens and N. Visser (eds), Johannesburg: Ravan (includes: "The Girl Who Killed to Save," "Cetshwayo," and "Moshoeshoe").

Dhlomo, H. I. E., Dhlomo, R. R., and Motsicloa, G. (1934) "Dramatic Display" for the Emancipation Centenary Celebration, unpublished materials in the SAIRR Collection, Witwatersrand University Library.

Dike, F. (1977) *The First South African*, Johannesburg: Ravan.

Dike, F. (1978) "The Sacrifice of Kreli," in S. Gray (ed.) *Theatre One*, Johannesburg: Ad Donker.

—— (1996) "So What's New?," in Z. Mda (ed.) *Four Plays*, Florida Hills, SA: Vivlia.

Drinkwater, J. (1925) *Collected Plays*, 2 vols, London: Sidgwick & Jackson.

Du Plessis, P. G. (1971) *Siener in die Suburbs*, Cape Town: Tafelberg.

Ellenbogen, N. (1999) "Horn of Sorrow," in D. Graver (ed.) *Plays for a New South Africa*, Bloomington: Indiana University Press.

Ellenbogen, N., Pearson, E., and Mkhwane, B. (1990) "iKisimus Box", unpublished playscript.

Fugard, A. (1974) *Three Port Elizabeth Plays*, New York: Viking.

—— (1978) "Orestes: an Experiment in Theatre as Described in a Letter to an American Friend," in S. Gray (ed.) *Theatre One*, Johannesburg: Ad Donker.

—— (1987) *Selected Plays*, Dennis Walder (ed.), Oxford: Oxford University Press.

—— (1991) *Blood Knot and Other Plays*, New York: Theatre Communications Group.

—— (1992 [1964]) *The Blood Knot*, Oxford and Cape Town: Oxford University Press.

—— (1993) *Township Plays*, Oxford: Oxford University Press (includes "Nongogo," "No-Good Friday," "The Coat," "Sizwe Banzi Is Dead," and "The Island").

——, Kani, J., and Ntshona, W. (1986) *Statements: Three Plays*, New York: Theatre Communications Group (includes: "Sizwe Banzi Is Dead" and "The Island").

Goethe, J. W. von (1959) *Faust II*, trans. P. Wade, Harmondsworth: Penguin.

—— (1981) *Faust II*, in *Werke*, 14 vols, Munich: C. H. Beck Verlag.

Govender, K. (1979) "Working Class Hero," unpublished playscript.

Govender, R. (1977) *The Lahnee's Pleasure*, Johannesburg: Ravan.

—— (1996) *At the Edge and Other Cato Manor Stories*, Pretoria: Marx.

Graver, D. (ed.) (1999) *Plays for a New South Africa*, Bloomington: Indiana University Press.

Gray, S. (ed.) (1981) *Theatre One*, Johannesburg: Ad Donker (includes: A. Fugard, "Orestes"; F. Dike, "Sacrifice of Kreli"; Pieter-Dirk Uys, "Paradise is Closing Down").

—— (ed.) (1981) *Theatre Two*, Johannesburg: Ad Donker (includes: Junction Avenue Theatre Company, "Randlords and Rotgut"; P. D. Uys, "God's Forgotten").

—— (1984) Introduction to S. Black, *Three Plays*, Johannesburg: Ad Donker.

—— (ed.) (1986) *Market Plays*, Johannesburg: Ad Donker (includes: M. Manaka, "Pula" and B. Simon *et al.*, "Hey, Listen!").

—— (ed. and intro.) (1993) *South Africa Plays*, London: Nick Hern (includes: S. Pam-Grant, "Curl up and Dye").

Grosskopf, J. W. (1940) *As Die Tuig Skawe*, Johannesburg: Afrikaanse Pers.

Hauptfleisch, T. and Steadman, I. (eds) (1984) *South African Theatre: Four Plays and an Introduction*, Pretoria: Haum (includes: P. G. du Plessis, "Christine"; A. Fugard, "Hello and Goodbye"; M. Maponya, "The Hungry Earth"; B. Simon *et al.*, "Cincinatti").

Joubert, E. (1981) *Poppie Nongena*, London: Coronet.

Joubert, E. (1981) *Die Swerfjare van Poppie Nongena*, Cape Town: Tafelberg.

Joubert, E. and Kotzé, S. (1984) *Poppie Nongena* (stage version), Cape Town: Tafelberg.

Junction Avenue Theatre Company (JATC) (1978) *The Fantastical History of a Useless Man*, Johannesburg: Ravan.

—— (1994) *Sophiatown*, Johannesburg: Witwatersrand University Press.

—— (1995) *At the Junction: Four Plays by the Junction Avenue Theatre Company*, M. Orkin (ed.), Johannesburg: Witwatersrand University Press.

Kani, J. (comp.) (1996) *More Market Plays*, Johannesburg: Ad Donker (includes: Simon *et al.*, "Born in the RSA," N. McCarthy, "The Rainshark," V. Cooke and N. Haysom, "The

Native who Caused All the Trouble," and Vuzisizwe Players, "You Strike the Women, You Strike the Rock").

Kavanagh, R. (ed.) (1981) *South African People's Plays*, London: Heinemann (includes: C. Mutwa, "uNosilimela"; G. Kente, "Too Late!"; M. Shezi, "Shanti"; Workshop '71, "Survival").

Kente, G. (1981) "Too Late!" in R. Kavanagh (ed.) (1981) *South African People's Plays*, London: Heinemann.

Kramer, D. and Pieterson, T. (1991) "District Six – The Musical," unpublished score and playscript.

Krige, U. (1939) *Magdalena Retief*, Cape Town: Nasionale Pers.

Ledwaba, J. M. (1994) "Jozi, Jozi," broadcast on NNTV, South Africa, 25 September.

Louw, N. P. van Wyk (1938) *Die Dieper Reg*, Cape Town: Nasionale Pers.

—— (1972) *Die Pluimsaad waai ver*, Cape Town: Human & Rousseau.

Mackey, W. W. (1986 [1971]) "Requiem for Brother X," in W. King and R. Milner (eds) *Black Drama Anthology*, second edition, New York: New American Library.

Mahomed, I. (1999a) "Purdah," in D. Graver (ed.) *Plays for a New South Africa*, Bloomington: Indiana University Press.

—— (1999b) "Cheaper than Roses," in K. Perkins (ed.) *Black South African Women Plays*, London: Routledge.

Manaka, M. (1980) *Egoli: City of Gold*, Johannesburg: Ravan/Soyikwa.

—— (1989) "Goree," unpublished playscript.

Maponya, M. (1986) "Gangsters," in D. Ndlovu (ed.) *Woza Afrika! An Anthology of South African Plays*, New York: Braziller.

—— (1995) *Doing Plays for a Change: Five Works*, I. Steadman (ed.), Johannesburg: Witwatersrand University Press.

Maqina, M. (1975) *Give Us this Day*, Johannesburg: Ravan.

Masinga, K. E. (1944) *Chief above and Chief below*, Pietermaritzburg: Shooter & Shuster.

Matheus, J. (1975 [1926]) "'Cruter," in J. Hatch and T. Shine (eds) *Black Theater USA: Forty-five Plays by Black Americans, 1847–1974*, New York: Macmillan.

Matshikiza, T. and Williams, P. (n.d.) *King Kong – Original Cast Recording*, Paris: Celluloid (under license from Gallo, South Africa).

Mda, Z. (1990) *The Plays of Zakes Mda*, Johannesburg: Ravan (includes "The Hill").

—— (1993a) *When People Play People*, London: Zed Books.

—— (1993b) *And the Girls in Their Sunday Dresses and Other Plays*, Johannesburg: Witwatersrand University Press.

—— (ed. and intro.) (1996) *Four Plays*, Florida Hills, South Africa: Vivlia.

Mekgoe, S. (1978) *Lindiwe*, Johannesburg: Ravan.

Mhlophe, G., van Renen, M., and Mtshali, T. (1988) *Have You Seen Zandile?*, London: Methuen.

Mkhwane, B., and Pearson, E. (1994) "A Boy Called Rubbish," unpublished playscript.

Moodley, V. (1993) "Got Green Chillies, Makoti," unpublished playscript.

Mqayisa, K. (1974) *Confused Mhlaba*, Johannesburg: Ravan.

Mtsaka, M. J. (1978) *Not His Pride*, Johannesburg: Ravan.

Mtshali, T. (1999) "Weemen," in K. Perkins (ed.) *Black South African Women Plays*, London: Routledge.

Mtwa, P., Ngema, M., and Simon, B. (1983) *Woza Albert!*, London: Methuen.

Ndlovu, D. (1999) "Sheila's Day," in K. Perkins (ed.) *Black South African Women Plays*, London: Routledge.

Ndlovu, D. (ed.) (1986) *Woza Africa!*, New York: Braziller (includes: M. Manaka, "Children of Asazi"; M. Maponya, "Gangsters"; P. Mtwa, "Bopha!"; M. Ngema, "Asinamali"; B. Simon *et al.*, "Born in the RSA'), New York: Braziller.

Ngema, M. (1995) *The Best of Mbongeni Ngema*, Johannesburg: Skotaville.

Nkosi, L. (1964) "The Rhythm of Violence," in G. Wellwarth (ed.) (1973) *Themes in Drama*, New York: Thomas Crowell.

Opperman, D. (1986) *Môre is 'n Lang Dag* and *Die Teken*, Cape Town: Tafelberg.

—— (1996) "Donkerland," unpublished playscript.

Pam-Grant, S. (1993) "Curl Up and Dye," in S. Gray (ed.) *South Africa Plays*, London: Nick Hern.

Perkins, K. (ed.) (1999) *Black South African Women Plays*, London: Routledge.

Pillai, K. (1995) *Looking for Muruga*, Durban: Asoka Publications.

Serpent Players (1967) "The Coat," *The Classic* 2, 3: 50–68.

Shezi, M. (1981) "Shanti," in R. Kavanagh (ed.) *South African People's Plays*, London: Heinemann.

Simon, B. *et al.* (1986) "Born in the RSA," in D. Ndlovu (ed.) *Woza Afrika!*, New York: Braziller.

—— (1996) "Born in the RSA," rev. edn, in J. Kani (comp.) *More Market Plays*, Johannesburg: Ad Donker.

—— (1997) "Black Dog/Inj'emnyana," in Simon *et al.* (eds) *Born in the RSA: Four Workshopped Plays*, Johannesburg: Witwatersrand University Press.

Slabolepszy, P. (1985) *Saturday Night at the Palace*, Johannesburg: Ad Donker.

—— (1994) *Mooi Street and Other Moves*, Johannesburg: Witwatersrand University Press.

—— (1998) "Fordsberg's Finest," unpublished playscript.

Small, A. (1965) *Kanna Hy Kô Hystoe*, Cape Town: Tafelberg.

—— (1973) "What about de Lô?" unpublished playscript.

—— (1990) *Kanna – He Is Coming Home*, trans. C. Lasker in association with the author, New York: Garland.

Smit, B. (1960) *Die Verminktes*, Johannesburg: Afrikaanse Pers.

—— (1962) *Putsonderwater*, Cape Town: Tafelberg.

—— (1976) *Die Verminktes*, second edition, Johannesburg: Perskor.

Sondhi, K. (1968) "Encounter," in C. Pietersen (ed.) *Ten One-Act Plays*, London: Heinemann.

Sowden, L. (1937) "Red Rand," unpublished playscript, Witwatersrand University Libraries, A406.

—— (1976) *The Kimberley Train*, Cape Town: Howard Timmins.

Storyteller Group (1994) *Heart to Heart*, Johannesburg: Storyteller Group.

—— (1996) *Heart to Heart: From Dream Love to True Love*, Johannesburg: Storyteller Group.

Themba, C. (1986) "The Suit," in E. Patel (ed.) *The World of Can Themba*, Johannesburg: Ravan.

—— (1996) "The Suit," unpublished stage adaptation by M. Mutloatse and the cast of the Market Theatre production.

Tremblay, M. (1972) *Les Belles-Sœurs*, Montréal: Leméac.

Uys, P. D. (1981) "God's Forgotten," in S. Gray (ed.) *Theatre One*, Johannesburg: Ad Donker.

—— (1983) *Selle ou Storie*, Johannesburg: Ad Donker.

—— (1995) *Funigalore: Evita's Real-life Adventures in Wonderland*, London: Penguin.

Vusisizwe Players (1996) "You Strike the Woman, You Strike the Rock," in J. Kani (comp.) *More Market Plays*, Johannesburg: Ad Donker.

Witbooi, M. (1984) "Dit Sal Die Blêrrie Dag Wies," unpublished playscript.

Workshop '71 (1981) "Survival," in R. Kavanagh (ed.) *South African People's Plays*, London: Heinemann.

History and theory

Akerman, A. (1977–78) "Why Must these Shows Go on?" *Theatre Quarterly* 28: 67–70.

Alexander, N. (comp.) (1996) *Final Report of the Language Task Action Group*, Pretoria: Dept. of Arts, Culture, Science and Technology.

Amato, R. (1977) "A Xhosa Woman's Serious Optimism," *Speak* 1, 1: 14–17.

Anderson, B. (1983) *Imagined Communities: Reflections on the Origins and Spread of Nationalism*, London: Verso.

Ashcroft, B., Griffiths, G., and Tiffin, H. (1989) *The Empire Writes Back: Theory and Practice in Postcolonial Literature*, London: Routledge.

Astbury, B. (1979) *The Space/Die Ruimte/Indawo*, Cape Town: Space Theatre.

Bacqa, S. (1997) *Investigation of the Play Sarafina II: Public Protector's Report*, Pretoria: Office of the Public Protector.

Bakhtin, M. (1987) *The Dialogic Imagination*, trans. Michael Holquist (ed.), Austin: University of Texas Press.

Ballantine, C. (1993) *Marabi Nights: Early South African Jazz and Vaudeville*, Johannesburg: Ravan.

Balme, C. B. (1995) *Theater im postkolonialen Zeitalter: Studien zum Theatersynkretismus im englischsprachigen Raum*, Tübingen: Niemeyer.

Barber, K. (1986) "Radical Conservatism in Yoruba Popular Plays," *Bayreuth African Studies Series* 7: 5–32.

—— (1987) "Popular Arts in Africa," *African Studies Review* 30, 3: 1–78.

Bate, J. (1989) *Shakespearean Constitutions: Politics, Theatre, Criticism, 1730–1830*, Oxford: Oxford University Press.

Bauman, R. (1989) "Performance," *International Encyclopedia of Communications*, New York: Oxford University Press, 3: 262–66.

Benson, M. (1977) "Keeping an Appointment with the Future: The Theatre of Athol Fugard," *Theatre Quarterly* 7, 28: 76–79.

—— (1997) *Athol Fugard and Barney Simon*, Johannesburg: Ravan Press.

Berlant, L. (1988) "The Female Complaint," *Social Text* 19–20: 237–59.

Berman, M. (1988) *All That's Solid Melts into Air: The Experience of Modernity*, New York: Penguin.

Bhabha, H. K. (1986) "Signs Taken for Wonders: Reflections on Questions of Ambivalence and Authority under a Tree outside Dehli," in H. L. Gates (ed.) *"Race," Writing, and Difference*, Chicago: University of Chicago Press.

—— (1991) "'Race,' Time and the Revision of Modernity," *Oxford Literary Review* 13: 193–219.

—— (1992) "Freedom's Basis in the Indeterminate," *October* 61: 46–57.

Bharucha, R. (1993 [1991]) *Theatre and the World*, London: Routledge.

Biko, S. B. (1978) *I Write What I Like*, New York: Harper & Row.

Bloch, E. (1977 [1933]) "Nonsynchronism and the Obligation to Its Dialectics," *New German Critique* 11: 22–38.

Boal, A. (1979) *Theatre of the Oppressed*, trans. C. and M. Leal McBride, New York: Urizen.

Boal, A. (1992) *Games for Actors and Non-Actors*, trans. A. Jackson, London: Routledge.

Bosman, F. C. H. (1969) *Drama en Toneel in Suid-Afrika: 1800–1962*, Pretoria: Van Schaik.

Bourdieu, P. (1993) *The Field of Cultural Production*, trans. R. Nice *et al.*, New York: Columbia University Press.

Bozzoli, B. (ed.) (1979) *Labour, Township and Protest: Studies in the Social History of the Witwatersrand*, Johannesburg: Ravan.

—— (ed. and intro.) (1983) *Town and Countryside in the Transvaal: Capitalist Penetration and Popular Response*, Johannesburg: Ravan.

Bozzoli, B. and Delius, P. (1990) "Radical History and South African Society," introduction to *History from South Africa*; *Radical History* 46–47: 13–45.

Branford, W. and Claughton, J. (1995) "Mutual Lexical Borrowings among some South African Languages," in R. Meshrie (ed.) *Language and Social History: Studies in South African Sociolinguistics*, Cape Town: David Phillip: 209–21.

Brecht, B. (1992 [1964]) *Brecht on Theatre*, trans. John Willett (ed.), New York: Hill & Wang.

Brickill, J. and Brooks, A. (1980) *Whirlwind after the Storm: The Origin and Development of the Uprising in Soweto and the Rest of South Africa*, London: International Aid and Development Fund.

Brink, A. P. (1973) *Kennis van die Aand*, Cape Town: Buren.

—— (1974) *Looking into the Darkness*, London: W. H. Allen.

—— (1979) *'n Droë Wit Seison*, Johannesburg: Taurus.

—— (1979) *A Dry White Season*, New York: William Morrow.

—— (1986) *Aspekte van die nuwe drama*, Cape Town: Human & Rousseau.

Brook, P. (1976) *The Melodramatic Imagination*, New Haven: Yale University Press.

Brown, J. A. (1982) Review of *The Blood Knot*, in S. Gray (ed.) *Athol Fugard*, Johannesburg: McGraw-Hill.

Buthelezi, Q. (1995) "South African Black English," in R. Meshtrie (ed.) *Language and Social History*, Cape Town: David Phillip: 242–50.

Butler, G. (1986) "English in the New South Africa," *English Academy Review* 3: 163–76.

Caccia, A. (ed.) (1982) *The Beat of Drum*, Johannesburg: Ravan.

Caldecott, C. H. (1853) *Descriptive History of the Zulu Kafirs*, London: John Mitchel.

Callaway, H. (1870) *The Religious System of the AmaZulu*, Pietermaritzburg: Davis & Springvale.

Caluza, R. (1992) *Caluza's Double Quartet. 1930*, with notes by V. Erlmann (ed.) Sussex: Interstate Music.

Campbell, R. (1949) *Collected Poems*, London: Brun.

Campschreur, W. and Divendal, J. (eds) (1989) *Culture in another South Africa*, New York: Olive Branch Press.

Carlson, M. (1989) *Places of Performance: The Semiotics of Theatre Architecture*, Ithaca: Cornell University Press.

Carmichael, S. [K. Ture] (1968 [1966]) "Towards Black Liberation," in L. Jones and L. Neal (eds) *Black Fire*, New York: William Morrow.

Celli, L. (1937) "South African Dramatists," *South African Opinion* (15 May): 13–14.

Césaire, A. (1972) *Discourse on Colonialism*, trans. J. Pinkham, New York: Monthly Review Press.

Chakrabarty, D. (1992) "Postcoloniality and the Artifice of History: Who Speaks for 'Indian' Pasts?" *Representations* 37: 1–26.

Chapman, M. (1989) "More than a Story: *Drum* and its Significance in Black South

African Writing," appendix to M. Chapman (ed.) *The Drum Decade: Stories from the 1950s*, Pietermaritzburg: University of Natal.

—— (1996) *Southern African Literatures*, London: Longman.

Chaudhuri, U. (1995) *Staging Place: The Geography of Modern Drama*, Ann Arbor: University of Michigan Press.

Chipkin, C. (1993) *Johannesburg Style: Architecture and Society, 1880s-1960s*, Cape Town: David Phillip.

Coetzee, J. M. (1988) *White Writing: On the Culture of Letters in South Africa*, New Haven: Yale University Press.

—— (1995) "Retrospect: The World Cup of Rugby," *South African Review of Books* 38: 19–21.

Colenso, F. and Durnford, E. (1881) *History of the Zulu War*, London: Chapman & Hall.

Comaroff, J. and Comaroff, J. (eds) (1993) *Modernity and Its Malcontents: Ritual and Power in Postcolonial Africa*, Chicago: University of Chicago Press.

Commission of Inquiry (1977) *Commission of Inquiry into the Performative Arts in South Africa*, Pretoria: Govt. Publication.

Cope, J. (1983) *The Adversary from within: Dissident Writing in Afrikaans*, Cape Town: David Phillip.

Coplan, D. (1985) *In Township Tonight!*, London: Longman.

—— (1993) "History Is Eaten Whole: Consuming Tropes in Sesotho Auriture," *History and Theory* 32, 4: 80–104.

—— (1994) *In the Time of Cannibals: The Word Music of South Africa's Basotho Migrants*, Chicago: University of Chicago Press.

Couzens, T. (1985) *The New African: A Study of the Life and Work of H. I. E. Dhlomo*, Johannesburg: Ravan.

Cronjé, G. (1945) *'n Tuiste vir die Nageslag*, Cape Town: Afrikaanse Pers.

Curtis, N. (1920) *Songs and Tales from the Dark Continent*, New York: Schirmer.

Davids, A. (1994) "The Contribution of the Slaves to the Generation of Afrikaans," in V. February (ed.) *Taal en Identiteit: Afrikaans en Nederlands*, Cape Town: Tafelberg.

Davis, P. (1996) *In Darkest Hollywood: Exploring the Jungles of Cinema's South Africa*, Johannesburg: Ravan.

De Klerk, W. A. (1975) *The Puritans in Africa: A Story of Afrikanerdom*, Harmondsworth: Penguin.

De Kok, I. and Press, K. (eds) (1990) *Spring Is Rebellious: Arguments about Cultural Freedom by Albie Sachs and Respondents*, Cape Town: Buchu Books.

Dell, E. (1993) "Museums and the Re-presentation of 'Savage South Africa' to 1910," Ph.D. thesis, School of Oriental and African Studies, University of London.

Dept. of Information (1969) *Performing Arts in South Africa: Cultural Aspirations of a Young Nation*, Pretoria: Government Publications.

Dhlomo, H. I. E. (1977) *Literarary Theory and Criticism*, N. Visser (ed.), special issue of *English in Africa* 4, 2: 1–76.

—— (1977a [1936]) "Drama and the African," *Literary Criticism and Theory of H. I. E. Dhlomo*, special issue of *English in Africa* 4, 2: 3–11.

—— (1977b [1939]) "African Drama and Poetry," *Literary Criticism and Theory*: 13–18.

—— (1977c [1939]) "African Drama and Research," *Literary Criticism and Theory*: 19–22.

—— (1977d [1939]) "Nature and Variety of Tribal Drama," *Literary Criticism and Theory*: 23–36.

Dhlomo, H. I. E. (1977e [1939]) "Why Study Tribal Dramatic Forms?" *Literary Criticism and Theory*: 37–42.

—— (1977f [1943]) "Masses and the Artist," *Literary Criticism and Theory*: 61–62.

—— (1977g [1946]) "Bantu Culture and Expression," *Literary Criticism and Theory*: 67–68.

—— (1977h [1949]) "The African Artist and Society," *Literary Criticism and Theory*: 71–72.

—— "The Evolution of Bantu Entertainments," unpublished manuscript, Killie Campbell Centre (KCM 8290/2).

Dikobe, M. (1979) "We Shall Walk," in B. Bozzoli (ed.) *Labour, Township and Protest: Studies in the Social History of the Witwatersrand*, Johannesburg: Ravan.

Dollimore, J. and Sinfield, A. (eds) (1985) *Political Shakespeare*, second editon, Ithaca: Cornell University Press.

Dominy, G. (1991) "Thomas Baines: the McGonagall of Shepstone's 1873 Zulu Expedition?" in "Notes and Queries," comp. M. Comrie, *Natalia* 21: 73–79.

Driver, D. (1990) "M'a-Ngoana O Tšoare Thipa ka Bohaleng – The Child's Mother Grabs the Sharp End of the Knife: Women as Mothers, Women as Writers," in M. Trump (ed.) *Rendering Things Visible*, Johannesburg: Ravan Press.

Du Bois, W. E. B. (1989 [1903]) *Souls of Black Folk*, New York: Bantam.

Dubow, S. (1987) "Race, Civilization and Culture: the Elaboration of Segregationist Discourse in the Interwar Years," in S. Marks and S. Trapido (eds) *The Politics of Race, Class, and Nationalism*, London: Longman, 71–94.

Erlmann, V. (1991) *African Stars: Studies in Black South African Performance*, Chicago: University of Chicago Press.

Esterhuysen, P. (1991) "'Heyta Ngwenya'. 'Sharp, sharp'. Popular Visual Literature and a New Pedagogy," in R. Ferguson (ed.) *Media Matters in South Africa*, Durban: University of Natal, 274–79.

Evian, C. (1992) "Community Theatre and AIDS Education," *Progress* (Summer): 34–37.

Fabian, J. (1993) "Keep Listening: Ethnography and Reading," in J. Boyarin (ed.) *The Ethnography of Reading*, Berkeley: University of California Press, 80–97.

Fanon, F. (1968 [1962]) *The Wretched of the Earth*, trans. C. Farrington, New York: Grove.

February, V. (1981) *Mind Your Colour*, London: Kegan Paul.

Filewod, A. (1990) "National Theatre, National Obsession," *Canadian Theatre Review* 62: 5–10.

Finnegan, R. (1970) *Oral Literature in Africa*, Nairobi: Oxford University Press.

Foucault, M. (1979) *Discipline and Punish*, trans. Alan Sheridan, New York: Random House.

Fraser, N. (1989) *Unruly Practices: Power, Discourse, and Gender in Contemporary Social Theory*, Minneapolis: University of Minnesota Press.

Frederikse, J. (1990) *The Unbreakable Thread: Non-racialism in South Africa*, Bloomington: Indiana University Press.

Freire, P. (1972) *Pedagogy of the Oppressed*, trans. M. B. Ramos, Harmondsworth: Penguin.

Friedman, G. (1992) "Puppetry and AIDS Education," *Progress* (Summer): 38–39.

Fuchs, A. (1990) *Playing the Market: The Market Theatre, Johannesburg, 1976–86*, Chur (Switzerland) and New York: Harwood Academic Publishers.

Fugard, A. (1982) "Sizwe Banzi Is Dead," in R. Harwood (ed.) *A Night at the Theatre*, London: Methuen, 21–33.

—— (1984) *Notebooks: 1960–77*, New York: Theatre Communications Group.

Fugard, A. and Simon, B. (1982) "The Family Plays of the Sixties," in S. Gray (ed.) *Athol Fugard*, Johannesburg: McGraw-Hill, 40–52.

Gatti, A. (1982) "Armand Gatti on Time, Space, and Theatre Event," trans. N. Oakes, *Modern Drama* 25, 1: 69–81.

Gedenkboek (1938) *Gedenkboek van die Voortrekker-Eeufees*, Johannesburg: Sentrale Volksfeeskomitee.

—— (1940) *Gedenkboek van die Ossewaens op die Pad van Suid-Afrika*, D. Mostert (ed.), Cape Town: Nasionale Pers.

Gérard, A. (1971) *Four African Literatures*, Berkeley: University of California Press.

Gerhart, G. (1978) *Black Power in South Africa*, Berkeley: University of California Press.

Gerwel, G. J. (1985 [1976]) "Afrikaner, Afrikaans, Afrika," in *Skrywer en Gemeenskap*, Pretoria: Haum Literêr.

Gevisser, M. (1994a) "SA's Reconciliation in Motion," *Johannesburg Weekly Mail* (13–19 May): 9.

—— (1994b) "A Different Fight for Freedom: A History of Gay and Lesbian Lives in South Africa," introduction to M. Gevisser and E. Cameron (eds) *Defiant Desire*, Johannesburg: Ravan.

Gilbert, H. and Tompkins, J. (1996) *Post-colonial Drama*, London: Routledge.

Glasser, M. (1960) *King Kong – A Venture in the Theatre*, Cape Town: Norman Howell.

Goldin, I. (1987) "The Reconstitution of Coloured Identity in the Western Cape," in S. Marks and S. Trapido (eds) *The Politics of Race, Class and Nationalism*, London: Longman.

Göle, N. (1997) "The Gendered Nature of the Public Sphere," *Public Culture* 10, 1: 61–81.

Gordimer, N. (1964) "Plays and Piracy," *Contrast* 3, 4: 50–59.

Govender, S. (1996) *Interculturalism and South African Fusion Dance* (Indic Theatre Monograph Series, no.3), Durban: University of Durban-Westville.

Gramsci, A. (1971) *Selections from the Prison Notebooks*, trans. and ed. Q. Hoare and G. N. Smith, London: Lawrence & Wishart.

Granville-Barker, H. (1922) *The Exemplary Theatre*, London: Sidgwick & Jackson.

Graver, D. (1997) Review of National Arts Festival, Grahamstown, *Theatre Journal* 49: 56–59.

Graver, D. and Kruger, L. (1989) "South Africa's National Theatre: The Market or the Street?" *New Theatre Quarterly* 19: 272–81.

Gray, S. (ed.) (1982) *Athol Fugard*, Johannesburg: McGraw-Hill.

Gready, P. (1990) "The Sophiatown Writers of the 1950s: The Unreal Reality of Their World," *Journal of Southern African Studies* 10, 1: 139–64.

Greenblatt, S. (1991) *Marvelous Possessions*, Chicago: University of Chicago Press.

Greenhalgh, P. (1988) *Ephemeral Vistas: The Expositions Universelles, Great Exhibitions, and World Fairs, 1851–1939*, Manchester: Manchester University Press.

Greig, R. (1993) "Time to Say Boo to the Bogeyman," *Johannesburg Weekly Mail* (16–23 July): 37.

Grundlingh, A. and Sapire, H. (1989) "From Feverish Festival to Repetitive Ritual? The Changing Fortunes of the Great Trek Mythology in an Industrializing South Africa, 1938–1988," *South African Historical Journal* 21: 19–37.

Grundy, K. (1993) *The Politics of the National Arts Festival* (Occasional Paper no. 34), Grahamstown: Rhodes University Institute for Social and Economic Research.

Guldimann, C. (1996) "The (Black) Male Gaze: Mbongeni Ngema's *Sarafina!*," *South African Theatre Journal* 10, 2: 85–99.

Gunning, T. (1994) "The Horror of Opacity: The Melodrama of Sensation in the Plays of

André de Lorde," in J. Bratton, J. Cook, and C. Gledhill (eds) *Melodrama: Stage, Picture, Screen*, London: British Film Institute.

Gwala, M. P. (1973) "Towards a National Theatre," *South African Outlook* (August): 131–33.

—— (ed.) (1974) *Black Review 1973*, Durban: Black Community Programs.

Habermas, J. (1989 [1962]) *Structural Transformation of the Public Sphere*, trans. T. Burger, Cambridge, Mass.: MIT Press.

Haggard, H. R. (1882) *Cetywayo and His White Neighbours*, London: Trübner.

Hamilton, C. (1985) "Ideology, Oral Traditions and the Struggle for Power in the Early Zulu Kingdom," M.A. thesis, University of the Witwatersrand.

—— (1998) *Terrific Majesty: The Powers of Shaka Zulu and the Limits of Historical Invention*, Cambridge, Mass.: Harvard University Press.

Harries, P. (1993) "Imagery, Symbolism and Tradition in a South African Bantustan. Mangosutho Buthelezi, Inkatha and Zulu History," *History and Theory* 32, 4: 105–25.

Hartshorne, K. (1992) *Crisis and Challenge: Black Education, 1910–1990*, Cape Town: Oxford University Press.

Hauptfleisch, T. (1997) *Theatre and Society in South Africa*, Pretoria: van Schaik.

Hegel, G. W. F. (1956 [1899]) *The Philosophy of History*, trans. J. Sibree, New York: Dover.

—— (1974) *Aesthetics: Lectures on Fine Art*, trans. T. M. Knox, Oxford: Oxford University Press.

Heugh, K. (1995) "Disabling and Enabling: Implications of Language Policy Trends in South Africa," in R. Meshtrie (ed.) *Language and Social History*, Cape Town: David Phillip: 329–50.

Hill, R. and Pirio, G. (1987) " 'Africa for the Africans': the Garvey Movement in South Africa: 1920–1940," in S. Marks and S. Trapido (eds) *The Politics of Race, Class and Nationalism*, London: Longman, 209–53.

Historical Sketch (1910) *Historical Sketch and Description of the Pageant Held at Cape Town on the Occasion of the Opening of the First Parliament of the Union of South Africa*, Cape Town: Pageant Committee.

Hobsbawm, E. and Ranger, T. (eds) (1982) *The Invention of Tradition*, Cambridge: Cambridge University Press.

Hoernlé, A. (1934) "The Bantu Dramatic Society of Johannesburg," *Africa* 7: 223–27.

Hoffman, A. and Hoffman, A. R. (1980) *They Built a Theatre: The Story of the Johannesburg Repertory*, Johannesburg: Ad Donker.

Hofmeyr, I. (1987) "Building a Nation from Words: Afrikaans Language Literature and Ethnic Identity, 1902–1924," in S. Marks and S. Trapido (eds) *The Politics of Race, Class and Nationalism*, London: Longman, 95–123.

—— (1988) "Popularizing History: The Case of Gustav Preller," *Journal of African History* 29: 521–35.

Holloway, M. (1988) "An Interview with Zakes Mda," *South African Theatre Journal* 2, 2: 88–92.

—— (1992) "The Crisis of Liberalism in South African Theatre," *Westerley* 3: 41–47.

Horn, A. (1985) "Ideology and Melodramatic Vision in Black South Africa and Nineteenth Century America," *English in Africa*, 12, 1: 1–10.

—— (1990) Introduction to Z. Mda, *The Plays of Zakes Mda*, Johannesburg: Ravan.

Hough, B. (1981) "Interview with Athol Fugard; Port Elizabeth, 30 November 1977," *Theoria* 55: 37–48.

Hughes, L. (1976 [1966]) "Black Influences in the American Theater, Part 1," in M. Smythe (ed.) *The Black American Reference Book*, Englewood, N.J.: Prentice Hall.

Huguenet, A. (1950) *Applous*, Cape Town: Haum.

Husserl, E. (1954 [1936]) "Die Krisis der europäischen Menschheit," in *Die Krisis der europäischen Wissenschaften und die transzendale Philosophie*, The Hague: Nijhoff.

—— (1970) "Philosophy and the Crisis of European Humanity," trans. D. Carr, in *The Crisis of European Sciences and Transcendental Philosophy*, Evanston: Northwestern University Press.

Inskip, D. (1977) *The Leonard Schach Story*, Cape Town: Timmins.

Irele, A. (1990) *The African Experience in Literature and Ideology*, second edition, Bloomington: Indiana University Press.

Jabavu, D. D. T. (1935) *The Findings of the All African Convention*, Lovedale, South Africa: Lovedale Press.

Jackson, S. (1996) "Civic Play-Housekeeping: Gender, Theatre, and American Reform," *Theatre Journal* 48: 337–61.

Jeyifo, B. (1990) "The Nature of Things: Arrested Decolonization and Critical Theory," *Research in African Literatures* 20, 1: 33–48.

—— (1996) "The Reinvention of Theatrical Tradition: Critical Discourses on Interculturalism in the African Theatre," in P. Pavis (ed.) *The Intercultural Performance Reader*, London: Routledge.

Joans, T. (1961) *All of Ted Joans and No More*, New York: Excelsior.

Johannesburg City Council (1936) *Official Guide to the Empire Exhibition*, Johannesburg: JCC.

Johnson, D. (1996) *Shakespeare in South Africa*, Oxford: Clarendon Press.

Johnson, J. W. (1991 [1930]) *Black Manhattan*, New York: Da Capo Press.

Joseph, H. (1993) *Side by Side: The Autobiography of Helen Joseph*, Johannesburg: Ad Donker.

Kabane, M. L. (1936) "The All-African Convention," *South African Outlook* (August): 185–89.

Kamlongera, C. (1989) *Theatre for Development in Africa: Case Studies from Malawi and Zambia*, Bonn: German Foundation for International Development.

Kani, J. and Ntshona, W. (1976) "Art Is Life and Life Is Art: an Interview with John Kani and Winston Ntshona of the Serpent Players, South Africa," *UFAHAMU: Journal of the African Activist Association* 6, 2: 5–26.

Kannemeyer, J. C. (1983) *Geskiedenis van die Afrikaanse Literatuur*, 2 vols, Pretoria: Academica.

—— (1988) *Die Afrikaanse Literatuur 1652–1987*, Pretoria: Human & Rousseau.

Karis, T. and Carter, G. (eds) (1977) *From Protest to Challenge: A Documentary History of African Politics in South Africa, 1882–1964*, 3 vols, Stanford: Hoover Institution.

Kavanagh, R. [Mshengu] (1982) "Political Theatre in South Africa and the Work of Athol Fugard," *Theatre Research International* 7, 3: 160–79.

—— (1983) "The Theatre of Gibson Kente," *African Communist* 95, 3: 91–103.

—— (1985) *Theatre and Cultural Struggle in South Africa*, London: Zed Books.

—— (1989) "Theatre and the Struggle for National Liberation," manuscript based on a paper reconstructed after discussion and submission by the theatre committee of Congress for Another South Africa (CASA), Amsterdam.

Kelly, M. (comp.) (1934) *Conference on African Drama. 1934*, London: British Drama League.

—— (1938) *Conference on African Drama. 1938*, London: British Drama League.

Kerr, D. (1995) *African Popular Theatre*, Portsmouth: Heinemann.

Khoapa, B. A. (ed.) (1973) *Black Review 1972*, Durban: Black Community Programs.

Koch, E. (1983) "'Without Visible Means of Subsistence': Slumyard Culture in Johannsburg, 1920–1940," in B. Bozzoli (ed.) *Town and Countryside in the Transvaal*, Johannesburg: Ravan, 151–75.

Kraai, N. (1973) "Black Theatre," *PET Newsletter* 1: 11–12.

Kruger, L. (1991) "Apartheid on Display: South Africa Performs for New York," *Diaspora* 1, 2: 191–208.

—— (1992) *The National Stage: Theatre and Legitimation in England, France, and America*, Chicago: University of Chicago Press.

—— (1993a) "Placing the Occasion: Raymond Williams and Performing Culture," in D. Dworking and L. Roman (eds) *Views beyond the Border Country: Essays on Raymond Williams*, London: Routledge.

—— (1993b) "Staging South Africa," *Transition* (N.S.) 59: 120–29.

—— (1995a) "The Uses of Nostalgia: Drama, History, and Liminal Moments in South Africa," *Modern Drama* 38, 1: 60–70.

—— (1995b) "So What's New? Women and Theater in the New South Africa," *Theater* 25, 3: 46–54.

Kruger, L. and Watson, P. (unpublished) "'Shoo, This Book Makes Me to Think': Education, Entertainment, and Life-Skills in South Africa," *Poetics Today*.

Krut, R. (1984) "The Making of a South African Jewish Community in Johannesburg, 1886–1914," in B. Bozzoli (ed.) *Class, Community and Conflict: South African Perspectives*, Johannesburg: Ravan.

Lagden, G. (1909) *The Basuto: The Mountaineers and Their Country*, London: Hutchinson.

Laing, R. D. (1969) *Self and Others*, New York: Pantheon.

Linscott, A. P. (1936) "R.U.R.," *South African Opinion* (14 November): 15.

—— (1937a) "Mr. van Gyseghem and the Bantu Players," *South African Opinion* (23 January): 15.

—— (1937b) "Mr. van Gyseghem and the Pageant," *South African Opinion* (23 January): 15–16.

Lloyd, T. C. (1935) "The Bantu Tread the Footlights," *The South African Opinion* (6 March): 3–5.

Locke, A. (ed.) (1992 [1925]) *The New Negro*, New York: Macmillan.

Lodge, T. (1985) *Black Politics in South Africa since 1945*, London: Longman.

Louw, N. P. van Wyk (1959) *Berigte te Velde*, Cape Town: Nasionale Pers.

Love, H. (ed.) (1984) *The Australian Stage: A Documentary History*, Sydney: University Press of New South Wales.

Lyotard, J.-F. (1977) "The Unconscious as Mise en Scène," in M. Benamou and C. Caramello (eds) *Performance in Post-modern Culture*, Madison: Coda Press.

McClintock, A. (1991) "'No Longer in a Future Heaven': Women and Nationalism in South Africa," *Transition* 51: 104–23.

—— (1992) "The Angel of Progress – Pitfalls of the Term 'Postcolonialism,'" *Social Text* 31–32: 79–92.

McGrath, J. (1981) Introduction to J. McGrath, *The Cheviot, the Stag, and the Black, Black Oil*, London: Methuen.

Madikizela, P. (1995) "Black and Chauvinist," *Mail and Guardian* (Johannesburg, Electronic Edition), 30 September.

Mahomed, I. (1993) "Theatre for Activists or Activists for Theatre?" paper delivered at Youth Theatre Conference, Cape Town.

Mailer, N. (1992 [1957]) "The White Negro," in A. Charters (ed.) *The Portable Beat Reader*, New York: Viking.

Maingard, J. (1997a) "Imag(in)ing the South African Nation: Representations of Identity in the Rugby World Cup 1995," *Theatre Journal* 49: 15–28.

—— (1997b) "Transforming Television Broadcasting in a Democratic South Africa," *Screen* 38: 260–74.

Maja-Pearce A. (1996) "Binding the Wounds," *Index on Censorship* 25, 5: 50–56.

Mandela, N. (1994) "A Time to Build and Heal the Wounds," *Sunday Nation* (15 May 1994), 4–5.

—— (1995) *Long Walk to Freedom*, Boston: Little, Brown & Co.

Manganyi, N. C. (1973) *Being-Black-in-the-World*, Johannesburg: Spro-cas/Ravan.

Mannoni, O. (1964) *Prospero and Caliban: The Psychology of Colonialism*, trans. P. Powersland, New York: Praeger.

Maponya, M. (1984) "Problems and Possibilities: A Discourse on the Making of Alternative Theatre in South Africa," *English Academy Review* 2: 19–32.

Marcuse, H. (1968 [1935]) "The Affirmative Character of Culture," in *Negations*, trans. J. Shapiro, Boston: Beacon Press.

Marks, S. (1986) *The Ambiguities of Dependence*, Johannesburg: Ravan.

—— (1989) "Patriotism, Patriarchy, and Purity: Natal and the Politics of Zulu Ethnic Consciousness," in L. Vail (ed.) *The Creation of Tribalism in Southern Africa*, Berkeley: University of California Press, 215–240.

Marks, S. and Trapido, S. (eds and intro.) (1987) *The Politics of Race, Class and Nationalism in Twentieth Century South Africa*, London: Longman.

Marx, L. (1994) Review of *And the Girls in their Sunday Dresses* and *When People Play People* by Z. Mda, *Southern African Review of Books* 6, 2: 20–21.

Matshikiza, T. (1953) "How Musicians Die," *Drum* (October): 38.

—— (1956) "Masterpiece in Bronze: Emily Motsieloa," *Drum* (May): 22–23.

—— (1957) "Jazz Comes to Jo'burg," *Drum* (July): 38–39, 41.

—— (1985 [1963]) *Chocolates for My Wife*, Johannesburg: Ad Donker.

Mattera, D. (1987) *Memory Is a Weapon*, Johannesburg: Ravan.

Maughan-Brown, D. (1989) "The Anthology as Reliquary: *Ten Years of Staffrider* and *The Drum Decade*," *Current Writing* 1, 1: 3–21.

Mazrui, A. and Tidy, M. (1984) *Nationalism and New States in Africa*, London: Heinemann.

Mbanjwa, T. (ed.) (1975) *Black Review 1974/75*, Durban: Black Community Programs.

Mda, Z. (1993) *When People Play People: Development Communication through Theatre*, Johannesburg: Witwatersrand University Press.

—— (1995) "Theater and Reconciliation in South Africa," *Theater* 25, 3: 36–45.

—— (1997) "When People Play People in Post-Apartheid South Africa" (interview by D. Salter), *Brecht Yearbook* 22: 283–303.

Mdhluli, S. V. H. (1933) *The Development of the African*, Marianhill: Marianhill Mission.

Memmi, A. (1965) *The Colonizer and the Colonized*, trans. H. Greenfeld, Boston: Beacon Press.

Merrington, P. (1997) "Masques, Monuments, and Masons: The 1910 Pageant of the Union of South Africa," *Theatre Journal* 49: 1–14.

Mesthrie, R. (ed.) (1995a) *Language and Social History: Studies in South-African Sociolinguistics*, Cape Town: David Phillip.

—— (1995b) "South African Indian English," *Language and Social History*: 251–64.

Meyer, P. J. (1940) *Die Afrikaner*, Cape Town: Afrikaanse Pers.

—— (1942) *Demokrasie of Volkstaat?*, Stellenbosch: Afrikaner Nationale Studentenbond.

Midgley, H. P. (1993) "Author, Ideology and Publisher – a Symbiotic Relationship. Lovedale Missionary Press and Early Black Writing in South Africa," M.A. thesis, Rhodes University.

Miller, J. (1980) "Listening to the African Past," in J. Miller (ed.) *The African Past Speaks*, Hamden, Conn.: Archon Press.

Millin, S. G. (1925) *God's Step-Children*, London: Constable.

—— (1954) *The People of South Africa*, London: Constable.

Mlama, P. (1991) *Culture and Development: The Popular Theatre Approach in Africa*, Uppsala: Nordiska Afrikainstitutet.

Mngadi, S. (1997) "'Africanization' or the New Exoticism," *Scrutiny 2* 2, 1: 18–22.

Modisane, W. (1986 [1963]) *Blame Me on History*, Johannesburg: Ad Donker.

Modleski, T. (1982) *Loving with a Vengeance: Mass-Produced Fantasies for Women*, New York: Methuen.

Mofokeng, J. (1996) "Theatre for Export: The Commercialization of the Black People's Struggle in South African Export Musicals," in G. Davis and A. Fuchs (eds) *Theatre and Change in South Africa*, Amsterdam: Overseas Publishers Association.

Mofokeng, S. (1996) "The Black Photo Album: Look at Me: 1890–1950" in *Standard Bank National Arts Festival: Souvenir Program*, Grahamstown: Grahamstown Foundation, 81.

Moodie, T. D. (1975) *The Rise of Afrikanerdom: Power, Apartheid, and the Afrikaner Civil Religion*, Berkeley: University of California Press.

Mosala, I. (1995) "Letting down Steve Biko," *Mail and Guardian* (Johannesburg, Electronic Edition), 23 September.

Mudimbe, V. I. (1988) *The Invention of Africa*, Bloomington: Indiana University Press.

Murray, C. (1981) *Families Divided: The Impact of Migrant Labour in Lesotho*, Johannesburg: Ravan.

Mutwa, C. V. (1974/75) "*Umlinganiso* – The Living Imitation," *S'ketsh*: 30–32.

Naidoo, M. (1997) "The Search for a Cultural Identity: A Personal View of South African 'Indian' Theatre," *Theatre Journal* 49: 29–39.

Nakasa, N. (1959) "The Life and Death of King Kong," *Drum* (February): 27.

Nandy, A. (1983) *The Intimate Enemy: Loss and Recovery of Self under Colonialism*, Oxford and New Delhi: Oxford University Press.

Naudé, S. C. M. (1950) "The Rise of the Afrikaans Theatre," *Trek: South Africa's Literary Magazine* (April): 8–10.

Ndebele, N. (1986) "The Rediscovery of the Ordinary: Some New Writings in South Africa," *Journal of Southern African Studies* 12, 2: 143–57.

—— (1987) "The English Language and Social Change in South Africa," *English Academy Review* 4: 1–16.

Negt, O. and Kluge, A. (1993 [1972]) *Public Sphere and Experience*, trans. P. Labanyi, J. Owen Daniel, and A. Oksiloff, Minneapolis: University of Minnesota Press.

Ngũgĩ wa Thiong'o (1986) *Decolonising the Mind: The Politics of Language in African Literature*, London: James Currey.

Nicol, M. (1991) *A Good-looking Corpse*, London: Secker & Warburg.

Nixon, R. (1994) *Homelands, Harlem, and Hollywood*, London: Routledge.

Nkosi, L. (1965) *Home and Exile*, London: Longman.

—— (1983) *Home and Exile and Other Selections*, London: Longman.

Nyatsumba, K. (1990) "Theatre in a Rut," *Tribune* (Jan.): 68–69.

O'Brien, A. (1994) "Staging Whiteness: Beckett, Havel, Maponya," *Theatre Journal* 46: 45–61.

Official Program of the Van Riebeeck Festival (1952) Cape Town.

O'Meara, D. (1983) *Volkskapitalisme: Class, Capital, and Ideology in the Development of Afrikaner Nationalism*, Johannesburg: Ravan.

260

—— (1996) *Forty Lost Years: The Apartheid State and the Politics of the National Party, 1948–1994*, Johannesburg: Ravan.

Omond, R. (1985) *The Apartheid Handbook*, Harmondsworth: Penguin.

Omotoso, K. (1991) *Seasons of Migration to the South: Africa's Crises Reconsidered*, Cape Town: Tafelberg.

Orkin, M. (1989) *Shakespeare against Apartheid*, Johannesburg: Ravan.

—— (1991) *Drama and the South African State*, Johannesburg: Witwatersrand University Press.

—— (1995) Intro. and ed. of JACT, *At the Junction: Four Plays by the Junction Avenue Theatre Company*, Johannesburg: Witwatersrand University Press.

Pelzer, A. N. (1966) *Verwoerd Speaks*, Johannesburg: Afrikaanse Pers.

Peterson, B. (1990) "Apartheid and the Political Imagination in Black South African Theatre," *Journal of Southern African Studies* 16, 2: 229–246.

—— (1993) Introduction to Z. Mda, *And the Girls in Their Sunday Dresses*, Johannesburg: Witwatersrand University Press.

Phillips, R. (1930) *The Bantu Are Coming*, New York: Richard Smith.

Polley, J. (1973) *Die Sestigers*, Cape Town: Human & Rousseau.

Proctor, A. (1979) "Class Struggle, Segregation and the City: A History of Sophiatown, 1905–1940," in Bozzoli (ed.) *Labour, Township and Protest*, Johannesburg: Ravan.

Purkey, M. (1993) Introduction to Junction Avenue Theatre Company, *Sophiatown*, Johannesburg: Witwatersrand University Press.

Purkey, M. and C. Steinberg (1995) "South African Theater in Crisis," *Theater* 25, 3: 24–37.

Rabie, J. (1985 [1975]) "Is dit ons erns – in Afrika?" in *Skrywer en Gemeenskap*, Pretoria: Haum Literêr.

Rambally, A. (ed.) (1977) *Black Review 1975/76*, Durban: Black Community Programs.

Ramphela, M. (1995) "Can Steve Biko Arbitrate from beyond the Grave?" *Mail and Guardian* (Johannesburg, Electronic Edition), 17 September.

Rassool, C. and Witz, L. (1993) "The 1952 Jan van Riebeeck Tercentenary Festival: Constructing and Contesting Public National History in South Africa," *Journal of African History* 34: 447–68.

Read, J. (comp.) (1991) *Athol Fugard: A Bibliography*, Grahamstown: National English Literary Museum.

Roach, J. (1996) *Cities of the Dead: Circum-Atlantic Performance*, New York: Columbia University Press.

Roberge, P. (1995) "The Formation of Afrikaans," *Language and Social History*: 68–88.

Robertson, H. (1994) "Feeling Our Way to the Future" (interview with Walter Chakela and John Matshikiza), *Tribute* (June): 76–78.

Rosenberg, J. (1995) "After Apartheid," *New York Village Voice* (17 January): 77–78.

Routh, G. (1950a) "The Johannesburg Art Theatre," *Trek* (September): 25–27.

—— (1950b) "The Bantu People's Theatre," *Trek* (October): 20–23.

Sachs, A. (1990) *Protecting Human Rights in a New South Africa*, Cape Town: Oxford University Press.

Sagan, L. (1996) *Lights and Shadows: The Autobiography of Leontine Sagan*, L. Kruger (ed.), Johannesburg: Witwatersrand University Press.

Sampson, A. (1983) *Drum: An African Adventure and Afterwards*, London: Hodder & Stoughton.

Samuel, R., McColl, E., and Cosgrove, S. (1985) *Theatres of the Left: Working Class Theatre in Britain and the United States, 1880–1935*, London: Routledge & Kegan Paul.

Schach, L. (1996) *The Flag Is Flying: A Very Personal History of Theatre in the Old South Africa*, Cape Town: Human & Rousseau.

Schadeberg, J. (ed. and comp.) (1987) *The Fifties People of Johannesburg*, Johannesburg: Baileys African Photo Archive.

Schauffer, D. (1994) *In the Shadow of the Shah*, Durban: Asoka Publications.

Schechner, R. (1985) *Between Theater and Anthropology*, Philadelphia: University of Pennsylvania Press.

—— (1988) *Performance Theory*, London: Routledge.

Schwartz, P. (1988) *The Best of Company: The Story of Johannesburg's Market Theatre*, Johannesburg: Ad Donker.

Sepamla, S. (1981) "Towards an African Theatre," *Rand Daily Mail* (2 April).

Shepherd, R. H. W. (1935) *Literature for the South African Bantu*, Pretoria: Carnegie Corporation.

Shohat, E. (1992) "Notes on the Postcolonial," *Social Text* 31–32: 99–113.

Simon, B. (1974) "Education through Respect," *The Leech* 44, 2: 84–85.

Simone, A. M. (1994) "In the Mix: Remaking Coloured Identities," *Africa Insight* 24, 3: 161–73.

Sitas, A. (1986) "Culture and Production: The Contradictions of Working Class Theatre in South Africa," *Africa Perspective* (N.S.) 1, 1–2: 4–110.

S'ketsh (1972) (Summer).

—— (1973) (Summer).

—— (1975a) (Summer 1974/75).

—— (1975b) (Winter).

—— (1975c) (Summer).

—— (1979) (Winter).

Skota, T. D. M. (ed. and comp.) (1931) *The African Yearly Register. Being an Illustrated National Biographical Dictionary (Who's Who) of Black Folks in Africa*, Johannesburg: R. L. Esson.

Skurski, J. and Coronil, F. (1993) "Country and City in a Colonial Landscape: Double Discourse and the Geopolitics of Truth in Latin America," in D. L. Dworkin and L. G. Roman (eds) *Views Beyond the Border Country: Essays on Raymond Williams*, London and New York: Routledge.

Slosberg, B. (1939) *Pagan Tapestry*, London: Rich & Cravan.

Small, A. (1961) *Die eerste Steen*, Cape Town: HAUM.

—— (1985) "Die Skryfambag en apartheid," in *Skrywer en Gemeenskap*, Pretoria: Haum Literêr.

Smit, B. (1985) "Skrywe – 'n ambag?" in *Skrywer en Gemeenskap*, Pretoria: Haum Literêr.

Smith, D. (1990) "The Anthropology of Literacy Acquisition," in B. Shiffelin and P. Gilmore (eds) *The Acquisition of Literacy: Ethnographic Perspectives*, Norwood, N.J.: Ablex: 260–75.

Smith, J. (1990) *Toneel en Politiek*, Bellville: UWC Press.

Sole, K. (1979) "Class and Continuity in Black South African Literature, 1948–60," in B. Bozzoli (ed.) *Labour, Townships, and Protest: Studies in the Social History of the Witwatersrand*, Johannesburg: Ravan.

—— (1984) "Black Literature and Performance: Some Notes on Class and Populism," *South African Labour Bulletin* 9, 8: 54–76.

—— (1987) "Identities and Priorities in Black Literature and Performance," *South African Theatre Journal* 1, 1: 45–111.

Stadler, A. (1993) "Bridewealth and the Deferral of Marriage: Towards an Understanding of Marriage Payments in Timbavati, Gazankulu," *Africa Perspectives* 1, 1: 1–11

Stead, R. (1984) "The National Theatre Organization, 1947–62," *The Breytie Book/Die Breytie-Boek*, T. Hauptfleish (ed.), Randburg: Limelight.

Steadman, I. (1985a) "Drama and Social Consciousness: Themes in Black Theatre on the Witwatersrand to 1984," Ph.D. thesis, University of the Witwatersrand.

—— (1985b) "The Other Face," *Index on Censorship* 14, 1: 26–30.

—— (1990) "Towards Popular Theatre in South Africa," *Journal of Southern African Studies* 16, 2: 208–228.

—— (1991) "Theatre beyond Apartheid," *Research in African Literatures* 22, 3: 70–90.

—— (1992) "Performance and Politics: Process and Practices of Representation in South African Theatre," *Theatre Survey* 33, 2: 188–210.

—— (1995) Introduction to Maponya, *Doing Plays for a Change*, Johannesburg: Witwatersrand University Press.

Stein, P. and Jacobson, R. (eds) (1986) *Sophiatown Speaks*, Johannesburg: Junction Avenue Press.

Steinberg, C. (1991) "Now Is the Time for Feminist Criticism: A Critique of *Asinamali*," *South African Theatre Journal* 5, 2: 22–39.

Stepan, N. (1985) "Biology and Degeneration: Races and Proper Places," in J. E. Chamberlin and S. Gilman (eds) *Degeneration: The Darker Side of Progress*, New York: Columbia University Press.

Themba, C. (1981) *The World of Can Themba*, ed. E. Patel, Johannesburg: Ravan.

—— (1983) *The Will to Die*, London: Heinemann.

Thompson, L. (1990) *A History of South Africa*, New Haven: Yale University Press.

Turner, V. (1982) *From Ritual to Theatre*, New York: Performing Arts Journal Publications.

Vail, L. and White, L. (1991) *Power and the Praise Poem: South African Voices in History*, Charlottesville: University Press of Virginia.

Vaillante, P. (1969) *Les Nègres blancs d'Amérique: Autobiographie d'un terroriste québécois*, Montréal: Parti pris.

Vandenbroucke, R. (1986) *Truths the Hands Can Touch: The Theatre of Athol Fugard*, Johannesburg: Ad Donker.

Van Onselen, C. (1996) *The Seed Is Mine: The Life of Kas Maine, African Sharecropper, 1894–1985*, Cape Town: David Phillip.

Vilakazi, B. W. (1942) "Some Aspects of Zulu Literature," *African Studies* 1, 4: 270–74.

Visser, N. (1976) "South Africa: The Renaissance that Failed," *Journal of Commonwealth Literature* 9, 1: 42–57.

Visser, N. and Couzens, T. (1985) Introduction to H. I. E. Dhlomo, *Collected Works*, Johannesburg: Ravan.

von Kotze, A. (1988) *Organise and Act: The Natal Workers' Theatre Movement, 1983–87*, Durban: Culture and Working Life Publications.

—— (1989) "First World Industry and Third World Workers: The Struggle for Workers' Theater in South Africa," *Brecht Yearbook* 14: 157–67.

Walder, D. (1985) *Athol Fugard*, New York: Grove.

—— (1993) Introduction to Fugard, *Township Plays*, Oxford: Oxford University Press.

Watson, P. (1994) "Does *Heart to Heart* Work as an Effective Resource in Sexuality Education? A Preliminary Research Report," Johannesburg: Storyteller Group.

—— (1998) *Producing a Rural Comic beyond the Learner Paradox*, M.A. thesis, University of the Witwatersrand.

White Paper (1996) *White Paper on Art, Culture, and Heritage*, Pretoria: Dept. of Arts, Culture, Science and Technology; http://www.polity.org.za/govdocs/white_papers/arts.html.

Wilentz, E. (ed.) (1960) *The Beat Scene*, New York: Corinth Press.

Williams, R. (1973) *The Country and the City*, London: Chatto & Windus.

—— (1977) *Marxism and Literature*, Oxford: Oxford University Press.

—— (1979) *Politics and Letters: Interviews with New Left Review*, London: New Left Books.

—— (1980) "The Bloomsbury Fraction," *Problems in Materialism and Culture*, London: Verso.

—— (1981) *Politics and Letters*, London: Verso.

—— (1995 [1981]) *The Sociology of Culture*, Chicago and London: University of Chicago Press.

Woods, D. (1986) *Biko*, London: Secker & Warburg.

Yuval-Davis, N. (1993) "Gender and Nation," *Ethnic and Racial Studies* 16, 4: 621–32.

INDEX

acting: amateur (white) 36, 52–55; Brechtian 69, 156–61, 180–81, 204–16; as cultural work 133–37, 145–47, 164–74; as education 129–31, 204–16

actors: Alli, Mohammed (m) 148, Bezuidenhout, Aletta (f) 168; Bryceland, Yvonne (f) 156,161,163; Buthelezi, Sipho (m) 137; Cooke, Vanessa (also writer) 168, 178–80, 241n12, 242n29; Curry, Bill 161; Dibeco, Stanley "Fats" (and producer) 138; Dube, Lillian 193, 240n4; Ebrahim, Vincent 161; Engelbrecht, Annette 118, 124; Flynn, Bill 230n20; Fugard, Sheila (also writer) 89; Gampu, Ken 89, 92; Huguenet, André (also director) 79–81; Kahn, Essop 148; Kekana, Fana (m) 236n15; Kente, Dambise (f) 194; Keogh, Danny (also writer) 169, 178; Khumalo, Leleti (also singer) 184; Khumalo, Stella 195; Klaasen, Tandi (also singer) 96; Kraai, Nomsisi (f, also writer) 134, 144, 146, 234n29, 234n30; Kwebulana, Timmy 180–81; Lamprecht, Don 107, 117, 127; Majozi, Kenny 139, 159, 175; Makeba, Miriam (also singer) 88, 93, 139, 182, 227n32; Maredi, Dan Selaelo 236n15; Masokoane, uJebe (m) 141, 144; Maythan, John 172–73; Mbuli, Letta (also singer) 96, 182–84, 241n11; Mdledle, Nathan (also singer) 92–94; Minaar, Dawid 126; Mkhwane, Bhaki 197–98; Mokae, Zakes 89, 103, 110 (see also Fugard); Mokoena, Ronnie 151–52, 159; Moloi, Stephen 89, 92 (see also Fugard); Mthoba, James (also playwright) 169, 187 (see also Workshop '71); kaNcube, Sello Maake (m, also writer)

195; Nhlapo, Eddie 187, 239n47; Norton, Terry (f) 179; Ntinga, Themba (m) 164, 236n15; Ntshinga, Thoko (f) 180–84, 238n39; Ntshona, Winston 13, 154, 157–59, 162 (see also Fugard, Kani); Nyembe, Nandi (f) 193, 240n4; Poho, Dan 89, 92; Ramsay, Fiona 179; Redelinghuys, Kita 105, 229n10 (see also Smit); Sebogodi, Seputla (m) 176, 192, 240n1; Sibanda, Seth 236n15; Sibisa, Gladys 89; Silwane, Hamilton Mahonga 170; Singana, Margaret (also singer) 141, 234n26; Snyman, Wilna 169; Thorndike, Sybil 55, 223n11; Tsira, Poppy 238n40; Weyers, Marius 168–69; see also Kani; Ledwaba; McCarthy; Mhlophe; Nkonyeni; Slabolepszy; Twala; Uys

African-Americans: and Beat Generation 131–33; and Black Consciousness Movement 129, 135–36, 142, 144, 233n8; and Market Theatre 164; and New African 28–29, 44–45; and New Negro 26, 220n12, 220n13, 220n14; and Sophiatown 87, 91–92; see also Black Consciousness Movement

African National Congress (ANC) 1–11, 23–25, 67–70, 72–74, 97–99, 178–80; and Defiance Campaigns 77, 96, 98, 200; and inauguration of Mandela 2–11; and post-apartheid society 191, 240n2; Umkhonto we Sizwe [Spear of the Nation] 131–32; women's league 237n34; Youth League 72

African nationalism 24, 27–29, 41–43, 46; African Resistance Movement (ARM) 132, 232n2, 235n3; Non-European Unity Movement (NEUM) 80, 229n8; Pan-African Congress (PAC) 100,

Bar and Ger (Aron) 163

Barker, Harley Granville 54, 61, 223n13

Barnard, Chris (playwright): *Pa, maak vir my'n vlieër, pa* 231n39; *Die Rebellie van Lafras Verwey* 101, 115, 117–19, 231n39, 236n13

Barnard, Lady Anne 24, 40

Beckett, Samuel 186–87; *Catastrophe* 172–73; *Waiting for Godot* 111, 169

Les Belles-Soeurs [Sisters-in-law] (Tremblay) 116

Berman, Marshall 85

Bernhardt, Ian (chairman of Union Artists) 88, 112, 138, 227n29

Beukes, Gerhard (author) 80; *Langs die Steitjies* 226n15

Bhabha, Homi 11, 127–28, 133, 176

Biko, Stephen (founding president of SASO) 129, 133–35, 166, 173, 195, 237n29

Black Consciousness Movement (BCM) 14, 128–53; and African diaspora 133–36; and Black Power rhetoric 132–33, 142–43; and gender 144–47, 234n27, 234n33; and Indian South Africans 129, 135–37; and Marxism 134–35; and multicultural organizations 137–39; and South African Students Association (SASO) 129–53

Black, Stephen (playwright) 20, 50–51; *Helena's Hope Ltd* 52, 229n16; *Love and the Hyphen* 51

Bloom, Harry (writer) 17, 88, 90–95, 227n36, 228n37; *see also King Kong*

Boal, Augusto 67, 205, 208; and theory of spect-action 208, 213–14

Bokwe, John Knox (composer) 45

Boucicault, Dion (playwright): *The Colleen Bawn* 142; *The Octoroon* 102, 106

Bourdieu, Pierre 12, 222n6

Boy Called Rubbish (Mkhwane, Pearson) 198

Brecht, Bertolt 67, 120, 162; and Junction Avenue Theatre 91; *Caucasian Chalk Circle* 130, 156–57; and *Lehrstücke* 60, 156–57; and Market Theatre 154, 166–69, 178–81; *Mother Courage* 228n41; *The Resistible Rise of Arturo Ui* 68; *St. Joan of the Stockyards* 97; *Threepenny Opera* 91, 227n34; *see also* acting

Brink, André (writer) 101; *A Dry White Season* 228n1; *Kennis van die aand* [Looking into Darkness] 229n5; *Die Verhoor* 230n30

British Commonwealth 34–38, 40–42, 53–55

British culture *see* neocolonialism

Brook, Peter (director) 156, 174, 235n2

Buckingham Palace, District Six (Rive) 226n26

Butler, Guy (poet and playwright) 20; *Die Dam* 81, 84–86, 90

Caluza, Reuben (composer) 25, 30, 32, 58, 69, 94–95, 220n14; "Sixoshiwe [emsebenzini]" [We are being expelled (from work)] 25; *see also* national anthems

Campbell, Roy (writer) 54–55

Camus, Albert 111, 129

capitalism 14–15, 34–35, 239n50; black 139; as dramatic theme 75–76, 111–19, 170–71, 188–91; and race 134–35, 194–95; and subsidy 87, 88–91, 154–68, 236n19, 237n24, 240n8, 241n12

Carlyle, Thomas 62,66

Carmichael, Stokely (Kwame Ture) 129, 135, 233n8

censorship; and Afrikaner ascendancy 101–3, 228n5; and anti-apartheid activity 110, 164, 172; and Black Consciousness Movement 136–37, 145–46, 233n14, 234n30–33; and the "emergency" (1984–85) 178–79, 238n35; and gay themes 161, 236n11; and miscegenation 105–7; and neocolonial tutelage 55–62, 223n12, 224n25, n28; and Soweto uprising 169

Césaire, Aimé (poet) 106, 135

Chakela, Walter (director) 15, 164, 186, 195; *Baby, Come Duze* 194

Chamber of Mines 30, 35, 52, 80, 97

Chekhov, Anton (playwright) 52; *The Seagull* 166

Chief Above and Chief Below (K. E. Masinga) 77

city: culture 28–30, 86–90, 154–56; post-apartheid 192–94, 209–11; vs. rural 72–78, 81–84, 110–14, 185–90, 225n1

class: as a category: 14–15, 26; and gentility 15, 52–55; proletarian 39, 74–76, 116, 134–35, 170, 221n30; "ruling" 52, 117, 188; *see also* New Africans; white; workers

Clegg, Johnny (singer and "white Zulu") 2, 11

Coetzee, J. M. 82–83

colonial history 6, 10–11, 25–28; in drama

Xuma, Dr A. B. (ANC leader) 23, 87

Zombie (Bailey) 21, 198, 203, 209
Zulu culture 62–66, 78–79, 224n22,
224n24; and tribal sketch 31–34, 40–43;
Zulu Cultural Society 27, 43, 219n8

Zulu language (isiZulu): in drama 18–20,
33, 53, 77–78, 94–95, 144, 181–82, 208,
238n37, 240n5

Zulus (amaZulu) 38, 45, 59–71, 78–79,
148, 221n26; white Zulus 10–11, 62–66